WITH

HITLER

AND

MUSSOLINI

WITH

HITLER

AND

MUSSOLINI

memoirs of a

NAZI INTERPRETER

*Translated from the German
by J. Maxwell Brownjohn*

EUGEN DOLLMANN

FOREWORD BY
DAVID TALBOT

Skyhorse Publishing

Skyhorse Publishing books may be purchased in bulk at special discounts for sales promotion, corporate gifts, fund-raising, or educational purposes. Special editions can also be created to specifications. For details, contact the Special Sales Department, Skyhorse Publishing, 307 West 36th Street, 11th Floor, New York, NY 10018 or info@skyhorsepublishing.com.

Skyhorse® and Skyhorse Publishing® are registered trademarks of Skyhorse Publishing, Inc.®, a Delaware corporation.

Visit our website at www.skyhorsepublishing.com.

10 9 8 7 6 5 4 3 2 1

Library of Congress Cataloging-in-Publication Data is available on file.

Cover design by Rain Saukas
Cover photo credit: Art Resource

Print ISBN: 978-1-5107-1594-3
Ebook ISBN: 978-1-5107-1596-7

Printed in the United States of America

CONTENTS

	Foreword	7
I	His Majesty	13
II	Arcadia	19
III	Contacts	44
IV	The Police Chiefs	76
V	The Honeymoon	100
VI	Interlude with a Courtesan	136
VII	The Two Corporals	185
VIII	Twenty-Four Fateful Hours	217
IX	The Snake-Pit	235
X	My Fight for Rome	262
XI	*Cur Non?*–Why Not?	305
	Index	347

ILLUSTRATIONS

Obersalzberg, 1939: Balbo, Dollmann and Hitler *frontispiece*
Hitler's visit to Rome–May 1938 *see insert*
Himmler in Tripoli–November 1938
Visit of Reichsfrauenführerin Scholtz-Klinck to Italy–1939
The Contessa Colonna, Duchessa di Sermoneta
Hitler with the Countess Attolico
The Duke and Duchess of Windsor with Hitler at the Berghof
The Crown Princess of Italy with the German Ambassador to
Rome, von Mackensen, and his wife
Reinhard Heydrich, chief of the Central State Security Bureau, in
Rome–October 1938
Count Ciano, Mussolini and von Hassell awaiting the arrival of
Chamberlain and Halifax in Rome–January 1939
Hitler, Dollmann, Ciano and von Ribbentrop in Berlin–May 1938
Mussolini and Hitler
Hitler, Mussolini, Ciano and Keitel in Florence–October 1940
Ricci's visit to Goebbels
Osteria 'Alfredo'–Rome 1938
The funeral of Bocchini in Rome–November 1940
Castle of Klessheim–April 1943
Mussolini at Kesselring's headquarters in Parma–August 1944

Obersalzberg, 1939: Balbo, Dollmann and Hitler

FOREWORD
BY DAVID TALBOT

SS COLONEL EUGEN DOLLMANN was not one of the most central figures in Hitler's inner circle, but he certainly was the most dishy. As the Rome-based interpreter who linked together the German-Italian axis during World War II, he had unique access to the Führer and his top henchmen, as well as the decadent milieu surrounding Mussolini. He was not as morally depraved as those he served, but his cynicism made him capable of accommodating himself to their baroque evils. Dollmann was a "self-serving opportunist who prostituted himself to fascism." That was the succinct historical judgment of Holocaust scholar Michael Salter. And yet, precisely because he did not drink fully from Hitler's poisoned chalice, Dollmann was able to observe his masters from a droll distance like the world-weary characters played by George Sanders. This perspective—intimate, but detached—makes his memoirs an utterly fascinating and disturbing reading experience.

Dollmann's companion volumes caused something of a sensation when they were published in Europe under the original titles *Call Me a Coward* (1956) and *The Interpreter* (1967). But they have long been forgotten, until now. With America's descent into its own bizarre nightmare, the discovery of these lost memoirs seems exquisitely well-timed. The inner world of fascist power that Dollmann reveals is both all too human and frighteningly monstrous.

The man who enabled Hitler and Mussolini to communicate with each other was a closeted homosexual, serving a regime that sent thousands of gay men to the gas chambers. This is just one of many ironies that defined Eugen Dollmann. To make things even stranger, Dollmann suggests that Hitler's own fondness for boy-ish-looking men was a well-known secret in certain German circles during his rise to power.

In one of the most memorable passages of the volumes, Dollmann recalls his frantic shopping sprees in Rome with Eva Braun, Hitler's companion. "She loved crocodile in every shape and form, and returned to her hotel looking as if she had come back from a trip up the Congo rather than along the Tiber." Dollmann was fond of the sweet and simple Braun, who confided her sad life to him. She confessed to him there was no sexual intimacy between her and the Führer. "He is a saint," she told her shopping companion. "The idea of physical contact would be for him to defile his mission."

Dollmann also writes—with chilling if bemused style—about the antics of the debased Italian royalty and the visiting Nazi dignitaries who saw Italy as their playground. His account of a debauched, late-night party at a decaying Neapolitan palazzo—enlivened by a troupe of performing dwarves and hosted by a duchessa whose twisted smile was the handiwork of a knife-wielding jealous lover—is right out of Fellini. And his chronicle of the evening he spent in a gilded Naples whorehouse with Reinhard Heydrich—the dead-eyed SS general known as "the Hangman" who was one of the masterminds of the Final Solution—is right out of Visconti's *The Damned*. Heydrich, who apparently recoiled at the idea of human touch, preferred to take his pleasure from the two dozen half-naked women displayed before him by scattering gold coins across the brothel's marble floor and making the women scramble on all fours to gather them.

As the war drew to its close, Dollmann remained a cunning navigator of power, working with a group of wily SS officers to cut a deal with future US intelligence legend Allen Dulles, whose own moral dexterity allowed him to defy FDR's orders and make a separate peace with Nazi forces in Italy. This unholy pact allowed Dollmann and a number of other even more culpable war criminals to escape justice at Nuremberg. But for years after the war, Dollmann was forced to scurry this way and that along the notorious Nazi "ratlines"—the escape routes utilized by fleeing German criminals, often with the help of Western intelligence officials.

Dollmann was a master at the Cold War game, offering his spy services to various and often competing agencies. He even tried to extort Dulles, by then CIA director, as his first memoir headed for publication, unsubtly suggesting that anything in the book the spymaster found embarrassing could be made to disappear if the two men reached an understanding.

Dollmann was shrewd enough to realize it was not wise to keep shaking down men like Dulles, and he got out of the spy game. He tried his hand at selling Nazi memorabilia of dubious authenticity. An ardent movie fan, he also put his translation skills at the service of the Italian film industry, providing the German subtitles for Fellini's *La Dolce Vita*.

You will find no deep moral self-reflection in Dollmann's memoirs. But like many morally compromised men, Dollmann has penetrating insights into the flaws of others.

There was little punishment for his sins. He spent some time confined, fittingly enough, in Cinecitta, the Rome film studio that was briefly turned into a prison after the war, and later at a POW camp on Lake Maggiore that he had the sheer gall (or perhaps sick humor) to compare unfavorably with Dachau, because of the camp's watery pea soup and its rain-soaked tents. "At least in Dachau they had wood huts," he observed.

Dollmann lived to the age of eighty-four, comfortably cocooned in his later years in a sunny garret in a blue-colored residential hotel in Munich, where he was surrounded by photos, books and memorabilia that recalled his past life. He was perfectly content to live in the past, he told an American visitor one day—after all, he had been begun his career as a European Renaissance historian, until he was kidnapped by history.

At one point, his visitor brought up the recently published Dulles war memoir, in which Dollmann was described as a "slippery customer." Dollmann, whose grasp of English was unsure, asked his guest to explain the meaning of the term and was told that it was someone who was shrewd, cunning, Machiavellian.

The old SS man's face lit up with a smile. "Oh! That is a compliment—for me."

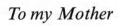

To my Mother

AUTHOR'S NOTE

My life has been decisively influenced by two
men from the former domain of the Habsburgs,
one a grand seigneur and the other an evil
genius. The first was Franz Joseph I, Emperor of
Austria, Apostolic King of Hungary, King of
Bohemia; the second, Adolf Hitler, born the
son of a customs officer at Braunau am Inn.

Both men were Austrians.

I

HIS MAJESTY

WE WERE greeted in the reception hall of the Emperor's villa by an ancient gentleman whom my mother addressed as 'my dear Count.' He kissed her hand gallantly and ignored me, possibly because he did not see me. In any case, my own attentions were claimed by a row of glass cases filled with stuffed birds of every description.

'Poor Rudolf's birds,' observed the elderly cavalier, turning to my mother, who later told me that Crown Prince Rudolf had shot and collected the birds in his youth.

We were conducted up a staircase and through a number of reception rooms, one in grey, another in red, and all—so I was informed in a whisper—formerly used for various purposes by the Empress Elisabeth. We were even allowed to peer into the study that had once belonged to the unhappy Wittelsbach princess. Every square inch of the wall was covered with pictures of the Empress's best-loved horses. What impressed me most was a large painting of a gorgeously attired zouave who had once, so the Count informed us, been favourite master of hounds to this most capricious of European princesses.

Emerging from this equine museum with its mixture of amiable and demonic-looking fauna, we entered a series of waiting-rooms, in one of which our escort left us. My mother was still nervously adjusting her own gown and my 'archducal suit' when the door nearest to us opened and the Count summoned us inside.

I saw a fair-sized desk in one corner, and standing in front of it an extremely old gentleman whose picture I had often seen before. His Imperial and Royal Majesty Franz Joseph I of Austria-Hungary approached my mother with a light tread, drew her to her feet from the low curtsey into which she had subsided, and conducted her to the other end of the room, where stood an old-fashioned sofa and a few armchairs. He beckoned to her to sit down with an inimitable gesture and left me standing where I was, optimistically hoping that he would ignore me just as his Aide-de-Camp General had done.

Not until we were outside again did my mother tell me that this was the celebrated 'Emperor's Corner', where the sovereigns of Russia, Germany and Austria had once held an historic conference.

While the low hum of conversation drifted across to me from the said corner, I stood politely near the door. The longer I stared at the old gentleman the more he seemed to resemble God, and I would no more have dared to approach or address him than I would have dared to accost the Almighty. He was as remote from me as if he were floating on a purple cloud and might ascend into Heaven at any moment.

I cannot recall what the Emperor and my mother chatted about. I only remember that the old man said he was glad the Empress had been 'spared this'. Presumably he meant the Sarajevo assassination and the risk of war, but he may have been referring to something else—I am not sure.

Suddenly, Almighty God said:

'So that's the lad, is it?'

He raised his hand a fraction and beckoned me over.

'What's your name?'

'Eugen, Your Majesty,' I stammered, remembering my lines.

'Well, Eugenio,' said the voice in my ear, 'be sure you grow up as a fine man as Eugenio of Savoy. He was a faithful servant of my house.'

I knew something about Eugene of Savoy, thanks to my Christian name. What I did not know was that, if it had not been for this faithful servant of the Habsburgs, the chair opposite me would probably have been occupied, not by His Majesty, but by a Turkish sultan or a descendant of some other arch-enemy of the archducal house in the days of Eugene of Savoy.

'When were you born?' was the next question.

I saw my mother bite her lip, but my orders were to speak up boldly, so I said:

'The twenty-first of August 1900, Your Majesty.'

Then I quailed. Almighty God passed a hand across his eyes as if trying to brush something away. He turned to my mother:

'Well, well . . . August twenty-first—just like poor Rudolf.'

I did not understand this, of course, but the moment passed quickly.

The Emperor opened one of his desk drawers with the slightly tremulous hands of old age. Slowly, he held out the picture of a very lovely woman whom I at once recognised. Thick coils of golden-brown hair were dressed low on her neck, her charming face was overlaid with an expression of gentle melancholy, and the pale-blue ribbon of an order lay draped across her peerless bosom. It was a copy of the famous portrait of Elisabeth of Austria as a young woman, painted by the masterly hand of Franz Schlotzbeck.

'How beautiful the Empress was,' Franz Joseph murmured almost inaudibly. 'Would you like to take your leave now, Baroness?'

He invariably addressed my mother as 'Baroness', which was correct only to the extent that he had made her grandfather a baron and privy councillor many decades earlier. She nodded with tears in her eyes, and the audience was at an end. She gave another curtsey and the old man gallantly escorted her to the door, where the Count reappeared. Then, for the last time, I heard the quiet voice of Europe's last great emperor:

'*Au revoir*, Baroness—until next year, perhaps. It was good of you to visit me. I much appreciated it.'

We were conducted past the antlers and horses' heads and through the Imperial Villa's suite of reception rooms, this time to a side entrance. We were soon to learn why.

When we neared the great fountain in front of the colonnaded portico we saw that the grounds were swarming with people— locals and townsfolk, farmers, foresters, soldiers, and countless children carrying bunches of Alpine roses and nosegays of Edelweiss. They stood there, hushed and silent, until the door to the balcony opened and the old, old man emerged as though descending from Olympus.

At that moment there came to our ears, softly at first, then ever louder, the strains of Haydn's old Imperial anthem:

'*Gott erhalte ...*'

We saw Franz Joseph raise a hand to his cap in salute. Not long afterwards he returned to Vienna, never to see his beloved Ischl, his stags and chamois again. It was 10 July 1914, and Europe stood on the threshold of the First World War.

The audience in the Imperial Villa at Ischl is my most vivid memory of the old Europe, whose last great monarch Franz Joseph was. I have never forgotten him, and to me, despite all subsequent encounters with the self-styled great, he has remained the embodiment of regal majesty.

My mother lived on in her native Munich, savouring her innumerable memories of the Habsburg-Wittelsbach era. She continued to give tea-parties accompanied by tarot, the bridge of the contemporary *beau monde*. Franz Joseph and his Aide-de-Camp General were no more, alas, but Bavarian ministers and generals seemed only too ready to fill the gap.

As for me, it was time to concentrate seriously on my studies, and I devoted myself to university life.

The years 1920–6 were rewarding years indeed. What a university, what teachers! When I tick off their names—the historians Marks and Oncken, the art historians Wölfflin and Pinder, Vossler and Strich in the fields of literature—I get the impression that Munich must have undergone a last humanist renaissance at this period. It was a time without mass-activity, without shortages of teaching space and accommodation—a time, moreover, when no motor shows were held in front of the University. Whether eminent or less eminent, celebrated or less celebrated, teachers still had time to spare for their pupils. They used it not only to acquire a personal knowledge of the young men who hoped to graduate under their guidance but to assess their human and intellectual qualities. Universities, and Munich's Ludwig Maximilian University in particular, had yet to become party-political training establishments or centres of advancement for budding technocrats.

Through Wölfflin, a man of Swiss calm and composure, I came into contact with his friend and kindred spirit Ricarda Huch. Their duologues on the political and artistic problems of the Thirty Years War afforded me hours of unadulterated pleasure. At the home of my tutor, Oncken, an old National Liberal whose small french beard gave him the look of a latter-day descendant of Napoleon III, I encountered the surviving representatives of German liberalism. Constitutional history figured as prominently in their conversation as the doctrine of the pre-eminence of foreign policy.

Just before Christmas 1926 I graduated under Oncken with a thesis on the problems of imperial policy during the second half of the sixteenth century—and graduated, much to my surprise, *magna cum laude*. If I have acquired any aptitude for logical and critical thought, I owe it to the distinguished man who was my tutor and patron.

However, the really memorable feature of my student days in Munich was provided neither by Oncken, Wölfflin nor Strich, despite the knowledge of history, art and literature which I derived from them. What endowed this period with true lustre was the integrated personality of Vossler, the Romance scholar. It is to him and his courses and lectures on the great French literature of the nineteenth century that I owe my acquaintanceship with two writers who have accompanied me throughout my life. One of them, Stendhal, was to be my constant companion in Italy. My studies in Parma were profoundly coloured by his *Chartreuse de Parme*, even though I never managed, for all my strenuous endeavours, to discover the location of the Farnese Tower.

The other, Balzac, became my life's greatest teacher. As an historian, I have applied myself to the Roman emperors and the Hohenstaufens and made the Roman Popes of the sixteenth century a special field of study. Thanks to my mother, I have preserved an undying regard for the strange and splendid figures of the house of Habsburg. Nevertheless, the world of great historical personalities has never endowed me with as much experience of life, as much knowledge of the human heart and its outward manifestations, as the French writer's immortal *Comédie humaine*. Vossler predicted—and hoped—that each of his students would sometime share the moment which fell to the lot of young Baron Rastignac after the burial of the unhappy Père Goriot. I shall never forget how he used to quote passages from this episode by heart:

> Thus left alone, Rastignac walked a few steps to the highest part of the cemetery, and saw Paris spread out below on both banks of the winding Seine. Lights were beginning to twinkle here and there. His gaze fixed almost avidly upon the space that lay between the column of the Place Vendôme and the dome of the Invalides ; there lay the splendid world he had hoped to gain. He eyed that humming hive with a look which foretold its despoliation, as if he already felt on his lips the sweetness of its honey, and said with superb defiance: 'It's war between us now.'

I was reminded of this passage on my arrival in Rome, as I stood on the Monte Pincio and watched the clouds in the gathering twilight, but I never formed any such clear-cut decision as Monsieur de Rastignac. To this day, I have no idea how to classify or define the bitter-sweet love for Rome which brought me so much joy and grief. Besides, I had too much of the anti-Rastignac, Lucien de Rubempré, in me to have plunged boldly into the fray. I preferred to leave such decisions to others, which is why I became no more than a Rastignac in Rubempré's clothing or vice versa.

Be that as it may, my tutor, Oncken, had adjudged me worthy of a grant from the Kaiser Wilhelm Society for the Advancement of Knowledge. My field of research, 'The history of Cardinal Alessandro Farnese and his family' (one of the most important and interesting Italian families of the sixteenth and seventeenth centuries), was an over-ambitious one. It still amazes me that a cool and rational scholar like Oncken should ever have sanctioned it, but he did. And so, armed with a thick wad of letters of recommendation, I made my way southwards.

It was spring 1927, and I was bound for Arcadia.

II

ARCADIA

ALESSANDRO FARNESE—'The Great Cardinal', as even his contemporaries called him—had long fascinated me. I had first come across him in Ludwig von Pastor's exhaustive but dry-as-dust *History of the Popes*. The Austrian scholar, whose close relationship with Pope Pius XI earned him the post of Austrian Ambassador to the Holy See, had pronounced Farnese to be well-deserving of a biography. Since the Cardinal belonged to my beloved sixteenth century, and since I was in urgent need of an historical victim to provide me with an entrée to the south, I settled on him.

He was, and still is, a worth-while subject for biography, but he had the good fortune to escape my own attentions in that respect. In 1945 Allied intelligence agents in Rome found a trunkful of documents, testimonials, written records and photographs referring to him. Probably under the impression that Cardinal Farnese was my 'contact' at the Vatican, they appropriated all my material on him. I have no idea where they took the trunk, but this is hardly surprising—the secret service is nothing if not secretive. I can, however, commend Alessandro Farnese to the younger generation with a good conscience. Anyone, whether art historian, literary historian or historian proper, could make something of him.

Alessandro Farnese was the eldest grandson of Pope Paul III, who ascended the papal throne in 1534, at the age of sixty-seven, and occupied it until 1549. All Rome wept when Farnese himself died in 1589, and even Pope Sixtus V, a harsh and austere man who cherished no great love for him, is said to have shed a few tears. He died a cardinal, having been a candidate for the papacy in seven successive papal elections. He left magnificent works of art, palaces, villas, and collections of all kinds. His finest property, which he commissioned from Vignola, was his summer residence at Caprarola, near Viterbo, a place famed for its countless fresco-adorned halls and rooms, its fountains and caryatids, gardens and grounds. Titian painted his portrait several times.

Such was the man to whom I proposed to devote my next few years in Italy. The years spun out into almost two decades and my book remained unwritten, but it would be unjust to pretend that the Allied secret service was exclusively responsible for that. I was equally to blame. Unhappily, I allowed myself to be seduced into concentrating on the story of our own time rather than on the past.

I have no idea how many letters of recommendation Goethe took with him when he travelled to Italy. Personally, I had a large number addressed to the heads of German academic institutes, cardinals and monsignors, professors, authors and scholars. I had some personal letters as well. These derived from my mother's non-academic but capacious private archives, and proved no less valuable to me. General von Lossow gave me a note for Badoglio, and Konrad von Preger, the Bavarian Ambassador to Berlin (an anachronism which still existed at this time), gave me some visiting-cards to hand in at the two German embassies.

I accordingly paid my calls, armed with some visiting-cards of my own. They were far too expensive, but I think my initial successes were largely due to them. Rome in those days was a veritable paradise for graduates and students, irrespective of their private means. If they had a lot of money, it merely meant that they did not have to cram their bellies as assiduously with the ample refreshments provided at academic gatherings as did those whose pockets were not so well lined.

The German scholastic triumvirate in the Eternal City was made up of Ludwig Curtius, Director of the Archeological Institute, Ernst Steinmann, owner and administrator of the world-famous Bibliotheca Hertziana, and Paul Kehr, head of the Prussian Historical Institute. It was to them that I turned first. Being a pupil of Oncken, Wölfflin and Strich, I was taken more or less seriously. All three men listened to my Farnese plans and each tried to coax me into a different field. Curtius urged me to devote myself to the Cardinal's archaeological excavations and collections and Steinmann to his artistic legacy, while Kehr wanted to see me bury my nose in the documentary treasures of the papal archives.

Of the three men who represented German erudition in Rome, Paul Kehr was undoubtedly the most considerable from the scientific point of view. His institute was dominated by the spirit of Mommsen, and it was no coincidence that Mommsen's grandson Theodor also worked there. Discounting the Hohenstaufen period, my knowledge of the Middle Ages had unfortunately been limited to the minimum necessary for passing my examination. I intended to pursue my Farnese studies, if not in the style of Emil Ludwig or Stefan Zweig, at least in an *a fresco* manner, and to confine my study of documentary records principally to the vast correspondence between the Cardinal and the great figures of his day, popes and cardinals, scholars, artists and other members of the Farnese family. I wanted to portray his role at the seven conclaves more from the aspect of personal ambition and human tragedy than through the medium of a study of written sources, a field in which von Pastor's labours had borne far more fruit than mine could ever have done.

Fundamentally, I believe that Kehr regarded anything which had not been gleaned from an intensive and unremitting study of written sources as suspect by definition. The archaeologist Ludwig Curtius was his exact scholastic opposite. He always needed a forum to dazzle, an adoring throng to spur him on. Where Kehr was dry, brittle and methodical, Curtius's lectures had the colour and brilliance of a firework display. If he spoke of Emperor Hadrian in the Villa Albani, a treasure-house of Roman baroque which was generally closed to the public, he *was* Hadrian. If, at the annual gathering in memory of Winckelmann, he paid tribute to that Nestor of archaeology, he transformed himself into Winckelmann. If he gave an address on Goethe—and he gave many, all of them brimming with wit and fire—one could almost believe that he was a reincarnation of Goethe in Rome. He had the great actor's gift of pausing for effect while his eyes roved over his doting audience. Not in vain did countless elderly ladies, especially those of the Prussian nobility, spend their winters in Rome in the late 'twenties and early 'thirties. Their hearts throbbed and their eyes shone in the presence of this erudite and glamorous man. I cannot pronounce upon his scientific work, but he, too, afforded me some memorable moments.

Curtius had a shrewd, slightly snobbish wife. I got on well with her and admired her ability, unique in contemporary Rome, to mix a social cocktail out of representatives of the intelligentsia and members of the fashionable society in which she and her husband delighted. The Curtiuses made a point of living in an ancient palazzo in the centre of the old quarter, which automatically endowed their receptions with the requisite atmospheric *je ne sais quoi*. Whether one had been invited there to meet the Russian émigré circle of Rome, in which case one felt eerily transported into the time of Rasputin and the ill-fated Tsar and Tsarina, or whether Furtwängler was playing—his sister, who was married to Scheler, the philosopher, also worked at the Institute —or whether the 'Georgianer', represented by Karl Wolfskehl, already half-blind, and Ernst Kantorowicz, were giving readings from their works, one could always count on enjoying a social or cultural feast.

I made a trip to the Bay of Naples with Kantorowicz, the German Jew who alone grasped the nature of that universal phenomenon, Frederick II, the Hohenstaufen emperor. His account of the Cumaean Sibyl and her prophecy to Aeneas was a blend of classical grandeur and modern intellect in which Virgil himself would have revelled.

In 1932 I attended Curtius's last major public lecture, delivered at the German colony's Goethe celebrations and entitled 'Goethe as a Phenomenon'. I should like to quote one passage from it. It has not lost its validity, though few people—and certainly not I myself—could have been struck by its tragic topicality at the time:

It is because our national education is still incomplete—indeed, because it only really begins with Goethe—that the idea of education occupies so central a role both in our world of ideas and in Goethe's work. Other nations, with the exception of the Russians, do not realise this. They recapitulate and delve deeper into what they already possess, whereas we seek to delve deeper into what we do not have. They mould what they have in common, whereas we are indefatigable in our efforts to formulate what divides us. This is the fundamental source of our present national misfortune.

The third member of the German academic triumvirate in Rome, Ernst Steinmann, was very much one of the older generation. To any connoisseur of Rome he remained inextricably associated with the Eternal City until his death in 1935, not because he was a great scholar but because his love for Rome was second to none. He loved the art and artists of the imperial and papal metropolis less with his mind, which modestly patrolled the frontiers of genius, than with his whole romantic German soul. He was a typical product of the Kaiser era, with its traditions of princely and feminine patronage. At the court of Kaiser Wilhelm II he had listened with deep emotion to Prince Eulenburg's *Rosenlieder*; in Rome he devoted himself heart and soul to Michelangelo, who was not really his meat. He lived in the Palazzo Zuccari, which had been bought by his two patronesses, the inseparable friends Henriette Hertz and Frida Nord, wife of the famous German-born chemist who emigrated to England. At great expense Henriette Hertz had restored the home of the Mannerist painter Zuccari at the beginning of the century and made it a worthy abode for her fine collection of Italian art and her extensive library of works on art history. The latter formed the basis of the celebrated Bibliotheca Hertziana, situated at the junction of two famous streets, the Via Sistina and the Via Gregoriana, where so many artists and authors from Northern Europe lived during the nineteenth century and where Gabriele d'Annunzio maintained the luxurious apartment in which he wrote *Il Piacere*, that still unsurpassed portrait of Roman *mœurs* in the 'eighties and 'nineties of the last century.

Steinmann was no d'Annunzio, but he did enjoy the pleasures of life—though in a milder and less voluptuous fashion than 'il Divino'. Before his final move to the Palazzo Zuccari, the German government had granted him the funds to complete his magnum opus on the Sistine Chapel, now slightly dated but still one of the standard works on Michelangelo's painting. He then began to collect the world-famous library on the Florentine artist which he later bequeathed, so I believe, to the Vatican.

His salons, adorned with lively Mannerist frescos, were frequented by old and aristocratic Roman society people of the vintage of Prince Bülow and his mother-in-law, Donna Laura Minghetti. Steinmann was a close friend of the ex-Chancellor. I recall seeing Bülow holding court beside his deaf and half-crippled wife—once one of the most fêted women in imperial Berlin—scattering quotations right and left and broadcasting malicious comments on friend and foe in the inimitable style of a latter-day St Simon. Another attractive feature of the receptions at the Hertziana, and one which found particular favour with the ladies, was the presence of the best-looking churchman in contemporary Rome, a Bavarian prince and grandson of Emperor Franz Joseph. After a lamentably brief marriage to an archduchess, Prince Georg bethought himself that the house of Wittelsbach had been entitled, from time immemorial, to a place in the hierarchy of St Peter's. It was an enviable post which not only entailed no expenditure but was well enough endowed to permit its incumbent an ample opportunity to lead the life of an abbé of the Winckelmann era. The Prince, who was dazzlingly handsome, bore a resemblance to his maternal grandfather in the days before he had become Almighty God in mutton-chop whiskers and was still dashing young Franzl. His soutane, with its small lilac neck-band, suited him perfectly. He accepted the admiration due to him and enjoyed the Library's Italian-style buffets in a far from purely Platonic manner. Handsome as a god and man of God withal, he used to stand in the centre of a circle of admiring females, mainly of Anglo-Saxon origin. They were not as beautiful as he was, but then the Church pays no heed to outward appearances. One man who enjoyed chatting to him in a slightly mocking fashion was Professor Nogara, director-general of the papal museums and art collections, another enthusiastic amateur of Michelangelo.

Ernst Steinmann bestowed his favour on me from my very first visit onwards, either because I resembled one of Michelangelo's slaves on the ceiling of the Sistine Chapel or, again, because I knew so many stories about Germany which reminded him of his friend Bülow. He not only took me seriously but, unlike Kehr, did his best to launch me on my forthcoming research into the life of Cardinal Farnese, the great art patron. Schudt, the real brains of the Library and an austere scholar who likened his chief's social functions to sessions with the dentist, gave me access to all the treasures the Hertziana had to offer on the subject of my cardinal. I was allowed to peruse first editions of Michelangelo's poems and contemporary descriptions of 'il Terribile', some erotic and some genuinely illuminating.

I divided the next few months between serious study and enjoyment. They were comparatively successful months, but success in Rome is short-lived, and I am convinced that the hatred which the Romans still bear for Mussolini is largely attributable to the fact that he was successful for so long. Though no Mussolini, I too enjoyed temporary esteem. Then, when my fund of anecdotes ran out, my star faded and I was forced to look around for new roads to success. I remembered in due course that my cardinal had been a great friend and patron of the Jesuits, and that I had been given a letter of introduction to the Chronicler of the Order, Father Tacchi-Venturi. I also remembered that the writer had conveyed in a mysterious whisper that, as father confessor to Mussolini, Tacchi-Venturi was the Jesuits' *éminence grise*.

I was relatively uninterested in the latter information. I had certainly seen large numbers of black shirts and several noisy parades since my arrival in Italy, but not a sign of Mussolini himself. The German and cosmopolitan academics who had welcomed me so hospitably behaved as though he did not exist. He did not annoy anyone, and everyone took care not to annoy him. Besides, what I wanted from Father Tacchi-Venturi was not an audience with Mussolini at the Palazzo Venezia but permission to use the Vatican's archives and libraries—and this I duly obtained.

The Father lived in the heart of Rome in a palatial baroque building near the Gesù, a church commissioned for the Jesuits by Cardinal Farnese and begun by Vignola in 1568. After passing through a monastery garden, silent save for the gentle plashing of a fountain and enclosed by ancient trees, I was conducted into an equally secluded study. Here a bald priest rose politely from his desk, which was covered with documents and parchment tomes. My letter of introduction lay before him. He spoke excellent German, and I soon found myself drawn into a conversation about my native land. One of his first questions was:

'Do you know a Signor 'Itler?'

I did not understand him to begin with, but as soon as I realised who he was referring to I told him what I knew about Hitler. He pressed me for details, and I was lucky enough to be able to give him some information acquired at second hand from General von Lossow. He went so far as to make notes, several times murmuring '*molto interessante*' to himself. We continued to converse about Signor 'Itler until I could think of nothing more to say.

Then he tugged an old-fashioned bell-cord and a deferential young priest appeared. Having dictated two letters on Compagnia di Gesù paper, Father Tacchi-Venturi gave them to me. They were addressed to the Prefect of the Vatican Secret Archives and the Prefect of the Vatican Library, two men with the identical surname of Mercati. The Father explained that the holders of these important posts were brothers. When I took my leave he pressed a thick volume of his history of the Jesuit Order into my hand and invited me to pay him another visit. Having bowed myself out, I decided to take a look at his church—my cardinal's church—together with the chapel dedicated to St Ignatius, the founder of the Order. The four lapis-lazuli pillars adorning the chapel and the huge effigy of Ignatius, apparently made of silver, did not quite accord with my preconceived notions of the saint's asceticism. However, I was highly impressed by what his followers had made of the place, and I also knew why my cardinal had taken so much interest in the Society of Jesus.

Next day, after a glorious morning stroll along the side and rear of St Peter's which took me through Bramante's courtyards and fresco-covered galleries, I handed in my two letters. Twice I was appraised by alert priestly eyes, and twice I was accorded a cool handshake. Then I was given two reader's cards stamped with the papal arms and made my way into the spacious halls beyond. They were thronged with busily writing priests of all ages, attired in robes of every hue. Having registered the fact that

I was in a temple of erudition, I started to look up 'Farnese' in the immense card index. My heart sank. I envisaged spending the rest of my days there, and, lovely though my morning journey to the tree of knowledge had been, the prospect of plucking its fruits seemed arduous in the extreme.

I was still rummaging desperately in the filing cabinets when I felt a light touch on my shoulder. Behind me stood a young, black-clad priest who looked like a converted Siegfried—slim, blond and blue-eyed enough to have excited the attentions of any modern film producer. I must have looked very German myself because he gave me an encouraging smile and offered to help me. He did, in fact, help me a great deal, and we became firm friends. He was living with a number of fellow-priests, most of them equally young, at the Camposanto Teutonico, or German Cemetery, behind the colonnades of St Peter's Square. Attached to this last resting-place of notable Germans who had died in Rome was a seminary at which young German priests pursued historical or theological research, either independently or in conjunction with the Prussian Historical Institute. There was nothing monastic or ascetic about the Camposanto. Once or twice a year a jovial crowd of German scholars, young and old, used to gather on the terraces of the college, which afforded a superb view of the dome of St Peter's. A barrel of Bavarian beer would be procured from home, much to the delight of the Italian guests, and everyone —from Curtius and his staff to the gentlemen of the Bibliotheca Hertziana and the Prussian Institute—put in an appearance. Towards midnight, when the Roman moon was shining above St Peter's, voices would be raised in song—profane rather than sacred. The close proximity of the slumbering Pope lent the scene a unique flavour. Next morning invariably brought caustic complaints and accusations from the eminent old monsignori who were spending the twilight of their days in an adjoining palazzo. They regarded these nocturnal symposia as works of the devil and meet to be condemned. However, since His Royal Highness Monsignor Prince Georg was a regular patroniser of such functions—if only because of the good Bavarian beer, ham and sausages—the devil prevailed after all.

Young students from the rest of Europe and America invited

each other to social gatherings with equal regularity. All the larger nations and many of the smaller possessed institutes of varying elegance, mostly in the Valle Giulia, a valley-like indentation at the foot of the Monte Pincio.

What I did not know at the time and only learned in 1945 was that the inmates of the English Academy in the Valle Giulia voluntarily co-operated with their justly renowned Intelligence Service. They did so for no reward other than an agreeable awareness that they were serving their country. Given the necessity for intelligence work, I find this approach to it far more appealing than later techniques of a fundamentally similar but far less lighthearted nature.

The grandest of these youthful gatherings were given by the French at their embassy on the Quirinal. This was situated in the Palazzo Farnese, begun by my cardinal's grandfather and completed by his grandson. Because my predilection for Alessandro Farnese had become something of a talking-point, I used to act as a retailer of anecdotes from the turbulent life of the greatest Roman art patron of his day, and, as I stood talking in those fresco- and tapestry-adorned rooms, his successes became my own.

Then, again, when I stood late at night in front of works by Michelangelo and other great names in architecture, my opinion of myself dwindled and I began to feel that it was time to bid the Eternal City a temporary farewell. After all, other parts of Italy were also closely associated with my cardinal and his house. His brother Ottavio had been the Duke of Parma and Piacenza, so the archives and libraries there would undoubtedly contain an abundance of material for my biography. In addition, the name Parma was redolent of violets, Stendhal's *Chartreuse de Parme* was one of my favourite books, and it would doubtless be amusing to pick up the trail of Marie Louise, Napoleon's pleasure-loving consort. It was as Duchess of Parma that she only too swiftly found a replacement for the man she had never been worthy of. In short, I had ample reason to embark on a voyage of discovery and exchange the gay and hectic life of the capital for the provincial calm of Northern Italy.

I have never regretted my six months there. Admittedly, the

violets turned out to be a snare and delusion. I never saw fewer violets than I did in Parma, and the scent manufactured from the few there were could only be described as pitiful. The same applied to Stendhal's celebrated Torre Farnese, the tower in which Fabrizzio del Dongo was incarcerated. It existed only in the author's imagination, though the palace of the Duchess of San-severina and many other enchanting features of his immortal novel were still in existence. I began by concentrating pleasurably on Fabrizzio's escapades and love-life—that is, until I discovered Maria Louise. Then I forgot all about violets, the Torre Farnese and the Carthusian monastery of Parma.

I am not, of course, referring to Napoleon's brainless bed-mate, who ruled her pretty little duchy reasonably well—with mild sensuality and the assistance of a man or two—from 1816 onwards. No, far from sitting with majestic ennui atop a monu-ment in Parma, my Maria Louise was very much alive. She worked as a librarian in the Public Records Office and had been instructed to initiate me into the archivistic mysteries of her personal domain. She had neither the silly china-blue eyes nor the egg-shell colouring nor the Habsburg lip of the Archduchess. She was as dark as one could have wished, and her velvety al-mond-shaped eyes had a besotting quality wholly appropriate to a romance in a North Italian duchy. She taught me a great deal. For instance, I still have an exact recollection of Parma—the vast palace of the Farnese; the Pilotta with its three courtyards and its art gallery containing famous paintings by Correggio, who was born in the vicinity of the city; and, above all, the equally famous Teatro Farnese, whose 4500 seats made it the largest theatre in the contemporary world when it was built by a pupil of Palladio in 1620.

Maria Louise knew every ancient street and palace. She drove with me to the summer residence of the Farnese—Colorno, whose peaceful rococo gardens, romantic, time-worn fountains and classical temples of love harmonised perfectly with our mood of youthful enchantment. She also initiated me—this being one sphere of interest which Maria Louise fully shared with her ever-ravenous namesake—into the mysteries of the culinary delights of Emilia, the province to which Parma belongs. My gratitude to her endures to this day. I have never yet eaten ham as tender as that of Parma, never tasted asparagus as delicate as in *asparagie alla parmigiana*, which is renowned throughout Italy, never encountered a cheese more delicious than fragrant golden-yellow Parmesan, never enjoyed *piatto bollito*, a dish compounded of tender *zamponi*, or pigs' trotters, stewed with beef and a diversity of sausages—a dish to be dissected with the fork alone, as at the court of His Apostolic Majesty in Vienna—more wholeheartedly than I did at Parma. There in the modest trattorias overlooking the small river of the same name, my enjoyment would be crowned by a white Albano or a dry and sparkling Lambrusco, which smacked of the fertile soil of Emilia itself—crowned, too, by the presence of Maria Louise, so blissfully unlike the picture of Italian women and Italian love affairs painted by German academics, romantics and classicists.

I had never been wholly convinced by German poets' and scholars' accounts of their affairs with foreigners, and my own experience with Maria Louise clinched the matter. The creatures who peopled their Arcadian idylls—Southern belles with smouldering eyes and the mentality of Campagna sheep, sentimental damsels whose interests were confined to baubles and finery, dream-girls whose thoughts had not yet turned to marriage and child-bearing—none of these existed outside their imagination. Disillusionment at the hands of Maria Louise was an enjoyable process.

Six months went by, and, despite all my efforts, nothing remained in Parma to justify my further presence there. Maria Louise's parting gift to me was a small book penned by herself and devoted primarily to her namesake's private life, which was nothing if not gay. The historical Marie Louise rediscovered in the arms of General Neipperg the joys that had once been bestowed upon her in such abundance by Napoleon, whom she quickly forgot. She survived the death of her lover, who later became her husband, with equal ease. A few years after his demise she married the Comte de Bombelles, another Frenchman with a turbulent past but not one who had succeeded in becoming Emperor of the French. Their marriage, as described by Maria Louise, pursued a harmonious course. The now aging Duchess of

Parma divided her time between embroidery and church-going. The only thing that survived her was her love of music, for which she made available a charming Late Empire opera house in her own residence. Giuseppe Verdi was so smitten with it that he dedicated one of his earliest operas to her.

Armed with this reading matter, I drove from Parma direct to Naples, whither the art treasures and documentary records of the Farnese had found their way in 1734 as a result of the complex and wearisome dynastic links between the Farnese, who had become unprolific, and the considerably more prolific Spanish Bourbons. Whenever I had broached my plans in Rome, every one had agreed that Naples was the true burial-place of my cardinal, and that his literary remains must lie interred somewhere in the city's archives, which were renowned for their profusion and disorder.

Having acquainted myself with the ritual which must be observed there, I knew that the first step to be taken by any foreign student who wanted to achieve results was to pay his respects to the city's uncrowned spiritual king, Benedetto Croce, the world-famous philosopher, critic, historian and scholar. While I was in Munich, Vossler had given me a letter of introduction to his friend, with whom he maintained a lively correspondence. In view of my wholly inadequate philosophical training, he expressed the hope that Italy's greatest living philosopher would not draw me into conversation on the subject, and Maria Louise had strongly urged me not to mention Mussolini or Fascism, which Croce uncompromisingly rejected. The fact that nothing had ever happened to him testified to the Italian dictator's magnanimity and humanity—qualities which distinguished him from his fellow-dictators. Croce lived in seclusion, surrounded by pupils of both sexes. His books continued to be published, however, and his review *La Critica*, which had gained him such a vital influence over the intellectual life of his country, appeared as regularly as if relations between the regime and the irascible philosopher were of the very best.

Croce lived in the old quarter of the city in one of those baroque Neapolitan streets which exist nowhere else in the world, and which foreigners—God be praised! —find unappetising. It was there that I first encountered the smell which has remained associated in my mind with Naples ever since: a mélange of sea air and fish, orange-blossom and garlic, which envelops the sun-burned bodies of the city's inhabitants in a stupefying aura of half-repellent, half-exciting sensuality. Croce's palazzo was a vast and gloomy building with courtyards which teemed with grimy children and shushing mothers. An elderly maid opened the door suspiciously and left me waiting in a passage crammed with book-shelves before ushering me into the great man's study. My first reaction was one of disappointment. Croce had neither the Frenchified elegance of my old tutor, Oncken, nor the Swiss masculinity of Wölfflin nor the oak-hewn nobility of his friend Vossler. A short, stocky man with an office-clerk's face and a small moustache adorning his upper lip emerged from behind a mountain of books. Indeed, books were all I saw at first. Lining the walls, scattered across the floor and piled on the green plush armchairs, they transformed the room into a veritable book-worm's paradise.

Croce shook hands with a cordial smile and told me to find a seat somewhere. A typewriter was chattering away next door, and I could hear the sound of approaching voices. They belonged to his pupils, an inelegant bunch of young men and women whose rather grubby linen and heavy horn-rimmed glasses were offset by intelligent eyes and splendidly unconventional manners. They immediately accepted me as one of themselves. Conversation turned to the position of German universities and university teachers, notably Vossler, whom Croce much admired. One of his pupils led me to a shelf which contained nothing but books by the master of the house—volume after volume, including historical works on the Kingdom of Naples and the baroque period in Italy, his celebrated *Logica*, treatises on Hegel and G. B. Vico and, standing beside them in long rows, bound vol-umes of *La Critica*. Such was the output of this small and out-wardly unprepossessing man. At this time, the beginning of the 'thirties, Croce was almost sixty-five and looked ageless.

Eventually they forgot about me and embarked on a fierce philosophical debate. I should have been hard put to it to follow them in German, and my knowledge of Italian, which I owed in no small measure to Maria Louise's stern criticism, proved totally unequal to their cascades of Neapolitan dialectic.

At the height of the discussion the grim old maid-servant appeared with a trayful of small coffee-cups. I quickly ascertained that the china was magnificent and the espresso truly divine. The maid reappeared several times with more cups. We sat on books, cushions and boxes at the philosopher's feet. The scene bore no resemblance to a debate between Socrates and his young men, but it seemed no less impressive to me.

The hours sped by, until all at once—it was now nearly ten o'clock and I had arrived at six—the party broke up. I later learnt from the men that the girls had to go home to supper, for which ten o'clock appeared to be the recognised Neapolitan hour. Croce asked me to send his regards to Vossler and urged me to call on Count Filangieri at the Grande Archivio in two days' time. It would be enough, he said, to mention his name.

Two days later I again sauntered through the old quarter, with its enchanted maze of alley-ways and myriad smells, this time bound for the Grande Archivio. It was romantically housed in a former Benedictine monastery and turned out to be a positive labyrinth of rooms, cloisters and courtyards. It, too, smelt of everything imaginable—not merely of files and documents—and the noise of the narrow streets surrounding it was deafening.

Count Filangieri himself smelt of fresh Eau de Cologne, was carefully manicured, and looked like a Spanish viceroy of Naples. He belonged to one of the city's foremost aristocratic families, and the street in which his ancestral palace stood bore a name which had given Naples an entire museum, a sizable art gallery, precious porcelain from the Capodimonte manufactory, and a valuable library.

The Count, who had been informed of my requirements by one of Croce's pupils, led me through a bewildering multiplicity of rooms and courtyards to some subterranean vaults heaped with dust-covered bales of documents which looked as if they had remained undisturbed for centuries. He put everything at my disposal—the documents, the dust of ages, and an old attendant who had trailed around after us, clad in a sort of livery. Don Gaetano—he set the greatest store by this mode of address—

resembled a bastard child of the Bourbons. He was to be at my service for the duration of my labours in the Archivio Grande. He behaved as if he were doing what I wanted: in reality, I did what he decreed. It was a mild but unmistakable form of tyranny. Every morning I would come upon him holding an immense chunk of bread laden with tomatoes, garlic or onion. He stared mournfully at me and conveyed, by means of one of the peculiarly Latin gestures which I mastered to perfection in the course of our acquaintanceship, that he had nothing to drink. The problem was eventually solved by the offer of a daily wine allowance, and Don Gaetano vanished. Visibly cheered and fortified, he re-appeared after a lengthy interval accompanied by two younger minions. Records of centuries of Farnese sovereignty were dumped on my desk. When the family archives were transferred from Parma to Naples in the eighteenth century, the documentary relics of everyone—kings and emperors, popes and cardinals, dukes and duchesses—had been bundled together higgledy-piggledy and tied up with cord. Now they lay invitingly before me, awaiting resurrection. It was an archivist's treasure-trove of unique importance, and my one regret was that I had not received any archivist's training. What was more, rather than cut the cords, Don Gaetano always ignored my eagerness and applied himself with endless reserves of truly Bourbon patience to the task of unpicking them. Since they were Farnese cords and had survived the centuries with supreme ease, I suspect that he converted them into one of his innumerable subsidiary sources of income.

At length, when he had collected a substantial hank of cord with many grunts and groans, he would announce that he had been summoned away on important official business and that he invited me to join him in a *colazione* at two o'clock. I dared not refuse, even though I had a pretty fair idea of who was inviting whom.

Having at least bought myself time to explore, to abandon myself to the joys of discovery, I rummaged at random in the papers, almost all of which were originals. For hour after hour, with flushed cheeks, I sat poring over letters which testified to a great age and a great career; but, whenever my excitement and sense of anticipation reached a climax, whenever I had come

upon a letter from Michelangelo, a note written by Charles V,
a sketch by Vignola, my dreams were shattered by Don Gaetano.
He wanted to eat. He knew superb, dirty, splendidly inexpensive
trattorias in the labyrinth of lanes and alleys round the Archivio.
He knew where the *baccalà*, or dried cod, was freshest, where
the cuttlefish was at its most tender, where the *mozzarella*—the
buffalo cheese from Salerno—was at its most succulent. He knew
the only establishments whose white wine really came from Ischia
and whose red wine hailed with equal certainty from the slopes of
Vesuvius. And, since it was he who issued the invitations, I had
to accept.

We ate copiously, well and cheaply, dispelling yet another
German professorial myth, namely, that Italian food is poor
and inadequate. After each of these bouts of self-indulgence came
il conto, the bill. My host would glance at me, then turn to the
landlord and tell him casually to debit it to the account of His
Excellency Count Filangieri, whose guests we were. This would-
be burdening of my protector prompted me, in turn, to demand
il conto. The landlord, who had undoubtedly seen through this
Neapolitan charade long ago, would hesitate to take my money
—the money of someone who was not an '*Eccellenza*'. I am
sure that this was how the courtiers, favourites and retainers of
the Neapolitan Bourbons used to settle their accounts, except
that in their day it was mainly the Inglesi, the friends of Lady
Hamilton, who footed the bill. I duly paid with money provided
by the Kaiser Wilhelm Society for the Advancement of Knowledge. No one—neither Don Gaetano, the landlord, His Excellency nor me—minded. The sums involved were so small, and it
was such a splendid, oft-repeated and ever-varied performance.
Confident that my cardinal would have behaved in exactly the
same way, I paid on historical grounds.

I did not eat with Don Gaetano every day, and I also avoided
eating with him and his Hydra-headed family in the evening.
One visit to his home was enough. He lived in one of those appalling Neapolitan basement flats known as *bassi*. His wife, who was
a cripple and had been confined to their huge iron-framed bed
for years, possessed the charm of a duchess and the soiled clothing of a pauper. In one corner, a toothless old grandmother was

kneeling before a reproduction of the over-popular Madonna of
Pompeii. She was praying, so my burgeoning knowledge of
Neapolitan dialect informed me, for a better life in the world
hereafter. Then a handsome young couple appeared. The woman
looked like a Greek goddess of fertility, which was not surprising
in view of Naples' past links with Greece. A naked infant slumbered against the alabaster curve of her bosom, and clinging to
her right hand were two more children, aged about three and five,
whose looks were far less classical. The man beside here would
have quickened the pulse of any American dollar millionairess
from the canning belt, any English governess willing to spend her
life-savings on a single night of bliss—any lonely queen of German
industry, who would have followed him down the basement steps
without a moment's hesitation. Peppino, as this idol was called,
was the adored son of Don Gaetano. His wife and, more particularly, the mother of his children, was named Marietta. Both
greeted me with the self-assurance which distinguishes the grub-
biest Neapolitan street urchin from a German academic, and
Peppino at once drew me into a lengthy conversation. He spoke a
smattering of German and English, and considered himself a man
of the world. His father proudly informed me that he was a *ragioniere*, an untranslatable term which covers a whole range of
masculine occupations in the commercial field. Peppino was currently employed as *ragioniere* to a duchess, *molto ricca, molto
strana*, and he assured me that it would be an easy matter for
him to secure me an invitation to one of her midnight receptions,
which were famed throughout Naples.

I politely declined this unconventional method of gaining access
to the night life of the Neapolitan aristocracy. Peppino was
offended and his manner became perceptibly cooler, but the atmosphere was restored by the appearance of a huge tureen of steaming *zuppa alla marinara*, which roughly corresponds to the French
bouillabaisse.

It was a lively evening. Several other children or grandchildren
emerged from the recesses of the basso, and the grandmother
was lured from the scent of the wax candles burning before the
Madonna of Pompeii by the aroma rising from the countless
fish-heads, tails and spices which floated in the tureen like a

Mediterranean fleet in review order. Don Gaetano waited on his crippled wife with touching solicitude and celebrated his first glass of Ischia by making a speech in my honour in which he promoted me *barone* and *professore*. When espresso was served I dispatched one of the boys with the requisite banknote to buy a cake named after Margherita, the Italian queen mother, thereby earning universal esteem.

At last, after an hour of pressing invitations to stay, I managed to take my leave. Peppino, the *ragioniere*, extended his hand with a regal gesture and assured me that we should soon meet again. As I quickly discovered, he was thinking of his rich and eccentric duchess: I was not.

Before long he turned up at the Archivio Grande bearing a perfumed black-bordered card inviting me to a reception at the Duchess Rosalba's town mansion at midnight on the coming Friday. I could do no more than express my gratitude and accept. In view of the secret power wielded by Neapolitan duchesses, especially when they boasted a *ragioniere* of Peppino's type, I did not dare to refuse a second time.

The palazzo at which I presented myself on the dot of midnight that Friday was quite as vast, gloomy and dismal as Benedetto Croce's. The entrance was adorned with the majestic busts of two Roman emperors, and visitors entering the courtyard were greeted by the sight of an enormous sculptured horse's head. Peppino, who was waiting for me at the foot of the soaring baroque staircase which led to the *piano nobile*, whispered to me not to be surprised at anything I saw. At the top of the steps, a hunch-backed dwarf welcomed me with a low bow. He was dressed from head to foot in black silk and wore court shoes with buckles. I wondered whether I was being ushered into the presence of a duchess or the manager of a circus act. Both suppositions were correct. I looked round helplessly for Peppino, but he had vanished and did not reappear until my departure. The dwarf conducted me through a suite of dimly lit rooms with painted ceilings. Man-size candelabra stuck with thick candles flickered in corners, their fitful light falling on ghastly scenes of torment from the richly imaginative treasure-house of Neapolitan baroque art. The lighting gradually increased in strength until I found myself standing in a drawing-room draped entirely in yellow silk in the style of Queen Maria Carolina of Naples, ill-fated daughter of Maria Theresa, whose likeness hung in Habsburg majesty on one wall. My last reserves of self-assurance evaporated. Reclining on a sort of divan in front of me, attired like one of the blue-blooded abbesses of the Counter-Reformation, was the lady of the house. At her feet, grinning slily, cowered two hideous and mis-shapen female dwarfs. A silver-coloured, silken-haired lap-dog of unfamiliar breed yapped furiously at me. It was like a bad dream. A white, slightly starched wimple perched bird-like on my hostess's black hair and was gathered round her long slender neck into a kind of Spanish ruff. The rest of her costume, which was black, looked like a cross between a Paris evening gown and a nun's habit, and the only jewellery she wore was an enormous black pearl on her left hand. Her youthful mouth smiled amiably at me. It was a simultaneously charming and inhuman mouth. Not until later, when I knew more about her, did I realise what lay behind that mouth and the Spanish masquerade.

Behind her, mute and motionless, stood another Peppino, but this one would not have been to the taste of a dollar millionairess or industrial magnate's wife. He stood guard over his mistress like a surly Campagna buffalo-herdsman who had been transplanted into a drawing-room. His immaculately tailored suit gave a hint of the muscles beneath, and I should not have cared to meet him on a dark night. Round the walls stood some young noblemen, a few foreigners who could only have been English, and two colourful monsignori who went admirably with the abbess on the sofa. The Duchess introduced me to the room with a sweeping gesture, a few names were murmured, and I exchanged bows with my fellow-guests. No women were present apart from Donna Rosalba and the two female dwarfs, nor did there seem to be any food and drink in evidence. I waited for something to happen.

The drawing-room slowly filled. A few more lordlings who resembled members of the Spanish viceroy's bodyguard appeared, as did another monsignore and several army officers. The ritual of welcome was the same in every case.

I grew very bored. No one seemed particularly anxious to talk to me, nor did the other guests exchange more than a word or two. It was an orgy of blasé indifference which recalled descriptions of similar functions at the court of Madrid—and Naples had long been ruled by Spain.

Then the dwarf usher appeared. He bowed to Donna Rosalba, who mercifully rose and gestured to us to follow her. A large folding door was opened, and we found ourselves on the threshold of a gilded hall which had probably been used as a ballroom in the days when Maria Carolina honoured the ducal mansion accompanied by her favourite, Lady Hamilton, and Lord Nelson. A stage, complete with delightful old scenery, had been set up in the background, transforming the place into a theatre. After standing around for so long, it was heaven to be able to relax at last in the heavy baroque armchairs. The female dwarfs had disappeared, but I soon saw them and others of their kind on the stage. One of the monsignori was kind enough to explain that we were to be privileged to witness a spectacle unique in Europe: the dwarf theatre of Her Excellency the Duchess.

Mussolini ruled at Rome and a man named Hitler was preparing to seize power in Germany, but in Naples, by candlelight and before a strangely assorted audience, a play depicting life in a long-forgotten world was being enacted by hunchbacked and malformed outcasts of fortune clad in the colourful costumes of the seventeenth century.

It was a complex story of intrigue taken from the so-called *Comedias de capa y espada* or 'Cloak and Dagger Plays' of the prolific Lope de Vega. The dwarfs might just as well have been performing it before one of the Spanish kings, who always delighted in the antics of these pitiful creatures. The general effect was of a painting by Velazquez, and the costumes might have hailed from the treasure-chambers of the Prado or the Escorial. Donna Rosalba presided in black and white like the widowed mother of one of the innumerable Philips.

The whole performance, with its meetings and partings, quarrels and reconciliations, ultimate rewarding of virtue and happy ending, lasted precisely two hours. It was now 3 a.m., which everyone appeared to find a highly agreeable hour of the morning. The aristocrats slept all day anyway, the priests and army officers could curtail their duties to God and the King respectively, and the English had slumbered so soundly that they were wide awake. It being long past my own bed-time, I warmly welcomed the reappearance of the troop of dwarfs carrying coffee in minute cups, violet candies and brightly coloured liqueurs. The latter were appalling beverages which made the Englishmen's gin- and whisky-seasoned lips writhe in agony.

The Duchess, who was as fresh as a daisy, chatted to everyone in turn. She placed her family archives at my disposal and graciously invited me to come to her future midnightly entertainments. I did, in fact, attend many other such functions at Donna Rosalba's palazzo. She always had some new surprise in store. On one occasion, ancient Neapolitan dances were performed by what was probably the last surviving troupe from the slopes of Vesuvius, and Donna Rosalba's dusky herdsman joined in the tarantella with the lithe grace of a panther. An elderly princess— ladies had been invited that evening—informed me in a whisper of the youth's true function in life. She mentioned a certain Donna Julia, and it gradually dawned on me that she was referring to the favourite daughter of Emperor Augustus. Taking it for granted that I was acquainted with the lady's notorious love-life, she embellished the subject with racy details concerning the predilection of 'Donna Julia the Second'—our hostess—for seamen's taverns and other places of entertainment frequented by the Neapolitan proletariat but never by ladies of high degree. On one such excursion Donna Rosalba had apparently received a frightful razor-slash across the throat from some jealous Don Juan of the people, who had wanted, in accordance with well-established custom, to disfigure her permanently. The doctors had managed to save her life, but her days of décolletage were past. For all that, whispered the old lady, the Duchess had never given up her nocturnal forays. The only difference was that she now went escorted by a sturdy cavalier recruited from the class of masculinity she favoured most.

As the principessa chattered on, I began to understand the cruel charm of Donna Rosalba's mouth. The historian in me was fascinated by this reincarnation of the imperial wanton from the

Julian clan. Our relationship grew closer, not that she guessed what I knew, and the standard of liquid refreshment at her parties considerably improved under my guidance.

Donna Rosalba could only have lived and died in Naples. She perished, as her stars ordained, beneath the ruins of a wretched harbour tavern destroyed by Allied bombing in the Second World War. The fatal bomb may even have been dropped by one of the cherubic Englishmen who had enjoyed her hospitality, but all this still lay in the distant future. My own stay in Naples gradually drew to a close. Its end came in the late spring of 1934, and was marked by another typically Neapolitan encounter whose future significance I did not suspect at the time.

I had treated myself to a farewell dinner at the well-known trattoria of Signor d'Angelo, once a celebrated folksinger who had earned the approbation of the great Caruso. His restaurant stood high above the city on the Vomero, with the blue sea and shining shores of Capri glinting in the distance. It was a lovely farewell scene, but my quiet enjoyment of it was not destined to last for long. A hubbub arose from the next table, which had been taken by a party of middle-aged men. All five were more or less of the same build, that is to say, short, tubby and unmistakably Neapolitan. They were followed by a chauffeur carrying some giant packages which were quickly borne away by a bustling and attentive Signor d'Angelo. The newcomers dispensed greetings in all directions and received respectful salutations in return.

Taking compassion on me—for what gregarious Neapolitan does not pity a lonely man?—they invited me to join them. They ordered vast platters of antipasto followed by no less impressive bowls of spaghetti and macaroni, lasagne and cannelloni. Then, proudly smiting their chests, they announced that they were manufacturers of all these wonders—spaghetti kings, as the padrone reverently called them. They ate with abandon, disliked the English and, fortunately for me, liked the Germans very much indeed. My references to the Grande Archivio impressed them deeply, but they had never heard of Benedetto Croce. I prudently refrained from mentioning Donna Rosalba because they would almost certainly have known something about her.

When, after disposing of various dishes of marine life floating in magnificent sauces, we reached the sweet course, the mozzarella cheese with its scent of fresh buffalo-milk, and the espresso, they started to question me about my life in Rome and asked if I had met His Excellency Don Arturo. My negative reply caused them profound astonishment. They whispered together, and Signor d'Angelo was set in motion once more. He brought out a tall bottle full of a golden liqueur. This, I was informed, was Strega from Benevento, Don Arturo's favourite drink.

I still had no idea who Don Arturo was, but I did know that Benevento was a peaceful provincial town in Campania, that it boasted a magnificent triumphal arch built by Emperor Trajan, and that the chivalrous Manfred, bastard son of Frederick II of Hohenstaufen, had lost both life and throne there during a san-guinary battle against the Anjous. My friends toasted me and the distant Don Arturo. When we said goodbye they asked where I was staying and made a careful note of the address. They in- sisted on sending me a letter of introduction to Don Arturo and urged me to make use of it, adding *'Non si sa mai!'*—'You never know!' I took leave of the spaghetti kings feeling at once grateful and intrigued.

Next day a huge carton full of spaghetti, macaroni and similar treasures was delivered to my small hotel, and with it a sealed envelope bearing the address: 'His Excellency Don Arturo Boc-chini, Senator of the Realm, Chief of Police.'

My hotel, where I was normally treated with cool civility, became transformed overnight—so much so that I honestly be- lieve I could have left without paying my bill. I studied the inscription thoughtfully and smiled. It was my first contact with the police, let alone with a senior member of the institution. Before leaving I questioned Don Gaetano about the authors of the letter. He went into raptures and informed me that they purveyed their wares to all the barracks, warships and ministries in Italy, also the prisons—not that I ever ascertained whether this was why they were on such intimate terms with Don Arturo. On the principle *'non si sa mai!'*, I resolved to present my letter on reaching Rome. His Excellency would probably decline to receive me in any case.

I was wrong. His Excellency received me many times. If it had been based on him alone, my opinion of the police would have remained untarnished. Unfortunately, there were other police forces and other police chiefs from other countries to contend with.

III

CONTACTS

IN ROME, Mussolini was still the man of the hour. His imperial ambitions were gradually focussing themselves on the Abyssinian Empire, and from now until 1936 Italy gave no sign of any bias in favour of Hitler's Third Reich. On the contrary: the salons and streets of Rome began to see more and more of a stylish Austrian aristocrat named Prince Starhemberg. Attired in a fantastic uniform designed by a leading Viennese tailor and wearing a sort of biretta jauntily adorned with a grouse-feather, he hurried from ministry to ministry, while his shrewd mother, a majestic figure in a black mantilla and lace veil, made a point of attending every Vatican ceremony, large and small. Independence was still Austria's trump card, and Chancellor Dollfuss still stood far closer to the Duce than Chancellor Hitler in Berlin.

Hitler's assumption of power on 30 January 1933 had caused a far greater stir among the German colony in Rome and the Germans in Italy as a whole than among the Italians themselves. For the German institutes in Rome and the young German students there in particular, the carefree days were past. Curtius threw open the doors of his salons more and more rarely, although he kept faith with the Jewish friends for whom he retained such a warm and unclouded affection. The Michelangelo worshipper, Steinmann, chose Swiss hospitality in preference to the rigours of Roman social functions. Opinions among the younger people were divided. From the very outset, many of them made no secret of their dislike, indeed, their bitter hatred for Hitler and his regime. Foremost among these was Theodor Mommsen, the grandson of the historian, who worked at the Prussian Historical

Institute. I had long discussions with him as to the best course to adopt. As early as 1933, Mommsen was firmly resolved to emigrate to America at the first available opportunity. Even though the Americans might confuse him with his grandfather, his name was sufficiently well-known to secure him a place at one of the innumerable American universities. Mine was not. I was confident that old Emperor Franz Joseph was still remembered over there—though even this was open to doubt—but the Lossows, Knillings, Schrenck-Notzings and other great figures of my youth would have made little impression. Mommsen blandly remarked that plenty of other young men had begun their careers on the other side of the Atlantic as dish-washers or bar-tenders and ended up as professors, but I was not attracted by this challenge.

After interminable discussions with visitors to the German institutes in Rome, people with whom I had spent gay and carefree times before my Arcadian years in Parma and Naples, I turned my attention to the place whose primary function was to set me and the numerous other Germans in Italy an example and provide us with a pointer to the future, namely, the German Embassy on the Quirinal. After a brief interlude, during which it was occupied by Stresemann's former Secretary of State, Herr von Schuberth, whose vineyards beside the Rhine were more attractive than their owner, Herr and Frau von Hassell had taken up residence there. Like his predecessor, the new ambassador was a career diplomat. He looked superb and knew it. The eyes of Roman feminine society dwelt pleasurably on his aristocratic countenance, and he suffered their gaze with equal pleasure. He used to give well-attended political lectures which agreeably enriched the Roman social programme. Mussolini and Fascism he appeared to regard with cool scepticism, but it was far harder to fathom his true feelings where Adolf Hitler and National Socialism were concerned.

His ambivalent attitude was welcomed by his wife, a daughter of Grand Admiral von Tirpitz, who, in company with Prince Bülow, had been one of Kaiser Wilhelm II's most dangerous and destructive advisers. Although it went without saying that Frau von Hassell was a lady, she had the misfortune to succeed Frau von Schuberth, née Countess Harrach, who was a *grande dame* to her finger-tips. She would have made an ideal Prussian Oberpräsident's wife, but Rome, unfortunately for her, was not the capital of Prussia. Although she certainly took no trouble to disguise her loathing and contempt for visitors from the new Germany, this was scarcely calculated to make a great ambassadress of her.

Her husband was somewhat more diplomatic. He snubbed the Nazis who turned up at his embassy with great finesse, forgetting —unwisely, as it turned out—that membership of the Nazi Party was not limited to drunks and petits bourgeois. Not even that would have mattered unduly. What was far more important was that he soon began to attend receptions in the the uniform of an NSKK Oberführer. He wore his cap cocked boldly over one ear, and the Heil Hitlers flowed freely, though with a hint of mockery, from his lips. One day, when I asked him what a German of my academic qualifications ought to do, he shrugged his shoulders with a look of weary resignation and replied comfortingly: *'Chacun à son ɡˌˌût.'*

This Delphic oracle would have availed me little if I had not been given a practical interpretation of it shortly afterwards. My friends and I were sitting, once more immersed in the topic of the moment, in the main square of the small but celebrated wine-growing town of Frascati, when an open embassy car drove past. In it sat Herr von Hassell, dressed as an NSKK Oberführer, and beside him, an apparition in black, a youthful general of the SS. One of us recognised him and excitedly whispered the name Heydrich. It did not mean much at the time, but at least we knew who was being shown the beauties of Frascati by the ambassador. The two men were plunged in seemingly animated discussion. The moral did indeed seem to be 'each to his own taste'.

This episode decided me against washing dishes in America. I made up my mind to follow the example set by the leading German in Italy and apply for membership of the Party. I did so without enthusiasm but, equally, without any ulterior wish to improve my personal prospects. I did not need a Party job, I could make a living without a membership number, and my work on a cardinal and his family were no particular recommendation. Before taking the plunge, I used my research on Alessandro

Farnese as a pretext to pay another visit to Father Tacchi-Venturi. As one of the men behind the reconciliation between Fascism and the Church and one of the instigators of the 1929 Lateran Treaty, he had enough experience to be able to advise me on how to establish contact with the dictatorial regime.

The Chronicler of the Jesuit Order received me with polite interest, as before. I found the transition from my sixteenth-century cardinal to the cardinals of the twentieth century a happy one, and was enlightened at length on the beneficial effects of the reconciliation between Church and State, Pope and dictator. The remainder of the visit proceeded virtually without any contribution from me. Alessandro Farnese and his great favourite, St Ignatius Loyola, would both have enjoyed the ensuing monologue immensely. It was a masterpiece of indirect allusion, the most important feature being Tacchi-Venturi's reiterated assurances that the reigning Pope, Pius XI, had gained positive results from his policy of rapprochement with Mussolini and Fascism, and that the Vatican was strongly counting on similar results from the concordat recently negotiated with the German government. There were certain inferences to be drawn from Tacchi-Venturi's hint that the Jesuit Order had never, in the course of its varied history, committed itself unreservedly to a specific regime or form of government, but had always striven to gain the co-operation of the younger generation in particular. I left him feeling thoroughly heartened, and received similar encouragement from people with whom I discussed my intentions at the Vatican Archives, Vatican Library and Camposanto Teutonico.

Accordingly, on 1 February 1934, I joined the Party and was allotted Membership No. 3,402,541. I do not know what number Herr von Hassell held, but cannot leave the subject without wondering, even today, what motives could have prompted him to adopt the attitude he did. I cherish the deepest respect for his tragic death and magnificent demeanour while on trial in 1944. On the other hand, if he was really so permeated with profound hatred for Adolf Hitler and the regime, why did he not draw the appropriate conclusion in 1933, and so give many Germans in Italy a lead in what he believed to be the right direction?

I have before me a file containing two facsmile letters from

the ambassador. The first, Document No. 11, is a letter from
Hassell to Herman Göring dated 23 December 1937. It reads:

> My dear and esteemed Herr Göring,
> The articles purchased by Professor Weickert are being despatched
> to you by today's courier. I rejoice that they have been acquired
> for Germany. Needless to say, no further reference must be made
> to their land of origin.
> I have advanced the sum of 120,000 lire, and should be grateful
> if I could have it back by the next courier, as current supplies of
> lire are extremely short.
> With best regards, Heil Hitler,
>
> > > Yours ever,
> > > > Hassell.

At the foot of the letter Göring noted:

> Many thanks and best wishes for the New Year.

The second letter, Document No. 30, likewise addressed to
Goering and dated 18 April 1938—i.e. after Hassell had been
relieved of his post—is headed 'Haus Tirpitz, Feldafing (Upper
Bavaria)':

Dear and highly esteemed Herr Göring,
On 11 March I crossed the Brenner and travelled through Austria
on my way back from Rome, so was almost an eye-witness of the
great events in which your vital part is known to no one better than
myself. It is equally apparent to me what your personal feelings
during those days must have been: I have only to think of Mautern-
dorf and your sister and poor Riegele, who was not, unfortunately,
there to witness it. From the political angle, I have been pleased to
note the attitude taken by Mussolini, and believe that my work
in that sphere has been useful.
It is only natural that affairs of moment should have obscured
my personal case. However, the new postings have now been largely
completed. You told me on 5 February that no one held anything
against me, that the Führer intended to employ me in another
post, and that I should undoubtedly hear something soon and be
received by the Führer. I have had nothing the past two-and-a-half
months apart from some futile instructions to hold myself in readiness. I cannot regard this treatment as justified. I do not know what

to do for the best—my furniture is in store in Munich. I propose to arrive in Berlin on the evening of the twenty-first, report to Herr v. Ribbentrop and request an interview with the Führer. I should be most grateful if you would spare me a moment and get someone to ring the Hotel Adlon and tell me when.

In loyalty, Heil Hitler!

Yours ever,

Ulrich Hassell.

Nothing ever came of these urgent requests for interviews, which Göring simply filed. There might have been a number of changes for the better, at least from the point of view of foreign policy, if Herr von Hassell's plea for further employment in the Third Reich had been granted. Ribbentrop, in particular, could have found ample use for his diplomatic skill and knowledge of foreign countries. Hassell certainly had a hard time of it in the years between 1933 and 1937. He despised the new rulers of the Reich and treated Italian Fascism with, at the most, chilly respect. He found himself faced on the one hand by a German colony which had become progressively split by Hitler's accession to power and, on the other, by the overt hostility of Mussolini and his associates towards the National Socialists.

The first personal encounter between the two dictators at Stra and Venice in June 1934 was a resounding failure, and had only confirmed the Duce in his tendency to regard Hitler as a sort of Roman governor of Germania. The gory liquidation of the Röhm putsch shortly afterwards and the murder of Dollfuss, the darling of Rome, on 25 July did nothing to improve mutual relations. Though subject to the normally alert scrutiny of the Propaganda Ministry in Rome, Italian newspapers were still able to describe the Germans as 'a nation of pederasts and murderers'.

Relations between the two countries did not begin to improve until during and after the Abyssinian War of 1935–6, thanks mainly to Germany's moral support of Italy when she had been ostracised by everyone else. Benito Mussolini was at the height of his glory during the early days of May 1936. I watched Rome's elaborate act of homage to him in the Piazza Venezia on the night when victory and the founding of the *Imperio* was celebrated. It was not, for a change, an organised or compulsory mass demonstration. The whole city turned out to see and hear the Duce of its own accord. If only the merciful gods had miraculously translated him from the balcony of the palazzo to some higher plane, how much both he and Italy would have been spared!

It was his finest hour, although I heard him say—only a few days before his murder in 1945—that the Munich Conference of 1938 had been the proudest day of his life.

The whole country shared fully in the war . . . Uplifted by the inspiring words with which our beloved King Emperor sent us forth to reward our endeavours, led by the Duce in all our feats of arms, we felt that the ardent soul of the entire nation was with us.

The children, our Balilla and Young Italian Girls, the government, the Party, the administration, the people in its entirety—all were by our side.

And this agglomeration of forces which is called a Fascist nation did, in company with us, rapidly transform the war into total victory.

Such are the closing sentences of *The Abyssinian War* by Pietro Badoglio, Marshal of Italy, Duke of Addis Ababa, a work which I translated into German. It was my first meeting with the man who was then Chief of the Grand General Staff of the Italian Army. I could not know that I would come across the same man again in July and September 1943, this time as a deadly enemy of Fascism and successor to the dictator whom he had once lauded to the skies, but I was, I think, the only German who really got to know him—in so far as it is ever possible to know a genuine Piedmontese. I later had repeated opportunities of meeting another Piedmontese whom Badoglio's victorious campaign had elevated to imperial rank, namely, His Majesty King Victor Emmanuel III. I can only deplore the fact that, while the Germans knew Florence and Tuscany as well as if their grandmothers hailed from there, while they have felt as closely associated with Rome, ever since the time of Goethe and Winckelmann, as if they had been born there, and while, thanks to the Hohenstaufen emperors, they looked upon Apulia and Sicily as a German imperial fief, they know nothing whatsoever about Piedmont.

The King and his marshal were parsimonious to the point of avarice, shrewd and cunning, averse to pomp and splendour of any kind, keener on preserving their personal authority than fulfilling their solemn obligations, born soldiers, and profoundly hostile to any form of dictatorship. They kept this to themselves, however, and in 1936 one of them calmly allowed himself to be crowned Emperor of Abyssinia by the ruling dictator while the other was loaded with the highest titles and honours Italy had to offer.

The conversations I had with the victor of Addis Ababa while I was translating his work were of the sort that Julius Caesar might have had with a German historian whom he had commissioned to translate his *De Bello Gallico*—not that German historians existed in his day. We were more closely associated at that period with reed huts, mead-horns, and forest life.

Badoglio was laconic and dignified in the traditional Piedmontese manner. He acknowledged our military gifts but feared them. He claimed that we won our battles principally by a ruthless expenditure of human life, and it irked me not to be able to retort that there had been one or two pretty sanguinary incidents during the Abyssinian War, the main sufferers being the soldiers of the Negus. When I had handed over the final batch of proofs at the close of our joint activities in the General Staff building in Rome, he gripped my hand with soldierly brevity and presented me with a signed picture—unframed, needless to say.

'I trust you realise that you have gained a friend in Marshal Badoglio,' were his words.

I hoped I had, as, in 1943, did many other Germans, notably Field Marshal Kesselring, supreme commander of the Mediterranean front. Our hopes were ill-founded. On the evening of 25 July 1943, His Imperial and Royal Majesty appointed Marshal Pietro Badoglio head of the new government and successor to the Duce. The Piedmontese had triumphed. The new premier's first proclamation contained an assurance that '*la guerra continua*'—'the war goes on'. Everyone had expected that, but I was less sanguine. Having translated his book, I had got to know Pietro Badoglio fairly well.

Such was the first result, from my point of view, of the campaign against the 'Lion of Judah', as the Negus had styled himself from time immemorial. The second took quite a different form and was closely linked with my farewell dinner in Naples, of which I have already given an account.

I well remembered the thoroughly nice, thoroughly Neapolitan gentlemen who had pressed me to accept a letter of introduction to Arturo Bocchini, chief of the Italian police. In late summer 1936 I received a telephone call asking me if I were prepared to call on His Excellency at the Ministry of the Interior.

Of course I was. Plenty of 'heroes' will claim today that they would not have gone, just as thousands and tens of thousands allege that they never joined the Party or, at most, did so under duress.

I went voluntarily. It was approaching midday, and His Excellency's ante-room swarmed, like the levee of a French king, with people of every condition, high and low, army officers, prefects, quaestors, industrialists and beautiful women. His Excellency was not only powerful but a ladies' man. I entered my name on the visitors' list and resigned myself to a long wait. Who was I, after all? I had certainly not been summoned on account of my seven-digit Party number, so I attributed it to the intervention of my Neapolitans, whom I occasionally met for a spaghetti orgy in Rome and who always regretted that military developments had prevented Don Arturo from seeing me.

I did not have to wait for more than a few minutes. Then, to the chagrin and annoyance of the mighty, an attendant appeared and whispered to me to accompany him. I smiled amiably and followed him into the police chief's office, a large airy room with a massive desk set against one wall. The man behind it had a still youthful face, but one on which burgundy and lobster already seemed to have left perceptible traces. He politely extended a soft, well-tended hand, exposing his small protuberant belly. I noted how well dressed he was, and remembered that his friends had mentioned this. He owned several hundred ties, eighty suits by Saraceni, the most expensive tailor in Rome, and countless pairs of shoes made for him by a bespoke bootmaker who was no less expensive and just as well known.

I was drawn into a conversation brimming with charm and bonhomie. Don Arturo told me how greatly his old friends from Naples had been delighted by my enthusiasm for their city. He further told me that Marshal Badoglio had declared himself extremely satisfied with my translation. He asked me how I liked Italy and how my work on the Farnese was going. He was very well informed, but this could not be the purpose of the interview. The ante-room was still swarming with people, all of whom were far more important than I was. Then it came.

His Excellency was going to let me into a great secret. My festive evening in Naples, coupled with my skill as a translator, had apparently inspired him with '*grande fiducia*' in me. He also knew that I was already '*molto italianizzato*', 'very Italianised'. Above all—and this was the crowning glory of His Excellency's rhetorical performance—I presumably intended to stay in Italy for a long time to come, and nothing would please him more than to make my sojourn there as agreeable as possible: his door would always be open to me. To a foreigner in Fascist Italy, this was pleasant hearing indeed. I said I understood, and politely asked him to disclose his secret. In brief, the Duce proposed to send him to Germany in the near future. He was to act as a sort of personal envoy, and his mission was to gain a first-hand impression of the attitude and views of leading National Socialists, now that Germany's conduct during the Abyssinian War had resulted in an improved climate of opinion. The pretext for this trip was the joint crusade against Communism, an operation which came within the sphere of the two countries' police forces and their various agencies.

This was all very interesting, but I still could not see where I came into it. Don Arturo asked me if I knew Signor Himmler, but I had to disappoint him. When he asked if I had met Signor Hitler I was at least able to help him out with my recollections of General Lossow and what he had said about him.

Don Arturo seemed highly entertained. Then he said something which no German police chief would ever have said. He told me that he would be interested to hear something about my compatriots—what they were like, what they liked to be told and what it was preferable not to tell them. In short, he asked me for a modern version of Tacitus's immortal *Germania, de origine, situ, moribus ac populis Germanorum*.

He openly confessed—and this endeared him to me for all time —that he thought little of Embassy or Foreign Office reports, that he had done his best to get to know Germany and the Germans from books, but that he largely dismissed what he had read as literary or journalistic tittle-tattle.

Accordingly, I gave him a lecture on my family home. I suspect that, like most unrehearsed and unscripted talks, it was an entertaining enough account, at least from an Italian's point of view. Groping for something to say, I seized upon that never-failing stand-by, Goethe. What was it he had said to Chancellor von Müller? As luck would have it, the remark came back to me because it had impressed me so deeply as a student: 'Who ventures to have a sense of humour when he considers the multitude of responsibilities incumbent on himself and others?'

Don Arturo was impressed. Not only was he renowned throughout Rome for his own often spicy sense of humour, but he also had a multitude of responsibilities, among them responsibility for Benito Mussolini's personal safety.

With Goethe's lack of humour and that of the Germans as my point of departure, I advised him to make the most of the fortunate coincidence that his home was at Benevento, near the famous battle-field where the valiant Manfred, favourite son of the great Hohenstaufen emperor Frederick II, had forfeited life and throne. The additional fact that Dante had applied himself to the subject would be bound to impress my culturally minded compatriots. I further advised him against exaggerated courtesy and excessive friendliness. What was considered a prerequisite of social intercourse in his native land was only too readily construed by northerners as weakness, effeminacy, smarminess and lack of proper solemnity. He must not be afraid to speak, however. His Excellency was a celebrated raconteur and after-dinner speaker, and would be able to employ his talents to the full in Berlin. In Germany, speeches were second only to Goethe as a key to success.

And so it went on. I found the situation amusing, though the notables in the ante-room may not have shared my amusement.

Don Arturo never stopped chuckling. After an hour he extended a diamond-adorned hand.

'I shan't forget our time together in a hurry, Signor Dottore. When I get back from your complicated country I'd like you to be my guest, but not here at the Ministry. *Tante, tante grazie!*'

He pressed one of the many buttons on his desk and the commissionaire reappeared. His manner struck me as considerably more deferential. I felt somewhat apprehensive about traversing the ante-room, but everything went off splendidly. I was scrutinised with a mixture of undisguised curiosity, envy and respect. Even so, I was quite happy to get outside again. You can never tell, with police chiefs, whether you will leave by the same route that took you to them!

His Excellency travelled to Berlin shortly afterwards. There he had a purely formal interview with Signor Hitler and also met Signor Himmler, who was deeply impressed by him. He delivered some elegant speeches and captured the hearts of German police officials of every rank because he was so utterly different from them. This trip paved the way for what later came to be called the Rome–Berlin Axis, but I can hardly be blamed for my own small contribution towards it.

United in the struggle against Communism, Bocchini and Himmler spent hours discussing the international situation, and complete unanimity reigned between them throughout Bocchini's stay in Berlin.

Don Arturo told me all this in the course of an intimate but elaborate dinner to which he invited me on his return. For the first time, and from the lips of an Italian *homme du monde*, I heard some informative comments on the new rulers of my native land. I also picked up some no less interesting tips on Italian cuisine of a standard which had hitherto been beyond my financial reach. What I did not know was the significance which this strange association was to hold for me at a later date.

Shortly afterwards I received an elegant card inviting me to get in touch with the sender. 'I hear you play bridge and do translations. I should be delighted if we could meet for the former and discuss the latter in the near future. Vittoria Caetani, Duchessa di Sermoneta.'

It was true that I played bridge with single-minded enthusiasm, but I played an extremely bad game. Perhaps my translations were better. I never discovered how I came to be invited to converse with one of the leaders of feminine society at her dreamlike palazzo in the ruins of the Teatro Marcello in the ancient heart of Imperial Rome, but I was. The Theatre, which had been begun by Julius Caesar and completed by Augustus, used to hold 20,000 spectators. Now it housed Donna Vittoria and her guests, but the latter were legion.

Donna Vittoria, née Princess Colonna, was connected with the English peerage on her husband's side. Her marriage to Don Leone Caetani, Duke of Sermoneta, had also linked her with another of the clans that made up Rome's *aristocrazia nera* or 'black aristocracy'. Just as others collected paintings, porcelain, books or carpets, so Donna Vittoria collected people—new, interesting people. Having 'bagged' Anatole France, Gabriele d'Annunzio and the elder Mommsen, she had now added Mussolini's daughter Edda and her husband Galeazzo Ciano, Mussolini's Foreign Minister, to her collection. All the film stars of her day, particularly those of the masculine gender, had drunk very dry Martinis amid her centuries-old art treasures and made obeisance to the reigning queen of the Roman salons.

She had also conversed with Mussolini (so charming!), but unfortunately the Duce scorned social chit-chat with princesses and duchesses. He might have done better to pay a little more heed to the hellish cocktails that were being brewed there to his detriment.

Signor Hitler had so far evaded Donna Vittoria, but she very much hoped to meet him some day. Curiously enough, her ambition was shared by many female members of the international set, both then and later.

Donna Vittoria's ducal spouse, who deeply abhorred social functions of any kind, had immersed himself in Islamic studies, a field in which his expert knowledge had earned him universal recognition in professional circles. He also administered some 7500 acres of land.

To quote the translation which I later undertook for the Duchess:

The vast domains of the Caetani family were still whole and intact in those days, and would have been far more aptly described as a small kingdom than a private estate. On the one hand, they extended southwards from Rome to Foce Verde and Fogliano, running along the coast as far as Monte Circeo; on the other, they were bordered by the slopes of the Monti Lepini, on which are situated the fortress and town of Sermoneta, and extended as far as Terracina. At my father-in-law's beck and call were countless devoted retainers and herdsmen, probably descendants of the medieval vassals of the house of Caetani. They wore a dark-blue livery, the tunic being adorned with a small silver badge engraved with the Caetani arms. It seemed almost incredible that scenery of such wild beauty should exist so close to Rome. The area was infested with malaria in summer, and thus uninhabited. The marshes lay there desolate and deserted, and the few employees of the Duke who had to stay behind—shepherds, buffalo-herdsmen and watchmen—were all consumed with fever.

The vegetation was positively tropical, and one of the loveliest spots in the whole area was actually called 'The Congo'. The Caetani owned the entire coast from Foce Verde to Cape Circeo—a landscape of indescribable beauty, with kilometres of golden sands bordered on one side by the dull green of the forests and on the other by the blue sea. After the death of my father-in-law my husband sold the whole vast estate which his ancestor, Pope Boniface VIII, had assembled with such loving care in the fourteenth century. The entire area—the former Pontine marshes—has now been turned into arable land by the State. Towns like Littoria and Sabaudia, with their farms and houses full of peasants, are situated in a region which I can still remember when it was a wide expanse of marsh and deserted woods, roamed by buffalo-herdsmen and cattlemen on long-maned horses. All that remains is the eyrie of Sermoneta perched on its mountain-top. Once, gazing down from its towers at the limitless plain at his feet, which extended from the mountains to the sea, Boniface VIII, the Caetani pope, exclaimed proudly: 'All that I can see is mine!'

Such was the ancient glory and present misfortune of the Caetani—although their brand of 'misfortune' was quite tolerable, even in 1937. The palace was an enchanted haven amid the bustle of the metropolis, and its works of art were worthy of a museum. It was easy to picture the haughty, arrogant, worldly woman who greeted me hunting wild duck and moorhen in her kingdom in the Pontine marshes, escorted by Caetani retainers riding long-maned horses with the long poles typical of the herdsmen of the Roman Campagna resting obliquely across their pommels.

The divine scourge of this feudal fief, malaria, was unpleasant in the extreme, but the Caetani never took any effective steps to counter it. Donna Vittoria was too busy collecting scalps, and her husband, the serious-minded scholar Don Leone, too preoccupied with his Islamic studies. The problem was finally and permanently solved by the draining and cultivation of the whole area on Mussolini's personal initiative. Not every dictator can boast such a clean page in the dark book of his life-story.

I kissed Donna Vittoria's hand, which evidently surprised her —perhaps because she had assumed that all Germans clicked their heels and bowed from the waist. An old but haughty footman with malaria-ravaged features offered me a whisky with the air of one conferring a special honour.

Having cursorily introduced me to the members of two bridge fours, Donna Vittoria drew me into the library, where all further talk of bridge ceased. She extracted a thick wad of manuscript from a drawer and thrust it into my hands with the words: 'My memories of Europe in the old days.'

She spoke of my publishing contacts, my translations, and my work on Cardinal Farnese. Like many *grandes dames* of the old Europe and unlike the so-called *grandes dames* of the new, she was a well-informed and skilful conversationalist. Her manner throughout our talk was simultaneously insufferable and appealing. She inquired about Hitler and his associates and expressed the hope that she would meet them if they ever visited Rome, implying that, however uncongenial she might find them, they still merited a place in her specimen cabinet. I had to disappoint her just as I had disappointed Bocchini, whose name was also mentioned.

'*Che simpatico signore. E uno dei nostri, un vero peccato che fa quel mestiere.*' ('What a nice man—one of us. Such a shame he pursues that profession! ')

Quite why she claimed him as one of her own totally escaped

me at the time, though I found out later on, just as I also discovered that his profession was wholly acceptable to her and
her ilk.

Then, with the capriciousness of a Pompadour who picks up a
favourite one moment and drops him the next, she had had
enough of me. I was requested to read her bundle of memoirs,
take an interest in them and obtain a contract from a German
publisher as soon as possible. She insisted on a fee because she
was plagued with so many '*opere di beneficenza*' or charitable
works. What I got out of it was, of course, a matter of indifference to her. Beckoning the malaria-ridden footman, she majestic-
ally gave me her hand to kiss. Our farewells were conducted in
English, as befitted the polyglot tone of her salon.

The bridge-players ignored me and I them. Once more outside
beneath the columns of the Teatro Marcello, I was reminded of
a great lady of the ancient world who had probably sat there and
watched many a command performance. The Lady Livia, prob-
lem-wife of Emperor Augustus, could have been Donna Vittoria's
sister.

Intrigued by the prospect of reading the memoirs of this Roman
matron from the house of Colonna, I dipped into her jottings
while seated on a shady bench in the Forum. As might have
been expected, they were in a hopeless muddle. However, they
did present a truly vivid picture of a Europe dying or already
dead, and if only she gave me a free hand I might be able to mould
them into a delightful collection of vignettes depicting the world
which had, with such charming abandon, committed suicide in
1914.

The fruit of my labours was a book entitled *Vittoria Sermoneta,
Recollections of the Old Europe*. It has long been out of print
and would arouse scant interest today, given the indifference of
the vast majority of modern readers. I can, however, recommend
literary gourmets to browse through the volume, which will repay
their attention. Extravagant parties, masked balls, service at court
as lady-in-waiting to the Queen from 1903 onwards, fox-hunting
in the Campagna—all these things become transformed by the
Duchess's memoirs into a colourful chronicle of contemporary
social life.

My first attendance at court occurred during the State Visit of the German Emperor, who came to Rome with his son the Crown Prince. Who among us could have guessed that the Great War would break out only a few years later? In those radiant Roman springtime days, all was festive and gay. His Majesty the King went with his retinue to the station, the streets along the processional route were decorated with laurel-wreaths, and German and Italian flags flew from every house.

The Queen, surrounded by an enchanting group of young ladies-in-waiting in bright and elegant gowns, waited at the Royal Palace in the so-called Cuirassier's Hall. We all wore Her Majesty's initials in diamonds on a blue sash fastened to the left shoulder and were, at this happy time, in a gay and relaxed mood. I still recall that the Queen had to ask us to remain serious during the solemn ceremonial and not to laugh. Such injunctions would, I fear, be unnecessary today.

The Emperor had come to Rome with an impressive retinue of officers. There was a noise of rattling sabres and jingling spurs as they ascended the great steps of the Royal Palace, all of more than average height and all resplendent in white uniforms, cuirasses, and silver helmets adorned with golden eagles. One handsome, very blond young man from the ranks of these gigantic officers looked exactly like Lohengrin. Sitting next to him at table, however, I discovered to my regret that his conversation was stiff and ponderous to a degree. All the others resembled him closely except the Emperor and the Crown Prince, who talked incessantly and were fond of jokes and witticisms. In consequence, it was among the persons of highest rank that the most unconstrained atmosphere prevailed during this official visit.

I was also summoned for duty at the great reception held at the Capitol by my uncle Prospero Colonna, who was then Mayor of Rome. The three Capitoline palaces had been linked for the occasion by means of temporary galleries decorated with magnificent tapestries. In this way, people could move from one museum to another through brilliantly illuminated halls filled with masterpieces of Greek and Roman art.

My uncle who was acting as cicerone, conducted us into the small hall housing the Capitoline Venus. The famous statue was bathed in a soft pink light which seemed, by some magical means, to imbue it with life.

'With Your Imperial Majesty's permission,' he said, 'I should like to present my official wife.'

The Emperor broke into appreciative laughter.

Next day a banquet was held in the Quirinal at which speeches and toasts were delivered in an atmosphere of extreme cordiality. The Emperor spoke in resounding German phrases of which I understood very little, but his concluding words were uttered in well-accented Italian:

'I raise my glass to the beautiful Italian sun and the prosperity of the delightful Italian people.'

Everything seemed so rosy. Who of us could have dreamt of war in those days?

A bare thirty years later Donna Vittoria Caetani was privileged to attend another gala dinner at the same royal palace, still as lady-in-waiting to Her Majesty. This time, instead of the jovial Kaiser and his gay Crown Prince, the guests of honour were Adolf Hitler and his entourage. It is improbable that the Duchess was as greatly entertained by the new cavaliers, who were devoid of silver helmets adorned with golden eagles and attended the function in sombre black and brown uniforms. The only gratifying feature from her point of view was that His Majesty King Victor Emmanuel III again presided. Having concluded a solemn alliance with his fellow-sovereign, Wilhelm II, he proceeded to extend the same offer to the brown-clad dictator. One toast ran:

To your people, Führer, which has given Europe so much in the way of civilisation and constructive energy, and which you are resolutely guiding towards a glorious future, I express my warmest salutations.

The other was delivered by Chancellor Hitler, this time entirely in German:

Our mutual friendship not only constitutes a pledge of our peoples' security but also represents a guarantee of universal peace. With this in mind, I raise my glass and drink to the welfare of Your Royal and Imperial Majesty, Her Majesty the Queen Empress and the Royal House, coupled with the success and prosperity of the great Italian nation.

A year later peace was at an end, and five years later Victor

Emmanuel slunk surreptitiously out of Rome to escape the ven-geance of his erstwhile Axis confederate, Adolf Hitler. During his flight, which dealt the Italian monarchy a blow as fatal as that sustained by the German concept of monarchy when his former ally, Wilhelm II, fled to Holland in a Pullman car, Victor Emmanuel may well have looked back on the banquet of 4 May 1938 and its pledges of eternal loyalty—who knows? All that is certain is that Donna Vittoria did not enjoy a repetition of the agreeably erotic little adventure that befell her during the Kaiser's and Crown Prince's visit:

The Crown Prince had been paying court to me, in the most innocent way, ever since his arrival. On the evening in question, while filing past in the royal procession, he whispered to me: 'I have kept a rose hidden in my helmet all evening, and would very much like to give it to you. Do you think this would be an appropriate moment? Please take it quickly, but in God's name don't let my father see!' The rose changed hands safely without our being caught.

Rudolf Hess, whose status as Deputy Fuehrer and Reichs-kanzler made him the 1938 equivalent of Crown Prince, certainly cherished no intention of conjuring a rose out of his uniform cap for Donna Vittoria's benefit. It is a pity she never wrote about the latter period of her life. Her salons at the Teatro Marcello became one of the two main centres of anti-German propaganda, and nothing was too foul or foolish, fictitious or malicious, to be retailed there with joyous abandon. She died in London a few years ago, at a ripe old age, a typical representative of the era which had long preceded her to the grave, its death heralded by the pistol-shots at Sarajevo.

The next author to employ my services as a translator was an-other representative of the good old days. After a soldier and a lady of high degree came a high-ranking diplomat. Count Luigi Aldrovandi-Marescotti, whose recorded recollections of the years 1914–19 were given to me to translate, had started his career in 1914 as a councillor at the Italian Embassy in Vienna. Its high-spot had been his attendance at the Paris peace talks of April–June 1919 as principal private secretary to the Foreign Minister, Baron Sonnino. In the interval he had also participated in the Inter-Allied Mission, the Western Powers' final contact with the Tsarist regime when it was on the verge of collapse. The charm of his memoirs lay in his vivid and elegant portraits of the notable personalities who crossed his diplomatic path.

Der Krieg der Diplomaten, as the German edition of Aldrovandi's book was called, may be recommended to anyone who wants to familiarise himself with the Machiavellian techniques and principles of Italian diplomacy. While engaged in translating it I was treated to some memorable lectures by the author, who was an informative and entertaining conversationalist as well as an ardent patriot.

What with my essays in translation and the human and objective lessons they taught me, my contacts with those who had recorded their memories of such varied worlds, and the revision and compilation of the Farnese material which I had accumulated in Rome, Parma and Naples, the years following my return from the Bay of Parthenope sped by in a flash.

At the 'white' embassy on the Quirinal, Herr von Hassell vainly strove to camouflage his loathing and contempt for the new regime beneath the uniform of an NSKK Brigadeführer. No such experiments took place at the enchanted oasis of the 'black' embassy which represented Germany at the Vatican. The Villa Bonaparte had once been the residence of Napoleon's favourite sister Paolina, a fact which was commemorated in the life-size statue of the Corsican in the entrance hall and the scantily clad goddesses attired in Directoire costume painted on the ceilings. Diego von Bergen had been appointed to the post shortly after the First World War, and, if diplomacy be the art of silence and subtle shades of meaning, he was *primus inter pares* among the cardinals at the Papal Court and the other diplomatic representatives accredited to His Holiness. Of course, he had an easier time of it than his colleague von Hassell, who was battered by the billows of National Socialism and Fascism, but he was correspondingly more bedevilled by the hatred which Hitler and his closest advisers entertained towards the Church. I still look upon him as my real politico-diplomatic mentor. Thanks to our mutual enthusiasm for the art and literature of the sixteenth century, of which he had a thorough knowledge, he took an interest in my activities which went beyond routine social encounters at the embassy. One or two evenings a month the ambassador used to receive me in his private study, whose walls were lined with priceless parchment incunabula from his personal collection. A butler would serve vintage port, and Don Diego, who had inherited Spanish blood from his mother, would proceed to tell me about the diplomatic career which had kept him in Rome for so many years. As he talked on in his quiet voice, the tall trees outside in the park where Paolina Borghese-Bonaparte had pondered on far different problems would rustle softly in the Ponentino, the sea-borne breeze which refreshes the sun-baked city towards evening.

Don Diego spoke of Winckelmann, Gregorovius, and his Royal Prussian predecessors at the Vatican—notably Kurd von Schlözer, whose once celebrated *Römische Briefe* are now, like so much else, forgotten—as if they were old and intimate friends. He did not speak of them in the style of Professor Curtius—'as I regard them, as I see them'—but as they might really have been. He described his fierce campaign against Prince von Bülow, who lived near the embassy in his magnificent residence, the Villa Malta, after the war. It was Bergen who, working discreetly in the background, had managed to prevent the greatest Byzantine of the Kaiser's court from becoming Chancellor for a second time after Bethmann-Hollweg's resignation. No published historical work has ever embodied the things I learned in the course of these conversations about the Kaiser's notorious camarilla, the Eulenburgs, Holsteins and Hardens, because, unlike many far less important figures, Herr von Bergen bequeathed no memoirs to posterity.

Yet another highly instructive episode whose details I learned from the old diplomat, amid old books and the aroma of old port, had to do with the concordat negotiations of 1933, which Hitler entered into for prestige reasons and the Vatican on grounds of expediency. Von Bergen had remained aloof from them in the belief that Berlin was playing a double game, and that active personal involvement would inevitably—and gravely—imperil his position of trust at the Curia. Instead, he had left the responsibility to Franz von Papen, the Don Quixote of German history, and to Monsignor Kaas, the ill-fated grave-digger of the German Centre Party.

Diego von Bergen was ably assisted in the fulfilment of his arduous duties by his wife Vera. The ambassadress was a daughter of Councillor von Dirksen, whose beautiful and palatial villa in the Margarethenstrasse had been one of the best-known haunts of Berlin court society during the reign of Wilhelm II.

The splendid reception rooms of the Dirksen home were adorned with great masterpieces of the Italian High Renaissance which had been acquired under the guidance of Wilhelm von Bode, reigning pontiff of the Berlin art world. The master of the house was a personal friend of the Kaiser, who used to meet his closest associates there for private luncheons. These were often attended by Grand Admiral Tirpitz of the impressive beard and even more impressive powers of persuasion, who all too often succeeded in drawing the Kaiser's favourable attention to himself and his calamitous schemes for naval expansion.

Another relic of the imperial era was Secretary of State Richard von Kühlmann, whose brilliant social gifts could often be observed at close quarters when he was a guest of the ambassadorial couple in Rome in later years. Unhappily, he was far less interested in politics than in beautiful women, exquisite dinners and his art collections.

Vera von Bergen was a born ambassador's wife, mainly because nobody ever noticed that she was or claimed to be one. With the clear-eyed courage of a thoroughbred steeplechaser which balks at no hurdle, familiar or unfamiliar, she boldly issued invitations to people from every sector of the political and social spectrum. Although everyone predicted inevitable disaster, her parties always went with a swing. Admittedly, members of the Sacred College and the senior Vatican nobility were amazed to find that others besides themselves were considered worthy of an invitation, but once they had recovered from their surprise they enjoyed themselves hugely.

I still recall an episode, taken out of context here, which clearly illustrates Vera von Bergen's diplomatic skill.

After his dismissal from the Foreign Ministry in February 1943, Count Galeazzo Ciano, Mussolini's son-in-law, became Italy's

Ambassador to the Holy See—a post to which any one of his 45,000,000 compatriots would have been better suited than he. His ebullient and highly intelligent wife Edda, the Duce's favourite child, thus became ambassadress at the Vatican, and it was Frau von Bergen's strange duty, as doyenne of the diplomatic corps accredited to the Pope, to introduce her to her female colleagues and the ladies of the 'black' aristocracy. Edda Ciano-Mussolini had hitherto been accustomed to living as her personality, tastes and inclinations dictated. Social functions at her house in the Via Angelo Secchi were noted for their lavish hospitality, and no one was ever bored. Her tea-time début at the Vatican presented a far less entertaining prospect. The ambassadors' and envoys' wives were hardly famed for their youthful charm, nor was it likely that the great ladies of the aristocracy would deign to throw off their stiff-lipped *grandezza* for the benefit of Edda Ciano.

The ambassadress asked my advice. Having met the guest of honour on numerous occasions, I suggested an invitation to tea *and* cocktails. (I had never seen Mussolini's daughter imbibing tea, with or without milk or lemon.) I further urged her to invite a few male members of the senior nobility—also to cocktails. Although my proposals encountered some initial opposition on grounds of protocol, an experiment in this direction was finally approved.

The solemn hour approached. It was a glorious afternoon in May, and the warmth was already summer-like. Birds sang and fountains splashed in the garden that had once belonged to Paolina Borghese, who had always been so amused by similar functions given on behalf of her imperial brother. The wives of the diplomatic corps, the princesses, duchesses and countesses, appeared. With few exceptions, they were sombrely clad, the predominant colours being black, grey and violet. All wore gloves and most were in high-necked dresses. Having greeted their hostess with as much warmth as they had at their command, they distributed themselves round the Yellow Salon, a spacious room adorned with a wonderful Perugino. Apart from the embassy staff and two or three of the more youthful princes employed by the Foreign Office, I was the only male outsider present. The guests, who were disconcertingly punctual, kicked their heels for a quarter of an hour while the cocktail jugs slowly frosted behind the scenes.

Then Edda swept in like a breath of spring, dressed as Paolina might have dressed. She was ungloved and wearing the gold sandals that had just come into vogue. There followed a ritual presentation worthy of the court of Philip II of Spain as the ambassadress introduced her to the assembled company. Stern eyes scrutinised the new-comer closely, lingering for a moment on the gold sandals and the modern jewellery which was in such stark contrast to the far more valuable but correspondingly more old-fashioned jewels of the other ladies. Edda's face brightened slightly when she saw me, and when I whispered to her that cocktails were also available she became noticeably more cheerful.

Tea with milk or lemon was served to the majority and a cocktail to the guest of honour. Edda sat uncomfortably but with dignity on her hostess's right, ringed by excellencies and princesses, but not for long. Frau von Bergen beckoned me over and commissioned me to show Edda Ciano round the Villa Bonaparte, which the other guests had known so well for so long. Edda looked visibly relieved and we set off on our tour. I chatted about Napoleon's charming and frivolous sister, pointed out the Directoire goddesses hovering on the ceiling and showed her the noted collection of miniatures which our hostess had inherited from her parents. Edda had some more cocktails and the other men drifted across to us. It was a gay and vernal half-hour.

Edda returned to the fray cheered and refreshed. She was like her father in that she could, when she wished, rivet the attention of everyone, friend or foe, partisan or opponent. Accompanying the ambassadress from group to group, she listened closely to the experienced doyenne's whispered remarks before crossing each feminine hurdle. She was courteous, modest and suitably appreciative. She enthused about her audience with His Holiness, the beauty of his gestures, the nobility of his hands. She put on a magnificent Vatican performance in the Mussolini manner, and the black-, grey- or violet-garbed guests hung with eager approval on her words.

The time sped by. Twilight was already gathering in the garden when the dictator's daughter took leave of hostess and guests with a graceful bow. I was privileged to escort her to her car. She glanced round at the twilit loveliness of the May evening and then turned to me.

'*Andato bevone, nevvero, dottore?*'

I assured her that it had indeed gone well, reflecting, not for the first time, that many wives make better diplomats than their husbands. Back in the Yellow Salon, the party was breaking up. The subject of Edda dominated the farewells, and Frau von Bergen received a spate of compliments on the analloyed success of her première. Yet another diplomatic steeplechase had been won—and an ambassador's wife has to know how to ride!

*   *   *

German-Italian relations had much improved in the interim, particularly since Bocchini's tour of reconnaissance. Now that the all-powerful Italian police chief had unobtrusively explored the terrain, Fouché-like, it was the turn of Italian youth. Here, too, Don Arturo had his finger in the pie. One day, after a number of seemingly casual invitations to his office at the Ministry of the Interior, I was introduced there to an uncommonly handsome man whose sole blemish was lack of hair. He fitted my schoolboy image of the Roman Emperors' Praetorian Guard. When I got to know him better I discovered that he really was what a true Praetorian ought to be—no genius, but a loyal and stout-hearted man. His name was Renato Ricci—or, as his friends called him, '*il silenzioso*'. Apart from being intelligent enough to earn this sobriquet, he was Under-Secretary of State at the Ministry of National Education and President of the Balilla, or Italian youth organisation. This meant, in practical terms, that he was Mussolini's Schirach, with the entire Fascist youth movement under his command.

Ricci had a long talk with me while the police chief went about his official business. Youth and police . . . It was a potent combination, though I failed to grasp my own connection with it. The question quickly resolved itself. Ricci and twenty-two young officers from all over Italy were to visit Germany between 24 April and 3 May as guests of Baldur von Schirach, the Reich

Youth Leader. Just as I had had to admit to Don Arturo that my knowledge of Signor Himmler was non-existent, so I had to confess to Ricci that I did not know Herr von Schirach, but I did know something about the Hitler Youth and its ramifications among young Germans in Italy. Instead of donning the uniform of an NSKK Brigadeführer, Diego von Bergen had done his bit by placing part of the park attached to the Villa Bonaparte at the disposal of the German youth of Rome. The result was a sort of club which had precious little in common with similar institutions in the Third Reich. It was run by a youth-leader who owned a chic little Mercedes sports car and was fond of taking the girls in his youth section for romantic drives in the Roman Campagna—a practice which was, I am sure, foreign to Hitler Youth activities in Germany itself. Since he could not understand a word of Italian, he invited me to join his 'staff'. My duties absolved me from further contact with the Party in Rome, which had fallen into the hands of a dangerous character who had received a sadistic upbringing in his youth and was now taking it out on his subordinates.

Whatever bearing my conversation with Bocchini may have had on the contacts between the German and Italian youth leaders, I received a summons to serve as interpreter to Reich Youth Leader Baldur von Schirach when he welcomed His Excellency Renato Ricci and his officers at 12.30 p.m. on 24 April.

I had not met von Schirach before, but one glance sufficed to tell me that he was very much a gentleman. He was good-looking, too, but over-aware of the fact. He was also well educated, and enthused about Napoleon and his valuable library dedicated to the Corsican dictator. I still cherish the conviction that, unlike many other Party functionaries, great and small, he genuinely believed in his mission and his leader. I am equally convinced that he never committed any offence save that of having been Reich Youth Leader, a crime which his sojourn in Spandau Prison has, in my view, sufficiently expiated.

Schirach and Ricci could only communicate through me. This trip taught me for the first time how exacting the job of an interpreter is and what a wealth of responsibility, and even power, it entails. No one has yet written a treatise on the interpreter's art, but I believe that it would be an extremely rewarding venture. All men of destiny, from Mussolini and Hitler to Kennedy and Khrushchev, have had to rely on their interpreters.

Our journey across the length and breadth of Germany was an enjoyable one, as journeys in the company of young people usually are. It took us from Munich to Münster and the Ruhr, and from there to Hamburg, Königsberg, Trakehnen, Rominten, Marien-werder and Berlin. Less enjoyable were the innumerable rapturous receptions and the endless torrent of flattery that flowed between the two youth leaders, straining my German-Italian vocabulary to the limit. I have long forgotten how many wreaths were laid, how many times the national anthems rang out, how many guards of honour marched past and how many glasses were raised in honour of the Italian King and Emperor and the German Fuehrer and Chancellor. It would have been worth while to keep a tally, just for the sake of the statistics so dear to the German heart.

In Berlin the delegation was greeted by Baron von Neurath, the Foreign Minister. Neurath had formerly been German ambassador in Rome, so at least I did not have to interpret for him. In addition, he was anything but an enthusiastic orator, quite unlike Dr Goebbels, who compensated for Neurath's brevity by delivering a five-page address at the Propaganda Ministry. It contained one passage which I have never forgotten:

Furthermore, it is a fortunate characteristic of the developments now taking place that what one does benefits the other, and vice versa. When the Duce of the Italian people conquers Abyssinia, for example, that gives us an opportunity to reoccupy the Rhineland; and when we reoccupy the Rhineland we thereby launch a diversionary offensive which assists Italy and her national leaders in the conquest of Abyssinia.

Baron von Neurath was not present at this simplified exposition of foreign policy, I am happy to say, but His Excellency Renato Ricci beamed with pleasure and found it quite in harmony with his own mental approach. The visitors from Italy were less impressed by Goebbels' unfortunate exterior—a club-foot brings bad luck there, as everyone knows—than by the timbre of his voice.

'*Parla come un tenore*' ('he speaks like a tenor') was their unanimous verdict, which had gratifyingly little to do with foreign policy.

In answer to a pressing request from the latter-day Praetorian leader, the Italians were also invited to inspect Hitler's Leibstandarte, or personal bodyguard. The latter duly marched, drilled, shot and swam for the benefit of the visitors. To a layman like me, the only incongruous feature of this martial display was the presence of Heinrich Himmler, Reichsführer-SS and Chief of the German Police, who spoke no foreign languages at all. I am quite sure Frederick the Great would never have made him a general, if only because of his rimless glasses. On the other hand, his manner towards the Italians—both then and later—was courteous, discreet and self-effacing, whereas von Schirach and his Italian counterpart wallowed in military ambition.

The Italians naturally attended the May Day celebrations of 1937. The disciplined masses, the ceremony in the Olympic Stadium before an audience of 120,000 Berlin boys and girls, the Herculean endeavours of the Third Reich's propaganda machine—all were calculated to impress Ricci's simple soldierly mind and those of his still more impressionable officers. Whereas Police Chief Bocchini had returned from his exploratory tour of Germany full of warnings to his intimates about the immense risks which Hitler and his associates were courting more and more recklessly, Renato Ricci did all he could to convince Mussolini of the unique and titanic greatness of his colleagues in Berlin. This visit, rather than the Duce's trip to Germany in September of the same year, was the real origin of the Palazzo Venezia's inferiority complex, which prompted the Duce to step up his own mass demonstrations and displays of military might to an extent which far exceeded the capabilities and wishes of the Italian people and accorded only with his morbid vanity.

The climax of these festivals of youth was a reception attended by 1300 male and female Italian youth leaders who had been staying at a youth camp near Berlin, also as guests of von Schirach. I returned from my trip feeling convinced that it marked the beginning and end of a brief career as an interpreter, but I was wrong.

Everyone selects the date of a celebration as best he can. Julius Caesar chose the Ides of March as his dying day involuntarily, and March has always been renowned for being Rome's worst month. For 'Italian Police Day', the wily Don Arturo settled on 28 October, which not only coincided with the anniversary of his Duce's march on Rome in 1921 but also fell within the Eternal City's loveliest month.

28 October 1937 was a glorious day in late summer. I was living in the Pensione Jaselli-Owen, a boarding-house named after the Englishman who had once owned it. Now run by a Signora Stefania, it was situated in the Piazza Barberini, with Borromini's and Bernini's joint masterpiece, the Palazzo Barberini, loftily enthroned across the way. Bernini's happy Triton still spewed his jet of water into the air in the middle of the square. A few decades earlier, herdsmen from the Campagna had watered their flocks of sheep and goats at the fountain, presenting a romantic picture which former generations of German pilgrims to Rome had duly admired.

Signora Stefania's boarding-house, while far from romantic, was very Roman. It was inhabited by a motley assortment of people, among them a Roman principessa who had seen better days and a commendatore who had lost his post after a clash with the Fascist regime. The happier present was represented by gay widows and some young provincial deputies, mainly from the south, who were not only enjoying their first taste of power and influence but making the most of it. The food was excellent and the wine flowed freely. The pet of the establishment was Signora Stefania's teen-age daughter, who was fussed over and showered with sweets and titbits by all the residents. Her name was Maria Celeste, though everyone called her Bibi. She looked like a pre-Raphaelite angel, but her character was thoroughly Roman. That one can go far with such an exterior and such a character is demonstrated by the fact that Maria Celeste is now a Roman princess and lives in one of the most magnificent palaces in Rome —but more of that later. At this period she was still little more than a child, and I was doing my best to teach her German at her mother's request.

We were earnestly engaged in this endeavour on 28 October

1937 when Signora Stefania rushed into the sitting-room, pale
with apprehension, and asked me what I had been up to. When
I looked blank, she told me that two senior police officers were
outside in the hall and had asked to speak to me on a matter of
urgency. However, when I was further informed that they were
not carrying handcuffs but wearing swords, full-dress uniforms
and a glittering array of orders, I felt reassured. No policeman
from any part of the world, with the possible exception of South
America, came to arrest someone dressed up like that. I asked
her to show them in. They sighed with relief when they saw me
and shook me warmly by the hand. Then they explained that
their chief, His Excellency Arturo Bocchini, apologised for disturbing me but hoped that I would do him a *grande favore*. At
that very moment, the European and non-European police chiefs
who had come to Rome for Italian Police Day were Bocchini's
guests at a seaside lunch in Ostia. Would I mind coming at once?

I replied that, though I was naturally prepared to comply with
His Excellency's urgent request, I was not a police chief myself.
This made no impression on them.

'Please understand, *caro dottore*. The gentlemen are in the restaurant at this minute. His Excellency Signor Himmler, the guest
of honour, is sitting beside His Excellency Don Arturo, and we
have forgotten to invite an interpreter—you know how these
things are. Their Excellencies can exchange smiles but they can't
talk to each other. That's where you come in. We know that you
are the *padrone*, the absolute *padrone* of both languages, so please
come.'

I glanced down at my clothes. I was wearing a very summery,
very Italian suit and a smart tie with a lot of stripes on it. The
two men noticed the direction of my gaze.

'It doesn't matter a bit. You look splendid. All you have to
do is speak.'

Signora Stefania gave me an imploring nod. Little Bibi asked
if she could come along for the ride and her request was granted
at once. The die was cast. Outside in the piazza the fountain was
splashing merrily and the Triton and his nymphs seemed wholly
indifferent to my fate. Bibi ensconced herself happily in the
luxurious limousine, a specially built Lancia belonging to His

Excellency. I had never covered the distance between Rome and Ostia at such speed.

The blue sea blinked peaceably at me as I pondered the problem of my ceremonial entry, but the short trip sped by like a dream. The name of the luxury restaurant in question was, I believe, La Rotonda, and the table to which I was conducted was semicircular in shape.

There they sat, encrusted with gold and silver braid, adorned with orders and decorations, swathed in coloured sashes, pampered and pomaded—the most powerful men on earth. I had a fleeting recollection of how greatly Sejanus had been feared by Tiberius and Fouché by Napoleon. Then I bowed, much as I had done in the imperial villa at Ischl before the worthy old Emperor Franz Joseph, one ruler who had certainly not feared his chief of police. In view of the latter fact, my bow was a touch less profound. I waited, and a moment later I was joyfully greeted by Don Arturo, who was dressed like a peacock for the occasion. I bowed again, and looked up to find myself staring into the cold, greenish eyes of Signor Himmler. He assured me that he remembered my admirable work as interpreter during the inspection of Adolf Hitler's Leibstandarte in May. His words sounded like an end-of-term report, but they soothed me. I sat down between the two supreme myrmidons of Europe's two greatest dictators, and Bocchini embarked on one of the anecdotes for which he was famed, first in Italian, then in French. All the police chiefs from France, England, Poland, the rest of Europe and elsewhere smiled—all, that is, except Signor Himmler, who had not understood a word. I tried to convey something of the Latin piquancy of Don Arturo's *bon mot*. I do not know that Himmler appreciated it, but he behaved as if he did.

The ice was broken. Needless to say, Himmler was not acquainted with the numerous varieties of sea-food which were set before us, so I had to lecture him on them. His neighbour plunged into a rather suggestive dissertation on the arduous love-life of some of the marine creatures on our plates. Lucullus would have been delighted by the meal, which consisted exclusively of fish dishes—two dozen of them, at a rough estimate. Although Himmler would probably have preferred a German beefsteak with gravy, he made the best of his colleague's epicurean pleasantries. The many-coloured wines in their assorted glasses also took effect, even though Himmler did scant justice to them.

I took care not to over-indulge in the wine, and I scarcely had time for food. It was sad, but my experience of interpreting ultimately taught me that a wise interpreter either eats a little beforehand or a lot afterwards. Drinking is an individual matter, but I find that my brain functions best if I stick to two kinds of wine and avoid sweet liqueurs.

After the meal, which lasted for hours, the guests adjourned to the terrace to survey the blue sea whose denizens they had devoured in such quantities. Himmler, who was evidently unaccustomed to heavy lunches, looked weary. True, he regaled me and his entourage with the ancient history of Ostia and other tales from Baedeker, but he was perceptibly relieved when the time came to climb in beside his host and drive back to Rome. Farewells were preceded by the appearance of an Italian champagne called *Principe di Piedmonte*, chilled, dry, and—fortunately —drinkable, which was served in honour of the guests and their assorted kings, emperors, presidents and dictators. I happily drained my glass in a private toast to my enjoyable life at the Pensione Jaselli-Owen and to my beautiful, beloved Rome.

IV

THE POLICE CHIEFS

THE young Lord Byron could say of himself that he woke up one morning to find himself a famous man.

I woke up one morning, the morning of 9 November 1937, to find myself in the SS.

I have no intention of presenting an apologia here, nor of attempting to shift the responsibility to the shoulders of others. It all stemmed from the fact that I was generally regarded by the Germans and Italians as an efficient interpreter, a reputation largely based on the police chiefs' banquet described above. If it had been the European ministers of education or agriculture who had employed my services at Ostia, things would probably have turned out otherwise. As it was, the men who had lunched together and conversed with my assistance were the police chiefs of Germany and Italy.

I could, of course, have declined to be enrolled as an Obersturmführer in the ordinary SS at the Hotel Vier Jahreszeiten on that November day, and most Germans would now claim that, in my position, they would have done just that. I accepted, first, because there would have been no absolute certainty of my returning to Rome unless I had, and, secondly, because my absence from Germany since 1927 and my experience of the very different circumstances prevailing in Italy had left me with only the vaguest conception of what Heinrich Himmler and his SS really represented. What was more, no form of limitation was imposed upon my current activities, both as a student of the Farnese and as a translator, in the course of my crucial interview with the chief of Himmler's personal staff and several of his aides. My new sphere of duty was confined to Italy and consisted in the further exploitation of my skill as an interpreter, in the maintenance and development of my Italian contacts, and in the closest possible co-operation with the two German embassies in Rome. The police sector was specifically excluded, though it was naturally suggested that I foster and extend my personal relationship with Don Arturo Bocchini.

Many qualified and unqualified observers have racked their brains as to the motives which prompted me to take this step. The world-famous expert on Florentine art and distinguished connoisseur of the Renaissance, Bernhard Berenson, dwelt on me at some length in his book *Rumor and Reflection*, published by Simon and Schuster (New York, 1952). He wrote, among other things:

He is a certain Dollmann, good-looking, in the early forties, cultivated, affable, a man of the world, and claiming to have spent sixteen years in Rome. In which capacity remains uncertain. Not in diplomacy, nor in the consular service. Neither in finance nor in trade. He speaks of the smartest society ladies as intimates, calling them by their Christian or pet names.

The doyen of art critics concluded his examination of me with the words: How can a civilian of such culture, sense and judgment be the lieutenant of Himmler?

A contemporary British historian (Gerald Reitlinger: *The SS. Alibi for a Nation*, Heinemann, 1956) writes:

It is uncertain what can have attracted Captain Eugen Dollmann, one of Himmler's intellectuals, to the SS. He was a Rome-bred art historian and spoke fluent Italian. He had access to the best houses and was on good terms with Count Ciano.

Motives are always hard to pin down. I can only say that I had no financial worries. I lived well and comfortably, and my life, after I had yielded to my so-called motives, was no better than before, only more arduous. I was not motivated by ambition, either. I have none, unfortunately, or my biography of Cardinal Farnese would doubtless have been completed by now. Apart from that, political ambition in an historian is tantamount to suicide. His studies afford him an ample opportunity of assessing the dire perils to which his political heroes expose themselves with such deliberate and truly valiant masochism. No, whatever prompted me to take the step I took on 9 November 1937, it was certainly not political ambition. Was it, perhaps, little Bibi's eagerness to see me in uniform? She undoubtedly liked me in uniform, but that was hardly an adequate reason. I think, looking back, that my motives were a mixed bunch—a compound of thoughtlessness, guilelessness, and, above all, a desire not to see my sojourn in Rome and Italy placed in jeopardy. Had I given the matter greater thought I might well have gathered, if only from my success at the lunch party in Ostia, that I was in the act of mounting a tiger from which it would be impossible to descend. That this did not occur to me was largely due to Arturo Bocchini. who had evidently taken a liking to me from the start. Despite the genuine esteem in which I still hold the memory of that grand seigneur and kid-gloved police chief, I cherish no great illusions about his motives. He had met German police officials of all ranks during his first visit to Berlin. He got to know them even better in 1938, when a man named Herbert Kappler was dispatched to Rome as German police attaché. In comparison with such people, I was pleasant and accommodating. I loved Italy with the doomed love of all German romantics and classicists, so I had an Achilles' heel—and what police chief has ever disliked someone who suffers from such an infirmity?

I should like to conclude my examination of motives and motivations by quoting the best available verdict on my new sphere of duties in Rome. It is given by no less a man than the former head of the American secret service, Allen Welsh Dulles, in his book *Germany's Underground* (The Macmillan Co., New York, 1947), and forms part of his account of the events at the Führer's Headquarters on 20 July 1944:

By a strange coincidence Hitler had granted Mussolini, who had long been importuning him, an interview for that very day. A few hours after the attack, Hitler, with his right arm bound up, met Mussolini and Graziani at their train. They had been accompanied from Northern Italy by an SS-officer, Sturmbannführer Eugen Dollmann, who can best be described as a diplomatic envoy in Italy of the SS (originally a Nazi elite guard and later practically a state within a state), and SS-liaison with Mussolini. Dollmann has given a vivid description of the macabre meeting.

Long and varied experience has left me far from convinced of the infallibility of secret service judgment or secret service verdicts, but in this instance Mr Dulles has given a broadly accurate account of my functions. He might have added that I gradually became a sort of Axis interpreter and translator, corresponding, again broadly, to Ribbentrop's well-known Foreign Office chief interpreter of French and English, Dr Paul Schmidt, who also, incidentally, held a rank in the ordinary SS.

I do not propose to give a detailed description of the numerous meetings between Heinrich Himmler and his associates and his Italian partner Bocchini, members of Bocchini's staff and other prominent Italians. I have no precise recollection of any but the most important interviews, in any case, and it seems to me far more interesting and informative to present a general comparison of the two men who held such key positions in two countries linked by a life-or-death alliance.

Dictators of every era have always been less powerful than those who know their secrets and can provide them, in their own dark ways, with the thing which none of the great ones of this earth can enjoy without their assistance: security. They are the only people whom dictators seldom if ever manage to dislodge, either by brute force or gentler means. Field marshals and generals, ministers, diplomats, party politicians and senior civil servants fall in swathes, but chiefs of police remain. The most powerful dictator of modern times, Napoleon, loathed and detested his own police chief, Fouché, but he remained 'true' to him until his own downfall. There were countless reasons why he never got rid of him, even though he was well aware that Fouché's career was founded on an unbroken sequence of treachery and betrayal.

Fouché knew a great deal—indeed, he knew too much. Since it was impossible to hide a secret from him, the Emperor was forced to trust him willy-nilly. And this knowledge of everything and everyone constituted Fouché's unique power over human beings.

This is how Fouché's masterly biographer, Stefan Zweig, attempts to explain the mystery of the greatest police chief of any dictatorship. The picture remained essentially unchanged under Hitler and Mussolini. Those who control a dictatorship's vast and ruthless police network simply know too much. Above all, they know that dictators, who have no legitimate or democratically based claims to sovereignty, are virtually compelled to rely on them to the hilt. Their soldiers will follow them only for as long as they lead them from one victory to the next, their civil servants are mute officials activated by a sense of duty rather than genuine conviction, their humblest followers dwindle in the course of the years: only their policemen remain pledged to them for better or worse.

Like their masters, most of them gain power by dint of treachery, betrayal and crime. Above all, though, they are custodians of secrets and of a diabolical institution known in Russia as the *sapiska*, which provides a complete dossier on the past and present activities of everyone, from the current Head of State to the most junior Party member. Fouché gleaned the most intimate secrets of the Emperor's marital couch from his own wife, Josephine, and Napoleon's extra-marital escapades were equally well known to him.

There is no doubt that Heinrich Himmler was just as well informed about his Führer's years of obscurity in Vienna and Munich. Why should he not have had access to police dossiers on the private life of the young and still almost unknown Adolf Hitler, when General von Lossow had a detailed knowledge of them at the time of the 1923 putsch and regarded them for the rest of his life as a form of personal safe-conduct?

Hitler, in his turn, knew that the shrewdest and most dangerous member of his police force, State Security Bureau chief Reinhard Heydrich, had a Jewish grandmother called Sarah—a diabolical quirk of fate which secured him the lifelong allegiance of a diabolical man. Every Italian knew and still knows that Bocchini played guardian angel to his lord and master's relationship with Clara Petacci, and that only his skilful management enabled Mussolini to devote himself to his passion undisturbed. The dramatic conflict between his mistress and his legal spouse, Donna Rachele, did not flare up until after the omniscient police chief's death.

Thus, ministers and chiefs of police watch over their masters day and night. They know all about them, remain true to them for as long as they consider their dictatorship secure, and will do everything, pull every one of the thousand strings at their fingertips, to keep their employers in power. The only thing they will not do is share in their downfall. They never entirely sever relations with their liege lords' mortal foes.

Heinrich Himmler, when the tide of victory began to recede, established contact with the enemy in Switzerland through the intermediacy of a Berlin lawyer named Langbehn. His role in the preparations for the assassination attempt on 20 July 1944 remains obscure to this day. To Hitler during the last days in the Chancellery, he was a convicted traitor who had only escaped execution because of the pressure of events.

Reinhard Heydrich would undoubtedly have tried to prevent the *Götterdämmerung* of the Third Reich by eliminating Hitler, and only Bocchini's premature death spared him the need to make a similar decision in Rome. From the very moment when his successor and most faithful disciple, Carmine Senise, assumed office, he started to play a cunning double game which kept him in his seat of power even after the collapse of July 1943.

Treacherous are the murky waters which form the natural habitat of the political police, and treachery—as their model, Fouché, has taught them—is what makes them mightier than the dictators they appear to serve so faithfully.

Since Germany's defeat in 1945, a vast quantity of literature has been devoted to Heinrich Himmler, his status and activities in the Third Reich. His Italian counterpart, Bocchini, also recurs in the background of historical works and accounts of Fascism. His smaller claim to international 'popularity' is attributable to a lack of the terror and dread which will always be associated with Himmler's name.

However, I am not concerned here with writing a history of the police under Hitler and Mussolini. My aim is to shed light on the personalities of these two distinguished mainstays of dictatorship and present a critical appreciation of their relationship, which was one of the most noteworthy features of the Rome–Berlin Axis.

Systematic comparison of the two men at once brings out the absolute dissimilarity of their philosophy and way of life. The full-blooded, all too full-blooded South Italian was an indefatigable worker like his German associate, but he was also, in complete contrast to the latter, a *bon vivant* of epicurean refinement, an unrivalled connoisseur and admirer of the fair sex, and a gourmet in the finest French tradition. He could be implacable when it was a matter of guarding Benito Mussolini's life, but in Italy such things are handled with an infinitely lighter touch.

While I am not trying to defend all Bocchini's police measures, who would seriously compare his deportation orders or latter-day *lettres de cachet* with the horrors of consignment to one of the German concentration camps? It was not, of course, pleasant to be deported 'to the frontier', i.e., to some lonely place, isolated province or remote island, but it was not fatal nor even injurious to the health. Italians, policemen included, always sympathise with the poor and unfortunate, never with the rich and successful. Hence, despite subsequent claims to martyrdom, the vast majority of deportees survived their sojourn in Calabria and Apulia or on Stromboli and Ponza passably well.

'*Il ira loin, il croit tout ce qu'il dit,*' Mirabeau once said of Robespierre, and these words might have applied equally well to Heinrich Himmler. Don Arturo Bocchini seldom believed what he said, but he, too, went far. However, to go far without believing what one says is possible only in Italy. In Germany, absolute faith in oneself and one's pronouncements is essential, and the results are correspondingly more frightful. This contrast was apparent both in the careers of the two police chiefs and in the gulf between their respective penal systems—the gulf between the German concentration camp and the Italian deportation order.

The other verdict on Robespierre which might also be applied unhesitatingly to the Reichsführer-SS and head of the German police comes from Grillparzer, who described 'the exaltation of a cold mind' as the most awesome of all dangers. Himmler was quite as profoundly convinced of the infallibility of his theories, the exemplary nature of his way of life and the inviolability of his principles as the virtuous lawyer from Nantes. Had his Führer won the Second World War, he would doubtless have instituted a 'Festival of the Supreme German Being'. *'C'était un enthousiaste, mais il croyait selon la justice'* was Napoleon's verdict on the sea-green Incorruptible. Heinrich Himmler would have been equally astonished if anyone had dared to question the absolute morality of his concept of justice.

I had more than one opportunity to discuss all this with the chief of the Italian police. It was as possible to converse with him about the most delicate and dangerous subjects as it was out of the question, at least for me, to do the same with Himmler. The latter made me give him detailed lectures on the Italian world which was so alien to him, briefing himself for every visit to Italy, every meeting with Italians, like a schoolboy preparing for a lesson. I cannot say that he ever disgraced me. He could not help his outward appearance, which was diametrically opposed to Latin ideals of beauty, but he followed my hints and suggestions like an apt pupil—at least in Italy. It was not my job to discuss German questions with him, and the police sphere was happily tabu where I was concerned.

The atmosphere that reigned after one of Bocchini's Lucullan dinners was quite different in tone. He relished stories and anecdotes about everything and everyone, including Himmler. He needed Himmler's friendship, in an Axis context, because his cordial relations with the most feared man in the Third Reich impressed the Palazzo Venezia and the rest of the Fascist hierarchy. That was the precise reason why he took so much trouble with a man whom he otherwise found ludicrous, uncongenial, boring, and exceedingly tiresome. Himmler never suspected this. He genuinely respected and admired Bocchini because he saw him as the possessor of all the things he himself lacked: elegance, sparkling wit, the manners of a grand seigneur, and a knowledge of the fair sex which was matched only by his success with them. Consequently, he was charmed and delighted when Bocchini invited him to his villa at San Giorgio, near Benevento, in 1938—again on 28 October.

Bocchini's chalet was quite unlike the Reichsführer's gloomy villa beside the Tegernsee, with its rustling pines and hoarse-voiced crows. Not everything was in the best of taste, and the blend of Louis Philippe and Jugendstil which dominated the establishment was wholly alien to the décor of a German Ordensburg. The whole place vaguely recalled descriptions of the homes of pleasure-loving villa-owners of the late Roman period, though I doubt if even they would have boasted a fountain whose centrepiece was a group of naked girls squirting coloured jets of water from their shapely breasts. These figures and similar artifices were Don Arturo's pride and joy. The small entrance hall, for instance, was crowded with smiling wax dolls whose physical charms the beaming host could reveal at the press of a button. I never discovered what Heinrich Himmler thought of this, and was spared the job of translating his impressions.

Don Arturo loved to stroll through his olive-groves and vineyards, accepting the humble salutations of his retainers and distributing silver coins with all the open-handed generosity of a Roman senator. There were guards, too, of course, but their civilian clothes, pomaded hair and over-colourful neck-ties were worlds away from the raven-black uniforms of the men who stood guard over Herr Himmler in Germany.

Nevertheless, Himmler joined in everything. He even allowed himself to be talked into an allegedly impromptu meeting with the Archbishop of Benevento at his cathedral, and spent some time in animated conversation with that prince of the Church. He devoted himself to his host's renowned table with a zeal which taxed his weak stomach to the limits of its endurance, and imbibed the heavy red and golden wines of the South as though they were *Apfelsaft* and mineral water. To me, he resembled a schoolboy who was trying to forget his lessons for a day.

Himmler was in his pedagogic element when visiting the battlefield near Benevento where Frederick II's favourite son, Manfred, lost his life and throne. I had urged Don Arturo to recruit a Dante expert for the occasion, so the German visitor was treated to those magnificent stanzas from the third canto of the *Purgatorio* which begin: 'I am Manfredi . . .' He was particularly gratified to hear King Manfred's bitter attack on the Cardinal Archbishop of Cosenza, who strewed his remains on unhallowed ground at the Pope's behest:

. . . Had this text divine
Been of Cosenza's shepherd better scanned,
Who then by Clement on my hunt was set,
Yet at the bridge's head my bones had lain,
Near Benevento, by the heavy mole
Protected; but the rain now drenches them,
And the wind drives . . .

Heinrich Himmler had no love for the Hohenstaufens but he liked the Pope and his archbishop even less. He asked me to translate the passage which had just been quoted, and although my impromptu translation can have done little justice to the original he seemed deeply impressed.

Cosenza, a town in Calabria, provided Himmler with a less happy experience. For once, his Italian colleague's arrangements went awry, although—as will shortly be seen—anyone's arrangements would have done the same. Cosenza stands on the low banks of a small river which Count Platen, a writer generally condemned on moral grounds, immortalised in his poem *Grab im Busento*. Heinrich Himmler and his entourage were spending the night there en route for a private visit to Sicily, and the local prefect was shocked to learn at supper that the early part of the following morning was to be devoted to the hallowing of ancient Germanic tradition—more precisely, to a visit to the site of the legendary treasure which King Alaric and his faithful Vandals had taken with them to their common grave in the Busento. What the prefect knew but Herr Himmler did not, was that this very site was currently being explored by a party of French archaeologists accompanied by a lady dowser.

Next morning the German police potentate duly set off for the dismal, muddy and wholly unheroic little stream. Great schemes were evolved for diverting the Busento and exposing its bed. It was then seen that mademoiselle and her male companions were already on the spot. Alas, what were the modern descendants of Alaric compared to a young French girl with a divining-rod?

To the ever-susceptible Italians, even Herr Himmler's vast personal importance was inadequate competition. The circle round him thinned progressively as the attendant heroes of the local

Italian administration, who were as indifferent to Alaric and his Vandals as they were attracted by the sight of mademoiselle's alluring bosom, drifted away to swell the admiring ranks round *la douce France*. Fascinated, the sons of the South followed the combined undulations of divining-rod and bosom. The supple twig acted like Circe's magic wand, causing the entire retinue of senior local dignitaries to leave Himmler's side on various pretexts and place their services at the disposal of archaeology and femininity.

In the end, only the grim and unwavering figures of the saddened prefect and his chief of police stood firm, and Italy's outraged allies were left with no choice but to propose the sending of an expert German research team to explore the site in the near future. King Alaric was allowed to slumber on in the bed of the Busento, surrounded by his mythical treasure, and the Reichsführer punished Platen by declining to lay a wreath on the poet's grave at Syracuse.

At Taormina, Bocchini made up for his lapse at Cosenza. Himmler, whose schoolmasterly instincts had been aroused by the indigenous inhabitants of the island, the Siculi, amused their descendants by demonstrating that they were at least partly of Germanic stock. Fascinated by Sicilian shepherds' crooks and pipes, he seized upon these relics of Sicily's ancient past with burning enthusiasm. His Roman colleague carefully ensured that his hobby made strides. Had the great god Pan not died long before, he would undoubtedly have met his musical end in Sicily at the hands of Heinrich Himmler. Very soon, there were no pipes left with which to accompany the dancing of dainty nymphs beside virgin springs, no divine staff of the Siculan era with which a shepherd could have tended his flock: Himmler had bought them all up. Where they came from was a secret known only to His Excellency in Rome, but he later revealed to me in high glee that they had been specially manufactured for the occasion.

I have already mentioned that Himmler did not like the Hohenstaufens. Henry the Lion was to blame for this, because it was he who monopolised the Reichsführer's devotion. To Himmler, the Guelph ruler and his Eastern policy were a shining example, whereas the Hohenstaufens were associated with the useless shedding of German blood in Italy, and Frederick II was a magnificent but reprehensible illustration of German rulers' instability and their fatal susceptibility to the South. He believed that, had it not been for the Hohenstaufens, the Guelphs would probably have pushed forward to the Urals, and he swore that not a single member of the SS would ever spill his German blood in the South. He was no prophet, only a schoolmaster, but he was reluctant to lay wreaths on the imposing Hohenstaufen tombs of Henry VI and Frederick II in Palermo Cathedral.

The fact that he did so after all was the result of a plot hatched by Bocchini and me. We both liked the Hohenstaufens, though His Excellency knew a great deal about Frederick II's glittering court in Sicily and Calabria, and next to nothing about Frederick Barbarossa and Henry VI. Indeed, I think he would rather have been Frederick II's chief of police than Benito Mussolini's. To cut a long story short, he told me to inform Himmler on our arrival in Palermo that the prefect of the city would be turning up with two huge laurel-wreaths for Himmler to lay on the Hohenstaufen tombs, and that the Duce would be deeply touched by the gesture. I am pretty certain that the Duce was never informed of it, but the hint was enough. To the surprise and secret exultation of the proud Sicilians, who felt personally honoured by these wreaths, the official ceremony took place.

Heinrich Himmler lingered before the huge and unadorned red porphyry coffins, outwardly moved but inwardly, I have no doubt, thinking of his beloved Henry the Lion and the way his Eastern aspirations had been thwarted by the house of Hohenstaufen. He could not know that, at the same moment, I was thinking of Ernst Kantorowicz's masterpiece and his fanatical devotion to Frederick II, of his glowing descriptions of the fairy-tale court at Palermo with its Late Classical, Arab, Hellenic and Germanic undertones. Once again, most Germans would demand to know why I did not leave Himmler standing beside the Palermo sarcophagi—as they, of course, would have done.

I did not abandon him because at the time I regarded his homage to the Hohenstaufens and my conspiracy with Bocchini as a victory for the Hohenstaufens. My thoughts went no further than that. I am no hero, and I still think that there were enough heroes who, by reason of their status, hatred and contempt, could have done what I did not do.

Outside, before the portals of the cathedral, the Hohenstaufen farce was finally concluded to everyone's satisfaction. A blond, blue-eyed boy stuck out his grubby little hand in Himmler's direction and stammered a *'Buon giorno, Eccellenza'*. The object of his attentions, who had mistaken the child for a scion of the Guelphs, was startled. The Germanic blood of the Hohenstaufens' mercenary army had indeed survived the passage of the centuries with notable success. Half touched, half saddened, Himmler shrugged his shoulders and expressed sympathy for the Hohenstaufens and the results of their ethnic policy in distant Sicily.

Bocchini was highly amused when I recounted all this over a glass of cognac dating from the zenith of Napoleon's career. In return, he told me a story of his own and urged me to pass it on to Himmler sometime. He thought it might amuse him, but he was wrong.

The delightful anecdote which Don Arturo told me, between sips of 1811 brandy, concerned the wife of an ambassador of one of the Great Powers. He sighed, remarking that it was fortunate there were so few amorous ambassadresses. What would have happened if the malicious gossips of Roman high society had found out that the lady in question had decided to fulfil her Roman dreams in a small and shabby suburb, or that her eye had lighted, with this end in view, on a youthful Adonis of ancient but plebeian stock? Even this episode might have passed off without incident, like so many others of its kind, had not an unfortunate *agente* of the brothel surveillance squad chosen this particular night to rouse the sleeping household with a hoarsely bellowed request for *'Documenti, documenti!'* The young man, who was only in possession of a long-expired taxi-driver's licence, vanished into a rickety wardrobe, leaving his scantily clad companion to battle with the policeman in her inadequate Italian. Every woman's patience has its limits, especially under exhausting circumstances like these, and the astonished guardian of nocturnal decency and good order eventually received an imperious ambassadorial injunction to get in touch with higher authority —the higher the better, or the consequences would be disastrous.

The Rosenkavalier atmosphere reached an even more novelettish pitch when, just at that moment, the wardrobe door burst open and the taxi-driver, bereft both of taxi and clothes, tumbled out. What does a well-trained policeman do under such circumstances? Precisely what our worthy *brigadiere* did. He shut the wardrobe door again, beat a hasty retreat, and made for the nearest telephone. Then, sweating with apprehension, he fought his way up through the whole hierarchy of the Roman police until his cry for help reached the secretariat and, from there, the private residence of His Excellency. Don Arturo was not alone—he seldom was at night. Rising with a sigh, he prepared to set his personal seal on an incident which might have had far-reaching diplomatic repercussions. He notified the great lady, who had now dissolved into hysterical tears, of his impending arrival, had the unfortunate taxi-driver, now clothed, thrown downstairs, and then appeared on the scene in person, accompanied by a few aides. Elegantly dressed as usual, wearing a superb silk tie and fragrant with lemon Eau de Cologne, he entered the lady's suburban love-nest. Kissing her hand gallantly, he apologised on behalf of the Italian police for the taxi-driver's imprudent choice of hotel, smilingly promised better service in future and recommended a small and discreet villa at Ostia, which was always available. He further declared himself only too willing to provide her with an alibi which would explain her late homecoming.

Don Arturo then offered milady his arm with the utmost gallantry and escorted her to a discreet saloon car which conveyed her safely home to her embassy. He smiled gently when he read, over his morning coffee, that Her Excellency had gone off to Paris for some days to visit her dentist. No war broke out, no notes were exchanged, no ambassador was recalled.

Such was Don Arturo Bocchini, and such was the story which I faithfully retailed to Himmler. Alas, what a difference! If only it had happened to him, what capital he would have made out of the scandal! In spite of Mussolini and Fascism, how lax the Italians were in matters of morality! And so on. It was the only time he ever evinced a total lack of understanding for his Roman colleague's methods and expressed grave doubts about the morale and stability of Germany's ally 'if the balloon goes up'.

In other respects, Himmler continued to admire Bocchini until the latter's death. Freud would probably have ascribed this to a father fixation. The Reichsführer had every reason to detest the schoolmaster father who had reared him with such Spartan harshness. Perhaps, at the back of his impenetrable mind, he sought and found in Arturo Bocchini a substitute for the paternal understanding he had never enjoyed. Like their lives, the two men's deaths were as dissimilar as only a capricious fate could have made them.

During his latter years, Bocchini found happiness with a young female relative from the Naples area. Night after night the ill-assorted couple used to meet on the terrace of the Pincio in the Borghese Gardens. Guarded with oriental care, superbly gowned and bejewelled, the signorina would descend from her car as Don Arturo's black police saloon drove up. The ageing cavalier extended his arm with the *grandezza* of a Bourbon dignitary. There would then follow a brief *passeggiata* beneath the star-spangled purple of the Roman night sky until His Excellency's car bore the pair off to a discreet but opulent *diner à deux*.

Alas, she was far too young and the dinners far too rich, and Don Arturo had never read Brisot's description of the way his fellow-voluptuary, Mirabeau, met his end:

Shortly before his death Mirabeau spent a night in the arms of the danseuses Helisberg and Coulomb. It was they who killed him, and there is no point in ascribing his death to other causes.

When I was summoned to Bocchini's private villa in the early hours of a dismal November morning in 1940, I found him already in his death-throes and little Maria beside his bed, golden hair loose and cheeks wet with tears. The dying man pointed at her as though he meant to commend her to my protection, and I believe I faithfully carried out his wishes during the ensuing difficulties over his will. It was an enviable death, and its memory has never deserted me from that day forth. I recalled our parting most vividly in June 1945, when the British gave me a detailed description of Heinrich Himmler's end. Between the last passionate kiss of a young girl and the vial of poison concealed in a hollow tooth

lay the same gulf which divided Don Arturo Bocchini and Heinrich Himmler during their lifetime.

Needless to say, the relationship between the two police chiefs
did not consist merely in episodes like those described above,
which might be augmented by many others of equal gravity or
entertainment value. In general, however, Himmler's visits to
Rome while Bocchini was still alive were devoted to an exchange
of civilities and presents, sight-seeing tours, and lunches. Don
Arturo only told his Nordic friend the unvarnished truth in regard
to two subjects: attacks on the Church and attacks on the monarchy. It was not that Don Arturo was a complaisant Catholic—
I suspected him of being a secret freemason—but he was a politician to his fingertips, and he knew what it had cost Fascism
in terms of strength and energy to wage war against the Church
until the Lateran compromise was reached in 1929. In this connection, he once asked me to give him a summary of Bismarck's
abortive Kulturkampf, and later made free use of it during a
conversation with Himmler. This was one of the things that later
exposed me to a charge of having served two masters.

It was different with the monarchy. As a genuine South Italian,
Bocchini was a convinced monarchist. His whole way of life was
diametrically opposed to that of the frugal, taciturn, faithful pater-
familias Victor Emmanuel III, but he regarded prominent Nazis'
highly tactless and impertinent attacks on 'King Nutcracker',
'Elena the Cook' and 'Sonny Boy Umberto' as an unseemly interference in Italian domestic affairs. His personal intervention did at
least ensure that Himmler adopted a considerably more moderate
tone when speaking about Church, monarchy, and the 'black
corps'.

From 1938 onwards, police liaison work between Rome and
Berlin was handled by two police attachés of whom the German
in Rome was Herbert Kappler, an avowed favourite of the chief
of the Central State Security Bureau, Heydrich, and thus a secret
but unmistakable foe of mine. I only learned later that Heydrich
would have liked to incorporate me in his own organisation,
and his subsequent campaign against me through Kappler may
have been attributable to the fact that Himmler's personal chief
of staff, General of the Waffen-SS Karl Wolff, had firmly opposed

any such transfer. I had taken out additional insurance against this by enlisting the support of Bocchini, who saw no reason to accommodate Heydrich in any way. Although he was fully alive to the irksome nature of the paternal act he had to put on for Himmler's benefit, he knew that direct collaboration with Heydrich would be both arduous and dangerous.

I acted as interpreter to the dreaded chief of the Central State Security Bureau on only two occasions, each time because his police attaché in Rome had not yet mastered sufficient Italian to be able to fulfil this function. The first occasion was in April 1938, when Heydrich visited Rome and Naples to check Italian security measures for Hitler's scheduled tour in May, and the second was in October 1939, when he represented Germany at the Italian Police Day celebrations because his chief, Himmler, was involved in the Polish campaign. To the interested eyes of the Italians and their womenfolk, Heydrich possessed all the outward advantages which his chief lacked. In complete contrast to the Germans, the Italians are a 'visual' people. Character and so-called inner qualities come second with them, but they very soon penetrated the hard, icy, blue-eyed shell of the second-in-command of the German police. After his departure, Bocchini said to me:

'In Himmler's place, I would never tolerate such a man near me.'

Heydrich displayed his most seductive side in Rome. He treated Bocchini as his direct superior, spoke with military crispness, behaved with courtesy and respect. His Lucifer nature did not emerge until he had completed his programme in Naples. He had taken his official leave of the authorities, seeming less interested in Hitler's safety than in the Police College at Caserta. The huge Bourbon château which I recommended him to visit impressed him little. He was anxious to get back to Naples as soon as possible—why, I was soon to discover. His manner became increasingly affable on the drive back, and he finally asked me if I knew anything about the night-life of Naples. Remembering Donna Rosalba, I steered us towards the red-light district. I knew it well. One went there with a party, chatted to the scantily-clad girls in their salotto, offered cigarettes and occasionally bought a round of drinks. That was as far as it went. If the ladies were summoned to their private rooms one bade them a polite farewell and emerged into one of the small side-streets leading off the Via Roma.

Reinhard Heydrich found this a novel idea—or, at least, he acted as if he did. He told me of his plan to open an establishment in Berlin where the nocturnal frolics of influential foreigners, diplomats and other VIP's could be monitored by him through listening-devices. This was how the notorious 'Salon Kitty' originated, though it was still a pipe-dream at this stage.

I told him that it was out of the question for him to visit any of the celebrated streets off the Via Roma, but that we might take a quick look at the best house in its class, namely, 'The House of the Provinces', where I was known. He seized on the name at once. 'Why "House of the Provinces"?' he demanded, and was highly diverted when I explained that it was an establishment in which girls were available by provinces. If one said 'Perugia', the rouged old crone sitting with her yellow tom-cat at the cash-desk would call out 'Perugia!', and a daughter of Umbria would appear at the head of the stairs leading to the interior of the temple of Venus. A request for 'Venezia' would, in the style of a Goldoni comedy, evoke a nod from a girl who hailed from the Queen of the Adriatic, a cry of 'Sicilia' the appearance of some dark-eyed, dark-haired island beauty. Most if not all the provinces were represented in this ethnological museum of Italian femininity. I still believe that Benito Mussolini and Fascism cannot be accused of undue moral severity, and most inhabitants of the present republic, in which free love has been officially prohibited by the puritanical legislation of Senatrice Merlin, are agreed on this point.

When we got back to Naples, Heydrich begged me to arrange the little treat I had spoken of. He merely wanted to inspect 'the Provinces' for half an hour—nothing more, he swore by all that was holy. Eventually I yielded, and my best friends have never forgiven me. Summoning one of the *agenti* who were hovering in the background at Heydrich's beck and call, I pressed a large banknote into his hand and explained the VIP's requirements. No member of the Italian secret police ever performed a more congenial duty. He disappeared, beaming all over his face, and had still not recovered his composure when he returned shortly afterwards with tidings of success. Even I quailed at the sum demanded for half an hour's visit, which must have been the equivalent of the policeman's annual salary, but Heydrich, who thought the price ludicrous and found Italy genuinely cheap, did not turn a hair.

'Think what it would cost at home, if it existed at all!'

He showed me a sizable purse filled with gleaming gold coins from every land, coins bearing the likeness of my old emperor, Franz Joseph, the moustachioed countenance of Wilhelm II, the prim features of Queen Victoria, the arms and emblems of various republics. What he proposed to do with them became clear to me a short while later.

Accompanied by two delighted *agenti*, we presented ourselves at the 'House of the Provinces'. On the door hung a grimy notice which read: '*Apertura fra un'ora—cause impreviste*' ('Opening in an hour—unforseen circumstances'). It was the work of the policeman who had been given the banknote, and he glowed with pride at his achievement. In the main salotto, with its glittering mirrors and painted ceiling covered with naked nymphs and demi-gods, we were greeted by a couple of dozen half-clothed girls whose looks betrayed the diversity of their provincial origins. Slim gazelles, buxom Rubenesque beauties, girls with brown hair, blonde hair, blue eyes, black eyes—all were in evidence. All de-manded Asti Spumante and cigarettes, which were then at a premium, all chattered at once, and all thought we were out of our minds.

Heydrich, in a well-tailored dark-blue suit which moulded itself to him like a uniform, seemed amused. He ordered Asti and produced cigarettes from his pocket. He did not fulfil any of the other functions which the crowd of girls presumably expected of him. Instead, he fished out his gold-lined purse and sent the devil's ducats jingling across the marble floor. They rolled under the plush sofas, under the chairs and behind the rickety piano on which the province of Naples was rendering an appallingly dis-cordant version of *O sole mio*. Then he jumped up, Lucifer personified, and clapped his hands. With a sweeping gesture, he invited the girls to pick up the gold. A Walpurgisnacht orgy ensued. Fat and thin, ponderous and agile, the 'provinces' scrambled madly across the salotto on all fours. Gold, gold . . . Who but this *pazzo tedesco*, this crazy German, had ever hurled it at their feet before? Even the old cashier lowered herself painfully on to her hands and knees, and only the yellow tom-cat, spitting satanically in one corner, declined to join in. The Bacchantes might have continued their performance indefinitely, losing more and more of their clothes in the process, if there had not been a sudden sound of heavy fists pounding on the front door as the 'regulars' of the establishment demanded their rights. Quick as a flash, the *agenti* led us through a side entrance just as sailors, students and other clients poured into the room. I never discovered whether they concentrated on the girls or the gold, but that was of secondary interest.

Heydrich, who looked pale and exhausted, thanked me coolly and presented his astonished escorts with two large banknotes. The ghost was laid. The fire had burnt itself out.

I went for a long walk in the 'villa', Naples' sea-side park, listening to the murmur of the waves and wondering why the evening's events rang such a bell in my mind. Then it came to me. In the course of my studies I had dipped into the generally rather tedious journal of a German named Bucardus, who was master of ceremonies to His Holiness Pope Alexander VI. Drily and unemotionally, Bucardus related that the Pope had, in the presence of his beloved daughter Lucrezia Borgia, amused himself by inviting a party of beautiful and scantily clad courtesans into the Borgia Chambers in the Vatican, which are named after him and can still be seen today. Father and daughter then watched with relish as a wild scuffle took place between these women and the most stalwart of His Holiness's guards, who had also been invited for the occasion. Like Reinhard Heydrich, Alexander VI made them scramble for ducats under armchairs and chests, tables and stools.

I discreetly questioned Heydrich on his knowledge of the house of Borgia next day. He had naturally heard one or two of the lurid tales in which the history of the Borgias abounds, but he knew nothing about the master of ceremonies or his diary. If it did nothing else, the scene in the 'House of Provinces' at least taught me that past history can be both topical and instructive.

This concluded my tour of duty as interpreter to Herr Heydrich. Of all the so-called 'great' men with whom I came into contact, he was the only one I instinctively feared. Hitler, Himmler, Mussolini and Bocchini never inspired me with terror, but this ex-naval officer with his Jewish grandmother, cold blue eyes and guardsman's figure struck fear into me. I do not know if his most recent biographer, the Swiss writer Carl J. Burckhardt, was afraid of him too, but I do not think so—at least, not to judge by the account which the former League of Nations High Commissioner for Danzig gives of his meeting with Heydrich in his recent book *Meine Danziger Mission*. This is the fullest description I have yet read of the real Lucifer of the Third Reich. Burckhardt was then, in 1935, a member of the International Committee of the Red Cross, and his German opposite number was His Royal Highness Duke Eduard of Saxony-Coburg-Gotha, Prince of Great Britain and Ireland, NSKK-Obergruppenführer, Reich Commissioner of the Voluntary Nursing Service and President of the German Combat Veterans' Association. The Swiss professor and the SS-Obergruppenführer had met to discuss, inter alia, Burckhardt's request to be allowed to inspect German concentration camps and interview detainees there without witnesses being present. Since this plan could only be realised with Heydrich's approval, Eduard von Sachsen-Coburg-Gotha invited the two men to a meal.

Then the folding doors burst open and Heydrich appeared in the first black uniform I had seen at close quarters, slim and blonde, with Mongol eyes staring out of a sharp, pale, asymmetrical face whose two halves were completely dissimilar in conformation. Briskly, but with effeminate delicacy, the notorious killer entered the Duke's drawing-room.

Heydrich sat on my left at table. I was particularly struck by his hands, lily-white pre-Raphaelite hands designed for protracted strangling.

Burckhardt's account ends with the words: 'Heydrich left the

male gathering shortly afterwards, a young and evil god of death.'
Heydrich was Himmler's evil genius, mainly because Himmler,
too, feared him—and with justification. If Heydrich had not
been eliminated by his Prague assassins at such an early stage
he would undoubtedly have instituted a Nazi version of the Bartholomew's Day massacre, and his first victim would have been
Reichsführer-SS Heinrich Himmler, whom he despised so
deeply. How far the latter permitted the conspiracy against the
chief of his Central State Security Bureau to proceed without
hindrance will never be known, but officers of the British Intelligence Service certainly mooted this possibility to me in 1945.

*   *   *

Don Arturo Bocchini's death on 10 November 1940 was followed by a tragic-comic squabble over who was to succeed him.
The real Minister of the Interior was Secretary of State Buffarini-
Guidi, though Mussolini was the nominal holder of that ministerial post. Like Bocchini, Buffarini had managed to retain his
grasp for what was, by Italian standards, an incredible number
of years. Born in Pisa and endowed with all the eloquence of a
true Tuscan, short, stout, and quite unlike Bocchini in his indifference to physical hygiene and sartorial elegance, he was a typical
barrister of the type which has survived from Cicero's day to
our own. Intellectually, he towered above all his ministerial colleagues with the exception of Dino Grandi and Italo Balbo.
Politics, intrigue and the secret accumulation of power were his
life and ruling passion. He had tolerated Bocchini because the
latter was persona grata at the Palazzo Venezia, but he greeted
the news of his death with perceptible relief.
Buffarini had long been gazing with covetous eyes at the large
safe in the police chief's office which contained the legendary
fondi segreti, the secret funds which were subject to no form of
audit. Arturo was still lying in solemn state at his villa when a
fierce battle broke out over the right of succession. Count Ciano,
Mussolini's son-in-law, had already lined up a candidate of his
own, as had the Party. In short, every prominent Italian was eager
to have his private life camouflaged by a police chief acceptable
to him.

Buffarini's leading candidate was a fellow-provincial of Boc-chini's from Naples itself. This was Carmine Senise, who had been Bocchini's vice-chief and was generally regarded as a run-of-the-mill policeman with a pleasantly amiable manner and a fondness for telling jokes in pure Neapolitan dialect. Buffarini saw him as a willing tool, and I, after the irretrievable loss of my friend Bocchini, was only too happy that one of his closest associates should be next in line. The Palazzo Venezia remained silent, although every line to the Ministry of the Interior hummed with recommendations, demands and requests. Buffarini sum-moned me straight from Boccini's death-bed, announced Senise's candidature, and, to my consternation, begged me to telephone Signor Himmler from his office and solicit the Reichsführer's ap-proval of his plan. I felt sorry that the Italians should have sunk so low as to require the help of one German, let alone two, in appoint-ing their own chief of police. I felt sorry for myself as well, because I had never telephoned Himmler in my life and disliked telephon-ing in general, but there was no way out. After a brief delay Himmler's startled voice came over the wire from Berlin. I ap-prised him of his Italian colleague's death and was informed, in return, that he and his personal staff would attend the funeral— a piece of news which far from delighted the listening Secretary of State for the Interior. I then explained the position and gave a verbatim translation of Buffarini's stammered arguments in favour of his Senise plan. Buffarini was in luck. Being as ignorant of the Neapolitan's true character as the rest of us, Himmler was delighted with Buffarini's suggestion and even asked him to acquaint the Duce with his desire for a new colleague recruited from the dead man's immediate circle.

That was my one and only telephone call to the Reichs-führer-SS. It was, as subsequent events proved, a resounding failure. Although I had succeeded in annoying Count Ciano, who liked me as little as I liked him, I had also helped to exchange Bocchini for a prime intrigant who disliked all of us, especially Buffarini. The Secretary of State never laid hands on the key to the safe he coveted so much nor gained access to the hoard of gold and securities inside. Carmine Senise continued to play the buffoon, but only on the surface. Behind the scenes, with all the sturdy

self-assurance and routine thoroughness of an experienced policeman, he began to pave the way for the events of 25 July 1943,
which cost Germany the Italian alliance and Mussolini his
dictatorship.

Senise did not have the cultural pretensions of his predecessor.
His favourite fare consisted of enormous dishes of *spaghetti alle
vongole* and similar Neapolitan specialities. His suits and uniforms were always crumpled, his shoes store-bought, his ties as
garish and tasteless as those of his detectives. He had but one
hobby, the opera, and spent evening after evening in Rome's
opera house, the Constanzi—not with a young and beautiful
woman, but with the head of the Italian censorship bureau, a
desiccated bureaucrat named Zurrlo.

They, too, were to be seen on the Pincio, but they lacked the
aura of Bocchini and his *bellissima*. They walked up and down
with the purposeful tread of men taking a constitutional, and none
of us guessed that what they were hatching in the Roman starlight
was the overthrow of the Duce and the ousting of the hated
Germans.

V

THE HONEYMOON

THE year 1938, from which my description of Heydrich's Borgia-style performance is taken, brought with it a whole series of other developments which clearly illustrate the stage-craft and histrionic ability of the leading actors.

To mention only the two most important events of which, as an interpreter, I was a first-hand witness: in May Adolf Hitler paid a State visit to Italy accompanied by a retinue of Tsarist proportions, a visit reciprocated by Mussolini in autumn of the same year; and in September 1938 Europe's leading exponents of the art of statesmanship performed their gala roles at the Munich Conference.

Prior to this, there had been a change in the management of the German Embassy on the Quirinal. Herr von Hassell left the Eternal City at the end of February, by which time even the most obtuse of National Socialists had at last grasped how unwelcome they were at the embassy which was financed out of their taxes. However, even that would have been insufficient to bring about Hassell's downfall, which only became inevitable when the Italian government turned against him as well. Count Ciano, Mussolini's Foreign Minister and son-in-law, gives a detailed account of the episode in his *Diaries, 1937–8*. He relates that on 30 October 1938 the Führer's deputy, Rudolf Hess, who was then visiting Rome, informed him 'with nervous agitation' that Frau von Hassell had 'indulged in some extremely anti-Italian remarks in his presence'. Hess wanted to demand Hassell's head from Hitler immediately, but Ciano, ever an advocate of indirect methods, merely observed that Hassell was indeed 'an enemy of the Rome–Berlin Axis and an opponent of Fascism' —which was undeniably true. He went to Mussolini and tried to patch things up.

'The Duce then spoke to Hassell, who bemoaned his fate and aroused the Duce's compassion. The Duce instructed me to intervene with Berlin immediately, this time in order to save v. Hassell.' The duet continued. On 6 January the Fascist Foreign Minister and the National Socialist ambassador had a lengthy interview, in the course of which the ambassador claimed to have been an Italophile at a time 'when everyone in Germany, including the Party, was the opposite'. It availed him nothing. On 25 February von Hassell had to take leave of Ciano, who made the following instructive entry in his diary:

25 February. Said Goodbye to v. Hassell. Cold, brief, hostile conversation. I feel not the slightest twinge of conscience at having engineered the recall of this individual, who has done his country and the cause of German-Italian friendship such disservice. It could be that he tried to overcome his hostile attitude and failed. He belongs, inevitably and by destiny, to the Junker world which cannot forget 1914 and, being fundamentally opposed to Nazism, has no feeling for the solidarity of the regime. Besides, Hassell knew Dante too well. I distrust foreigners who know Dante. They try to hoodwink us with poetry.

I am sorry that I was not acquainted with Galeazzo Ciano's diaries at the time. Neither Herr von Hassell nor I ever knew the reason for His Excellency's dislike. I know it now, but too late. I should never have revealed my modest knowledge of Dante had I been aware of Ciano's subtle fears, but he only recorded his misgivings and true convictions hurriedly, at night, and on paper. If he had only adopted a different approach he might have rendered his country inestimable service, because his key status in Mussolini's household would, if coupled with a little more courage and drive, have made him an unbeatable proposition. As it was, the bitter fruit of his failure to take a clear line was his execution at Verona in January 1944.

Herr von Hassell's successor was Hans Georg von Mackensen,

previously Secretary of State at the Foreign Office, which had been headed by his father-in-law, Foreign Minister Baron Konstantin von Neurath, until 4 February 1938. Only two days earlier, on 2 February, Adolf Hitler had shaken Neurath fervently by the hand and declined to accept his resignation with the words: 'I cannot let you go yet. You are like a fatherly friend to me— I still do not have enough experience in foreign policy.' It was a touching scene, but only to the unwitting Swabian nobleman. Actually, Hitler had already signed the papers dismissing him in favour of the most calamitous German Foreign Minister since 1870. Why Hitler indulged in this emotional performance is still obscure to everyone, including the Neurath family. A 'Secret Cabinet Council' was created especially for Herr von Neurath's benefit, but it never met and the Baron would have been better advised not to accept its chairmanship.

His son-in-law, von Mackensen, was a son of the celebrated field marshal who had so charmed two members of the Triple Alliance, Wilhelm II and Franz Joseph. To Hitler, with his brilliant talent for stage management, the old field marshal represented an indispensable link with the military traditions of the Reichswehr, and he was always handled with kid-gloves. At his advanced age, he probably failed to realise that his own death-knell had struck on the day of General Fritsch's trial, but there were dozens of younger generals and senior officers who also failed to grasp this fact and only now claim to have done so 'at the time'.

The new ambassador, who was devoted to his old father, was a first-rate lawyer and had been a perfect aide to August Wilhelm, the Kaiser's son who later became an SA-Obergruppenführer and an ardent National Socialist. Diplomacy was not his real intellectual bent, as he himself realised, but he was a devout Prussian and had been reared in a Lutheran and unwavering respect for authority. Although he was not a Nazi he preserved belief in Hitler's essential decency until 1945, and nothing grieved him more when he lay dying in 1946 than the realisation that he had succumbed to a vast confidence trick. His family motto was 'Ich dien', and he would, like his friend Field Marshal Kesselring, have looked upon any form of opposition as high treason.

He kept his feelings hidden beneath Prussian armour plating, but those who knew him realised that he also had a soft heart and an infinite capacity for loyalty. A conventional Prussian gentleman, he had developed a strange passion for that most unconventional of all empresses, Elisabeth of Austria, and this formed a bond between us. It surprised everyone, because we certainly had nothing in common in Prussian terms. I acted as Hans Georg von Mackensen's interpreter on numerous trips of varying length, including one which took us deep into the Ukraine, and I shall never forget his upright and gentlemanly nature. He was no Metternich or Talleyrand, and his father-in-law was undoubtedly the better diplomat, but he was just the man to thread his way through the erotically perfumed maze which Italy's foreign policy had developed into under Ciano's influence. Mussolini respected him highly and so did the King, whom he always treated with the deference of an experienced courtier. Most of his embassy colleagues credited themselves with far greater political acumen, possibly with justification, but I doubt if any one of them could have survived immersion in the Roman witch's cauldron between 1938 and 1943 with such poise and authority.

His wife was, as I have said, the daughter of Foreign Minister von Neurath, who had previously been ambassador in Rome. Born in London and bred to the world of diplomacy, she had accompanied her much older husband from Brussels to Madrid and from there to Budapest. She always reminded me of the goddess of the chase, and managed to preserve this Diana-like image without losing her native Swabian characteristics. She had been happy in Budapest. Like Empress Elisabeth, she loved the country, its inhabitants, and the chivalrous traits of a once great but now declining race about whose fate she cherished no illusions. She permitted Admiral Horthy, former aide of the late-lamented Emperor Franz Joseph and Imperial Administrator of the Kingdom of Hungary, to pay court to her, and vainly strove, like the good Swabian she was, to persuade the Hungarian princes to lavish a little thought on the lot of their peasants, who led a life of medieval squalor.

Frau Wini von Mackensen returned reluctantly to Berlin, whither father Neurath had summoned his son-in-law to become

Secretary of State at the Foreign Office. At this period, i.e. in the years immediately following 1933, the Mackensens' path often crossed that of Adolf Hitler, who was doing his best to acquire a modicum of social poise and the environment that went with it. Frau Goebbels was trying to establish a salon frequented by people other than film stars, actresses and secretaries, a salon where Hitler could display his best side to the lady members of high society—which, as an Austrian, he was well able to do. The Duchess of Windsor found that out at a meeting with Hitler at the Berghof, as did Countess Attolico, the bewitching wife of the Italian Ambassador to Berlin. Hitler swallowed unfavourable comment from such quarters with good grace. For instance, far from taking umbrage at Frau von Mackensen's withering criticism of the New Chancellery's large gallery when he proudly showed it to her, he merely admired her refined taste. He also took her under his wing when Frau von Ribbentrop clashed violently with her during his visit to Italy, and quietly overlooked the ambassadress's far from pro-Nazi remarks, which were no doubt faithfully reported to him. Unlike Hassell's bellicose utterances, these remarks were always made openly, whether in the presence of Himmler, Ribbentrop or other leading National Socialists.

In April 1938 the new ambassadress, whose still fluent Italian was a legacy of her father's tour of duty in Rome, found herself plunged into the chaos of Hitler's forthcoming 'honeymoon trip' to Italy. Only when this storm had abated could any thought be given to the problems of Italo-German relations. The Foreign Minister was Count Galeazzo Ciano. His Foreign Office, centrally located in the ancient Palazzo Chigi, which had until the First World War been the Austrian Embassy in Rome, was only used for the transacting of routine diplomatic business. His real base of operations was not in the gilded halls of the Palazzo Chigi, but in the fresh air of the golf-club outside the gates of Rome, facing the Campagna and the imperial aqueducts. This was hardly the right milieu for an ambassadress of the style and background of Madame Mackensen-Neurath, and she could hardly join in the diplomatic frolics which were held there under Ciano's untiring aegis. The members of the Roman *chiaccheria*, as his coterie was called, were frivolous, promiscuous, irresponsible, and as amply endowed with physical charm as they were deficient in intellectual qualities. Matters of moment were settled at the nineteenth hole or between dips in the swimming-pool, and there was no State secret which was not broached and discussed there, as in Marie Antoinette's boudoir at the Petit Trianon. No, it was not the place for Frau von Mackensen, as she made very clear to Herr von Ribbentrop when he earnestly requested her presence at the Acquasanta golf-club. The Reich Foreign Minister never expressed such a wish again, and sought around for another solution.

Frau von Mackensen rightly regarded it as more seemly and important to maintain contact with the royal court to which, after all, her husband had been accredited, even if Berlin tried to ignore the fact. Miraculously, she established cordial relations with Victor Emmanuel III, normally so suspicious, unsociable and untalkative. She chatted to him in his native tongue about his great hobby—his unique collection of coins—and engaged him in table-talk at court functions with an ease which none of her predecessors had ever achieved. Contact with Her Majesty the Queen, a native of Montenegro who had been brought up at the Tsarist court and whose interests, like those of Empress Augusta Viktoria of Germany, were limited to the three Ks—Kinder, Küche and Kirche—was quite impossible from the outset. Instead, Frau von Mackensen managed to establish contact with the tiresome, temperamental and highly intelligent Crown Princess, Maria José. This liaison might have developed into a connection of real importance if her royal mother-in-law had not ultimately interfered, but the Crown Princess derived some benefit from it nonetheless. In July 1943, when the royal family were in dire peril, Frau von Mackensen managed to send her a warning—an episode in which I was not uninvolved.

The ambassadress gave no golf-club parties. The unforgettable Edwin Fischer, who was an old friend of the family, occasionally played at her home to a select audience recruited from the old Roman aristocracy and personal friends of the ambassadorial couple. On her initiative the embassy sponsored a last delightful evening of German opera in the grounds of the Villa Massimo,

seat of the German Academy. An old baroque fountain was transformed into the island of Naxos, and, as the sun set, nightingales
in the neighbouring Roman gardens joined the singers in their
love-duet. This performance of *Ariadne auf Naxos* took place
on 2 July 1940, shortly after Italy entered the war. It was directed
by Clemens Kraus, and the cast included Frau Ursuleac as Ariadne, Patzak as Bacchus, Frau Hüni-Mahascek as the Naiad
and Luise Willer as the Dryad. All the leaders of Roman society
attended, and even Count Ciano postponed his evening round of
golf.

Richard Strauss's letter of thanks to the ambassador read as
follows:

Garmisch, 22.6.40.
Your Excellency,
Permit me, through my friend Clemens Kraus, the masterly interpreter of my work, to send my warmest regards to you at the beautiful venue of the Adriadne performance, where I have often had the
pleasure of staying as a guest. I am particularly grateful to Your
Excellency for having chosen my work for the gala performance on
2 July, as a fresh token of the cultural ties between our two countries. Sincerely regretting my inability to attend the first open-air
performance on the sacred soil of Rome, I remain, with deep respect
and a Heil Hitler, Your Excellency's most humble servant,
                                        Dr Richard Strauss

This was the last major artistic event to occur before Italy
became ever more deeply embroiled in a war which exceeded her
military and moral, political and financial capabilities. I shall
never forget the historic moment when, on 10 June 1940, standing
on the same Palazzo Venezia balcony from which he had proclaimed the founding of the Abyssinian Empire under the sovereignty of the King, Mussolini announced Italy's entry into the
Second World War at the side of the Third Reich. What a difference! Gone were the jubilant, genuinely jubilant masses who had
thronged the spacious square and the streets leading to it. This
time, Mussolini's unconvincing speech was tepidly received by a
few thousand policemen and claqueurs. Frau von Mackensen and
the shrewd wife of the even shrewder President of the Chamber,

Signora Grandi, witnessed the ceremony from the palace opposite. Both women had tears in their eyes, and the ambassadress whispered to me that it was 'the end'.

She was an accurate prophet, as she again demonstrated at an embassy Christmas party in 1941, when, beneath a glittering Christmas tree from the Abruzzi, she described her vision of the future to a few intimate friends. Cassandra-like, she predicted that the Führer and the Duce would be dragged through the streets of New York, chained and caged, for the edification of a howling mob, that German and Italian cities would be reduced to smoking rubble, and that all of us who had served the Third Reich in any capacity would be hauled from one tribunal to the next. Even she failed to guess that the first victim of this persecution would be her own father, Neurath, whose release from the war-crimes prison at Spandau she ultimately secured after a heroic battle lasting many years.

But the year was still 1938, peace still reigned, and Mussolini and Fascism were preparing to welcome the Führer and Chancellor of the Third Reich with all the pomp and splendour of imperial Rome. Their best ally was the Mediterranean climate. The rain had teemed down in Berlin during Mussolini's famous speech in laborious German the previous September, but the rulers of the Third Reich had anaesthetised him against the appalling weather with their parades, manœuvres, Krupp tours and gargantuan demonstrations. Mussolini returned to Italy intoxicated by the sight of so much naked power and envious of the rival whom he had only a few years earlier regarded as insignificant and contemptible. Megalomania is infectious. From now on, everything in the Duce's domain had to be bigger, more powerful, more dictatorial. He and his associates wanted to show Italy's Nordic bridegroom what Fascism could do when it chose to.

They set to work. The official hosts were His Majesty the King Emperor and his court—yet another token of Mussolini's political expertise, even though the Third Reich laughed up its sleeve and Hitler indulged in some of his most tactless remarks. The Führer would have preferred to visit the Duce when the latter had overthrown the monarchy and become, like him, emperor, king, leader and dictator all rolled into one. His Majesty was in an extremely bad mood and so were the members of his immediate circle. There were drops of gall in the champagne consumed on this honeymoon trip to the South, as the entry in Count Ciano's diary for 7 May clearly shows:

What is more, the King is prejudiced against him, and tries to represent him as a mentally and physically degenerate sort of man. He tells the Duce and me that at about 1 a.m. on the first night of his stay at the Palace Hitler asked for a woman. Boundless amazement. The explanation: it seems he cannot go to sleep unless a woman turns down the bed before his eyes. It was difficult to find one, but the problem was solved by recruiting a chamber-maid from a hotel. If this were really true it would be weird and interesting, but is it? Isn't it just a piece of spite on the part of the King, who also alleges that Hitler has himself injected with stimulants and narcotics?

Was it true? King Victor Emmanuel III was a master of compromise and minor tactics, and he was certainly malicious— everyone in Rome knew that. Even if he was playing the host against his will, it would, I think, have been in better taste not to spread gossip of this kind. On the other hand, the everlasting gaffes made by Hitler's entourage had touched him on the raw. Goebbels, for instance, enlivened a visit to the palace throne-room by pointing to the throne and suggesting that the Duce would become it better than the pint-sized King. Hitler's private name for His Majesty was 'King Nutcracker', and Ribbentrop declared that the only good thing the German Social Democrats ever did was to abolish the monarchy. Himmler, who had either forgotten or wanted to forget that his father had once tutored a Wittelsbach prince, described the royal palace as an antiquated museum ripe for auctioning—and so on. It goes without saying that all these elegant sallies were promptly relayed to the court via the usual channels. An old courtier who had seen service under Queen Margherita unburdened himself to me on the subject. He told me that, although the court had hitherto regarded the Kaiser as the *ne plus ultra* of tactlessness, his record had been decisively smashed during the present State visit.

His Majesty was not the only one to gossip. Hitler's bosom friend Benito Mussolini, kept *au courant* by his son-in-law, was convinced that his guest enhanced his naturally sallow complexion with rouge. The golf-club, too, hummed with unsavoury stories. It was said that Hitler's armed escort had tried to safeguard him from assassination by militarily occupying the palace. According to current estimates, the alcohol consumption of these gentlemen rivalled the requirements of a full-strength division. Much to my glee, Galeazzo Ciano's male and female favourites were disappointed when it came to things erotic. Since Hitler, Ribbentrop, Frank and Himmler provided no material in this respect, golf-club rumour eventually had it that all the leading guests were linked by pederastic ties, and references to Röhm and his entourage abounded.

Lying before me as I try to recall this honeymoon trip to fleeting life are the sumptuously bound blue volumes which the Foreign Ministry issued to everyone before the start of the tour. With a precision more Prussian than Italian, they listed the participants in the peaceful State visit—five hundred of them loaded on to three special trains—their daily programme, hotel accommodation, the festivities and receptions to which they were invited and the uniforms or civilian attire to be worn at them.

Many a German king emperor of the Middle Ages would have been happy to muster as many knights and mercenaries for a military expedition across the Alps. None of the attendant interpreters found himself overworked during the visit. On one occasion I think there were four of us ready to step into the breach if need arose, including His Majesty's son-in-law, Prince Philip von Hessen, Oberpräsident of Hessen-Nassau, SA-Obergruppenführer, and holder of the Party's Gold Badge. For all Ribbentrop's desperate endeavours, there was very little top-level political discussion, and the Reich Foreign Minister's attempt to bind Italy to the Third Reich on a contractual basis was coolly ignored. Mussolini, who had not yet succumbed to Freudian love-hate complexes where the Germans were concerned and was still far removed from his subsequent state of abject servitude, went so far as to tell Count Ciano that 'Herr von Ribbentrop belongs to that category of Germans which brings Germany misfortune. He talks constantly to everyone of waging war without having a specific enemy or definite objective in mind'.

The only event of political importance was Adolf Hitler's speech at the State banquet given by Mussolini at the Palazzo Venezia on the evening of 7 May, at which the South Tyrol was presented to the host as a sort of mountainous wedding gift. This time the Fascists and National Socialists were alone together, having been abandoned to their fraternal fate by the 'royal museum'. The Germans, with Adolf Hitler at their head, radiated good-fellowship, and one could have heard a pin drop in the Palazzo's huge banqueting hall when Hitler rose to thank Mussolini for his address of welcome and hand over his territorial gift.

'It is both my firm wish and political testament that the German people should regard the natural Alpine frontiers between our two peoples as eternally inviolable. I am certain that a glorious and flourishing future will accrue to Rome and Germany as a result.'

This was, as I have said, the sole event of lasting importance to come out of these days in May. Even Count Ciano was forced to concede that 'the Führer had a greater political success than I assumed he would. Although he encountered universal hostility on his arrival, and although a certain amount of pressure was brought to bear on him by Mussolini, he was extremely successful at melting the ice around him. Last night's speech contributed greatly to this.'

What had preceded this speech and what followed it was a veritable orgy of theatricality in which every part of the nation—the court, the Fascist Party machine, the three armed services, artists, beautiful women and, as general accessories, the lovable Italian people themselves—played a role.

The indispensable military displays, notably the great military parade in the Via dei Trionfi and the naval review in the Bay of Naples, presented—to the layman, at least—a highly impressive picture of the strength of Fascist Italy. According to the official programme, the column which paraded past Hitler, his entourage and his hosts consisted of 30,500 soldiers, 2500 quadrupeds, 600 motor vehicles, 320 motorised vehicles, 400 tanks and howitzers, 400 pieces of artillery and a representative body of Libyan troops.

No one, apart from a few sceptical German military observers, thought of assessing the real military value and combat readiness of the units in this parade. Only the Second World War would show whether they were Potemkin villagers or genuine instruments of war. The splendour of the age-old architectural back-cloth towering into the Roman sky, the jubilant crowds and the colourful picture presented by the parading troops were all far too impressive to permit of any such misgivings on 6 May 1938 —especially as the visitors had just returned, full of admiration, from the grand review of the Royal Italian Navy which had been held in the Bay of Naples the day before.

On that equally glorious spring morning in the loveliest bay in the world, where once cruised the galleys and triremes of the Greeks and Romans, the sailing ships of the Saracens and Lord Nelson's frigates, Benito Mussolini received the King, the Crown Prince and the great ones of the Third Reich, Adolf Hitler at their head, on board the *Cavour*. The crews of all the ships in the two battle squadrons had turned out in review order to give the German visitor a naval welcome. Ships' guns boomed out at the approach of two squadrons of submarines—ninety vessels in all—which carried out a brief close-formation exercise designed to illustrate their crews' high standard of training. This exercise had a truly hypnotic effect. The ninety submarines dived simultaneously under the mass of heavy and light cruisers, pocket-battleships, modern destroyers and torpedo-boats, to re-emerge on the other side of the fleet four minutes later, still in perfect formation. This was the signal for a lively cannonade which endowed the manœuvre with warlike overtones.

Cheeks flushed with excitement, Adolf Hitler expressed his admiration to the King Emperor—an admiration which persisted during the final parade of seventy-five warships and ninety submarines. Never had King and Crown Prince, admirals and naval officers, been in higher spirits. The fleet was royalist to the core, royalist by tradition and conviction, and Adolf Hitler, to his sorrow, had no navy to compare with what he had seen. In the midst of all this jubilation I ventured to suggest that, in the event of war, Mussolini and his Fascists would never prevail on His Majesty to commit the fleet in its entirety. My only reward was ridicule, disbelief and allusions to my lack of military knowledge. I was involuntarily reminded of this Bay of Naples review in 1957, while reading the best account of the Italian Navy's role in World War II, a book graphically entitled *The Betrayed Fleet*. The author, an Italian airman named Trizzino, testifies to the extensive and, as far as the Mediterranean war was concerned, fatal sabotage engaged in by large sections of the Italian naval high command—sabotage which led in September 1943 to the surrender of naval vessels totalling 266,000 tons. Trizzino concludes his book with the words: ' "A splendid prize," says Churchill, "The betrayed fleet, the tragedy of the African fighters," says history.'

'I am proud of you,' read Mussolini's order of the day to his royal master's fleet, and, however sceptical a few connoisseurs of the Italian scene may have felt, no one would have ventured to speculate that evening on the likelihood of impending disaster.

The evening was notable for two events: a performance of the first two acts of *Aïda* in the most beautiful opera house in Italy, and a less musical performance in German by Adolf Hitler.

Thousands upon thousands of white roses filled the air with their heady scent as, at nine-thirty, the royal party entered their box, resplendent in full-dress uniforms and glittering evening gowns. The mightiest man in Germany surprised everyone by appearing in tails, unadorned save for the Party's Gold Badge. He resembled a hotel receptionist and looked appropriately ill at ease. It was plain to see how glad he was to wave away the pomp and splendour round him and draw his bosom friend Benito Mussolini, the last of the Romans, into the seat beside him. Crown Princess Maria José, who was wearing a superb evening dress encrusted with jewels, took no trouble to conceal her aristocratic and intellectual aversion to the visitor from the North. She later recorded (*La mia vita nelle mia Italia,* Oggi, 1959) an account of the banquet which preceded the opera performance, at which, as throughout the visit to Naples, she represented her royal mother-in-law.

'I sat next to Hitler at dinner. He spoke only German, and I naturally made not the slightest effort to follow what he said.

I myself have only a very general knowledge of the German language. He ate nothing and drank nothing. They say bad people drink no wine, and if I may pass judgment on Hitler, I can only state that the saying holds good. He nibbled chocolate throughout the meal, and his stiff and over-reverential gestures made a ludicrous impression.' (*Oggi*, Milano, 1959). Such was the Belgian king's daughter's description of her guest, written while living in exile beside the Lake of Geneva.

Her guest had no reason at all to feel happy in the royal box. The thought of assassination leapt to everyone's mind during Aïda's great aria, when a beam crashed to the stage just in front of the celebrated Gina Cigna, who bravely went on singing. Nothing —neither the enchanting voices of Pederzini as Amneris and Benjamino Gigli as Rhadames, nor a magnificent production which conjured a whole menagerie of animals on to the stage—succeeded in raising Hitler's spirits.

The Führer vented his annoyance at the obvious loathing and contempt of his royal table-companion on the innocent head of von Bülow-Schwante, German chief of protocol. Von Bülow-Schwante did not ensure that his lord and master had sufficient time after the *Aïda* performance to exchange his unwanted suit of tails for the more usual uniform. Consequently, when the guard of honour paraded at the train which was to convey Hitler back to Rome, His Majesty had the additional malicious pleasure of watching his guest inspect the ranks like a bare-headed wine-waiter. Hitler fumed with rage, and the head of protocol rolled, figuratively but irrevocably, on the red carpet leading to the special train.

Needless to say, the whole court quickly learned of the incident and were, in the fullest sense of the word, royally entertained— especially Crown Princess Maria José, who welcomed it as a perfect complement to her chocolate-nibbler's portrait.

What with parades, operatic performances, gala dinners, public celebrations and a minimum of top-level discussion, the May visit drew to its close. I propose to round the picture off by singling out two more items on the official schedule. One was an evening show in Rome's wonderful pine-fringed Piazza di Diena. The programme, which included folk dances and a mounted display by the Royal Carabinieri, closed with a cavalry charge, a general salute and Puccini's *Hymn to Rome*. The ceremonial chairs reserved for Victor Emmanuel and Hitler were located in the front row, Mussolini's seat and those of the Italian ministers in the row behind. Outraged that his best friend and fellow-dictator should play second fiddle to 'King Nutcracker', Hitler made a gesture as if inviting Mussolini to come forward. However, the Duce was still independent and statesmanlike enough to frown and shake his head, and a new crisis was safely averted.

Then came the final day in Florence. Hitler had drunk his fill of Roman grandeur and imperial splendour, past and present. He was alone at last with his chosen bride in the city of the Medici, and it was there that the most incongruous political marriage of recent times enjoyed its acme of nuptial bliss. Florence was an avowed favourite of Hitler's from this day forth. He found everything wonderful, the palaces and museums, the cheering crowds, the streets lined with figures dressed in historical costumes, the farewell dinner at the Palazzo Riccardi—even the society of the great ladies of Florence, who were more to his taste because even the loveliest of them had innumerable children and were far removed from the snobbism of their Roman and Neapolitan sisters. He was genuinely enchanted by them, and made some mournful allusions to the German aristocracy's half-hearted approach to procreation.

He could not be torn away from the Uffizi, where he lingered in front of Early and High Renaissance masterpieces for far longer than his hosts had envisaged. 'When I had time to look at pictures I was too poor,' he reflected sadly, 'and now I am in a position to do so I don't have time.'

Mussolini, who was accompanying him, greeted such remarks with incomprehension. He blithely admitted that he was visiting this treasure-chamber of Italian art for the first time in his life, and suggested that the tour had better be cut short because the descendants of Lippi, Botticelli, Ghirlandaio and Bronzino were already waiting in the Piazza della Signoria to pay homage to the distinguished admirer of their city and its art treasures. Only Count Ciano and his youthful companions would have liked to linger. They were so absorbed in the physical traits of certain fourteenth- and fifteenth-century Florentine ladies that they irritated the Duce by dawdling behind.

This day, too, drew to a close, but to Hitler Florence remained the high-spot of his honeymoon trip. Even on 30 January 1943, when the imminent fall of Stalingrad had plunged him in gloom, he drew the Florentine members of an Italian delegation into a long and nostalgic conversation about their native city. It was the only happy feature of a dismal tea-party held at the Führer's Headquarters on a day when, far from the Arno and surrounded by ice and snow, his encircled army awaited its inevitable doom.

The crossing of the Alps was enlivened by a special surprise concocted by Donna Eleonora Attolico, the delightful and intelligent wife of the Italian Ambassador to Berlin. Donna Eleonora, who resembled Bronzino's portrait of Eleonora of Toledo, was Adolf Hitler's favourite among the ladies of the diplomatic corps and was held up to the younger and more eligible bachelors in the German Foreign Office as a shining example of what a senior diplomat's wife should be. Hitler always beamed at the beautiful woman when offering her his arm after a reception, and she knew better than anyone else how to keep him in a good mood by listening with angelic patience to his effusions on the subject of women, education, posterity, art, and the theatre. I am sure she only understood half of what he said, but she never betrayed her incomprehension.

In brief, Donna Eleonora aroused wild enthusiasm among the leading ladies of the Third Reich by suggesting that they also take a trip to the South. Frau von Ribbentrop, Frau Hess, Frau Frank, Frau Keitel, Frau Bouhler and a few others were to join in the State visit unofficially, keeping well in the background. Most of them were wholly unsuited to such a venture. My own connection with this Valkyrie ride across the Brenner was minimal, I am happy to say, but it provided me with some amusing moments. The women did not like each other particularly, and were jealous of their husbands' relative power and status. They were inquisitive, like all their sex, but quite unwilling to make sacrifices in order to satisfy their curiosity. They naturally wanted to be received at court by Her Majesty the Queen Empress but had no intention—initially, at least—of observing court etiquette.

No comic dramatist could have devised a scene as side-splitting as the curtsey rehearsal at which the bewitching Countess, seconded by the German Ambassadress, taught them to fulfil their ritual obligation. The two graceful women gave the first ladies of the Third Reich a really impressive demonstration of this charming obeisance, but in vain. First, they were physically incapable of it, and, secondly, who was this jumped-up Montenegrin with her undersized king emperor of a husband? They eventually settled on a compromise consisting of a half-bow with right hand raised, and my only regret is that I was not at the palace to witness their performance.

It was equally difficult to convince Frau von Ribbentrop that Frau von Mackensen—not she—was Germany's first lady in Italy and thus entitled to sit on Her Majesty's right. They were still at odds over the problem of precedence when they were received, with a noticeable lack of enthusiasm, by the dark-haired, matronly queen. Her Majesty solved the point at issue by gesturing to the ambassadress to sit on her right. She then proceeded to address herself almost exclusively to her in Italian, which did nothing to improve Frau von Ribbentrop's mood.

The German ladies felt like queens but simultaneously congratulated themselves on the absence of a German monarchy and the existence of the Third Reich. As I had foreseen, they became split up during the trip through Naples and found themselves and their handbags delivered over to the tempestuous enthusiasm of a populace whose Greek ancestry was unknown to them but whose sweat, fish, and garlic-laden proximity filled them with repugnance. The trip was torture, especially for Frau von Mackensen, and culminated in an embarrassing clash between her and Frau von Ribbentrop in Florence which almost shattered Hitler's Medicean idyll.

However, the anxieties occasioned by the unofficial visit of the official mistresses of the Third Reich were of a relatively minor nature. I was far more worried when, shortly after Hitler's arrival in Rome, Don Arturo Bocchini asked me if I knew Fräulein Eva Braun. I was able to reply in the affirmative, even though we had only met once while I was having coffee with Hitler's aides. His Excellency was very anxious to know what she looked

like and what the 'position' was. I said she looked like a typical
secretary, modest and unassuming, blonde and quite attractive—
but why did he want to know?

Eva Braun came too, but in an even more unofficial capacity
than her distinguished countrywomen. All she wanted to do was
see the nice ships in the Bay of Naples, stay at a nice hotel and
do some nice shopping. The first requirement was not easy to
fulfil. She could hardly cruise around on a pocket battleship
because her blonde presence would probably endanger the whole
manœuvre. The chartered luxury steamer which accommodated
the ladies of the Third Reich was equally out of the question.
However, there were one or two smaller vessels available 'for
special use', and it was from one of these that she observed her
Adolf aboard the flagship in all his glory. But shopping was far
more important. She loved crocodile in every shape and form,
and returned to her hotel looking as if she had come back from a
trip up the Congo rather than along the Tiber. Nevertheless, she
was sheer delight compared with the uncrowned queens of the
Third Reich, and when I introduced her to Don Arturo at a
private meal he assured me that he would 'never have given Herr
Hitler credit' for such good taste. A magnificent crocodile handbag was the fruit of this brief, gay and highly unofficial encounter.

By midnight on 9 May they had all departed, confident that
Italy was a world power, Fascism indestructible and the monarchy
a museum-piece. They doubtless dreamed of the Rome-Berlin
Axis on their return journey, forgetting all about His Holiness
and the Vatican. Pope Pius XI had retired to Castel Gandolfo
for the summer, closing the Vatican museums and generally be-
having as though the Third Reich and its regime did not exist.
The fault did not lie with him, but with the organisers of the State
visit. It had always been customary in the past for foreign mon-
archs or heads of government to devote one day at the end of
their stay in Italy to an official visit to the Vatican. The Third
Reich did not consider this necessary, and all Don Arturo's hand-
wringing went for nought.

One person who was thrilled by the State visit was little Bibi
from the Pensione Jaselli-Owen, whom I had provided with
plenty of blue, green and yellow tickets for operas, concerts and

other functions. She was impressed by the good looks and better manners of the young ADCs who were introduced to her, even though their lords and masters bore no relation to her ideals of male beauty and were not to be compared with the masterful Mussolini or the Don Juanesque Ciano.

Not being a King's son-in-law like my fellow-interpreter, the Prince of Hessen, I had not over-exerted myself. I had seen some beautiful things, wined and dined excellently, amused myself variously and inexpensively. When I realised that my reservations about the Italian frenzy which had seized everyone were not only misunderstood but unwanted, I held my peace. If my duties as an interpreter had never been more arduous than they were during this visit, my future would have been cloudless indeed. Unfortunately, things turned out otherwise.

The unpleasant personal consequences of the May visit soon manifested themselves. The new watchword was: any National Socialist with any claims to importance must go to Italy, and any Italian Fascist with similar pretensions to Germany. The annual pilgrimage to Mecca must be child's play compared to the orgy of human ambition and vanity which now broke out. The Germans wanted Italian medals, Italian gifts, Italian sightseeing tours. Italians who had scarcely been abroad before developed a burning desire to realise the same ambitions north of the Brenner, not the least of their requirements being German women. Blonde Gretchen became an Italian idol, and many romantic tragi-comedies occurred as a result.

I have neither the space nor the inclination to enlarge upon this bazaar of human emotions, most of them rather primitive. Suffice it to say that, with the friendly assistance of the Italian Ministry of the Interior and of Bocchini in particular, I was able to evade some of the less agreeable assignments. Thanks to the 'star interpreter' status which I slowly but surely attained, I was able to frustrate numerous German requests to make at least one trip to the South at government expense. In the end, I was left victorious on the battlefield of the Italo-German crusades, and my services as an interpreter were only enlisted on special occasions such as guest appearances by Benjamino Gigli and other giants of song.

My duties naturally brought me into contact with some memorable people. Having already spoken of Don Arturo Bocchini in these terms, I should now like to summon up another figure from the past.

I do not know if Italo Balbo means much to the modern reader, but his memory lives on intact and undiminished in the Republican Italy of today, having survived the war years and the fall of the monarchy. Balbo the Fascist took second place to Balbo the coloniser of North Africa and Balbo the daring trans-oceanic flier, whose exploits stirred the imagination of the world in 1928. His death in the skies above Tobruk on 28 June 1940, shortly after Italy's entry into the Second World War, is still shrouded in obscurity, but to a legend-loving people like the Italians it has only enhanced the myth surrounding him. To me, who knew him for many years, he was that rare type, the congenial hero. He never bragged of his daring flight across the Atlantic with a squadron of sea-planes at a period when aviation was technically unequal to such a hazardous venture. He was vain, of course, like many heroes, but it was a virile and agreeable type of vanity. The conquest of a beautiful woman—and his conquests were legion—meant quite as much to him as a storm in mid-Atlantic. He was a Teutophobe and Anglophile, and showed it plainly in a way which also demanded courage, since from 1936 onwards it was undesirable not to like the Germans. In November 1937 he invited Himmler to Tripoli, where he was Governor-General, and vainly tried, with my assistance, to convince him of the long-term impossibility of holding North Africa and the Abyssinian Empire in any war which involved the Mediterranean area.

Balbo's Assyrian beard and love of ostentation made him suspect in the eyes of Hitler's entourage, and I did all I could to ensure the success of his trip to Germany in August 1938.

He was a brilliant writer. I still possess an autographed copy of his *Diario della rivoluzione* (1922), which tells the story of the March on Rome and the bloodless conquest of Italy by Mussolini and Fascism. I should like to quote one passage from it which Tacitus himself could not have moulded with greater dramatic economy. It was 28 October 1922, and Balbo, a member—with

Bianchi, De Vecchi and De Bono—of the so-called quadrum-virate which was destined to be most closely associated with Mussolini's triumph two days later, was already in Rome:

I find Rome in a state of military preparedness. Armed patrols in the streets, carabinieri and royalist guards occupying the city's strategic points, helmeted troops hauling machine-guns and even a few pieces of artillery into position, barbed wire draped round the Tiber bridges. The King conferred far into the night. Has a state of siege been proclaimed or not? It is announced and then denied, but the military preparations instituted in the Roman divisional area clearly show that, to all intents and purposes, it is already in force. Rome will wake up tomorrow to find itself in a state of war, like a border town threatened by the enemy.

The political situation is still dominated by uncertainty on the morning of the 29th, but we now have accurate estimates of our strength. 52,000 Fascists stand before the gates of Rome. Then the news spreads like wildfire: the King has asked Mussolini to form a government. An indescribable evening spent among jubilant black-shirts, an evening of victory, of repose and relaxation.

At 7 p.m. on the 30th I am back in Rome (*Balbo had organised the March on Rome from the north*) and go straight to the Hotel Savoya, where Mussolini is staying. The hotel is ringed by large crowds of people. Officers in command of Fascist units give the salute. In a large room on the top floor I find our leader surrounded by Bianchi, De Vecchi, De Bono and a number of politicians.

His face is radiant.

Not a word—just an embrace.

Anyone who gives this sort of description of an historic event in which he played a central role must be a congenial hero, but Italo Balbo's heroic hours were numbered. He possessed a mortal enemy in Mussolini's son-in-law, who, backed by a handful of princesses, numerous countesses and countless baronesses, had appointed himself Crown Prince of Fascism. Ciano looked upon Balbo as his keenest rival and did his utmost to cast suspicion on him and discredit him with Mussolini, even trying to inspire the Duce with fear of his former comrade-in-arms. Balbo told me a good deal, including the fact that he had to be on guard against attacks from the Ciano quarter. He did not, of course, envisage the possibility that an Italian coastal battery would shoot him down on 28 June 1940, while on a reconnaissance flight over Tobruk, nor that many Italians would suspect—as they still do—that Ciano was at the bottom of it. I should like to quote Ciano's reference to the dead man in his diary for 29 June 1940. It reads as follows:

Balbo is dead. His death was the result of a tragic misunderstanding. The anti-aircraft defences of Tobruk fired on his plane under the mistaken impression that it was an English machine. The news has distressed me deeply. Balbo did not deserve such an end. He was a restless, exuberant character. He loved every aspect of life. His verve was stronger than his intellect and careful reflection less his forte than temperamental decisions. The Italians will remember Balbo for a long time to come, primarily because he was, above all else, a true Italian endowed with all the characteristics of our race, good and bad.

Thus wrote the now undisputed heir to the Fascist throne in 1940. He could not know that exactly three years later, in July 1943, he would have gambled away his position in a vain attempt to oust his father-in-law and remain in power himself.

I believe that Balbo liked me, possibly because of our mutual dislike of Galeazzo Ciano. When the prospect of a Mediterranean war began to make him increasingly apprehensive about the safety of the North African domain to which he had been semi-exiled as a result of petty Roman jealousies, I advised him to invite one of the leading figures of the Third Reich to pay him a visit.

His choice fell on Heinrich Himmler, who happened to be visiting Sicily '*privatamente*' with his wife Marga in November 1937. Himmler was spontaneously delighted; his wife, about whom I should like to say a few words, less so.

Frau Marga was an odd woman. She undoubtedly took little pleasure in the manifold advantages which Himmler's position afforded her. She was much older than her husband, had been a nurse, and would, I think, have been perfectly at home as matron of a women's hospital. I must say that, in Italy, she took great pains to understand the alien South, though she undoubtedly understood her East German homeland better. When a mad German monk at the Convent of Santa Chiara in Naples clasped her round the knees and begged her to flee from the blandishments of his Neapolitan fellow-monks, the spirit of understanding deserted her.

She felt her best when at home and out of the social limelight. She had no wish to play an important role like her husband, nor was she an entertaining life's companion, but what was that to Heinrich Himmler? On the other hand, things might have turned out differently if she had been more amusing, more alluring, more stimulating—who knows?

Obediently but unenthusiastically, Frau Marga joined her husband in the luxurious special plane which was to convey them to Tripoli. On their arrival, Italo Balbo did his best to entertain them with big receptions, a tour of the souks and an Arab fantasia. Signora Balbo, who played hostess, was an equally unamusing person. Being an Italian, however, she possessed the sort of innate *savoir vivre* which is not indigenous to East Germany. The two ladies found little to talk about.

Heinrich Himmler, by contrast, was in his element. He could not wear uniform because this would have marred the unofficial image of his lightning visit, but he was able to inspect troops and take the salute garbed in a frightful sports suit and long stockings. His host delighted him still further by conducting a war-game on a map-table in the Governor's Palace. Balbo, who appeared with a staff of officers drawn from all the armed services, was determined to show that, in the event of military embroilment with England, the game would be lost from the outset. It could only be a matter of time before the whole of Libya and the even less defensible Abyssinian Empire fell prey to the British. With prophetic accuracy, he stressed the difficulty of keeping troops supplied from the other side of the Mediterranean.

Himmler did not give up so easily. Pointing to Hitler's gigantic arms programme and the ever-growing strength of Hermann Göring's pride and joy, the German Luftwaffe, he suggested that the Air Marshal and Governor-General should pay a visit to Germany in the near future in order to familiarise himself with current plans and potentialities.

The day which had been devoted to this gloomy game culminated in a grand evening reception at the palace, radiant with all the colours and hues of North Africa and graced by the presence of the colony's loveliest women.

Balbo had achieved his object after all, and so had I. Himmler flew off in a thoughtful frame of mind. He was delighted with his new-found friend and determined to secure him a cordial invitation to Germany. Balbo's jealous adversary in Rome organised some vigorous opposition to the proposed visit, but not even Ciano could prevail against an invitation from Göring's Luftwaffe when Himmler was backing it and Adolf Hitler had given it his blessing.

On 9 August 1938 Italo Balbo duly boarded a three-engined Savoya and flew, escorted by seven of his most distinguished trans-oceanic fliers, to the air station at Staaken. The plump Reich Marshal was waiting to greet him, resplendent in summery white. The two men's bemedalled chests gleamed and glittered and their satrap-like personalities harmonised immediately. At Karinhall, Göring welcomed his guest as 'one of the Duce's paladins and the man who has re-created the Italian Air Force', successfully transforming the Assyrian-looking Balbo into a Ferrarese condottiere of the cinquecento, a period when beards such as his were commonplace in his native city!

On 13 August the Italian air squadron landed safely and in glorious weather on the Obersalzberg. The fact that Balbo had only been invited to take coffee in Hitler's picture-crammed drawing-room seemed unpromising, especially as the coffee was, by Italian standards, poor. There were no women present either, though I vainly hoped for the appearance of the blonde Eva. However, we then adjourned to the famous terrace with its broad alpine panorama. Obediently following a tip I had given him, Balbo admired the mountain range in front of us and the view of Austrian territory.

Austria . . . That was Hitler's cue. He forgot his beard-born misgivings and any disreputable stories he might have heard about Balbo's private life. Stirred by the sight of his guest gazing reverently in the direction of Salzburg and stimulated by the thought that here was an Italian with the heart of an Austrian, he plunged into a long discourse on Austria while the evening sun shone gently down and two eagles—birds whose heraldic association with the Habsburgs was fortunately lost on Balbo—circled in the air high above us.

The meeting, originally intended to be a brief one, dragged on and on. Adolf Hitler's eyes glowed, Italo Balbo's eyes sparkled, a most successful photograph was taken on the terrace, later to receive wide press publicity, and tea was served, together with French cognac which would have satisfied the most exacting palate.

Finally, in a grave voice, the Führer said:

'I hope to see you again before long. Göring and Himmler have informed me of the Africa problem. We shall win there too, Excellency, because, unlike the democracies, we have the will to win. Convey my greetings to my friend, your great Duce, and to your beautiful Italy.'

Balbo had safely traversed another ocean. Back in his Munich hotel he hugged me fiercely and begged me to regard Libya as my second home from then on. Thanks to the underrated democracies, I was never able to take advantage of his invitation.

The second phase of the festive programme for 13 August 1938 began. We were greeted at the Hotel Vier Jahreszeiten by that doyen of European hoteliers, Adolf Walterspiel, who whispered to me that he had sent a dinner to the Tegernsee complete with chefs, waiters and all the trimmings. This was reassuring news, even though the accompanying circumstances of the dinner were less so: Heinrich Himmler had reciprocated Balbo's Tripolitanian hospitality by inviting him to dine at his villa in Gmund on the Tegernsee at 8.30 p.m. precisely. I had already hinted to Wolff, his Chief of Staff, that while the quality of the fare was important the quality of the lady guests was vitally so. I described the wide range of feminine pulchritude that had been offered us at the governor's palace in Tripoli and confirmed that Balbo and his gallant companions would be expecting some dewy Tegernsee maidens, preferably in low-cut party dirndls. General Wolff assured me that he was an expert in these matters and that nothing would be lacking.

I was still uneasy. Knowing the sort of ladies Frau Marga Himmler liked to consort with, I spoke frankly to Balbo. We agreed that a single glance in my direction after he had surveyed the guests would suffice to cut the ceremonial dinner short. He remained grateful to me for the rest of his life—not that he had long to live.

We arrived. Fir-trees rustled around us, hiding the lake from view. The villa was furnished in bourgeois peasant style, but without warmth. In the garden we fondled some dainty bronze gazelles, copies from Herculaneum which a sad fate had sent to graze here among Alpine violets. Once a birthday present from Bocchini, they now repose among the reeds of the Tegernsee, just behind the villa's bathing platform.

Frau Marga, clad in an evening dirndl, greeted us with the distant affability which was so characteristic of her. She did not radiate much warmth, but she radiated more than the women friends she had invited. Ah, sad autumnal flowers of Tegernsee femininity! There were plenty of attractive young baronesses in the villas lining the shores of the lake, and few were so 'anti-Nazi' that they would have refused to partake of a Walterspiel dinner in the Himmler household, but Frau Marga's contemporaries looked like Victorian ladies-in-waiting on holiday at a Tegernsee resort.

Balbo shot me the prearranged glance, and I immediately knew what to do. Before the gastronomic revelries had even begun I informed our regretful host that his guest of honour had just received instructions via the Italian Consulate-General in Munich to report to Mussolini as early as possible next day. There was not a word of truth in the story, but Himmler swallowed it without demur and Balbo recovered his spirits. Herr Walterspiel had surpassed himself, and I would not be surprised to learn that his famous cookery book lists the main course as *Saddle of Venison à la Balbo!*

Barely two hours later, a Maybach Super was standing outside the door with Himmler's personal driver, Bastian, at the wheel. Balbo said his adieus, making frequent use of the words 'Mussolini' and 'urgent'. The other trans-oceanic fliers stayed behind, willy-nilly. I accompanied him.

The night was clear and starlit when we reached the Brennerstrasse. At the pass itself we were challenged by a drowsy sentry. *'Sono il Maresciallo Balbo'* was the reply, and we crossed the frontier without having to produce papers or any other such inventions of the devil. After sleeping soundly in the luxurious government saloon, we were greeted in the early light of dawn by the sight of the Lago di Misurina. The driver wanted some leather trousers from the South Tyrol and I asked for a signed picture dated 13.8.38. A pair of *Lederhosen* made of the finest chamois arrived in Munich soon afterwards. The photograph, dedicated to 'My friend Eugenio Dollmann', is still in my possession. The various secret service agencies with which it was my subsequent pleasure to cross swords did not even rob me of the silver frame.

The Air Marshal and Governor-General returned to North Africa glowing with satisfaction, despite his visit to the barren flower-garden beside the Tegernsee. In Rome, Count Ciano was vastly irritated, as his notes show:

In other respects he is delighted with his trip, with the Germans, the Luftwaffe, everything. Now that his vanity has been tickled he talks like the most dedicated supporter of the Axis. The crux of his report: an extraordinarily powerful German air force, far more advanced than ours from the technical point of view.

Balbo is an overgrown schoolboy, spoilt and restless, high-spirited and ignorant, a man who may prove troublesome some day—but not dangerous, I think, because he isn't capable of it.

Galeazzo Ciano was capable of much more, as he proved at the famous session of the Fascist Grand Council on the night of 24–25 July 1943, when he basely betrayed the father-in-law to whom he owed everything.

The official Roman communiqué on Italo Balbo's trip was cool and terse:

The Duce received Air Marshal Italo Balbo, who reported to him on his recent visit to Berlin. Balbo described, in particular, the strides made by the German Air Force and the extremely cordial reception accorded him by the Führer, Göring, the officers of the Luftwaffe and other services, and the German population.

I can only say, in conclusion, that even after his return Balbo never for a moment underestimated the enormous dangers to which a Mediterranean war would expose Italy and, more especially, her African colonial possessions. If Mussolini had tolerated more Balbos round him and fewer Cianos, and if the Air Marshal's plane had not mysteriously crashed in flames so soon after the outbreak of war, the fortunes of Italy might well have changed for the better.

I do not propose to give a detailed description of the international drama which the year 1938 brought in its train. Personal impressions and experiences are all I have to add to the whole libraries that have been written about the Munich Conference of 28 September. However, the essential point that emerges from my observations is that, while the British and French managed to save the peace yet again, their feeble, diffident and irresolute attitude inevitably paved the way for the Second World War. The Western democracies had finally forfeited the fear and respect of the two dictators, who henceforth felt convinced of their omnipotence and invincibility. Hitler never expressed his dominant idea with greater clarity than he did before the start of the conference, during the trip from Kufstein to Munich in Mussolini's special train:

'The day will come when we shall have to take the field together against France and England. All will depend on whether this happens while the Duce and I are still at the head of our peoples and in full possession of our authority.'

It saddens me that my pen does not have the mordant power of a Saint Simon or Cardinal de Retz. How much material Munich would have given both men for what, as Ranke says, 'in the normal way passes only fleetingly from mouth to mouth'! Never have 'world figures' seemed more puny to me, and never have I cherished less respect for them than I did during those hours in the Prinz-Karl-Palais, the Führerbau and Hitler's private flat in Munich's Prinzregentenplatz.

Daladier alternated between apathy and tearful agitation. Not the least of his worries was that there should be an adequate supply of Pernod in the conference hall, and Herr Walterspiel delivered it with the same nonchalant efficiency he had shown when supplying Himmler's Tegernsee kitchen. Ciano felt sorry for his colleague from Paris and devised 'frivolous trifles' to amuse him and François-Poncet, the smooth, subtle schemer who was then French Ambassador to Berlin. Chamberlain, whose umbrella bearing arrival had evoked delighted grins from the élite troops who ringed the airport, certainly seemed to be in close communion with some invisible Anglican or Puritan deity, but he had none of the imperial aura of Benjamin Disraeli, who had so greatly impressed Bismarck at the Congress of Berlin. He played the martyr, and one can only speculate sadly as to what might have happened if the dictators had been confronted by a man like Churchill.

The dictators, too, were in very different moods. Adolf Hitler obviously lamented the frustration of his war aims from the outset, and his disappointment was shared by all the other Nazi leaders with the single exception of Hermann Göring, whose delight at the success of the conference struck me as genuine and sincere. Mussolini, who had engineered the conference almost single-handed, obviously felt that he was at the zenith of his fame and glory.

Years later, when his fame and glory had evaporated, he talked to me about Munich. It was my last private audience with him, only a few days before he was lynched at Dongo in April 1945. A miracle had happened, he told me, and the miracle's name was Munich. The still impressive eyes glowed with their old fire and the weary, shrunken figure with the balding head of a Roman emperor drew itself erect in memory of the day. I remembered it too. Mussolini had, in effect, been chief interpreter at the Conference. His laborious English, Italianate French and questionable German were the linguistic high-lights of a gathering at which none of the other three participants spoke a language other than his own. The Duce was, of course, able to enlist the services of the indefatigable Dr Schmidt of the Foreign Office, but this did not prevent him from scintillating, from mediating, from holding Europe's trembling scales in balance.

Mussolini himself was far from comprehending the real significance of his finest hour. The acclaim which he enjoyed throughout his trip—and which the usually cynical inhabitants of Munich showered on him even at two o'clock in the morning—was as incomprehensible to him and his fellow-dictator as was the frenetic jubilation which greeted him on his return to Italy. For a brief moment, the two men had become symbols of peace. Unbeknown to the cheering crowds, Hitler was deeply offended at all this pacifist hubbub, nor did his friend seek to repeat the theatrical performance which had met such initial success.

I took advantage of the lunch at Hitler's rather grisly private apartment in the Prinzregentenplatz to savour the bad taste of the devoted Party members, male and female, who had paid homage to their idol by presenting him with frightful specimens of home-handiwork and countless other souvenirs and tributes of every description.

Mussolini, who was not overburdened with an aesthetic sense, found the sight quite undaunting, and his wife Donna Rachele would doubtless have revelled in it.

Through the good offices of an aide whom I knew, I was able to take a quick glance at a room which was generally kept locked. Standing on a pedestal in this brightly furnished room was the bronze bust of a smiling girl. The girl, a niece of Hitler's named Geli Raubal, was the victim of a tragedy which the dictator had never forgotten. On 17 September 1931, in this same room, she had shot herself with a pistol taken from her uncle's desk.

Geli Raubal was the eighteen-year-old daughter of Hitler's stepsister Angela. In the home of her uncle, who worshipped her, she studied music and dreamed of forthcoming engagements at Bayreuth. She accepted Hitler's adoration but failed to cherish the feelings for him which, as a man not over-accustomed to womanly love, he expected of her. Her heart belonged to one of her uncle's constant companions, a man named Maurice who later proved to be sadly deficient in the racial requirements of Nazidom.

Out of this tangled web of human emotion came quarrels and jealous scenes. One day, after yet another clash, Hitler left for the North on one of his regular propaganda tours. He only got as far as Nuremberg, the scene of future Party rallies, where he was shocked to hear the news of Geli's suicide. The girl had slowly bled to death from a bullet-wound in the heart, and he never saw her alive again. He never got over her death, a fact which helps to explain his peculiarly diffident attitude towards the countless women who later competed for his favours. Gone was the

Hitler who had stood for hours beside a young girl's grave with a wreath of red roses in his hand. If it had not been for Geli's suicide, his subsequent life might have been more human, more relaxed and less inhibited. He brought women no happiness in later years. Between the suicide of Unity Mitford, the fanatical Englishwoman, and Eva Braun's tragic end in the Chancellery bunker lay a long road devoid of joy and fulfilment. Hitler later pronounced on the subject of love and marriage with an arrogant bitterness which was probably rooted in the tragedy of 17 September 1931:

I do not believe that a man like me will ever marry. He has—intellectually—constructed himself an idealised picture in which the figure is taken from one woman, the hair from another, the brain from a third and the eyes from a fourth, and he submits every woman he meets to this criterion. No such person exists, however. A man ought to be glad if a girl has something nice about her. Nothing is finer, after all, than to rear a young creature. A girl of eighteen or twenty is as malleable as wax. A man must be able to put his imprint on any girl—nor does a woman want anything else.

Sadly reflecting that the girl whose smiling effigy I had just glimpsed had not been malleable enough, I returned to the dining-room where the German and Italian leaders had assembled during a break in the conference.

After lunch, world history resumed its course. Thanks to the fact that Benito Mussolini was acting as interpreter-general, I did not find myself overworked. I spent most of the time standing around in corners with the Prince of Hessen or other members of the Italian party, watching with amusement as the Duce, striking a faintly bored dictatorial pose, paced up and down the room with his hands in his pockets. He was so carried away by his role that one would not have been surprised to see him don the imperial purple and plant a laurel-wreath on his bald pate. Daladier, fortified with Pernod, vented all his annoyance at the Munich fiasco on Beneš and the Czechs. The people of Munich having given him a wild ovation outside the Vier Jahreszeiten, where he was staying, he had now donned the pose of a Parisian barrister whose case is lost but whose rhetorical brilliance is bound to win the court's acclaim. The British premier still awaited divine intervention and took comfort in his sense of personal decency, little realising that in this company such a quality spelt mortal danger.

Just when things were getting interesting I was summoned from the room. A security guard outside the door told me excitedly that a veiled woman had appeared in the guard-room and demanded to speak to me on a matter of the utmost urgency. There was something intriguing and romantic about this feminine intrusion into the rude masculine world. Since my presence at the conference had not so far averted war or saved the peace, and since I knew nothing about the demands of the Sudeten Germans or Czechs, justified or unjustified, I hurried to the guard-room.

There, surrounded by a group of young men of heroic stature and Nordic appearance, stood an extremely elegant lady of unmistakably Latin appearance. A dense black veil obscured most of her face. The uniformed youngsters continued to ogle her until she greeted me with a 'Caro Dollmann—finalmente! I knew at once who it was. Only Donna Eleonora Attolico would have ventured so far along the corridors of power. A respectful circle formed round us. Then I had to laugh. She insisted that I ask Herr Hitler 'immediately and without delay' how the conference was going. Although I was much further from events than her husband, the Italian Ambassador, she seemed to find it entirely natural that I should step into the breach. The guards trembled with awe. I sent for a chair and asked her respectfully why the matter was so urgent. The mystery was soon solved: she had promised her favourite Madonna, the Madonna in the Pilgrims' Church at Loreto, that she would bring her a fat golden candle in person if the conference went well and the peace of the world were assured. Her train left in half and hour, hence the urgency of her request. I told her that it would be out of the question for me to accost Hitler, but that I would gladly ask Benito Mussolini or Galeazzo Ciano. This did not suit her at all. With a meaningful glance, she instructed me to ask Heinrich Himmler, who knew everything.

I went in search of Himmler and found him standing around looking important. Like his lord and master, he was not in a

rosy mood—a nice gory war would have suited him better—but
Donna Eleonora's name, coupled with an allusion of her proposed pilgrimage and the candle, put him in a more indulgent
frame of mind. His initial surprise gave way to amusement. He
authorised me to announce that peace was assured and further
instructed me to take one of the guards on duty—one who was
equipped with all the necessary permits—and convey the Lady
Attolico to her sleeping-car with his compliments.

I transmitted the joyful tidings. To the renewed astonishment
of the guards, who may have been Christians but may equally
have been devotees of Wotan, Donna Eleonora crossed herself.
There was a brief argument as to who should drive us—an
argument won, needless to say, by the man with the largest number
of official passes. We climbed into a beflagged Maybach and
raced through the crowded streets to Munich's main railway
station. My companion had relapsed into silence and was probably praying. I do not know who the crowds thought we were,
but they cheered us enthusiastically. The sleeping-car for Italy
and Loreto was on the point of leaving when we arrived. The
ecstatic driver received a handshake and I, to the amazement of
the bystanders, a light kiss, Roman-style, on both cheeks.

That was my chief contribution to the world-famous Munich
Conference of 1938. I found on my return that the Western
Powers had retired, worn out and dispirited, to their hotels to eat,
while the representatives of the Axis-to-be settled down to an
excessively long and substantial dinner. Mussolini cheerfully
ignored the chilly mood of his confederates. He ate and drank
with relish, his only kindred spirit at the table being Hermann
Göring. Ciano, who had taken me aside at the beginning of the
conference and begged me, as a native of Munich, to show him
the city's night-life, became increasingly taciturn as the meal
dragged on. I never managed to take him on a conducted tour,
as it happened, nor did he get a chance to satisfy his curiosity.

It was approaching 1 a.m. by the time everything was signed.
The crowds cheered again, far more loudly than they had done
during my ride with Donna Eleonora Attolico—in fact I had
never heard the inhabitants of Munich cheer louder, even during
the Oktoberfest or at carnival time. Benito Mussolini, who rel-

ished his triumph, bore the peace of the world home with him like a trophy. He was in a bountiful mood, but it did not last. His next bequest to the world was war, which destroyed not only Italy's prosperity but his own.

Two days later I was back at Munich's main station again, bound for Rome. Coupled to the regular Rome Express was a superb Pullman car of Italian origin which had, I was told, been used by Queen Margherita in the days of the Kaiser. The walls were hung with pink silk embroidered with marguerites. Beside the coach stood an oldish, bespectacled gentleman who held himself badly, and beside him, looking even more hunched and un-Latin, a somewhat younger man. The former was His Excellency the Italian Ambassador to Berlin, husband of the beautiful woman whom I had just helped on her way to the Madonna of Loreto, and the latter Signor Pittalis, Italian Consul-General in Munich, who was seeing him off. I knew both men and respected them highly. Unattracted by the prospect of travelling home alone, Don Bernardo Attolico promptly invited me to join him among the marguerites, and promised me an Apulian dinner. He was as ugly as his wife was beautiful, and ungrudgingly —wisely, too, in all probability—left the social side of their duties to her. They were an incongruous couple, but even the malicious gossips of Roman high society failed to discover any blemish on Donna Eleonora's reputation.

Don Bernardo had embarked on his diplomatic career in 1919. After representing his country in Brazil and, from 1930 onwards, in Moscow, he was sent to Berlin by Mussolini in 1935. The Attolicos were a great success in Soviet Russia, where the ambassador's commercial ability won him and the Italian automobile industry a great reputation. Donna Eleonora was the only foreign envoy's wife who succeeded in obtaining permission to attach a father confessor to the embassy staff. She was also the only one of her colleagues whom Stalin signally honoured by asking her to sit beside him in his box during a ballet performance.

In Berlin, Attolico became the cautious advocate of a rapprochement between his country and Germany, but he soon recognised the magnitude of the long-term dangers which would beset Italy as a result of the Third Reich's military superiority and her own exaggerated pretensions to power. From the time of the Munich Conference onwards he became a fanatical opponent of Hitler's military aims, believing that his only chance lay in a victorious Blitzkrieg, and that any struggle of longer duration would inevitably spell the joint downfall of Germany and her Italian ally.

Mussolini's non-intervention in September 1939 earned Attolico the bitter enmity of Ribbentrop, who from then on did all he could to engineer his recall. When Mussolini finally consented, Ciano's terse comment on Berlin's request was:

'Of course! He's an Italian and a gentleman.'

So I journeyed southwards with Attolico. We had the whole Pullman car to ourselves, complete with a staff which included a chef from Apulia. I do not recall the menu in detail, but I remember that there was an enormous bowl of *ricotta*, or sheep's cheese, and that every dish was accompanied by onion and garlic. It was an orgy of garlic-eating, and I fear that the lingering fragrance of Queen Margherita's perfumes must have been banished for good.

His Excellency was highly diverted by my account of his lovely wife's descent upon the Munich Conference. Whether or not it was the garlic that made him so unusually talkative, he spent hours after the meal discoursing upon matters of top-level policy. With profound pessimism, he implored me to do what I could to convert the temporary boom in peace prospects into a permanent state of affairs. Everyone, he declared, whatever his political convictions, ought to regard this as the need of the moment, though he personally was anything but confident of success. He looked upon Ribbentrop, whom he despised, as Hitler's evil genius, and pinned his hopes on Hermann Göring. Far from regarding Heinrich Himmler as the strong man of the Third Reich, he feared the worst from Heydrich and his cronies at the Central State Security Bureau. Finally, he stressed that he was only being so frank with me because of my friendly relations with Bocchini, for whom he had the highest regard.

It was far into the night when I took my leave. The whole carriage reeked of onion, garlic and sheep's cheese, and no soap or Eau de Cologne proved an adequate or effective counter-aroma. His Excellency told me smilingly that he seldom had a chance to indulge his taste for Apulian cuisine because Donna Eleonora strongly objected to it, but he had been lucky this time and I was not to give him away.

There was no need for betrayal. Towards morning, as the train pulled into Orte, about an hour's run from Rome, I saw an elegantly dressed woman pacing up and down the platform. It was Donna Eleonora, who had driven out to meet her husband so that she could brief him on the latest developments in Rome. I raced along to his compartment, to be met by a wave of Apulian effluvium. He blenched when he heard my news. Since I smelt less obnoxious than he did, having already washed and shaved, I complied with his fervent request that I should keep his wife company over a cup of coffee until he was fit to appear.

Donna Eleonora was redolent of Paris. Being the perfect lady, she said nothing—merely embraced Don Bernardo with an indulgent smile. I discreetly withdrew.

Attolico did not forget the small favour I had done him, and I remained a firm friend of the family until his untimely death in February 1942. Ever since 1938, the Munich Conference has been inextricably associated in my mind with Apulian cooking, sheep's cheese, onions and garlic.

VI

INTERLUDE WITH A COURTESAN

DURING the interval between the Munich Conference of 1938 and her entry into the war in June 1940, Italy was in the enviable position of a courtesan in universal demand.

Strong, vigorous, ruthless men wooed La Bella Italia as ardently as did less energetic but more refined and sensitive suitors, the former penniless and the latter well endowed with worldly goods. The Third Reich on the one hand and the Western democracies on the other seemed to be competing in an attempt to anticipate her every whim and fulfil her every requirement in the hope that she would decide to accept their passionate attentions.

It was a magnificent opportunity for a politician of real stature, but that was just what Benito Mussolini was not. For all the merits which even his detractors still acknowledge today—his restoration of peace and good order in the years after the March on Rome, many of his reforms, and his undeniably humane treatment of most of his opponents—he has never become an historical figure of the first magnitude. I had many opportunities of observing him at this period, and he never seemed less virile and more feminine than he did then. His martial bearing, rolling eyes and imperatorial mien did not disguise the fact that he was less like a *condottiere* from the golden age of his native Romagna than the reeling helmsman of a ship tossed by a storm of emotions, of sympathies and antipathies, personal inclinations and aversions. If he had only taken a few lessons from Franco, and adopted his much-ridiculed Spanish colleague's admirable tech-

nique of evasion and procrastination in the face of ardent court-
ship, he might still be at the Palazzo Venezia today.

His son-in-law, Galeazzo Ciano, was entirely in his element.
Whenever he could do so without risking unpleasant repercussions he snubbed and ridiculed the Germans—particularly his
opposite number, Ribbentrop. On the other hand, he allowed
them to court, flatter and pay homage to him so as to be able
to rush off and tell his international flower-show of femininity at
the golf-club what he had had to endure in the way of tactlessness and tastelessness at the hands of the Nordic barbarians. He
listened in silence to Mussolini's outbursts for and against the
Third Reich, and then, with terrifying frankness, committed his
views to the pages of his diary late at night.

Even Ciano had a brief moment of heroism when, at Obersalzberg in August 1939, he did his utmost to hinder the approach
of war, but this was only a flash in the pan: by the following
day all was forgotten. He skated gracefully along the razor's edge,
quickly repenting of his sounder judgements in the arms of some
Roman duchess or princess.

His wife Edda was indifferent to his behaviour. She had all
the makings of a political figure of the first order, but she was
too much of an individualist and far too involved in her strenuous
private life to want to play such a role. She, too, vacillated between partiality and dislike for the rude but occasionally congenial sons of the North, but her clear-cut, if disastrous, attitude
—at least where war was concerned—was far more masculine
than the Freudian complexes of her father in the Palazzo Venezia
and the hysterical emotional outbursts of her husband in the
Foreign Ministry. To quote Galeazzo Ciano's entry in his diary
10 May 1940, exactly one month before Italy's disastrous declaration of war:

Edda has been to the Palazzo Venezia too. With her usual vehemence, she told him that the country wants war and that continued
neutrality is tantamount to dishonour. This is just the kind of talk
he wants to hear—the only kind he takes really seriously.

The only surprising feature is that a woman of Edda Ciano-
Mussolini's high intelligence could have been so misled as to the

mood of her own compatriots. Apart from the radical wing of
Fascism, a few air force officers and the usual venal or corrupt
sections of public opinion, I myself came across no one who
wanted the war. Though disunited as only 50,000,000 indivi-
dualists can be, the Italian people were virtually unanimous in
their willingness to do anything rather than fight a war on
Germany's side.

The royal family was equally at one. Victor Emmanuel had
deposited his enormous private fortune with the Bank of England
and had hated the Germans ever since Kaiser Wilhelm's day.
Her Majesty still dreamed of the vanished Tsarist court in which
she had grown up, and was largely uninterested in politics. The
Crown Princess, like all German or half-German princesses who
have married abroad, cherished everything that was anti-German
and, more especially, anti-Nazi. Her husband would readily have
adopted a mediatorial attitude compatible with his urbane and
conciliatory nature, but he was used to regarding his father's
wishes as law, and he was naturally no friend of the Germans.

Pope Pius XI, with the memory of his Munich and Berlin
nunciatures still fresh in his mind, had done all he could after
1933 to find a modus vivendi with the Third Reich. His endeavours had, however, foundered upon the fanaticism of the Nazi
right-wing and the bitter hatred of Martin Bormann. Thanks to
Bocchini's influence, Himmler had shown a greater readiness to
make concessions, but he was, of course, far too loyal to the
Party line to engage in any effective co-operation. Even so, the
Vatican did everything within its power to stave off disaster.

The *beau monde* of Rome and Italy picked its way through
the currents and cross-currents set up by these vain attempts to
preserve the peace with the graceful indifference of a whore
ready to sell herself to the highest bidder. The good old days
were back again! Every embassy, from West to East, wooed the
Roman aristocracy with an endless succession of lavish parties.
Neither the Russian salons of the Rasputin era nor the French
salons of Marie Antoinette's day can have been more luxuriant
hotbeds of gossip, scandal and sensationalism than the palaces
of Princess Isabella Colonna, the Duchess of Sermoneta, and
other bearers of Italy's most ancient names, both in Rome and

elsewhere. Led by Count Ciano, the members of the aristocracy dabbled in top-level politics. Most of them were related to the noble families of England and many had gilded the crumbling façades of their palazzi by taking American ladies of the canning, automobile or commercial aristocracy to their bosom. Hence their natural sentiments, and hence their burning desire, while avoiding a direct alliance with the Western democracies, to rid themselves of the troublesome Huns of the Third Reich.

Being anything but martially inclined, however, the members of fashionable society were so filled with voluptuous terror by Germany's strength that they flattered the barbarians much as the Roman patricians had done in the time of the barbarian emperors. And so they danced from one party to the next, from Western ground to Nordic, confident that they could tip the scales in either direction, disliking Mussolini and his—by their standards—common little wife, praying for the perpetuation of the monarchy, and dreaming of Count Ciano as a future prime minister of Anglophile tendencies.

Naturally enough, I derived considerable entertainment from this chaotic situation. I was received everywhere. It is improbable that anyone trusted me entirely, but wholehearted trust was no more a characteristic of pre-war Italy than it is, I suspect, of the Italy of today. My duties as an interpreter encouraged the mystery-loving Italians to associate me with secrets of which I knew absolutely nothing. I was photographed hundreds of times beside the great ones of the earth, and who loves being photographed more than the Italians? I was seen at the side of Ambassadress von Mackensen, and everyone in Rome knew how much personal and public independence she had won from the Third Reich. I dined with the Catholic aristocracy at the German Embassy to the Vatican and was simultaneously employed as a translator by the Northern antichrist. What more mysterious and intriguing game, in the eyes of a true Italian, than mine appeared to be?

I naturally did all I could to protect my beautiful, much-wooed Italia from the threat of war. From Don Arturo Bocchini I extracted verbal and written references to the increasingly unwarlike and unsoldierly spirit which his agents reported from all over the peninsula, and relayed them to the ever-growing tide of visitors from the north. I described Italy's internal situation to the aides of the ministers, Gauleiters and other German dignitaries who visited Rome. They listened politely, but their minds were already on the girls they hoped to meet the same evening. I spoke to the ambassadors and their wives, but Herr von Mackensen's view was that Bocchini ought to take his defeatist remarks to Mussolini rather than to me. The good Prussian in him regarded what I was doing as unseemly interference in the internal affairs of another country. Don Diego von Bergen of the Vatican embassy implored me not to prejudice his daily struggle to maintain a truce with the Curia by making warlike noises. The two ladies, who were wholly unwarlike by nature but overburdened with social duties and obligations, readily transmitted to me all they heard about Italy's need for peace at their receptions, cocktail parties and dinners, but they were as much at a loss as I was to know whom to pass it on to.

My best spy and informant on the real spirit of the Italian people, which the Duce was bent on remoulding into an all-conquering warrior tribe, was Maria Celeste, otherwise known as Signorina Bibi. For a variety of reasons, her mother had by now exchanged her boarding-house in the Piazza Barberini for a smaller but far more romantic establishment in the Piazza di Spagna. Everyone who has been to Rome knows the flower-bedecked stone cascade of the Spanish Steps. He may even have bought a gardenia for his buttonhole from the floral treasures on display there—or possibly, as a prelude to a romantic adventure, acquired one of the salmon-coloured roses of Rome, genuine but dyed. Members of my own generation will know that the reddish *casina* on one corner of the steps was where Keats died of tuberculosis in 1821, at the age of twenty-six. Young people of today may remember that Axel Munthe, the legendary Münchhausen from Sweden, lived and loved in the same house.

Such was the typically Roman site of Signora Stefania Rossi's new abode. There were fewer deputies there, fewer widows and fewer gay evenings. The *pensione* was inhabited by the friends of a young man called Afredo, to whom, with all the fervour of a true daughter of Rome, little Bibi had lost her heart. Alfredo was not a prince or a marchese, though this would have been far more to her mother's taste. He was a young Roman from Trastevere, the most genuine but not the most genteel quarter of the Eternal City. He made a good living by buying and selling forest-land owned by palace-dwelling Roman aristocrats who were so blasé that they scarcely knew of its existence. He was far from being a Fascist, even though his twenty-five years and stalwart appearance would have earned him immediate admission to one of the Fascist praetorian guards.

Alfredo from Trastevere provided me with some deep insights into the ideas of another section of Italian youth—not the one I had seen under canvas, on parade or taking part in Fascist demonstrations. Its members were nearly all young people of humble background.

My accounts of the golf-club and other patrician distractions amused them, but they also prompted criticism, veiled at first, of Mussolini and the regime. They knew all about Mussolini the former Socialist, the blacksmith's son from Predappio, the friend of Communist Russian émigrés in Switzerland, but what had happened to him in the interval, and what had manifested itself so clearly during Hitler's 1938 visit, excited their hatred and derision. They described him as an ageing idol with absurd delusions of imperial grandeur, and assured me that they had no intention of taking his sabre-rattling seriously. During nocturnal wine sessions in dim Trastevere hostelries unknown to foreigners, whither I escorted young Bibi at her mother's request, they waxed sarcastic at the other Party bigwigs, skilfully mimicking their vanity, ostentation and arrogance. Almost all of them had passed through the Fascist educational mill, but they kicked against the pricks whenever they could. Their main ambition was to lead a quiet life, and nothing was more repugnant to them than Mussolini's celebrated dictum that it was better to live for a single day as a lion than vegetate for a hundred years as a sheep.

Squeezing me and my youthful companion into their rickety cars, they bore us off on timber-, sheep- and buffalo-trading expeditions. They frequented outlandish taverns where the evil but romantic days of the Campagna brigands seemed to live on. They were the Teddy-Boys of the Fascist era, except that they worked hard and did not affect drainpipe trousers. Instead, they generally wore high leather boots, and when their decrepit cars would go no further they vaulted on to the backs of reluctant mules, donkeys, or shaggy Campagna ponies.

They were on terms of rough intimacy with pretty innkeepers' wives and lonely countesses in dilapidated *castelli*, and they were not averse to settling amatory disputes in the traditional manner, with fists or knives. I ate and drank nobly in the company of these young Campagna traders. They scorned the epicurean refinement of my lunches and dinners at embassies and palaces, and my increasing skill at mixing cocktails merely evoked pitying grins. On the other hand, they knew where to find the tenderest lamb, the famous Roman *abbacchio* dressed with spicy herbs, the freshest buffalo cheese, the plumpest chickens and, last but not least, the most genuine wine. Everything they bought was fresh and acquired at source, and many were the times I returned to the Piazza di Spagna laden with culinary treasures whose preparation Signora Stefania undertook with an expert hand, winning an ever-widening clientele among the so-called 'top ten thousand', who had long been sated with the refinements of international cuisine.

Such were the representatives of 'the other' section of Italian youth in the years immediately preceding the war. As disaster drew near, they predicted its outcome with mathematical accuracy. They knew far more about Italy's lack of fighting spirit and concomitant lack of military preparedness than the men in the Palazzo Venezia. They knew which defence contracts had been bungled or not carried out at all, and they were extremely well informed about the mood of the General Staff and the contacts existing between service chiefs and anti-Fascist circles at home and abroad. They had friends and henchmen in subordinate positions everywhere, they guaranteed—on the basis of their wide agricultural experience—that food supplies would quickly break down, and they were unanimously resolved to avoid military service at all costs.

I was able to save them a good deal of trouble, thanks to my numerous friends in the Ministry of the Interior, who were glad to do me a favour by cancelling or deferring their call-up notices.

I could not, of course, save them from being called up when war broke out, but they never bore me a grudge on that account. Not only did my contacts upwards and downwards make me *persona grata* with them, but I was the oldest friend of Signorina Bibi, whom they idolised. They remained on good terms with me even after the tribulations of 1940, 1943 and 1945. I should have spent all my time with them instead of squandering it on polite society, most of whose members cold-shouldered me when I failed to channel *permessi*, foodstuffs or petrol coupons in their direction.

I might even have managed, by devious means, to shield my new friend and Bibi's great love, Alfredo, from the rigours of military service. Having secured a long spell of deferment through my good offices, he was summoned to his regimental depot at Verona to 'sign off'. On the way there he was killed in a car crash. It was my sad duty to escort Bibi and her mother to the venerable Church of Santa Maria in Trastevere, in front of which we had so often drunk genuine Frascati 'for the Romans of Rome' on warm summer nights.

All Alfredo's friends were there—buffalo-herdsmen, lumber-jacks and pretty innkeepers' wives from the Campagna included. Only the lonely countesses were missing. I never saw as many beautiful human beings at the Rome golf-club, at any glamorous gathering, at any embassy or reception held in honour of the great, as I did at Trastevere on that flawless summer morning. Two mourners made very dissimilar resolutions during the funeral. One was the frozen-faced Bibi, who decided, in that moment of farewell, that her life was going to diverge from the course it had taken while Alfredo was with her. The other was me. I resolved never to leave these true-born Romans in the lurch if danger threatened, and silently promised the dead man that his friends would always be mine, even if they were not ministers, ambassadors, princes or Party bigwigs. We both honoured our promises. The girl called Bibi now bears one of the proudest names in Rome, and I shall have some more to say about my own resolution in a subsequent chapter.

I could not, to my regret, spend every evening in the Roman Campagna, neither before Alfredo's death nor thereafter. Berlin-

Rome trips were still gaining in popularity among officials of every rank. Meetings, conferences and sightseeing tours multiplied to an alarming extent, and so, unfortunately, did the calls on my services as an interpreter—even though, as I have already faithfully reported, neither the honeymoon trip of May 1938 nor the Munich Conference in autumn of the same year gave me any particular opportunity to shine.

My growing indispensability to the success of the Italo-German love affair still puzzles me to this day. There must have been plenty of expert interpreters who were far better at supplying good, sound, faithful translations than I, who was generally regarded as anything but an exponent of literal translation. Perhaps my success was due to my ability—and this was Adolf Hitler's view—to 'photograph' well. This may sound a little odd, so I will endeavour to explain.

A 'photographic' interpreter not only renders words, sentences and speeches, but captures the whole tone of what has been said and embodies it in his translation. On this principle, a really first-rate interpreter has to participate or simulate participation in all that is enacted in his presence, from light-hearted interludes and formal exchanges of every shade to so-called historic decisions taken in deadly earnest. It is like a theatrical performance in which everything depends upon the producer.

I seem to have been well suited to this role, because I spent the two years between autumn 1938 and Italy's entry into the war in June 1940 shuttling back and forth between Rome and Berlin. It was tiring, despite lengthy breaks in Rome, where I was also in demand. It was exceedingly boring, too, because my duties seldom if ever varied. To cheer myself up I devised an outlet, and the name of that outlet was Venice.

What could have been more relaxing after State banquets and ghastly speeches which never gave one a chance to eat or drink, after soporific protestations of mutual esteem, after the greedy scramble for orders and decorations and the eternal talk of Fascist and National Socialist vigour and democratic senility, than to visit a city which had long been indifferent to such things? The ex-Queen of the Adriatic was past taking offence at anything provided she was left in peace, and it is to my friend Bocchini's eternal credit that his police left the city alone as far as it was humanly possible.

Surrounded by crumbling palaces alive with memories of former occupants and a society which was busily enacting its final role, a visitor could genuinely do as he pleased. I, for example, rediscovered an old passion for Lord Byron, who had fascinated me in my young days. I amused myself by retracing the tortuous path of his Venetian life and loves. It was a diverting pastime. Devoid as I was of his genius and the seductive magic of his personal appearance, I too found a Marianna with the grace of an antelope. Like him, I drove every morning to visit the Armenian monks on their dreamlike island and returned at nightfall to Marianna, my 'child of the sun'. I sought and found refuge in the enchantments of that old and immortal cocotte, Venezia. I also visited the city's uncrowned queen, knowing that to be received by her constituted an entrée to all the glories of Venice, past and present.

Although over seventy-four years old at the time, the Contessa Anna Morosini was still indisputably the most beautiful woman in Venice. With a figure as slender as a reed, luxuriant black hair and starry emerald-green eyes which had earned her the nickname 'La Salamandra', she drew every visitor into her orbit. She was not even a native of Venice. Her father had been a noted Genoese banker, and it was from him that she inherited her Genoese parsimony and business sense. She bore one of the proudest names in Venice, though her union with Count Morosini, whose family-tree included numerous Doges, had been a *mariage de convenance*. Donna Anna had consoled herself with the diversions of social life in her magnificent palazzo. Her salon was a picture-gallery of the celebrities of her day, an assortment of kings and politicians, diplomats and artists ranging from Alfonso XIII of Spain and Lord Asquith to Paderewski, Maurice Barrès and Paul Bourget, from King Fuad and the King of the Yemen to Queen Elena of Italy, whose lady-in-waiting she had been, and countless other members of high society.

Enthroned in majesty above them all was a photograph in full-dress uniform, complete with regal signature, of the greatest of them all: Kaiser Wilhelm II. I rather suspect that Anna Morosini was the Hohenzollern emperor's only extraterritorial *affaire de cœur*. Catching sight of her on the loggia of her palace during a Venetian encounter with the Italian royal couple in 1893, he forgot all about his homely consort Auguste Viktoria and paid her a visit. Venice talked of their friendship for years to come and Donna Anna for the rest of her days. They saw each other several times under circumstances known only to the *chronique scandaleuse* of Venice, not to me, but I doubt if rumour was correct. What man, even if he were Emperor of Germany and King of Prussia, would give his mistress a keepsake in the form of a leather-bound copy of the New Testament? This was not the only gift which failed to gladden the Contessa's Genoese heart. In 1911, when her daughter married, her royal and imperial friend sent two of his aides to Venice in full-dress uniform, bearing a jewel-case. Donna Anna expected it to contain a diamond tiara at the very least. Instead, all she found inside was a coral necklace, which prompted her to appraise the luckless envoys of her amazement and indignation at the fact that they had been obliged to transport a coral necklace to the home of coral.

Anna Morosini received me dressed like a *dogaressa* and wearing an enormous straw hat which concealed everything but her salamandrine eyes. I imagine she must have taken me for a Prussian, because she indicated the picture of her imperial friend with a gesture worthy of a reigning monarch and announced:

'*Ecco il suo imperatore!*'

He was not my emperor, but I forbore to enlighten her or tell her of my loyalty to the memory of a true emperor, namely, Franz-Joseph of Austria-Hungary. She would not have understood. Besides, she was too much of an Italian patriot not to hate the Habsburgs. She proceeded to tell me about Wilhelm II—or rather, she tried to. The telephone, which seemed to be her whole life, rang incessantly. She did no telephoning herself because she never spent money unless she had to, but this did not prevent her from keeping in touch from noon to midnight with everyone of rank and substance in Venice—not to mention those of the international set who had made the city the scene of their orgies and dissipations. Between calls she drew my attention to some untidy rows of books, all expensively bound in tooled leather or parchment and all inscribed with handwritten dedications. From the divine Gabriele d'Annunzio downwards, almost the whole of contemporary or near-contemporary Italian and French literature was represented by first editions—uncut. Donna Anna saw me smile and burst into laughter. It was Venetian laughter, like eighteenth-century music.

'Books, *mio caro*,' she said, 'what are books to someone who knew the authors as I did?'

She had a point. Before I took my leave she gave me a few addresses which she hoped would amuse me.

'*Tutti pazzi*—they're all crazy, but they're part of Venice. I never go there myself, of course, but at your age ... *perché no?*'

Why not indeed? I bent over the old hand, covered with moles and magnificent rings, gazed into the ageless emerald-green eyes, and knew that I should never forget Anna Morosini.

One of her introductions brought me an amusing and saddening evening—amusing because none of what I saw was intended to be funny, and saddening because it opened my eyes to a world of blasé and enervated decadence which seemed to vindicate what I so often saw and heard on my official trips.

The performance—and I use the word advisedly—took place in a palazzo beside the Grand Canal. Only the ground floor was intact, but it had that Venetian rarity, a superb garden. It was inhabited by an immensely wealthy American woman whose splendidly predatory teeth and boyishly Michelangelesque figure are all that I remember of her personal appearance. She was called Rita, but for her parties she used to adopt the name of the Amazon Queen, Penthesilea. Her money came from her parents' canning factory in Chicago, and she spent it with truly majestic prodigality. Spurred on by her predilection for young women with girlish breasts and gazelle-like thighs, she had founded a cult which she christened—loosely in the extreme—the Cult of Adonis. Festivals of the cult, which were under the artistic direction of Rita herself, called for the services of a youth whose sole duty was to don a gold lamé loin-cloth, recline on a flower-bedecked bier, and impersonate the moribund Adonis. The fee for this evening's work was a thousand lire, a considerable sum in those days. All the young gondoliers competed for the chance to earn a thousand lire, for which figure they gladly and gracefully simulated death and suffered themselves to be mourned by international virgins of the Adonis Cult without blinking an eyelid. It was far less strenuous and more profitable than guiding their gondolas through the turbid canals.

When the new Adonis was duly stretched out on his flower-adorned bier the priestesses came in wearing fantastic costumes designed by Rita and made by one of the leading Paris fashion houses. They processed round their idol, weeping, wailing, and scattering flowers on his inert body. At their head walked the high-priestess from Chicago, leading a leopard on a golden chain. It looked peevish and rather elderly, and its evident yearning to devour the succulent Amazons was sadly frustrated by a golden muzzle.

Convulsed with grief, the women gathered round their handsome young god and mourned him with passionate embraces. Their orgy of grief culminated in the singing of some words set to a genuine ancient Greek melody arranged by an American composer. The only passage I recall went something like this:

'Handsome Adonis dies!
Handsome Adonis is dead!
Wail ye and weep!'

Actually, I think that was all there was to it. The priestesses then performed some Bacchanalian dances to the strains of an unseen orchestra while handsome Adonis dozed off in spite of all the noise and the leopard scratched itself meditatively. Finally, the dead man was carried out and handed his thousand lire, after which he no doubt went home to his little Lucia, told her how easily and unerotically he had earned his money, and assured her how much he yearned for the arms of a real woman.

The rest of us, who had been watching the orgy ensconced in heavy gilt chairs, were now at liberty to stretch our legs. This gave me a chance to survey my fellow-guests. The Amazons had temporarily disappeared, and everyone seemed to know what they were up to. Now that the light from the Murano chandeliers allowed me to see the woman who had been sitting next to me more clearly, I at once recognised her from Donna Anna's des-

cription. She wore chalky-white make-up. Everything else about
her—hair, eyebrows and eye-shadow—was black. The diamonds
in her pallid ears and on her fingers must have been worth a
fortune. It was the Marchesa Luisa Casati, celebrated throughout
the *beau monde* as the subject of innumerable legends, one of
which concerned the huge Negro who never left her side and
whose function by day was to hold a golden umbrella over her
head. Like the leopard, the Negro understood nothing of the
Adonis Cult, but he may well have shared the lithe beast's longing
to sink its gleaming fangs into a few Amazons. That, however,
was not part of his job.

During the interval Donna Luisa told me something about our
hostess and her proclivities. It was unnecessary, since even a sexual ignoramus would have understood the implications of the
scene we had just witnessed. Then she pointed to an apparition
sitting by himself in a corner, lost in thought. He looked like the
picture of Dorian Gray after the knife has slashed it.

'Lord X, the famous historian. You must meet him. Anna
Morosini tells me you're interested in history.'

Before I could demur she dragged me across to the elderly
profligate, who came to with a start and waved me into the chair
beside him.

'Idiotic creatures!' he snapped, effacing the memory of the
foregoing scene with a weary gesture. He went on to invite me
to visit him in his palazzo—everyone at the party seemed to own
a palazzo—and described his unique library of 20,000 volumes,
all of them devoted to a single subject. I politely asked my fellow-
historian what it was, but he responded with a counter-question:

'Did you know Phili?'

I did not, which seemed to disappoint him. Phili, who had apparently been a bosom friend of his, turned out to be Philipp,
Prince Eulenburg, ex-Knight of the Black Eagle, ex-Ambassador
to Vienna and an ex-favourite of Wilhelm II, the monarch whose
picture I had recently seen on Donna Anna's writing-desk. I
failed to follow his drift until he explained that he had been
working for decades on an encyclopaedia of homosexuality, aided
by a staff of youthful historians. With a sigh, he told me that he
had only got as far as the letter E, but accounted for his slow

progress by explaining in a low voice that at least two-thirds of all the stars in the political, military and artistic firmament had succumbed to the common passion of Michelangelo, Leonardo da Vinci, Winckelmann, Frederick the Great, etc., etc.

I suspect that he wanted to enroll me as one of his staff, but I declined the invitation. I may have missed something—20,000 books would have been a sight worth seeing. Historical literature doubtless suffered as a result of his death a few years later, and I do not know what became of the A to E material. It was probably purchased from his heirs by such of his 'entries' who were still in the land of the living. His historians inherited the books, but I never heard what they did with them.

Our conversation was interrupted by the return of the Adonis disciples, who were now wearing Parisian or Roman evening gowns and matching garlands of flowers in their hair, a fact which excited his Lordship's renewed scorn. There followed a huge and elaborate Venetian dinner during which Donna Luisa Casati, slightly under the influence of champagne, related one or two episodes from her private life which would have enchanted Boccaccio and Casanova.

Everyone paired off as they pleased. I preferred to go home alone, and the sight of Venice shimmering in the silver moonlight was the best company I could have had. I decided that, rather than take up any more of Donna Anna's dubious introductions, I would go back to my other lord, Byron, to my little Marianna, and to Titian, Tintoretto and Veronese, none of whom was scheduled to appear in His Lordship's encyclopaedia.

Back in the Roman witch's cauldron once more, I recalled the ladies of Venice—Anna, Marianna, Luisa, Rita—with nostalgic regret, and my nostalgia was never more pronounced than during my most arduous tour of duty as an interpreter, this time for a German female with an ultra-German name.

Gertrud Scholtz-Klinck, the *Reichsfrauenführerin,* or Reich Women's Leader, had decided to pay her Italian sisters a long overdue visit between 27 February and 3 March 1939. I cannot recall where this bright idea originated, but I believe that its author was the Segretario del Partito, Achille Starace, an uncommonly stupid man but second only to Count Ciano in his good looks.

He was extremely susceptible to feminine charms, and Frau Gertrud's Wagnerian appearance appealed to him.

Starace's counterpart in the Italian Fascist women's organisation greeted the prospect with far less enthusiasm. The Marchesa Olga Medici del Vascello was a leading member of the aristocracy and the wife of a Secretary of State. It was my impression that she only took part in the Party's womanly high jinks (which Italian males leered at with their habitual sense of the erotic) because her activities brought her, at least occasionally, into contact with her idol. This idol was not Starace, whom she regarded as a buffoon, but Benito Mussolini, whom she admired with passionate fervour.

I told myself, even before Frau Gertrud's arrival, that the Marchesa would be my salvation, and I was not disappointed. She was a witty and sharp-tongued *belle laide* who resembled an Italian version of Princess Pauline Metternich, once the queen of the Viennese drawing-rooms. She was also a woman of sternly monarchistic views—yet another of the anomalies which the Duce permitted under his regime. To my secret delight, she included an audience with the Italian Crown Princess in Frau Gertrud's extensive programme. The Reich Women's Leader was obliged to make an entry in the protocol book at the royal palace, and in Milan the Marchesa treated her to the unaccustomed sight of a woman in Party uniform curtseying before a princess of the house of Savoy.

Most excited of all was the handsome Achilles of the Party. With uniquely Italian skill, he decorated an entire railway station in honour of her visit, swamping Frau Gertrud, whose world of German femininity was unaccustomed to such courtesies, in a sea of dark-red roses. His Excellency was quite bowled over by her palely gleaming crown of thick golden braids, her slim athletic figure and the tailored costume which fitted it so unexpectedly well. His confusion was apparent at the banquet which he gave for her at the Hotel Quirinal. To the amazement of his compatriots and the consternation of Ambassador von Mackensen he invited Frau Gertrud to occupy a tent of honour at the next mass rally of Fascist youth, and offered to stand guard over it in person.

I was in fairly good odour with Starace, possibly because, unlike anyone else in Italy except the more block-headed members of the Party, I pretended to take him seriously. I accordingly took the liberty of adding, to the uproarious amusement of the guests, that the Reich Women's Leader ought to have a German as well as an Italian protector during her sojourn in the tent, and nominated His Excellency Hans Georg von Mackensen for the job.

The Prussians are always reputed to have no sense of humour, but this is as fallacious as all generalisations are. The ambassador shook with laughter and Starace joined in. Frau Gertrud, whose womanly vanity was tickled, even though she was totally unused to hearing such remarks at a Party gathering, seemed amused. All in all, the banquet was a great success. It was one more item to add to my photographic interpreter's repertoire, and I believe that these flashes of stage-managerial inspiration were the secret of my apparent indispensability.

Next day came the visit to the Crown Princess, who received the visitor in her capacity as Honorary President of the Italian Red Cross, with which Frau Scholtz-Klinck had no connection. Like all women of Wittelsbach blood and Bavarian ducal lineage, Maria José was shy and unsociable. What was more, all her inbred instincts must have prejudiced her against the Scholtz-Klinck type. I shared the Marchesa's conviction that the audience would be a complete—if interesting—fiasco, but we were both wrong. Maria José resembled her charming and melancholic great-aunt, Empress Elisabeth of Austria-Hungary, in that she always did the opposite of what one expected of her. Having warned Frau Gertrud to be prepared for a cool, arrogant, eccentric *grande dame*, I was disconcerted when the Crown Princess revealed diametrically opposed characteristics. She seemed to be as little irritated by the blonde crown of plaits as by the black tailored costume and white collar which the visitor had, to our horror, considered appropriate to the occasion.

Having taken footmen, a suite of reception rooms and an aristocratic lady-in-waiting in her stride, Frau Scholtz-Klinck was soon chatting knowledgeably to the Crown Princess about mothercraft, baby care and other fields of feminine activity which taxed my vocabulary to the limit.

The audience, which was only supposed to last for thirty minutes, dragged on for nearly two hours. Back at her hotel, Frau Gertrud declared that the Fuehrer was absolutely right, as usual, in pronouncing Maria José to be the only man in the royal house of Savoy.

The remainder of her stay was devoted to visiting women's physical training establishments, among them the celebrated Girls' Academy at Orvieto, whither the Adonis-worshippers of Venice had travelled at their own expense and where I also managed to lose Frau Scholtz-Klinck—a dereliction of duty for which I was graciously pardoned in view of my efficiency as a guide hitherto.

Frau Scholtz-Klinck was genuinely hard to handle. Whenever people treated her as a woman she became 'the *Führerin*', and whenever they adapted their behaviour to her official status she began to feel feminine. It was like a vaguely erotic game of hide and seek, and although she did her utmost to make a pleasant and agreeable impression I was happy when she recrossed the frontier. At Verona she received another bouquet of dark-red roses from His Excellency Achille Starace together with a note which read: '*A rivederci nel Campo Dux*'—the Campo Dux being the site of the largest Fascist youth camp. However, the Reichsfrauenführerin's summer sojourn under canvas and the aegis of her two guards of honour, Starace and Mackensen, was frustrated by the advent of war.

The Marchesa found Frau Gertrud '*molto intelligente, ma molto fredda*'. Starace, by contrast, told me that she was '*una vera donna, e ché donna*'—a real woman, and what a woman! In view of opinions as divergent as these, it may well be imagined what a difficult task it was for me to steer the Reichsfrauenführerin between Scylla and Charybdis without coming to grief.

The Roman spring that followed would have been glorious if it had not been for the May-time love-duet between the Foreign Ministers of Italy and the Third Reich. I had planned an extensive series of trips to the Campagna with Bibi and Alfredo, but nothing came of them.

Ribbentrop and Ciano were the deities who ruled this spring, and I am still doubtful as to which of them I found less congenial.

Neither of them ever did me any harm, but each was the exact opposite of my historian's preconception of the Foreign Minister of a great nation. They were as alike as the representatives of two such dissimilar countries could possibly be. The numerous snapshots I took of them lie before me as I write. They were passionately fond of being photographed, and my pictures show them inspecting serried ranks of troops with Caesarian mien, waving to cheering crowds with polite condescension, shaking hands with exaggerated cordiality, and exchanging radiant smiles to disguise the fact that they could not endure each other. No surviving photograph of Bismarck shows him in a remotely comparable pose, but then, of course, Ciano and Ribbentrop would have considered him a far less distinguished exponent of foreign policy than they were.

Both men were immeasurably vain, presumptuous and arrogant. On reflection, I think I liked Ciano better. He was the more human of the two, for all his faults, and the aura of sex appeal and scandal that emanated from him was far preferable to the masklike demeanour and gelid affability of Herr von Ribbentrop, whose private life was doubtless far less open to reproach.

The German was better brought up than his noble colleague. Ribbentrop's manners were flawless, whereas Ciano used to outrage Hitler by his eating-habits and, worse still, by the way he blithely scratched himself in places where Ribbentrop would have endured an infestation of fleas without moving a muscle.

I never understood why the German Foreign Minister always stood on his dignity instead of letting go and enjoying himself occasionally. An Italian woman of wide and varied experience once told me that her mind baulked at imagining Ribbentrop in dressing-gown and pyjamas, whereas she found it only too easy to picture Ciano in the same garb. These are hardly suitable criteria for the student of foreign policy, however, and the spring, summer and autumn of 1939 did not lend themselves to such frivolous speculation. The month of May witnessed the birth of the Rome-Berlin Axis, a painless and surprisingly easy process. Oddly enough, no labour-pains manifested themselves until August, well after the event, when the warlike intentions of Hitler and his Foreign Minister became apparent. They reached their climax in September, thanks to Ciano's so-called 'minor betrayal' of Germany at the outbreak of the Second World War.

As Ciano's interpreter and travelling-companion I witnessed all these phases, most of them at first hand. It was the first time I ever felt a modicum of respect for the political acumen of Benito Mussolini's son-in-law. It was also the last, and I should like to talk about it here.

The most calamitous alliance of modern times, the Axis, came into being in Milan on 6 and 7 May 1939. There is no doubt that Mussolini took the crucial decision when he heard of the surprisingly warm reception given to Ribbentrop by the inhabitants of Milan, unemotional by nature and Teutophobes since the time of the medieval emperors. In actual fact, the two foreign ministers had only met to conduct a *tour d'horizon* of the general situation and discuss joint problems, but Arturo Bocchini's agents had done their work too well. They conjured up a cheering mob whose enthusiasm was taken seriously by all concerned. When Ciano telephoned his father-in-law on the evening of the first day and told him how ecstatic everyone had been, the Duce flew into an ecstasy too and instructed him to conclude the alliance or, rather, take the first steps in that direction.

Mussolini signed his own death warrant in the process, and Ciano paraded none of his usual objections to the Germans in general and his colleague from Berlin in particular. On the contrary, for the first time in his life he was charmed by Ribbentrop and even with his entourage, little realising that the object of his short-lived affections was a mortal enemy.

It was spring-time in Milan, but Milan is not a city whose mood is determined by the seasons, as are Rome and Venice. Back in Rome once more, Ciano was 'joyfully' welcomed by Achille Starace, who had likewise been carried away by the exultant cheers of massed Party supporters. Bocchini regretted what he had done, but too late.

Now that Mussolini was prepared to sanction the alliance, the die was cast. The official signing of the so-called Pact of Steel took place in Berlin shortly afterwards, accompanied by all the cold and sombre splendour characteristic of National Socialist ceremonies in the days of the Third Reich.

Between 21 and 23 May I escorted the Italian Foreign Minister to the capital of the Third Reich. The weather was cool, but the crowd which greeted Ciano at eleven o'clock that Sunday morning rose to the occasion with a warmth which he clearly appreciated. He strutted along the ranks of the inevitable guard of honour like an exotic Southern peacock, while his German colleague tried, much as it must have hurt him, to register delight and gratification. In the afternoon Adolf Hitler received his friend's envoy at the Chancellery. Everyone beamed, I remember, but conversation did not range beyond the usual protestations of mutual esteem. The only point of interest was that, under the terms of the new pact, Hitler guaranteed his Italian allies hegemony in the Mediterranean.

Count Ciano described his own impressions of the meeting as follows:

'I found Adolf Hitler in good health. Very serious, less aggressive. Slightly older. The creases round his eyes have grown deeper. He sleeps less and less.'

The same evening the dictator gave a large banquet at the Old Chancellery. He instructed me to stand beside the Attolicos while he was welcoming his Italian guests, so I had a good opportunity to observe him at close quarters. I remember that I found his gestures and whole manner, notably his lavish bestowal of hand-kisses on the ladies, very reminiscent of a *chef de reception* at the Hotel Sacher in Vienna. His eyes ran repeatedly over the elegant woman beside him, whose perfect charm and courtesy contrasted so strongly with the fruitless attempts of the German women guests to emulate her.

This contrast became even more striking at the long dinner-table. The enchanting Donna Eleonora sat on the host's right and Frau von Ribbentrop on his left. He spent all his time facing in the former direction, where smiles and conversation flowed freely, rather than in the latter, where the stiff and frozen atmosphere of a State funeral reigned. Opposite him sat the guest of honour, who would much have preferred to be seated between two of the few young women present. To his chagrin, he found himself flanked by Frau Göring and Frau Goebbels, neither of whom spoke any Italian and both of whom found it hard to cope with their table-companion's pronounced sexuality.

As at all social functions given by Hitler, the food was far removed from the Lucullan luxury which Roman society was used to on such occasions. The menu consisted of hors d'œuvres, bouillon, sole, saddle of venison, a sweet, and cheesecake—fare which would make any modern Ruhr industrialist blush with shame.

Scanning the guest list, I feel that it might be a good idea—and certainly a sensational one—to write an account of the transient glory and subsequent downfall of those present under some such title as 'The Fateful Banquet'. It would have the macabre flavour of those Shakespeare tragedies in which most of the dramatis personae are doomed to die. Hitler, Goebbels, Bormann, Schirach, Ribbentrop, Canaris, Speer, Todt, Himmler, Weizsäcker, Göring, Mackensen, Ley . . . All were still proud of their new-found ally that evening, still confident that they were the masters of Europe. Who would have thought, as the glasses clinked in honour of the King Emperor in distant Rome, that one of the principal actors would commit suicide in the bunker of the Chancellery six years later, or that the other, ignominiously tied to a chair, would be shot in the back on the orders of his own father-in-law? No shadow of doom clouded the brows of Mesdames Ley, Goebbels, Bouhler and von Braun-Stumm, née Countess Antinori: they all smiled and chatted, unaware that only a few years hence they would go to a death of their own choosing.

The official programme of the visit, which lies before me as I write, scheduled the following items for next morning:

10.55 a.m. Arrival of H.E. the Royal Italian Minister of the Exterior at the New Reich Chancellery. Ambassador Kiewitz will await the Royal Italian Minister of the Exterior and H.E. the Royal Italian Ambassador to Berlin at the entrance of the New Reich Chancellery and conduct them to the Marble Gallery, where they will be greeted by Minister of State Dr Meissner, Chief of the Presidial Chancellery of the Führer and Reich Chancellor, and SA-Obergruppenführer Brückner.

10.58 a.m. The Reich Foreign Minister will await H.E. the Royal

Italian Minister of the Exterior and H.E. the Royal Italian Ambassador to Berlin in the Great Reception Hall of the New Reich Chancellery.

11.00 a.m. Formal signing of the German-Italian Pact of Friendship and Alliance by H.E. the Royal Italian Minister of the Exterior and the Reich Foreign Minister. In conjunction with the signing, H.E. the Royal Italian Minister of the Exterior and the Reich Foreign Minister will announce the formal conclusion of the Pact of Friendship and Alliance between Germany and Italy.

11.30 a.m. The Führer will receive H.E. the Royal Italian Minister of the Exterior and H.E. the Royal Italian Ambassador to Berlin in his study, with the Reich Foreign Minister in attendance.

They clasped hands with deep solemnity and the inevitable look of mutual devotion. I remember avoiding Galeazzo Ciano's eye while translating the words of the Führer, who was visibly moved. I was too conscious of his true feelings towards his new allies to have kept a straight face.

The men who had forged the Pact of Steel then strode in solemn procession through the echoing halls of the Chancellery and out on to the terrace, where they received the acclamations of an enthusiastic crowd. Count Ciano behaved as though he had just conquered Berlin. The only person to look depressed was Hermann Göring, who, unlike the Reich Foreign Minister he despised so deeply, had not been designated 'Cousin of the King Emperor of Italy'—an honour which went with the award of the highest Italian order, the Collar of the Annunziata.

That afternoon Göring received the exalted visitor who had brought nothing for him and proclaimed in emotional tones that he was the sole author and originator of the alliance. He was genuinely affected by his own words, and took advantage of a lull in conversation to draw me aside and go over the whole story again. Since I lived in Rome and knew pretty well everything there was to know about Italian orders, my contacts might —he hinted—be useful.

I could only smile at this. He had quite enough orders and decorations strung across his ample chest already, but somehow, looking at him in all his finery, I felt sorry for him. I advised him to take his troubles to Ambassador von Mackensen, who was the right man for such a job. He did so, and Count Ciano assured him before leaving that next time he would be a 'Cousin of the King Emperor' too.

The same evening the Ribbentrops gave a big marquee party at their residence in Lentzeallee, Dahlem. There was Marquee A for the cream of society and Marquee B for lesser mortals. Braziers had been installed in the garden because the weather was cold and damp, just like the party atmosphere. Ciano's spirits slowly sank. He took exception to his place on the seating plan and hissed angrily to me that he saw enough film stars and prima donnas in Rome without having them thrust upon him in Berlin as well. His ambition was to sample the night-life of Berlin at the earliest possible moment, in particular the notorious 'Salon Kitty', that temple of sexual gratification which also, unbeknown to him, served Heydrich as a political listening-post. The numerous girls who had been graciously invited for his benefit were beneath his dignity. Besides, he was cold, and no Italian likes that. No one managed to thaw him out—not even Olga Tschechowa, nor Princess Carmen, nor Edda Wrede, nor Frau Clemm von Hohenberg, nor Princess Christoph von Hessen, nor Brigitte Horney, nor Frau Jannings, nor the delectable Fräulein von Laffert, nor Leni Riefenstahl, then at the zenith of her film career, nor the Mesdemoiselles Margot and Hedi, Nora and Erika, Liselotte and Hildegard, Rosemarie and Esther, Eva and Susi, Christa and Ellinor—or whatever their names were.

Even less capable of raising Ciano's spirits were the distinguished male guests present. Neither the Hohenzollern charm of August Wilhelm, Kaiser's son and SA-Obergruppenführer, nor the sardonic intelligence of theatrical director Gustav Gründgens, nor the devilish fascination of Reinhard Heydrich, nor the martial dignity of General Kesselring, nor the foxy cunning of Admiral Canaris, nor the theatrical talents of Werner Krauss, nor the English traditionalism of the Duke of Saxe-Coburg-Gotha, a grandson of Queen Victoria, succeeded in summoning a smile to the sensual lips of the shivering co-signatory of the Pact of Steel. He disliked his hostess, who had expended so much wasted effort, and he found Frau von Mackensen equally uncongenial. His

Salon Kitty glances in my direction became more and more frequent.

I was as incapable of getting him there as I was of securing Hermann Göring the Collar of the Annunziata. By the time he managed to get away it was too late for a sortie into the night-life of the capital because his private train was due to take him back to Rome early next morning—back to Rome and its not over-enthusiastic inhabitants.

His own account reads as follows:

Returned to Rome. Warmly welcomed at the station by Party chiefs and a large crowd. However, I get the impression that the Pact is more popular in Germany than Italy. People here are convinced of its expediency, but limit themselves to decorous acquiescence. The Germans, on the other hand, welcome it with feelings which are absent here. I reported the details of my trip and my impressions to the Duce. He was very pleased and (uncharacteristically) expressed his satisfaction several times.

His Excellency then hurried off at top speed to his harem at the golf-club, where there was no need to shiver in the company of film stars and stage idols, and where he was assured of a warm welcome by his princesses and countesses. His description of the 'assorted goods' in the Ribbentrops' marquees at Dahlem was a *tour de force*. What the charming cynic unfortunately forgot was that history would inevitably hold him responsible for the signing of the Pact of Steel, even if he had acted against his better judgement and out of slavish subservience to his father-in-law.

This marked the beginning of Ciano's campaign, at first overt but later clandestine and concealed, against his opposite number and fellow-ally in Berlin. In August he took advantage of an opportunity to show that he, too, had moments of wisdom and gravity. Then, in September, he revenged himself on Herr von Ribbentrop and his unenjoyable parties with a subtle piece of treachery which earned him the German Foreign Minister's undying hostility and may well have recurred to him just before the bullets ripped into his back at Verona in 1944.

Prior to the Count's fateful meeting with Hitler and Ribben-

trop at Schloss Fuschl and the Berghof in August 1939 came my
first encounter with the art of the new Germany. The Italian
Propaganda Minister, Dino Alfieri, had accepted an invitation
to the 'Tag der Deutschen Kunst', or Day of German Art, on 18
July 1939. Signor Alfieri was a slightly ageing professional char-
mer, and his very membership of the Fascist ruling class was
yet another token of the far more human atmosphere which
prevailed under the Italian regime. He was a very good-looking
man who cherished an implicit belief in his devastating effect
on women, a fact which became all the more widely known
because it was scornfully alleged by his fellow-ministers that he
had never got beyond the amatory preliminaries. Indeed, entire
cabinet meetings were devoted to the discussion of stories in this
vein. Whenever visiting Germans came to Rome, Alfieri's
Ministry ensured that State banquets were followed by some
light relief, and these post-prandial hours spent in the company
of elegant and entertaining women were infinitely gayer than
Ribbentrop's brand of social cocktail, with its mixture of film
stars and society women.

With me beside him, Alfieri stood on the rain-lashed rostrum
in the Odeonsplatz, clutching an official programme which bore
the words:

Munich, capital of German art, celebrates the Day of German
Art with festive splendour and heartfelt joy, in company with its
guests from the Reich and abroad. While the warlike clamour of
turbulent masses and hysterical politicians in the outside world
expresses itself in the strangest ways, Greater Germany celebrates
its artists' festival. In the serene language of German art and the
rejoicing of the entire nation, the German desire for peace has
once again manifested itself to all people of good will.

Under this slogan, which was invalidated only a few weeks
later by the very man who now watched 'his' art go parading by,
group after group representing scenes and figures from German
cultural history filed past the Führer's dais and the two Propaganda Ministers, Goebbels and Alfieri. The Daughters of the
Rhine wore raincoats, much to Alfieri's regret, and the only item
which moved him to admiring applause was a scantily clad fairy

borne along by some stalwart fauns from Giesing. He showed little interest in a huge cannon dating from the time of Frederick the Great, and only recovered his dampened spirits during a performance of the *Merry Widow* at the Gärtnerplatztheater, where Hitler made some extremely adverse comments on Gustl Waldau, the darling of Munich, and demanded his dismissal.

At noon there was an informal Propaganda Ministers' lunch at Hitler's private apartment in the Prinzregentenplatz. Goebbels, who liked to be able to do everything but could not speak Italian, was forced to rely on my services. He spouted words like a fountain, trying to convince his guest of the military advantages of a lightning Italian attack on Greece, but the handsome Dino was so distracted by pretty Frau Bouhler's lavishly displayed charms that he lost the thread of the conversation. After this diverting meal we adjourned to a neighbouring room and played with bricks, crawling around the floor like children. We built a new Berlin, a new Munich, a new Germany. Although Alfieri manfully swallowed the fact that the new victory column in Berlin promised to overtop the dome of St Peter's, he grew more and more weary. No espresso had been served, and he was visibly relieved when the time came to leave. So was I.

Arriving at the Hotel Vier Jahreszeiten, he sighed and told me that he had to write a report for Mussolini on the Day of German Art. Why didn't I write it for him? He was too tired, he had forgotten everything, the day had been too exhausting— in fact, the Germans were exhausting in general. He ordered a large number of *café cognacs* and I wrote his report. I hope the Duce enjoyed reading it. When it was finished he embraced me warmly and swore eternal friendship. He kept his promise when he came to Berlin in 1940 in place of Attolico, who had been ousted by Ribbentrop, and we remained on good terms even after Mussolini's downfall. He wrote me a touching letter at that time which gives a better picture of his character than any historical study could possibly do:

Rome, Foreign Ministry, 2 August 1943.
Dear Friend,
     If you should have an opportunity of seeing any of my German

friends in the next few days, please give them my very warmest regards and explain my position to them. I hope to see you again soon. With a firm handshake,

Dino Alfieri

For all his sending of warm regards to his German friends, Alfieri's position was ambiguous in the extreme. He had helped to topple the Duce at the Fascist Grand Council meeting on the night of 24–25 July, and his remarks about his German comrades had been anything but friendly. The Duce had been overthrown and imprisoned, but Alfieri was still nominally Ambassador to Berlin. He had never been a man of decision. What ought he to do—stay put or resign? He had no idea, and I was quite unable to help him. In the end he went down with the sinking ship of Badoglio's new regime. I shall always remember him as one of the most likeable representatives of Fascism, and so will many members of the fair sex who enjoyed his charming and innocuous protection in Rome and Berlin.

The German 'desire for peace' of July 1939 was merely a phrase in an official programme. I was happy to be able to abandon German art for Italian and return to the Piazza di Spagna. No one knows Rome who has not spent high summer there. Only then does Rome really belong to those who love her, and only during the torrid summer nights does the Roman miracle fully reveal itself. There are no foreigners, no parties, no receptions, no social calls. It is too hot for that. Only the true Romans remain, as Alfredo and Bibi and Alfredo's friends did. We had discovered a summer paradise known to the ancient Etruscans and associated with the Farnese family. The name of our little frequented retreat was Isola Farnese, which consists of a family castello perched on the acropolis of Etruscan Veii. Close at hand are the excavations of the Etruscan metropolis where the celebrated Apollo was discovered, a statue whose international fame now far exceeds that of its rival from Belvedere.

The area was still as romantic as it had been in the days of Gregorovius, and at the season of the nightingale, murmuring brook and flower-filled meadow, it recalled an ode by Horace. Needless to say, this Teutonic interpretation of the Roman summer was lost on Alfredo and his friends. They celebrated the ancient seasonal festivals in the local *osteria*, where the brigands of the Campagna had once met in an atmosphere redolent of blood, rapine, love, garlic, onions and wine. Everything was still more or less as it had been in those happy and accursed days. The tavern was ruled by a young, raven-haired, curvaceous padrona who looked like Feuerbach's Nana. My friends were not familiar with Feuerbach either, but they revelled in the dark threats that flew back and forth across the inn's smoky kitchen. Annina's husband was a corpulent old Silenus who always wore his trousers half-undone—for convenience's sake, he used to quip —and who was never seen without a full-bellied clay pitcher of dry wine. He was madly jealous of his beautiful spouse, and there were frightful scenes when, despite the seductive call of the nightingale and the summer serenade of the cicadas, he tried to lock her up in their stuffy bedroom. Alfredo and his cronies joined in these scenes delightedly, steering a course which avoided real disaster by a hair's breadth. In the end, Silenus would subside into a drunken stupor in one corner, and Annina would climb out of the window, bound for freedom and the arms of a stalwart goatherd.

It may well be imagined what my feelings were when the co-signatory of the Pact of Steel, Galeazzo Ciano, asked me to attend him at Obersalzberg on 12 August 1939. He would undoubtedly have been as glad to dispense with my presence as I with his. Alfredo, Silenus, Bibi and Annina were far closer to my heart than the bad food and uneasy atmosphere of Obersalzberg even if Eva Braun did occasionally alleviate the gloom by taking coffee with Hitler's aides and reminiscing about her trip to Italy the year before.

I was absolved from putting in an appearance at Schloss Fuschl, whither Ciano repaired on 11 August for a far from cordial meeting with his colleague Ribbentrop. The prevailing mood must have been dismal indeed, to judge from the Count's description:

The weather is chilly, and this coolness was echoed in our meeting. We did not exchange a word during the meal. Each of us mistrusts the other—the only difference being that I at least have a clear conscience and he does not.

Ribbentrop—and no subsequent attempt to clear him of this charge can succeed—was in a highly bellicose mood. As Dr Schmidt, who bore the main brunt of the Fuschl and Obersalzberg meetings, rightly says:

Ribbentrop was already in a state of feverish excitement, like a hound waiting impatiently for its master to unleash it at the prey. He indulged in convulsive and exaggerated attacks on England, France and Poland, made grotesque statements about German strength, and was quite intractable.

In the Italian view, the Pact of Steel had presupposed that several years of peace lay ahead of the Axis. Mussolini was well aware of Italy's calamitous position in regard to military preparations and raw materials, and he knew what an unmitigated disaster war would be. Hence the German Foreign Minister's 'bad conscience' and Ciano's even worse mood at the two meetings.

Hitler's conscience seemed no easier and his mood no brighter when he eventually emerged from his bedroom at about noon and came downstairs, looking wan, tired and fidgety, to greet Ciano and his entourage. An aide whispered to me that he had not got off to sleep until morning, and I could well believe it. On the other hand, he was far more civil than his Foreign Minister, who was patently irritated by the visitor from the South.

Lunch was served at speed and eaten without appetite. Hitler picked listlessly at his ill-prepared vegetables and ill-dressed salads, prompting Ciano to remark, with his usual tact, that in Italy such foods were prepared without flour and vinegar. He went on to poke fun at the floral decorations, which were of bright cottage-garden flowers and had been quite nicely arranged, probably by Eva, and sighed for the sight of some gardenias and tuberoses. Everyone was relieved when the meal was over and the host and his guest, in company with Ribbentrop, Schmidt and —inexplicably—me, were at liberty to adjourn to Hitler's private study for talks.

Immediately after the meeting I recorded an account of it which, for all its blemishes, I should like to quote here:

'The weather matched the mood. The celebrated view of the Führer's Austrian homeland was obscured by thick cloud, and this was the first such occasion on which the preliminaries, at least, were conducted standing up. Such were the circumstances under which Ciano delivered his great anti-war speech. His remarks were those of a responsible statesman and, thus, diametrically opposed to what the German side wished to hear at that juncture.

'His central theme was the fact that it was impossible, materially and politically, militarily and psychologically, for Italy to participate in a war at this early stage. She had, in effect, been waging war for years on end. What with intervention in the Spanish Civil War and the conquest of the Abyssinian Empire, the Italian people had been pushed into one armed conflict after another, and the result was a pronounced degree of war-weariness. In addition, these years had virtually exhausted Italy's scanty stocks of material. Her arsenals were empty and her reserves of gold and foreign exchange too slender to permit of an arms build-up.

'A further point to be considered was the position of the navy, which was currently engaged in adapting itself to modern war requirements, particularly in respect of capital ships. Here, too, a few years should be allowed for the implementation of the programme. Finally, Ciano mentioned the World Exhibition which was scheduled to take place in Rome in 1942, a pet project of Mussolini and the Fascist regime and one on which they pinned great economic and political hopes. It all amounted to a solemn and earnest declaration that, in view of the current mood of the masses, Fascist Italy could not take part in a warlike venture at this point in time.

'The reaction was predictable. The Count, who remained quite calm and composed, was bombarded with references to German disgrace, German humiliation—and all at the hands of the Poles. Seconded by Ribbentrop, Hitler enlisted the aid of a terrestrial globe which stood ready to hand. As on the occasion of the Day of German Art, the prospects of an Italian surprise attack on Greece and the almost undefended British bases in the Eastern Mediterranean were painted in bright and alluring colours. Hitler displayed considerable military knowledge, but this Fata Morgana, too, proved ineffectual. Ciano responded by asking for a glass of mineral water, a request which I hastened to fulfil so as to avoid the seemingly inevitable storm to come.

'But the storm never broke. In the nick of time, as Hitler was pacing nervously up and down and Ribbentrop stood wrapped in antique grandeur like a Homeric god of war and Ciano was starting to scratch himself—always a sign of extreme agitation—the miracle occurred. The door opened and Hewel of the Foreign Office rushed in. He whispered to his chief, who in his turn whispered to Hitler. Brows cleared and hostilities were postponed. What had happened? Neither Ciano nor I found out until much later. In fact, deliverance had come from Moscow. Someone in the Russian Embassy in Berlin had vaguely broached the possibility of direct East-West negotiations to a member of the Foreign Office. There was no suggestion of a trip by Ribbentrop to the Kremlin as yet, but the very prospects of such a thing pushed the fortunes—or misfortunes—of the Axis into the background. Hitler and his faithful shadow finished their mysterious confabulation while Ciano drained his bottle of mineral water.

'The talks were adjourned until next morning. Hitler suggested —war or no war, Italian military aid or no Italian military aid —that we make a trip to his beloved Eagle's Nest, his dream-world among the crags.

'He was in the best of tempers when we emerged from the bronze lift-gates at the top of the 425-foot-high shaft. There was no further mention of politics. Instead, the spacious room resounded to the voices of Richard Wagner's Valkyries. The Italian guest was propelled towards the vast window. At his feet lay a mountainscape which did not appeal to him, and above him circled two eagles which he would probably have shot down with relish. Hitler expatiated on the beauty of the scene as he had done during Balbo's visit. As an interpreter I was relieved, but Ciano was obviously cold. I never remember his being anything else in Germany, and even in Italy he tended to get cold in the absence of feminine warmth. In view of this, it was hardly surprising that he shivered at a height of over three thousand feet, drinking hot tea, which he disliked, and listening to the Valkyries, who had absolutely nothing to offer him in the way of sex appeal.

'He controlled himself with an effort, but heaved a sigh of relief when eagles, mountainscape and the view of Austria were swallowed up by evening mist. Then he made for the *Oesterreichischer Hof* in Salzburg, where he telephoned his father-in-law:

' "The position is serious. Further details in Rome by word of mouth."

'Next morning there was a final meeting on the Obersalzberg. Ciano was a changed man. All the cool decisiveness and statesmanlike discernment of the previous day had vanished. He seemed totally inert, and listened apathetically to Hitler's renewed assurances that England and France would never go to war on Poland's account—assurances which Ribbentrop confirmed with a vigorous nod. Then he uttered his parting words, a depressing swansong:

' "May your prophecy prove right once again, Führer—perhaps you see the position more clearly than we do in Rome." '

Count Ciano had never been a friend of Germany. I do not think he would have understood—or tried to understand—the Germans of the Kaiser's day or the Weimar Republic any better than he understood his National Socialist allies. From the moment of his return from the Obersalzberg, he became an avowed enemy who baulked at nothing in his efforts to sabotage the pact which he himself had negotiated.

In Rome, he aired his views to Party Secretary Starace and Arturo Bocchini. Don Arturo, in his turn, made no secret of his anti-war attitude and assured me that he would leave Mussolini in no doubt as to the true mood of the Italian people. The *contesse* and *principesse* at the golf-club made a point of speaking English when I was in their vicinity, and Princess Isabella Colonna, née Sursok from Beirut, started to refuse invitations from the German Embassy to the Vatican.

Such were the outward symptoms of a crisis which merely evoked smiles in Berlin. Was not Mussolini, that great friend of the Axis, on the German side, and were not Hitler and the Duce bound by mysterious ties of friendship? But Berlin did not smile for long. Just before war broke out the handsome Count did what the entire golf-club set had known he would do for months past, and performed a charming little waltz on the slippery dance-floor of international diplomacy.

On 31 August 1939, less than three weeks after his momentous meeting with Hitler and Ribbentrop, Ciano committed his *'indiscrezione'*, as he chose to call his conversation with Sir Percy Loraine, the British Ambassador in Rome.

The European crisis was at its height and the attack on Poland imminent when Galeazzo Ciano received His Britannic Majesty's representative at the Palazzo Chigi. It was between nine and ten o'clock at night. Rome was in darkness, and an uncanny silence reigned throughout the city. A faint glow of light came from the Pope's private apartments, where Pius XII, in concert with believers in countless Roman churches, was praying for peace.

By contrast, Ciano's study with its heavy baroque furniture was brilliantly lit. The Count was in high spirits when he received Sir Percy Loraine, who did not conceal his extreme agitation. Then came the soothing remark:

'Haven't you yet grasped the fact that we shall never start a war against your country and France?'

The ambassador understood. Radiant, he took both his host's hands in his and shook them warmly before making a hurried but happy departure. Ciano was no less happy when he telephoned his father-in-law at the Palazzo Venezia. He had taken his revenge for the August meeting and, above all, settled accounts with Ribbentrop.

All Rome rejoiced when Mussolini gave orders for the black-out to be lifted. Ciano had only secured another nine months of peace, but who realised that at the time? He hurried off to the Palazzo Colonna to be hailed as the victorious Crown Prince of Fascism by Donna Isabella and all the other princesses and coun-tesses, who lost no time in informing their British and American friends of their idol's magnificent little indiscretion.

Future students of the Second World War may well lay even greater stress on the historical significance of Ciano's interview with the British Ambassador on the night of 31 August 1939. Until that moment, France seems to have flatly refused to join Britain in hurrying to Poland's aid because Daladier and his Chief of Staff, Gamelin, were unwilling to risk a war on two fronts. Only when Paris learned of Rome's decision not to march at Germany's side did the French government give its consent. What would have happened if it had not been for Ciano's 'indiscretion'? Would the Western Powers have sacrificed yet another Eastern ally, as they did at Munich? Would Britain have gone to Poland's aid alone?

It is not my intention to pronounce upon these questions here. I only know that the Italian Foreign Minister regarded his nocturnal interview as a great diplomatic achievement. How far it contributed to his tragic death at Verona in January 1944 will be discussed elsewhere in due course, but it is certain that Hitler and Ribbentrop never forgave Ciano his indiscretion, which very soon came to their ears.

Rome now entered the celebrated period of *non-intervento*, during which Italy was courted by the rest of Europe like a beautiful girl who has still to give her final consent.

At about this time, Don Arturo Bocchini summoned me to his office and silently pushed a file across the desk for me to read. I did so and marvelled. It contained reports from quaestors and agents all over Italy, reports which made it clear that the Palazzo Venezia could not have relied on the Carabinieri and police in the event of Italy's entering the war at Germany's side. So far from lifting a finger to suppress demonstrations in favour of Italian neutrality, said the reports, they would actually have made common cause with the people. I ventured to ask His Excellency whether he and this file had, between them, dictated Mussolini's attitude, but my tactless question met with no response. Since I was not enjoined to keep quiet about what I had read, I followed my usual practice and passed the information on to Herr von Mackensen. I have no idea what he did with it, nor—happily—was it any concern of mine.

My time was largely claimed by the contest for Italy's favour, which I found far more to my taste. The two rivals, Germany on the one hand and the Western Allies on the other, surpassed themselves in their efforts to pay court to her, mainly in the social sphere, and Ciano's smiles and frowns became the focus of diplomatic interest in Rome.

The most improbable situations arose during this marathon contest. While the embattled armies faced each other on the Western Front, guns at the ready, attendance at a reception in Rome could bring one face to face with H.E. the French Ambassador, André François-Poncet, who had been posted there after the expiry of his tour in Berlin. He had always struck me as a Frenchman who displayed the less admirable characteristics of his great compatriot, Voltaire, without possessing his genius. His macabre and cynical witticisms did not go down well in the Eternal City, his strenuous efforts to ingratiate himself with Mussolini failed, and even Ciano cold-shouldered him. There were also bizarre encounters with Englishmen and representatives of other nations with whom one had consorted socially before the outbreak of war, and whom one now met under the auspices of Italian non-intervention as if nothing had happened in the interim.

Thanks to Ciano, his circle, and an aristocracy which had extensive links with Britain and America, it was, on the surface at least, a brilliant season. Many ancient palazzi which had hitherto been closed became venues for magnificent parties. Eventually, even Ribbentrop realised that he had to do something. In the spring of 1940, having failed in his attempt to persuade Ambassadress von Mackensen to take a more active part in Roman *chiaccheria* and golf-club revelries, he gave the embassy a facelift by sending it two ladies who were more suitable from that point of view—or, more precisely, he posted their husbands to Rome.

The first of the two new men thus favoured by fortune was Prince Otto von Bismarck, a grandson of the Iron Chancellor. He moved into an elegant villa in the best quarter of Rome with his beautiful wife Ann-Mari, née Tengbom of Stockholm, and before long the entire Ciano coterie was buzzing round them.

The Prince bore no outward resemblance to his grandfather. He looked far more like his Hungarian mother, Countess Hoyos, whose father, a Mr Whitehead, had founded the large torpedo factory at Pola. Although he combined diplomatic ability with political discernment, he was not Bismarckian enough to be able to act on his own excellent judgement, but made every effort not to irritate the Wilhelmstrasse in any way. He was also handicapped by his youngest brother, Count Albrecht, a deadly enemy of National Socialism who differed from most of his compeers in that he retained this abhorrence during military service and ultimately deserted.

The Princess loved social life. Her parties were dominated by the sound of her bell-like laugh and the sight of her blue eyes and blonde hair, and many were the Romans, young and old, who gazed at her entranced as she drove down to the sea clad in a sort of Swedish sailor suit. It is unlikely that the Iron Chancellor would have shared their admiration, nor would his wife, Princess Johanna. Her verdict on her unfortunate daughter-in-law, Countess Hoyos, had been: 'If you take away all her Viennese dressmakers' ribbons, frills and bows, what is left for my poor Herbert?' I dread to think what she would have said about Ann-Mari!

Foremost among the chic and charming princess's admirers was Filippo Anfuso, Ciano's principal private secretary. He was justly considered to be one of the handsomest men in Rome, and, unlike others of his sort, he was a person of courage and intelligence. The two were often seen together, which naturally caused tongues to wag with genuine Roman malice. However, the Princess was a true lady and an exemplary mother, and I never for a moment believed that their relationship was anything more than a sincere and platonic *entente* between North and South.

Ciano and his female admirers were frequent visitors to the Via Nicola Porpora, and his wife Edda could be seen there as well. The villa was an amusing blend of Bismarckian traditionalism and fashionable décor. At the foot of the stairs hung Franz von Lenbach's finest portrait, a picture of Pope Leo XIII, the only politician who ever worsted the old Chancellor in his Kulturkampf campaign. In the drawing-room, further Lenbach masterpieces depicted Bismarck surveying the social whirl at his feet with stern composure. The wall separating the drawing-room from the room next door was pierced by a glass case glittering with gifts—most of them appallingly over-ostentatious—which had been presented to the founder of the Reich by sundry sovereigns and governments. Rhenish tankards rubbed shoulders with silver Tsarist troikas, mute testimony to the bad taste of the Bismarck era. The Iron Chancellor would, on the other hand, have been extremely pleased with his grandson's dinners and their liberal accompaniment of French champagne. Food and drink were both excellent, and Roman society far preferred them to the Bismarckiana, whose existence they hardly noticed.

I spent many evenings at the Bismarcks' home. I suspect that the Princess took me for an unsuccessful academic whose Italian contacts were worth an invitation, and His Highness was glad to find an interpreter who did not eat peas with his knife. Being a friend of the ambassadorial couple and an admirer of his grandfather, I was classified as socially acceptable.

Despite the signed photograph of Hermann Göring displayed on their piano, both the Bismarcks were decidedly anti-Nazi when conversing among themselves and with Ciano and Anfuso. The Princess earned applause from the Ciano circle by saying that she was pro-German, 'because she had married Otto', but anti-Nazi. The Prince used to tell Italian Foreign Office officials much of what he knew, but, as Ciano discovered, 'he was hellishly afraid of being found out, and implored me in Heaven's name not to pass his confidential information on to anyone'. He was convinced of the inevitability of Germany's defeat but did not, unfortunately, mount the big political guns which had so often enabled his grandfather to avert disaster.

A visit to the Bismarcks' was always amusing and entertaining. People danced, gossiped, and called each other by their Christian or pet-names, after the style of imperial Vienna. The women were charming, malicious, superbly dressed and exceedingly fond of frivolous jokes. I could go a long way with Otto von Bismarck when I was alone with him, probably because each of us knew that there would be no indiscretion on the other's part.

At Ribbentrop's behest, another equally fashionable couple arrived in Rome almost at the same time. Herr Carl F. Clemm von Hohenberg, a relative of Frau von Ribbentrop, was employed by the Foreign Office as an economic adviser. It was in this capacity—as well as in the interests of Ribbentrop's social policy

—that he was posted to the German Embassy in Rome. He had no political functions, and his duties as an economic adviser were never very clear to me. He and his smart and attractive wife moved into a delightful medieval palazzo which became another favourite haunt of the Cianos. Edda Ciano-Mussolini seemed to feel particularly at home there, which fulfilled one of the main purposes of the Clemm-Hohenbergs' invitations. Galeazzo Ciano was not over-impressed by his hostess's political acumen, to judge by his reference to a conversation between her and his faithful henchman Anfuso:

Baroness Clemm told Anfuso that the Germans were entitled to a warm-water access, and that they would one day claim Trieste for themselves. Anfuso's advice to the Baroness was twofold: not to concern herself with politics, and to apply herself to another activity in which, as everyone knows, she has more experience.

No one knows the full truth of this but Anfuso himself, still a well-known Roman figure and now Senator of the neo-Fascist Party, nor is it of interest save as an indication of the malicious propensities of the Ciano circle. I remember the Clemm household for quite another reason. It was there, at an intimate supper à trois in autumn 1940, that I formed an acquaintanceship which was to prove of great importance five years later, not only to me but to international relations. Carl Clemm made these notes of the encounter:

Dollmann met Gero von Schulze-Gaevernitz at the home of the latter's old friend, Carl F. Clemm von Hohenberg, in autumn 1940. Their friendship dated from the years they had spent together in the USA. Clemm had returned to Germany at the end of the 'twenties and had since occupied a number of important administrative posts. Gaevernitz had become a naturalised American and divided his time between New York, Ascona and South America, where he had some valuable connections. Early in 1940 Clemm had been 'requisitioned' by the Foreign Office and sent to the German Embassy as an attaché with special responsibility for economic questions. Despite the deteriorating relations between the USA and Germany, Clemm and Gaevernitz had kept up their former friendship—not that this was surprising in two such liberal-minded and cosmopolitan men. I found the evening's conversation extremely informative, since we compared production figures in the USA with those of the Nazi-dominated part of Europe. Our talk, which was faintly pessimistic in tone, concluded with the expression of vague hopes that it would be possible to keep the USA out of the war this time. We thought a great deal about this conversation later on. Since Kappler was pretty well informed about all foreigners who were staying in Rome at that time, our private meeting at the Clemm home was not without its dangers.

So much for Clemm's notes. Kappler was the attaché with overall responsibility for police questions whom the Central State Security Bureau had sent to Rome in 1938. Herr von Gaevernitz became a close associate of Allen Dulles, head of the US Office of Strategic Services, Central Europe, which was based in Switzerland. It was through Gaevernitz that I first made contact with the Americans at Lugano in March 1945, a move which led, after protracted and difficult negotiations, to the surrender of the German armies in Italy at Caserta on 28 April 1945.

It would need a greater pen than mine to describe the atmosphere of Rome during these last few months of peace, the mysterious comings and goings, drawing-room intrigues and cabals, the feverish activity of secret service agencies and the groping bewilderment of most of the embassies. The battle for war or peace was not waged by fashionable hostesses, politicians and diplomats alone. Large numbers of outsiders, large numbers of mystery-men appeared on the scene and threw dazzling parties whose cost was undoubtedly borne by other pockets than their own. I am thinking, for instance, of a man who was soon to win the admiration of Europe and whom no less a mortal than Heydrich, chief of the Central State Security Bureau, regarded as the most dangerous spy of all: Felix Kersten, medical adviser and personal physician to Heinrich Himmler.

Kersten has been the subject of numerous books and articles of varying merit, but anyone who wants to gain a true picture of this masseur-magician should consult the pages of his memoirs.

Of all the people dispatched to Rome by the Third Reich, Kersten was without doubt the most original and the most endearing. He was not, of course, the tedious knight in shining armour which contemporary biographers choose to paint him, but everything about him—from his position of trust with the Reichsführer-SS to his services to humanity—was strange and inimitable. I only knew him in Rome, but a few words about his previous history may serve to illuminate his personality.

Eduard Felix Alexander Kersten was born in the Livonian university town of Dorpat on 20 September 1898. His father was a prosperous Baltic land-owner of German extraction. When the Kaiser's troops supported the Finns in their fight for freedom against the Russians during the First World War, Kersten served with them and was granted Finnish nationality at the close of hostilities. He subsequently studied scientific massage. The turning-point in his budding career came in Berlin in 1919, when he met and became the trusted disciple of a Chinese doctor named Ko, who initiated him into the theory and practice of Oriental massage. Dr Ko convinced him that many apparently incurable ailments stem from nervous tension, and that their cure consists in relaxing the nerves involved.

The fingers are the only instruments used in such treatment, and I well remember Kersten's unique hands. They looked at first glance like the soft, sensitive, well-manicured hands of a woman, but this impression was misleading. Once in their grasp, one felt them turn into relentless, steel-bladed knives which probed one's knotted nerve-ends with inexorable strength. There were moments when one yearned for an operating-table and an anaesthetic rather than Kersten's couch, but these moments were succeeded by a wonderful sense of release from all pain.

Kersten called his technique, which I often discussed with him, 'physio-neural therapy', and it proved to be a sovereign remedy for all forms of neuralgia, gastric and cardiac nervous disorders, migraine, debility and—last but not least—male impotence.

When Dr Ko returned to Tibet, Kersten inherited the majority of his practice. His international reputation continued to grow until, in 1928, he was summoned to the court of Queen Wilhelmina of Holland. As court masseur to the house of Orange, he found that the world was his oyster, and even if one discounts a few of his more colourful stories there is no doubt that his clientele included some of the most notable financiers, aristocrats and politicians in Europe. He owed his introduction to Heinrich Himmler to the far from altruistic recommendations of two German industrialist patients. On 10 March 1939, Kersten established that his new patient was suffering from a disorder of the sympathetic nerve-system which subjected him to spasms of agonising pain. He was able to dispel them with a few minutes of deep massage.

'I have consulted a large number of German specialists,' Himmler told him, 'but none of them could do anything for me. Please go on helping me.'

Felix Kersten continued to help him—for so long and with such success that he soon became indispensable to the most feared man in the Third Reich. Himmler knew most things, but he did not know that his new medical favourite had contacted the Finnish Embassy in Berlin before continuing to treat him and received a go-ahead on the grounds that 'it may sometime be possible to exploit this connection in some way'.

So Kersten went on massaging Himmler's pains away, simultaneously alleviating the rather disparate agonies of countless people in prisons and concentration camps or saving them from consignment to Buchenwald and Auschwitz. It was probably a unique occurrence in the history of medicine and one which, thanks to Dr Ko, had a very Chinese flavour. Kersten not only saved lives but coaxed Himmler to talk. As he lay there, racked with pain, the Reichsführer-SS felt a burning desire to unburden himself of his secrets. The 800-page diary in which Kersten recorded these revelations has little prospect of being published in full, but he did publish extracts from it in the book mentioned above. They rank among the most important sources of psychological and historical information about the Third Reich. To quote what is, perhaps, the most interesting passage of all:

Field Command Post, 12 December 1942.
I have just had my most exciting day since Himmler became my patient. He was very nervous and restless, and I could tell he had

something on his mind. When I spoke to him about it he responded by asking: 'Could you treat a man who is suffering from severe head-aches, attacks of giddiness and insomnia? Here, read this. It's the secret file on the Führer's illness.' The report ran to 26 pages, as I ascertained when I first leafed through it. It was obvious that they had used the hospital report dating from the time when he lay blinded in the hospital at Pasewalk. Proceeding from this period, the reports stated that as a young combat soldier Hitler had succumbed to a poison-gas attack. He had been inefficiently treated, with the result that a danger of temporary blindness arose. Symptoms of a syphilitic infection also manifested themselves. He was treated at Pasewalk and discharged as cured. In 1937 symptoms appeared which implied that the syphilitic infection was continuing its sinister work of destruction. In early 1942 the appearance of further such symptoms left no doubt that Hitler was suffering from progressive paralysis, all the symptoms being present with the exception of pupillary fixity and blurred speech. I returned the report to Himmler and told him that I was afraid I could not do anything in this case because I was a specialist in manual therapy, not mental disorders.

Kersten arrived in Rome in the spring of 1940, as a bread-and-butter offering from Himmler to his Roman friends. Before the wonder-man's arrival, his deadly enemy Heydrich warned me against him via his henchman in Rome, Police Attaché Kappler. It was the only time Heydrich ever tried to enlist my co-operation. He got Kappler to inform me that the Central State Security Bureau believed Felix Kersten to be an enemy intelligence agent, and that his forthcoming contact with prominent Italians was viewed with deep misgiving. I replied that Heydrich ought to take the matter up with his chief, Himmler, and that, anyway, I had only been asked to look after Kersten's personal needs in Rome and arrange for his professional attendance upon Ciano, Buffarini-Guidi and others.

The miracle-worker arrived, plump and gentle as a Buddha, and was installed in ex-King Alfonso's suite at the Grand Hotel. I am quite sure the Bourbon monarch never had as many visitors. Ciano consulted him at once, as did the Secretary of State for the Interior, Buffarini-Guidi, whose nerves were understandably frayed by persistent over-involvement in Donna Rachele's private battle with Clara Petacci and by Mussolini's lightning changes of mind and mood. Ciano was delighted with Kersten, whose drawing-room in the Grand Hotel was soon crowded with ladies from the golf-club. Kersten was discretion itself, so I never learned what they were all suffering from. Only in the case of Ciano did he permit himself a meaningful smile and some obscure allusions to Tibetan love-lore.

All sorts of people consulted him, among them the Duke of Spoleto, a nephew of the King and scion of the house of Aosta, and Count Volpi, the Venetian financier and diplomat. Bibi, no longer so little, offered to guide him round Rome at my suggestion, but he was far less interested in relics of the Ancient World than in sweet-shop windows, which displayed treasures no longer obtainable in Hitler's Germany.

Sweets and chocolates were Kersten's ruling passion, and it was not long before his patients were bringing him *pralinés* by the pound in the hope of keeping him sweet, both before and during treatment. These he would devour with evident satisfaction while his hapless victims waited for their next bout of torture. Being part of Germany's attempt to win the favour of a still neutral Italy, he had been expressly forbidden by Berlin to accept fees from anyone. In fact, Kersten was very fond of money. He sadly confided to me that he often wondered why he had not deserted Berlin in 1939 and thrown himself into the welcoming arms of his dollar-millionaire patients. I have often pondered the same question, and can only conclude that he was prompted by humanitarian motives. I was even more astonished by his fierce yearning for senior rank in the ordinary SS. As a Finnish Medical Councillor and former personal consultant to the house of Orange, he really had no need of added status. Felix Kersten was vain, however. Once, when I arrived to escort him to a reception, I found him attired in a tail-coat plastered with the most unlikely hotchpotch of decorations, ranging from Dutch orders to American gold medals and Italian *commendatore* crosses. He was very cast down when I advised him to go dressed as an ordinary citizen.

Himmler had hoped that he would treat Mussolini, but he never did. I discussed the matter with Bocchini, and we agreed that an unsuccessful massage might well endanger the survival of the Axis. Bocchini himself needed no massages. He soothed his nerves with lobsters, oysters, capons and vintage burgundy, and his migraines were spirited away by the gentle hands of his young blonde niece quite as effectively, if not more so, than they would have been by the Sino-Finnish manipulations of Felix Kersten.

Was Kersten a spy? I am as certain today as I was then that he was not. In the first place, he was far too lazy and too much of a coward; secondly, he was well aware that Heydrich and his Bureau hated him and kept him under the closest possible surveillance, and, thirdly, Heinrich Himmler was not such a fool as to lose his sixth sense for espionage, even when his judgement was blurred by excruciating pain. Kersten loved talking, of course. Ciano, who had once been Consul-General in Shanghai and knew something of the East, admired his esoteric knowledge and told me of interesting conversations with him on the subject of Chinese and Tibetan culture. It goes without saying that Kersten gleaned a great deal of information from his distinguished clientele, but his beloved estate, Harzwalde, and his cinema in Poznan were within the Third Reich's sphere of jurisdiction, and he was not the man to risk his neck and personal possessions unnecessarily.

His role during the last months of Nazi rule, his great Jewish rescue operation and his contacts with Count Bernadotte have already been described in detail elsewhere and are not connected with his activities in Rome, so I can now bid him a grateful farewell. He certainly caused me some pain during a nerve-massage which only a masochist could have described as enjoyable—and I have never been a masochist. However, he did save me from having to undergo a dangerous operation which had been recommended by a number of more conventional specialists, and I am eternally indebted to his skill and that of his great Chinese mentor.

Galeazzo Ciano gave Kersten a memorable farewell dinner. Since he was not allowed to pay him anything, much to Kersten's sorrow, he presented him with the largest available photograph of himself in an equally large silver frame which I procured for the occasion, the frame being worth something in itself. Kersten left Rome sans cash but no poorer. Berlin had not forbidden him to accept presents, so his private suite became heaped with bolts of silk for shirts, framed photographs, items of male apparel, gift parcels from the ladies of the golf-club, and box after box of his favourite chocolates and marrons glacés from Rosati's in the Via Veneto.

The guests at Ciano's Roman apartment consisted largely of the healed. Portly ministers and financiers whose nervous tension had been dispelled, or at least diminished, embraced their saviour for the last time. Migraine-afflicted ladies smiled at him, their headaches banished, and dukes who had been cured of fashionable ailments such as sciatica or gout turned out to bid him farewell. The Count occupied two floors in the smart Via Angelo Secchi. The reception rooms, which were on the first floor, were an amusing jumble of styles. The best things were some fine Chinese porcelain and a magnificent Zuloaga which had been presented to Ciano by the Spanish government. The champagne, I regret to say, was a gift from his colleague Ribbentrop. It arrived by the case each Christmas from the ample cellars of the House of Henkell, which belonged to Frau von Ribbentrop's family. If only her husband had continued to represent the firm in America instead of devoting himself to foreign policy, the world would have been spared a great deal of tribulation and we—as our host mockingly remarked—would have been able to drink French champagne instead of German *Sekt*.

The after-dinner atmosphere was as informal as usual. Countess Edda held court over a group of young people while the Count put his arm, in turn, round a contessa, a principessa and a sexy damsel of no ancestral pedigree. The Buddha-like guest of honour devoured mountains of sweetmeats and entertained his malicious audience by gossiping, with my assistance, about the members of royal and princely houses whom he had treated, with special reference to the legendary meanness of the Dutch Queen Mother. He prudently skirted the subject of Himmler, but left us in no doubt as to the power he wielded over him. Police Attaché Kappler had not been invited, which facilitated conversation a great deal.

I had visited the Ciano household on a number of occasions. I accompanied Himmler and von Schirach there and was sometimes invited in a private capacity. Edda Ciano-Mussolini never failed to make a strong impression on me. She was a true child of the Duce, whom she resembled both in manner and appearance, despite rumours that she had been fathered by a Russian émigré whom Mussolini had known during his Socialist days in Switzerland. She was tartly intelligent, capricious as a wild mare and endowed with a thoroughbred ugliness, but her Mussolini eyes irradiated everything and everyone they looked at. It still pleases me to think that in August 1943, when all the light had gone out of those eyes, I was able to repay the hospitality I had enjoyed in the Cianos' home by helping them to escape.

With the advent of spring 1940, Mussolini's state of mind remained that of a charger which hears the trumpet sound of the charge but prefers to linger in its warm stable for a while longer. He read Bocchini's increasingly depressing reports on the real mood of the country—or did not read them, as the case may be. The King, court and army leaders wooed Ciano with flattery and compliments, rightly regarding him as the personification of the anti-war front. They were mistaken only as to the strength and courage of his convictions. In this rumour-laden spring, Italy's last few months of peace, the King could have assumed personal command of the army and navy, persuaded Ciano to go along with him and, if necessary, forced Mussolini to resign. It was not enough to hope for the best, however. Someone had to be prepared to act for the best, and Victor Emmanuel III was quite as reluctant to do that as Ciano himself. The more imminent an offensive in the West became, the greater the nervousness and vacillation among the Italian leaders. Eventually, on 18 March 1940, while the mimosa was blossoming in Rome, the two dictators met at the Brenner. It was snowing, needless to say, and I still shudder as I recall the encounter. The Italian leader, so much the more intelligent, human and fascinating of the two men, listened to the interminable speechifying of his opposite number with a mixture of sorrowful humility and envious admiration. He had told us on the journey that he had had a remarkable dream, as he often did before critical moments in his career. He did not divulge the nature of this particular dream, unfortunately, but mentioned that before settling the Fiume question he had dreamt of wading through a river. This did not seem unduly revealing, and we all preserved a mystified silence.

The Brenner meeting, which left everything as much in the air as ever, marked the beginning of Benito Mussolini's 'silent' era. Determined as he was, while en route for the meetings and conferences which continued until his downfall in July 1943, to speak out, assert himself and make the voice of reason heard, the sight of his hypnotic colleague usually reduced him to silence. It was a truly pathological condition which one of Felix Kersten's neuro-massages might have relieved. Mussolini's Achilles' heel was anything with a military flavour—and Hitler reeked of the old soldier. He held his mute friend spellbound with martial perorations, demonstrated his strength by means of statistics, and vaunted of victories which the Duce, to his sorrow, could not match.

I found the increasingly one-sided nature of their relationship distressing, but the responsibility did not lie with my translations. After all, I could not translate what had not been said. The best verdict on this first conference of the 'silent era' comes from Mussolini's son-in-law:

'Mussolini is furious because Hitler did almost all the talking. He had intended to say a lot of things to him, but was reduced to silence most of the time. It really doesn't fit in with his role as a dictator, let alone as the "doyen" of these two dictators.'

The Western Powers were extremely disturbed by the news of this meeting, but Count Ciano hastened to inform his old friend Sir Percy Loraine that nothing of note had occurred. I, on the other hand, could have reported that a significant incident occurred on the return journey. The Duce, who had found his tongue again, pointed to the heavy snow-flakes and declared that he would need snow as far south as Etna if he were ever to turn his Italians into a race of warriors.

How right he was, but how much poorer the world would be if he had managed to overlay the sunny, lovable and endearing characteristics of the Italian people with a film of cold military ice!

For the moment, the sun still shone down on the much wooed courtesan beside the Tiber. Hitler's guns would thunder in the West soon enough, colouring the Duce's dreams and filling him with a nightmarish dread that he might arrive too late to share in the spoils of victory.

VII

THE TWO CORPORALS

IN SUMMER 1945, when I was privileged to be an involuntary
guest of the Intelligence Service Centre in Rome, a senior British
officer asked why I had not prevented Italy from entering the
Second World War. I endeavoured to explain that any such intervention would have far exceeded the scope and potential of an
interpreter. I should like to have seen Mussolini's face if I had
gone to him with such a suggestion! I got on very well with him,
but he only credited me with political influence when things
began to go badly for him. Dictators do not listen to their advisers
until they are at their wit's end. If I had realised how utterly at a
loss Mussolini was in spring 1940 I might even have tried to do
something about his hysterical bewilderment and pathological
indecision. What I had been told by the two strong-men of the
Italian Ministry of the Interior, Police Chief Arturo Bocchini
and Minister of the Interior *de facto* Buffarini-Guidi, about their
liege lord's hourly and daily changes of emotional tack was indeed
food for thought, but it was not enough to justify a suicide attempt
on my part!

The members of Count Ciano's harem, high-ranking and low,
made no secret of the detestation which their dashing golf-club
president felt for the Germans and his colleague Ribbentrop in
particular. Nevertheless, whenever I tried, in a casual and humorous way, to alert Mussolini's son-in-law to the potential dangers
of Italy's participation in the war, he promptly assured me of his
admiration for Adolf Hitler, whose judgement had always proved
so infallible in the past. Our conversations left me in no doubt

about one thing: the Italian Foreign Minister hated us and prayed that we should be defeated, preferably before Italy emerged from her indecision. His hatred was shared by the great salons of Rome, the 'top ten thousand' and the *chiaccheria*, as the feminine exponents of *la dolce vita* were called in those days.

Ciano's sentiments were also shared by the royal house of Savoy, but all concerned—whether in the remote royal residences, in the labyrinthine passages of the Palazzo Chigi or on the golf-course at Acqua Santa—nursed their hatred and hopes in secret. They would have been as reluctant as Arturo Bocchini or Buffarini-Guidi to venture on an open rebellion against the man who still reigned supreme at the Palazzo Venezia. The shrewd and violently temperamental Edda disliked us too, but the Fascist Amazon in her rallied to the banner of honour and, consequently, war.

Turning my attention to the Vatican, I called on my friends in the Vatican Library, the Papal Archives and the Camposanto Teutonico. I even paid another visit to Father Tacchi-Venturi, the Chronicler of the Jesuit Order and Mussolini's father confessor. He gave me the heartening information that everyone was opposed to entering the war at the side of Hitlerite Germany, and I was urged to pass the news on to Berlin. I was further informed that His Holiness was praying with devout fervour, night and day, for the peace of the world and of Italy in particular, but there was no intimation that he was contemplating an official crusade against the infidels of the Third Reich. As I well knew, Mussolini was currently following the disastrous example set by his friend Hitler. He was on the crest of a wave of hatred for the Vatican, and the Pope and Church were now subjected to his hysterical outbursts of fury as often as the King and monarchy.

Baulked at every turn, I remembered the 'Alfrediani'. Alfredo himself had gone to the happy hunting-grounds by now, but his cronies were still in evidence. I arranged to meet them, this time unaccompanied by Signorina Bibi. Bibi was concentrating on higher things, and her pretty head was filled with rosy-hued pictures of embassy receptions, cocktail parties and golf-club romances. She pursued her chosen social career with the tough single-mindedness of a budding dictator on the lower rungs of the political ladder—at least one respect in which women resemble ruthless demagogues of the opposite sex. She declined '*con tanti ricordi e tantissimi saluti*' and left me to go alone to the trattoria in Trastevere where she had spent so many happy hours in the past.

I was received in oppressive silence. Then the storm broke. The petty thieves of the Roman Campagna all shouted at once, prophesying their own certain doom as well as Italy's and mine. They evolved fantastic schemes for evading mobilisation and sabotaging the war-effort, swore that they would seek refuge in attics and mountain hideouts, and predicted that Benito Mussolini would die an agonising death. Although they were right in the latter forecast and would willingly have pressed a revolver into my hand so that I could shoot the man they had once followed with such enthusiasm, they would have been as incapable of pulling the trigger as I was. We finally decided, over innumerable *fiaschi* and plates of fat sucking-pig, on a policy of tacit collaboration. I promised to do what I could to assist them in their forthcoming brush with the military authorities, and they guaranteed that they would help me when Mussolini and Hitler, Fascism and Nazism, had bitten the dust. Both parties kept their word, and who knows where any of us would be today if it had not been for our exchange of pledges at Trastevere?

This concluded my private peace talks. I renounced any further attempt to hinder Italy's entry into the war, first, because it was useless, and, secondly, because I did not see why I should sacrifice myself on the Italians' behalf. I was fond of them and even fonder of their country, but it was up to them—King and Queen, Ciano and harem, Pope and Church, generals and admirals—to extricate themselves from the mess into which, whether by design or force of circumstance, they had got themselves.

On 10 June 1940, heedless of my unspoken disapproval, the Duce declared war and prophesied victory to a dispirited crowd. Italy's funeral march was preluded by a solemn drum-beat when Balbo crashed mysteriously over his own lines on 29 June. It got under way properly when Italy launched her disastrous attack on Greece on 28 October, news of which was conveyed to an astonished Hitler on Florence station, shortly before his special train departed.

I am not a war historian, nor was I even a war reporter. There is no need for me to describe Italy's fateful and tragic role in the Second World War. The lost battles, the sabotage and treachery, the mounting surge of hatred for the regime—in short, the whole desperate attempt of the least warlike and most war-weary people in contemporary Europe to opt out of a war of their own choosing—are well known enough already. I could give a chronological account of all the meetings, conferences, tours of inspection and scenes of mutual recrimination which I witnessed as an interpreter at Schloss Klessheim, at the Führer's Headquarters, in Italy and elsewhere, but it would be a monotonous story indeed.

What I found far more interesting, and still do today, was the game of toy soldiers in which the two dictators engaged, both in concert and opposition. Their favourite peace-time hobby had been to relive their glorious years of army service, during which each had risen to the rank of corporal. Then, they had dreamed of being reincarnations of Napoleon and Caesar; now, at the head of gigantic armies, they seemed to see their dreams transformed into reality. Mussolini, in particular, had achieved his most heartfelt and imbecile ambition: he had always yearned to be a general, and now—in his eyes, if in no one else's—he had become one.

I should like, therefore, to reproduce a few impressions of the two corporals 'at play' which I managed to salvage from my papers. They were written while I was still under the immediate impact of the events in question, and are anything but literary gems. Whatever their demerits, however, they are genuine and unadorned.

The first of these excerpts concerns the dictators' joint trip to Russia between 23 and 30 August 1941, when they were at the zenith of their martial glory and success. I entitled the episode 'Alexander weeps for the moon':

'Like huge eagles, the metallic birds soared eastwards across the endless forests and blue mountains of Carpathia. The two dictators sat safely ensconced in one of Hitler's enormous Kondor planes, bound for the Ukrainian theatre of operations. Thanks to the achievements of modern engineering, the tour, which was scheduled to cover roughly 15,000 kilometres, had so far gone well.

'The Duce had boarded his special train at Riccione on 23 August, pale and still grieving for his favourite son Bruno, who had died in an air crash shortly before. The journey to the Führer's Headquarters at Rastenburg had passed off in a human and untheatrical atmosphere. To Hitler's annoyance, Mussolini wasted time in the still smoking ruins of the largest Russian frontier fortress, Brest-Litovsk, by requesting translations of some charred Russian field post office letters wrapped in red and blood-spattered cloth. He was enough of an Italian to mourn the fate of the poor young Russian soldiers who had been overtaken by death with the eternal and international language of love next to their hearts. He was never more sympathetic than at moments like these, when he dropped his general's pose.

'Late that afternoon the dictators boarded the special trains which conveyed them, separately this time, to Wisniowa in Galicia, where they arrived on 27 August. Gently sloping green hills framed by mountains and virgin forest met the eye at every turn. A halt for rest and refreshment was called at a dilapidated hunting-lodge on a small hillock, where we were welcomed by grey-bearded foresters with mutton-chop whiskers in the style of Emperor Franz Joseph. This had been a favourite hunting-preserve of Archduke Franz Ferdinand, who often came there to indulge his passion for the mass-slaughter of game. Emerging timidly from the green woods to graze, gentle-eyed deer stared down in surprise at the special trains of Europe's new masters as they stood, one inside and the other outside a neighbouring tunnel.

'Next morning a long cortège of cars conveyed the party to the airfield at Krosno, where take-off was scheduled for 5.30 a.m. At this somnolent hour, many of the Italians would have preferred to abandon their trip to the Ukraine altogether, but Mussolini was quite the corporal-general again, and they eventually boarded the Kondors at his imperious urging. Friend Adolf was also treated to a sample of his 'Caesarian' mood. Tired of German victories and conquests but unable to produce any of his own, the Duce sought refuge in Italy's past history and roused the illustrious Trajan from his immemorial slumbers. Since the region we were flying over was more or less where his legions had fought, Hitler was forced to listen patiently to an account of the battles won by the emperor who had Romanised and colonised modern Romania. This was followed by a description of the feats of engineering performed by the Roman legions when building their celebrated bridge across the southern reaches of the Danube— an achievement scarcely to be equalled by troops with modern equipment. Hitler steadfastly ignored the Duce's pointed allusions to the difficulties which had beset Trajan when the enemy whom he had defeated in pitched battle withdrew into the inaccessible mountains and began to wage a brisk and extremely damaging guerilla campaign, but nothing could cloud the new Trajan's cheerful mood.

'Delighted at the obvious annoyance which his imperial mono- logue had caused, Mussolini begged to be allowed to take over the controls of the plane—a piece of typically Latin irresponsibil- ity which threatened to jeopardise the Third Reich and, with it, world supremacy. In vain did Hitler and his apprehensive aides try to discourage this whim by referring to the unpredictable squalls which were especially common over the Beskids and Car- pathians. The Führer's personal pilot, who looked alarmed, muttered something about "crazy Italians" and "welcome to crash on his own". In the end, subject to innumerable safety pre- cautions and the assistance and supervision of the Germanic crew members who hemmed him in on every side, the Roman guest got his way. Adolf Hitler could hardly have imagined in his wildest dreams that he would be piloted into his newly-conquered Ukraine by an Italian, of all people, but he was obliged to grind his teeth in silence and defer vengeance until the machine was safely back on terra firma.

'With the two dictators in the lead, the long convoy of cars got under way. The Ukrainian plain with its head-high sunflower plantations, fields of golden grain and white farmhouses—echoes of Tolstoy and Turgenev—glided past in the brilliant late summer sunlight. Slim birches bowed in the eternal wind of the wide and unprotected expanses, and the blue horizon resembled a distant sea. It was an unforgettable picture, and one which affected the two conquerors in very different ways. The magic of the scene prompted the Duce to reminisce about Russian literature, which he knew well and esteemed highly, whereas Hitler launched into a passionate tirade against it. Singled out for special abuse was Tolstoy's *War and Peace*, which was consigned to the bottomless pit of the Führer's contempt for being not only unheroic but a clumsy piece of Communist propaganda. Hitler had suffered too much from Emperor Trajan and his friend's aeronautical technique to be able to resist holding forth himself. He outlined the future status of Russia and the Ukraine under German sovereignty: an escape-proof slave-system—supervised by local, district and regional administrators armed with unlimited disciplinary powers—beside which the Tsarist regime would resemble a lost paradise. What aroused the German Tsar's particular displeasure was the sight of dilapidated roads and semi-cultivated fields. He proposed to import some German Communists so that they could see for themselves how their Russian idols had allowed the fertile soil to deteriorate. His mood did not grow any mellower even when blonde Ukrainian girls emerged from their wretched, shell-shattered villages bearing humble offerings of sunflower-seeds—unlike his friend, who accepted these tributes with evident pleasure and no less pleasurable glances at the girls' figures, which were in full accord with Latin conceptions of beauty.

'Behind the dictators, like two silent gods of war, rode Field Marshals von Rundstedt and Messe, the latter being the commander of the Italian corps serving in Russia. Behind them, again, came the numerous members of the German-Italian entourage.

'All at once, Hitler's monologue was brusquely interrupted and his words drowned by a storm of cheering which broke out on all sides as the party rounded a bend in the road. Mussolini's face glowed. There they were at last: his own troops—even if they had been posted to Russia mainly for propaganda purposes. Motorised units of every kind drove past the the proud and erect figure of their imperator. It was as though Trajan's glorious days had come alive once more, except that instead of heavily armed legionaries it was Bersaglieri with waving feathers in their steel helmets who roared past on motor-cycles. For the first time in its millenial history, the motionless and glittering Ukrainian plain rang to enthusiastic shouts of *"Duce!"* Victory still beckoned these sons of the South, and each of them dreamed of a hero's welcome at home before the Russian winter set in.

'It must, I think, have been the most enjoyable moment Mussolini had so far experienced in the Second World War. As a former corporal in the Bersaglieri, he would have liked nothing better than to mount a motor-cycle and join in—nor would Hitler and his staff have been surprised if he had. They paled as the sun-tanned soldiers raised their wholly unmilitary cry of "Duce, Duce! ", watching their allies' strange and increasingly ragged parade with narrowed eyes and sceptically surveying their summery attire.

'I thoroughly enjoyed it all, and if I had not been nudged by Hitler's chauffeur, Kempka, who was sitting beside me, I am afraid I might have cheered too.

'Then the Italian opera came to an end.

'With the visionary exuberance of a conqueror, Hitler boldly outlined his future strategic plans. While the procession of cars rolled slowly towards Uman, he totted up the distances covered by the armies of the great generals of the past, demonstrating to his wholly uninterested companion that Frederick the Great had covered 4000 kilometres with his troops in seven years, Napoleon 15,000 kilometres in twenty years and Alexander about the same distance in thirteen.

' "But who has yet estimated the number of kilometres which my incomparable soldiers have covered between Narvik and the Pyrenees, Africa and here? Who can estimate the distance that still lies before them? The whole of Russia will fall to them before winter, and they will await new conquests in the spring on the borders of the Urals, Persia and the Caspian Sea. Asia will at last be within reach of the Axis, and the dying democracies will have been struck a mortal blow! "

'Benito Mussolini listened to this torrent of verbiage without enthusiasm. When I had finished translating, there came a tired and melancholy echo:

' *"E allora? Piangeremo come Alessandro Magno per la luna?"*

'I hesitated for a moment before giving what I trust was a fair translation:

Hitler's visit to Rome—May 1938 (*from left to right*) Hitler, Mussolini, Goebbels, Himmler, Adjunct Schaub and Dollmann

Himmler in Tripoli—November 1938 (Collmann in the center)

Visit of Reichsfrauenführherin
Scholtz-Klinck to Italy—1939:
(Dollmann and the
Marchesa Olga Medici on her left)

The Contessa Colonna, Duchessa
di Sermoneta

Hitler with the
Countess Attolico

The Duke and Duchess
of Windsor with
Hitler at the Berghof

The Crown Princess of Italy with the
German Ambassador to Rome, von Mackensen, and his wife

Reinhard Heydrich, chief of the Central State Security Bureau, in Rome—
28th October 1938

Count Ciano, Mussolini and von Hassell awaiting the arrival of
Chamberlain and Halifax in Rome—January 1939

Hitler, Dollmann, Ciano and von Ribbentrop in Berlin—May 1938

Mussolini and Hitler

(*from left to right*) Hitler, Mussolini, Ciano and Keitel
in Florence—October 1940

Ricci's visit to Goebbels: (*from left to right*)
Goebbels, Dollman, Ricci and Schirach

Osteria 'Alfredo'–Rome 1938: (*from right to left behind table*)
von Hassell, Rossoni (Minister of Agriculture), Dollmann and Darré

The funeral of Bocchini in Rome–November 1940: (*from left to right*)
General Karly Wolff, Heydrich, Serena (Secretary of the Facist Party),
Himmler and Dino Grandi

Castle of Klessheim—April 1943:
General Ambrosio,
Hermann Göring and Dollmann

Mussolini at Kesselring's
headquarters in Parma—
August 1944:
(*from left to right*)
Dollmann, Mussolini,
Major Zolling and
Kesselring

' "What then? Shall we weep for the moon like Alexander the Great?"
'Adolf Hitler looked first at me, then at his friend, as though we were mad. He told me to ask Mussolini what he meant. Instead of an explanation, he got a poem:

> ' *"Giungemmo: è il fine. O sacro Araldi squilla!*
> *Nun altra terra se non là, nel,' aria,*
> *quella che in mezzo del brocchier vi brilla."*

'This was more difficult, but the Duce helped me with it, hardly giving me time to explain that it was the opening of Giovanni Pascoli's famous poem on Alexander. This describes how the insatiable Macedonian, having reached the borders of the conquerable world with his faithful companions, bewails the sad fate that forbids him to gain mastery of the moon as well.

'The Duce was feeling cheerful again. He had noticed that his friend was as irritated by Alexander and the moon as he had been by Trajan and the Danube bridge. Besides, he had proved himself a man of culture. Who in the heart of Ukraine apart from me—and that was coincidental—had ever heard of Giovanni Pascoli?

'Adolf Hitler had not heard of him and he probably considered Alexander the Great insane to boot, but he controlled himself with a visible effort. It was a unique scene set in the midst of the biggest battlefield in Europe, and I enjoyed it enormously. While his victorious armies advanced upon Asia in a series of encircling battles, like Alexander's, Hitler was obliged to sit listening to the Greek's lunar schemes as related by his friend from Rome. He was too shrewd not to read between the lines, but Mussolini was his only friend, and so, silent but furious, he forgave him Alexander just as he had forgiven him Trajan a few hours earlier.

'We had now arrived in the smoking ruins of Uman. This time it was Hitler who was encircled by his victorious soldiers. Wounded men asked to see their supreme commander, generals delivered lectures on successful battles, and squadrons of fighters zoomed over our heads. Hitler had won the war-game after all.'

Both before and after this visit to the Eastern armies, several things had occurred in Rome which taxed my abilities as an individual and an interpreter. In November 1940 Don Arturo Bocchini died in the arms of his youthful mistress after an over-abundant dinner—not a death merited by many police chiefs but one which was fully in keeping with Bocchini's way of life. I still welcome the fact that I was able to help his niece during the dispute that broke out over the terms of his will, a service which endeared me to her but not to the Bocchini clan, who saw several million lire slip through their fingers.

The last time I saw Donna Anna Bocchini she very nearly threw away an official gift to her husband from Heinrich Himmler. The Reichsführer-SS had celebrated his friend's birthday by sending an aide to call on him clad in full-dress uniform and bearing a large box. Never averse to receiving valuable presents, Don Arturo turned the presentation into an official ceremony. He was in his office, surrounded by senior colleagues resplendent in medals and gold braid, when I opened the box. It contained another box, and inside the second box was a leather case. What could it be —a diamond-studded dagger, a gold chain? I opened the mysterious case and gave an involuntary start of surprise. Then I took out the enclosed letter and asked for a brief recess. Skimming through the handwritten note, I learned that His Excellency's birthday present was the shrivelled piece of wood which I had seen reposing on red velvet inside the case. It was a fragment of bark from a Wotan oak, and Herr Himmler's letter of birthday greetings dwelt at length on its prehistoric, spiritual and divine significance. A fragment from the Germans' sacred tree . . . If only it had been set with precious stones, but it was nothing of the sort!

Rough, wrinkled, bleached, and far less valuable than its sumptuous bed of velvet, it waited mutely for me to resurrect it with a few well-chosen words. The right words refused to come. Instead, holding Wotan's oak gingerly between thumb and forefinger, I delivered a humorous address which would doubtless have outraged Heinrich Himmler. I compared his piece of bark with the sacrificial gifts once offered to the Gods of Rome, citing it as evidence of how modest and unpretentious the Germans had

been before they became corrupted by the luxurious deities of
the Roman metropolis. Unlike the piece of bark, my speech
enjoyed quite a success. The birthday-boy chuckled, clasping his
little pot-belly, and the decorations on his colleagues' chests
jingled merrily in concert. Then Don Arturo asked:

'And who is Signor Wotan, actually?'

What little I knew about him I owed to Wagner, but it was
enough to allow me to expatiate on the glories of the ancient
Germanic pantheon. It then occurred to me that the ancient Germans might have regarded such a piece of bark as an amulet. This
was a brainwave. The superstitious Don Arturo suddenly took
Wotan and his tree seriously, and Wotan's oak—or as much of it
as the case contained—was a success after all.

To resume, it was a cold winter's evening some time after Don
Arturo's death, and I was sitting opposite Donna Anna, watching
her sort through his old papers and feed them into the stove.
Suddenly, she held up Himmler's case with an exclamation of
delight:

'What a pretty box!'

Picking out the piece of bark, she made as if to sacrifice Wotan
to the gods of the Roman hearth—an act of sacrilege which I
only just managed to avert. Being a true Neapolitan, she knew
nothing about Wotan and his cult. She wanted to make me a
present of the sacred bark, but I declined the offer with thanks.
After all, it had not brought my good friend Don Arturo much
luck!

Himmler came to Rome for Don Arturo's funeral accompanied
by his whole general staff. Behind the bier, with heads bowed
and commanding tread, walked the Reichsführer-SS himself,
Wolff, his Chief of Staff, Heydrich, head of the Central State
Security Bureau, and General Daluege, head of the *Ordnungs-
polizei*. They effectively succeeded in turning an Italian State
funeral into a German one, a piece of tactlessness which did not
enhance their popularity. In the interval between Bocchini's death
and their arrival, I had, as I have already recounted, been dragged
into the dispute over the right of succession by my new patron
and protector, the Secretary of State for the Interior. For his
sake and that of my own peace of mind, I had done all I could

to ease Carmine Senise into Bocchini's vacant post. It was a mistake on my part but an excusable one, since Benito Mussolini also laboured under the delusion that the jovial Neapolitan was a Fascist and a friend of the Axis.

The only times I took any notice of Senise were when he or I was bored, in which case I would drop in and listen to a few Neapolitan anecdotes or catch up on the latest jokes. Police Attaché Kappler would undoubtedly have formed suspicions about Senise in the course of these interviews, but I was not as sharp as Kappler. It does not worry me that I never saw through his act. Senise deceived me and the whole Fascist hierarchy with all the histrionic skill of a Bourbon police chief, but I do not bear him a grudge. I had many a good laugh in his company, and how many policemen are good for a laugh?

When 1942 arrived, Germany started to take a more intensive interest in her Italian partner. In October of that year the Reichsführer-SS, who was already putting out the clandestine peace-feelers which have never been fully publicised to this day, was seized by an urge to visit Count Ciano. His proposal unleashed a storm of protests from Herr von Ribbentrop, who regarded it as an intrusion into his personal domain. Telegrams and telephone calls flew back and forth, but I had fortunately made all arrangements through the proper embassy channels, so everyone was satisfied of my loyalty.

Himmler arrived, fresh from a visit to the Russian front. His looks had not improved, but weariness had made him quieter and more cautious. Ciano had received me in private a few days before and announced his intention of trying to mollify Himmler's attitude towards the Vatican and monarchy. He greeted his guest at the Palazzo Chigi with that in mind, and I translated for him with the same end in view. The two men told each other what their requirements were and what information was to be passed on to their respective masters, Mussolini in Rome and Hitler at the Führer's Headquarters. Himmler endured a lecture on the 'loyalty' of the house of Savoy and the 'discretion' of the Vatican, and each wanted to know if the other was Hitler's successor-designate or Mussolini's heir, as the case might be. They evidently regarded themselves as such, because they parted under the agreeable impression that they were the future inheritors of their respective regimes. Knowing that Ciano would inform Crown Prince Umberto of what had been said at the interview immediately after it was over, I translated accordingly. An interpreter can sometimes exert influence, especially when his victims are as reliant upon him as mine were. Himmler declared the question of the Italian monarchy to be an internal concern of Germany's Axis partner, which was not strictly true but sufficed for the time being. He felt more reassured on this score when the Count charmingly hinted that the Palazzo Venezia possessed a secret file on certain private matters relating to the royal family and, more particularly, to the Prince of Piedmont, i.e. the Crown Prince. I secretly wondered why Mussolini had not appointed his son-in-law to succeed Bocchini, but kept the thought to myself.

That evening there was a gala dinner at the Ciano home. Edda not unnaturally absented herself, and her place was taken by a venerable lady-in-waiting who bored Himmler with interminable stories of life at court. On his other side sat a veritable Ninon de Lenclos, who irritated him by asking whether he always carried a pistol when he went out to dinner. It was a joyless occasion rendered even more so by the fact that, before setting forth, the guest of honour had suffered a mishap during a wash-and-brush-up in the private bathroom of the Villa Madama. This State guest-house with its Raphaelesque frescos had formerly belonged to an Italian marchese who had married an eccentric American woman and the millions that came with her. The bathroom was equipped with a multitude of taps and levers, and Himmler had accidentally pressed the perfume-button, enveloping himself in a cloud of jasmine scent. It was undoubtedly the first and last time that any uniform of his smelt of jasmine! He was very distressed, especially when the countesses and princesses present wrinkled their noses and asked indelicate questions. It was these questions which saved the evening, however, because I eventually came out with a discreet story on the subject of perfume which caused universal hilarity. For want of a better alternative, even Himmler joined in the laughter.

Next day Himmler had another meal in surroundings which

were equally repugnant to him, namely, the golf-club, where his host's harem and Princess Bismarck entertained him to lunch. It was as warm as only a Roman October can be, and the imperial aqueducts shimmered distantly in the Campagna as we drove out to Acqua Santa.

Himmler halted the car and sat down on a boundary-stone—an ancient one, of course. He polished his glasses carefully, listening to the fortissimo of the cricket orchestra around him. He looked even more pale and weary than he had done on his arrival, and was visibly depressed by the prospect of what lay ahead. Pointing to the aqueducts, he questioned me about their imperial builders. I mentioned Caligula and Claudius. Being the son of a Bavarian schoolmaster, he knew far more about these gentlemen than I did, though his knowledge derived from school-books rather than Suetonius. Mopping his moist brow with a handkerchief which, though clean enough, would have been disdained by the Caesars, he bemoaned Caligula's insanity and praised the skilful assurance with which Claudius had retained his seat on the tottering throne in spite of Messalina. He waxed quite melancholy, presumably comparing their fate and that of the aqueducts with his own and that of the Third Reich, which was already showing signs of dilapidation. Replacing his glasses, he assured me that I would not be so cheerful if I knew all that he did. I only grasped the terrible truth of this remark in 1945.

The imminence of our arrival at the golf-club spared me any further revelations, and the silvery laughter of the golf-club belles put paid to Himmler's historical reminiscences and topical disclosures. Instead, he made a few uncalled-for comments on the capitalistic basis of golf. Princess Bismarck blenched, but he was civil enough to acknowledge its status as a sport and pronounce it a suitable game for a Party élite to play.

Before he left Rome I lent him Signorina Bibi's assistance in buying Christmas presents from a smart and appropriately expensive Roman scent shop. She alone knows what Himmler bought for the ladies of the Third Reich, but she is a princess today and no doubt prefers to remember other shopping expeditions. All she told me, giggling, was that the counter had been piled with boxes of perfumed flowers of every hue, scent-sprays in Murano glass and perfumes of an aphrodisiac potency unknown in Germany. Himmler suffered himself to be addressed as 'Excellency' and allowed Bibi to talk him into buying everything she found most elegant and least practical. I have never heard what effect these presents had when placed beneath German Christmas-trees, but I suspect they must have caused as much of a stir as the jasmine scent in the bathroom at the Villa Madama.

On 8 November, after Rommel's glorious advance had been halted, the Allies landed in North Africa, and on 20 November Reich Marshal Göring paid a surprise visit to Rome. There followed a monster conference at the headquarters of the Italian Grand General Staff, attended by every available Italian field marshal and general and by my new friend Buffarini-Guidi. In view of the military character of the proceedings Buffarini-Guidi desperately sought my moral support against the German military leaders present, who were headed by Rommel and Kesselring as well as Göring.

The de facto Minister of the Interior—Mussolini only assumed the title for prestige reasons—was as usual wearing a heavy platinum ring set with a superb diamond such as only an Italian Fascist Minister could afford. When Hermann Göring demanded a mass levy on the Italian people in view of the increasingly threatening situation in the Mediterranean area, the plump little Secretary of State wriggled uncomfortably and asked me in a whisper if I thought the Reich Marshal would accept his ring as a souvenir and a substitute for the mass levy. I did not translate the proposal, despite the Reich Marshal's covetous glances in the ring's direction, and devoted myself to less agreeable but more military subjects. The conference was a Göring-size affair lasting nearly two hours, throughout which time I had to translate statistics and technical points of which I understood nothing in German, let alone Italian.

I soon clashed with Field Marshal Rommel, who took an immediate dislike to me and whose attitude towards the Italians encouraged me to believe—erroneously, as history has since demonstrated—that he was an out-and-out Nazi. I had already been of service to Hermann Göring on several minor occasions, but this was the first time I had interpreted for Field Marshal

Albert Kesselring. My first impression of him was a pleasant one, and the fact that I remained his favourite interpreter until the war's end seems to indicate that he found me equally congenial.

After this conference, which produced a lot of talk and very little action, I accompanied the Reich Marshal to Sicily on a tour of inspection. For all his military sins and human failings, Göring was a human being and not a high-precision machine like Himmler. He prepared to descend from his luxurious special train in a uniform worthy of Lohengrin, but when I pointed out that a few well-aimed tomatoes flung by members of the starving population would soon turn his gleaming white tunic another colour he went off and changed it without a word. Despite the many things about him which the ever-critical Italians found to laugh at, his love of pomp and his imperatorial mien endeared him to them more than any of the other German leaders. Having boosted his popularity with them by broadcasting his fame as a prince of peace at the Munich Conference of 1938, I felt obliged to ensure that his extravagant manner did not grate too harshly on their strained nerves at the present time.

Once, at a meeting with the Italian Minister of Transport at the Villa Madama, I noticed that Göring was bored to tears. I was just as bored, but Cini, one of the wealthiest and most influential industrialists in the country and a grand seigneur to his fingertips, deserved better treatment. I shot him a glance—any interpreter worthy of the name can afford to do so occasionally —and the Count-Senator-Minister bellowed at the dumbstruck Reich Marshal and demanded his attention and co-operation.

Everyone froze except the Minister and me, who had provoked the outbursts, but Göring mended his manners immediately. He sat up, became more alert, pestered me with points of detail, and took notes. The meeting was a success, and even produced a few results, one of them being that Göring pronounced Count Cini to be the only Italian, apart from Mussolini, who had ever impressed him.

Shortly before Christmas, of all times, the Führer's Headquarters requested conferences, first with Mussolini, who showed no eagerness to visit the snow-girt forests of Rastenburg, and then with Ciano and Count Cavallero, Chief of the Italian

General Staff. Quite why I should have been taken along still escapes me. The main purpose of the visit was an Axis confrontation with the ill-fated Laval, but Ciano's perfect French rendered my presence superfluous.

Presumably, I was supposed to entertain the travellers during the long journey in Mussolini's special train. They certainly needed entertaining. Things were going wretchedly for the Axis in Africa, Russia and elsewhere. Mussolini favoured negotiations with Russia, Laval's problems were legion, and disaster was looming ever more clearly over Stalingrad. Although the special train was grossly over-heated, its refrigerators contained enough fresh flowers for a new set of table decorations every day. The table itself was kept supplied with choice Italian fare, and each passenger had his own steward. The handsome Count and the wily Chief of Staff detested each other, so there was no lack of edifying incident. I had several days in which to observe Ciano's appalling table manners and Cavallero's gourmandise. His native Piedmont was the home of the white truffles of Alba, and every day after meals I was obliged to write down under his direction, not a formula for remedying the desperate military situation, but a recipe for preparing these delicacies in the subtlest possible way. It was all too reminiscent of Tsar Nicholas II's last journey in the imperial train, with life continuing as usual in the luxurious drawing-rooms and sleeping-car while, outside, the established order collapsed in ruins.

For the first time on one of these special-train journeys, I was afraid—afraid in spite of the perverse luxury surrounding me. I would gladly have bidden farewell to the Count, the Field Marshal, the table decorations and the rich food, and gone to eat spaghetti and drink golden Frascati at Isola Farnese.

The visit was soon over. There were no negotiations with Russia, of course, and Ciano was furious that Laval had enjoyed more success than he, whom no one at Headquarters could endure. Duly embittered, he went back to the golf-club, there to entertain his frolicsome lady-friends with descriptions of Rastenburg's evil-smelling huts and divulge State secrets which they promptly passed on to their Anglo-Saxon relatives. I myself travelled back to Rome to unpack the crates and chests crammed with over-lavish Christmas presents which had been bestowed on the Italians by their Axis colleagues in the North. I had just finished arranging a superb Nymphenburg '*Gelbe Jagd*' dinner service on the presentation table of an Italian minister when the bells of Rome rang in Christmas Eve. Now that the regime was starting to fall apart at the seams, I had a distinct feeling that I would not be unpacking any ministerial crates and chests at the same time next year.

Germany's position at the beginning of 1943 was equally depressing, as I had a chance to gauge on 30 January, when Hitler received a delegation of Italian Fascists at the Rastenburg headquarters to mark the tenth anniversary of his accession to power. Back in Rome, Mussolini had just taken his first step towards political suicide by dismissing Marshal Cavallero and replacing him as Chief of the Grand General Staff by General Ambrosio. The new appointee may have been more suited to the post militarily, but it must have filtered through, even to the Duce's ears, that Ambrosio was a confidant of the King and anything but a loyal Fascist. The move was even worse from the German angle. Cavallero, who resembled a captain of industry in uniform, had been an uncritical admirer of the German military leaders and a lethargic yes-man. Ambrosio detested us, like all Italy's senior army officers, and it was obvious that he would make serious trouble for us before long.

The appointment of this ardent royalist, soon to be followed by the dismissal of Buffarini-Guidi, was a clear sign of Mussolini's growing isolation. However, this did nothing to dampen the youthful enthusiasm of the Italian delegation mentioned above.

I reproduce my description of the afternoon's proceedings in the form in which I recorded it at the time. It may still serve to give a picture of the gloomiest anniversary celebrations I was ever privileged to attend. I called it 'Frederick the Great before Stalingrad':

'It was late afternoon on 30 January 1943, and beechwood logs were crackling peacefully in the hearth of the Führer's room at the Rastenburg headquarters. The room, simply furnished in pale wood throughout, was only half-heated because Hitler abominated any form of warmth as debilitating and enervating. The dire exigencies of the moment were as little apparent in the varied assortment of beverages and refreshments on the groaning tea-table as they were in the clean-shaven, white-jacketed young SS orderlies, whose blue eyes watched their idol's lips with unremitting devotion. Hitler had just welcomed the Fascist delegation which had come from Italy to congratulate him on the tenth anniversary of his accession to power. Nothing in this ritual act, which was witnessed by Reich Foreign Minister von Ribbentrop and the Italian Ambassador to Berlin, Alfieri, distinguished it from similar ceremonies held in previous years, although these had been accompanied by the cannon-roar of victory.

'Mussolini had sent a fair number of regional administrators from the various provinces under the leadership of General of the Militia Tarabini, who looked like a retired senior civil servant. Gorgeous new uniforms had been tailored for them at home. Countless thousands of their compatriots at the front, virtually unprotected against the icy blizzards of the Russian winter, would have been saved from frostbite by these tall riding-boots and high-necked, ankle-length greatcoats of heavy black cloth, but no one at the Palazzo Venezia had thought of that.

'Only the specially privileged *Federali* or gauleiters of Turin, Florence and Leghorn sat with Hitler himself. Their colleagues were regaled at a separate table and consoled with assurances that Hitler would address them personally before they left. The Führer gave no outward indication of what was conveyed to him by the pale-faced and agitated aides who hurried in with brief reports from time to time, namely, that Stalingrad was on the point of collapse. Tea-table conversation was centred on the three cities whose representatives were sitting with the host. Hitler launched into rapturous reminiscences of the last day of his Italian visit in May 1938, which had been spent in Florence.

' "I shall never, never permit the loveliest city in Italy to be bombarded by ruthless criminals," he declared, and went on to promise that the latest anti-aircraft guns would be dispatched to the Arno. Neither Turin, capital of Piedmont and cradle of the royal house, nor Leghorn, home of the Ciano dynasty, could compete with Florence in this respect. Hitler disliked both the King and Count Ciano, so there was no talk of any special military protection for their native cities.

'Herr von Ribbentrop did not consider such measures necessary either. In his best know-all manner he disclosed some top-secret information about America. According to his contacts, feeling there had become so anti-Roosevelt that the downfall of this "criminal in the criminal hands of a small clique of Jews and freemasons" was only a matter of time—exactly how much time his eager listeners were not told. Instead, they were treated to a lecture on America and the Americans in general:

' "I know them, I know their country. A country devoid of culture, devoid of music—above all, a people without soldiers, a people which will never be able to decide the war from the air. When has a Jewified nation like that ever become a race of fighters and flying aces?"

'He knew America, certainly, but he omitted to tell the young Italians who hung upon his words, while Alfieri smiled maliciously, that he had gleaned his knowledge as a champagne salesman for Henkell, his wife's family firm. He could not have even if he had wanted to, because Hitler leapt into the breach with eyes aglow:

' "America! America equals Jews everywhere—Jews in literature, Jews in politics, Jews in commerce and industry and a completely Jewified President at the top. It cannot be the will of Providence that I and my people should be seriously obstructed by this nation of shopkeepers and traders. History decrees otherwise, and I shall not rest until I have changed the face of the world in collaboration with you, my Italian friends. Please tell your great Duce that! "

'Heedless of such prophecies, more and more grave-faced aides and senior officers had been coming in to report the latest news. Adolf Hitler got up to show his guests Anton Graff's portrait of Frederick the Great, who had been staring down at this highly un-Prussian tea-party like an astonished eagle.

' "How often, when labouring under the heavy burden of responsibility laid upon me, have I derived consolation and renewed strength from looking into this man's eyes! I have felt ashamed of my own weariness each time, remembering how much the great king, standing alone against a hostile world, endured in sacred self-sacrifice on his people's behalf, and ultimately achieved.

To stand before this picture and request victory for the fulfilment of my historic mission is like praying."

'Der Alte Fritz continued to gaze down at his successor and
the latter's Italian guests with undiminished astonishment, but
his gaze had a tonic effect. Pale-faced and consumed by some
inner fire, Adolf Hitler bore down on the group of Italians that
had assembled in one of the passages of the Führer's bunker.

' "At this solemn hour, when you bring me the good wishes
of Allied Fascist Italy, my young Germans are fighting and dying
at the Thermopylae of Stalingrad for the survival of Europe and
its civilisation. No one knows better than I what enormous sacrifices I must demand from my people in order to prevent the
barbaric hordes from invading our ancient and cultural domain.
The dead of Stalingrad will sow seeds of a better and more equit-
able future and a new Europe in whose reconstruction you, my
young Italian friends, are destined to have a prominent share
under your Duce. In this, my men's hour of supreme trial amid
ice and blizzards on the borders of Asia, never forget what the
greatest German in history wrote to the English Prime Minister
Pitt in summer 1761, at the most critical moment of his career:
'Two guiding-stars direct me in my labours: honour, and the
welfare of the State with whose government God has entrusted
me. These are what place me under an obligation never to do
anything which might redound to my shame in the eyes of
the nation, and to pledge my last drop of blood for its deliverance
and renown. Armed with such principles no man ever yields to
the foe, and with them alone Rome maintained her existence after
the battle of Cannae.'

' "I shall never yield either, nor will the battle for Stalingrad
become a Cannae. The spirit of Frederick the Great fights beside
us, and Providence will not desert us, just as it did not desert him
in his darkest hour. Tell that to my friend, your great Duce, and
proclaim it, when you are back home again, whenever you are
summoned to lead at the Duce's behest." '

Thus spake the Führer and Supreme Commander of the German forces, on land, sea and in the air, only two days before the
final collapse of Stalingrad and the greatest military defeat Ger-

many had so far sustained under his leadership. I was not present when the members of the unhappy delegation reported to Benito Mussolini on their return, but they certainly did not rush off to Stalingrad to fight, nor, on 25 July of the same year, did they evince any willingness to fight and die for their Duce, let alone Frederick the Great.

On 5 February, whether or not their report had any bearing on his unexpected decision, Mussolini terminated Galeazzo Ciano's seven years' tenure of office at the Foreign Ministry and added the Palazzo Chigi to his own collection of ministries. My personal guess was that the Count would be far more dangerous in his new role as Italian Ambassador to the Vatican than he had been at the Palazzo Chigi. Surrounded by female admirers of high and low degree, he could now hatch plots, instigate cabals and indulge his wanton ambitions under far less supervision than before, but this was none of my business. I was not paid to spy for Ribbentrop or anyone else, I am glad to say. I was delighted to note, when I met Ciano at the golf-club after his resignation, that the ladies had not deserted him as men would have done if one of their number had fallen from grace. After greeting me with his usual spurious bonhomie, he gave me a highly coloured account of how he had taken leave of his father-in-law and stressed the immense contributions he had made to the Axis war-effort during his term at the Foreign Ministry. I listened with well-disguised amusement, and was even more amused later on when I read the precise opposite in his diaries.

I come now to the two meetings which took place between Hitler and Mussolini in the months immediately following. They were the last occasions on which the Duce met his friend in his capacity as head of the Italian government, leader of the Fascist Party and incumbent of numerous ministries. I christened my original description of these meetings 'Swan-song', and will retain the title now, even though zoologists have long ago consigned the swan's death-song to the realm of legend.

'Schloss Klessheim, Salzburg, 6–7 April 1943.

'Mussolini's health had gone from bad to worse since his visit to Russia in August 1941. His old sickness was far too deep-seated to be cured by gruel and rice-soup, optimistic bulletins and coveys of whispering doctors. Victory and success would, perhaps, have been the best remedies for this schizophrenic phase of the neglected youthful ailment which Arturo Bocchini had once referred to when we were alone together, but victory and success were precisely what had been lacking since the loss of Stalingrad and the Axis setbacks in Africa during the spring of 1943.

'Mussolini's mental state could be gauged from the regime's latest "changing of the guard", which took place early in February 1943. The Duce had dismissed two loyal henchmen, Buffarini-Guidi and Renato Ricci, and entrusted the Ministry of the Interior to the born traitor Albini, whose brow bore the mark of Cain for all the world to see. Although he could still have kept an eye on Ciano's escapades if he had left him at the Foreign Ministry, he preferred to replace him by a typical Foreign Office official who was not only not his son-in-law but anti-German as well.

'The Duce had done it at last. Voluntarily, and by the exercise of his absolute power, he had surrounded himself with men who, like Bastianini, Prefect Albini and General Ambrosio, Cavallero's successor, yearned for nothing so ardently as his own downfall. When informed of this reshuffle—after the event, as usual—the King rubbed his hands with glee and gladly allowed his prime minister to go and see Hitler, gaze deep into his eyes in the old manner, and state his requirements. Benito Mussolini boarded his special train accompanied by his new Chief of the General Staff, Foreign Minister and private secretary, De Cesare. Also invited to join the party were Ambassador von Mackensen, General von Rintelen, the German military attaché in Rome, and myself.

'The official purpose of the trip, behind which—as anyone who knew the Italians could see—lurked the spectre of a separate peace, was to advocate an armistice with Russia if at all practicable, propose a grandiose new 'European programme', obtain more military aid, and secure the withdrawal from Russia of the Italian Second Army Corps. The Duce seemed firmly determined to achieve results this time, and I did my best to strengthen him and his entourage in that resolve—with what success it will be seen.

'Under these auspices, with no floral decorations and a far less ambitious cuisine than in the past, the special train travelled northwards to Schloss Klessheim.

'It was a tired, ageing man with sunken cheeks and a pallid face increasingly dominated by large dark eyes who was greeted by his German opposite number. The two dictators gazed deep into each other's eyes and exchanged a long, firm handshake, reminding me of Manzoni's *Promessi sposi*. Mussolini at once disappeared into his private quarters, while members of his personal bodyguard, under the command of Inspector Agnesina, infuriated their German colleagues by searching the cellars of the Schloss for potential threats to the Duce's life—though it never became clear who might have wanted to poison him.

'Unpoisoned, nourished on soups and vegetables, and inaccessible to virtually everyone, the Italian dictator kept to his rooms throughout his time at Klessheim. The only person he saw was Hitler, with whom he conferred at great length once or twice a day. I was not present. The two men conversed in private, with results which were—in view of Mussolini's rudimentary knowledge of German—predictable. The only time I was called in I had to listen to a two-hour lecture by Hitler on the historical importance of Frederick the Great's father and Frederick the Great himself, a dubious pleasure which I had already sampled at the Führer's Headquarters on 30 January.

'Mussolini's Foreign Office advisers assailed me with requests to translate the terms of their series of new European programmes, and the newly fledged Chief of the General Staff, Ambrosio, did his best to convince Göring and Field Marshal Keitel, through me, of Italy's disastrous position in relation to the threatened invasion of Sicily. The German military leaders shrouded themselves in a rose-coloured fog of optimism, especially Grand Admiral Dönitz, who prophesied the inevitable success of his submarines and submarine warfare programme in truly rapturous vein.

'In the course of one conference, Hitler gave vent to the following assurances:

' "Rest assured, Duce, there will be no invasion of Sicily. The fortress of Verdun withstood every onslaught for months on end during the last world war, and I shall ensure that our enemies meet with as little success this time, on the shores of the Mediterranean: Tunis must become the African Verdun!"

'The Italian military leaders present paled visibly, but Keitel gave a deferential nod of agreement and Reich Marshal Göring concluded the discussion with the portentous words:

' "You will undoubtedly succeed, my Führer, as always." '

'Benito Mussolini expressed a sudden wish to see Heinrich Himmler. The idea appealed to no one but himself, but this time he was adamant. Delighted with this proof of his importance and relishing the annoyance which the meeting would cause everyone, especially Herr von Ribbentrop, Himmler came hurrying over from nearby Obersalzberg and spent two hours alone with the Duce and me.

'The main question submitted to him concerned the measures he had taken or proposed to take to counter the internal unrest which the long duration of the war must be causing within the Reich as well as Italy. Himmler impressed his questioner by promptly ticking off the steps he had taken to this end. He laid particular emphasis on the the far-reaching security measures which had been devised to safeguard Adolf Hitler and his headquarters. Having described the élite SS units assigned to this task, he astonished the Duce by proposing the formation of a new Italian division destined for his own personal protection. He offered some top quality matériel from Waffen-SS stocks—Tiger tanks, flame-throwers, mortars, anti-aircraft guns, etc.—together with some first-class, highly experienced SS instructors. In short, he suggested the setting up of a brand-new Italian *Leibstandarte* recruited exclusively from young members of the Fascist militia. The Duce glanced at me in frozen silence before declining with thanks. He appeared to feel the ignominious nature of the offer deeply, even though I exerted all my diplomatic skill in an attempt to gloss over the tactlessness of the suggestion. He then asked Himmler's opinion of Carmine Senise, his Neapolitan police chief. I mentally wrung my hands as Himmler sang Senise's praises in fulsome tones, thereby sealing his fate. The Duce could not hear a foreigner eulogise one of his minions without nourishing the sort of dark suspicions which used to breed in the mind of a Roman emperor.

'This concluded the audience. Himmler had grasped none of its implications. The Duce had grasped a great many, and so had I, but I received the cordial thanks of both parties. I was also a delighted witness of the scene outside the door as a deeply suspicious Ribbentrop tried to induce his rival to divulge something of what had gone on inside.'

On that note, the Klessheim visit came to an end. Thanks to the indispensable and indefatigable Dr Meissner, State Secretary in the Presidential Chancellery, it had been anything but a success for Benito Mussolini and his associates. Apart from a historical survey of the Prussian kings, the submarine optimism of Admiral Dönitz and Reich Marshal Göring's conviction that the Führer would 'pull it off' yet again, all the Italian dictator secured was the withdrawal of his mauled and battered Russian army corps. There was no talk of putting out any peace-feelers in Russia's direction, and Ribbentrop's watering-down of the Italian proposal for a European programme turned it into a shadow of its original self.

I wondered if Mussolini would resist Himmler's tempting suggestion of a Roman bodyguard indefinitely, decided that he would not, and prepared myself accordingly. The near future would show whether or not there was to be a return to the days when German mercenaries served on Italian soil.

Only a few weeks after the sick man of the Tiber had visited Schloss Klessheim, my suspicions were confirmed. I was not unduly busy at this period, having had little contact with the new men of the Italian regime since the death of Arturo Bocchini and the ousting of Buffarini-Guidi and Renato Ricci. Carmine Senise's dismissal shortly after the Klessheim visit and his replacement by Renzo Chierici, ex-chief of the forest militia, ex-Prefect of Pola, and a man unknown both to me and Italy at large, had absolved me from my routine chats at the Ministry of the Interior. I occasionally met Galeazzo Ciano disporting himself with undiminished sex appeal amid the green pastures of the golf-club, but this was a form of amusement, not a job. Ambassador von

Mackensen confided his growing concern with Prussian thoroughness and friendly candour, but I could do little to help him. All
in all, there was virtually nothing for me to do as an interpreter
during the months between April and July, so I decided to improve
my sadly neglected mind by spending more time at the opera.
Senise had been as fanatical a music-lover as only an Italian
police chief can be, and I still had a seat permanently at my
disposal because Signor Chierici had perpetuated Senise's con-
cession on the ubiquitous principle *non si sà mai*—'you never
know'.

I was at the opera house one evening early in May, far from
the hurly-burly of war and politics, listening to Orpheus pour
out his grief for Eurydice, when I heard a commotion which
formed no part of the Monteverdi opera in question. Doors were
flung open and slammed shut, provoking universal indignation,
and my first thought was that the Allies had carried out their
long-awaited landing on the coast near Rome. Then footsteps
thundered into my box and I was seized upon by Bastianini,
Ciano's successor. His voice rang with excitement, like that of
Orpheus reunited with his beloved spouse on the stage.

'There you are at last—in the theatre, of all places! Really,
Dollman!'

I invited him to sit down and at least hear Orpheus complete
his aria, but my suggestion was brushed aside. Bastianini could
scarcely speak for agitation.

'The Duce has been expecting you for the past hour—we looked
everywhere for you. You must come along at once.'

I rose with a sigh and accompanied my pale and reproachful-
looking escorts to the Palazzo Venezia.

I had no idea why Benito Mussolini had disturbed me in the
middle of the opera. He was sitting in his huge office, and I could
see the whites of his eyes as I set out on the long walk from the
door to his desk. But nothing happened. As always when he was
without an audience to impress, his manner was mild and polite.
He asked me to sit down. I think he was secretly amused that
any German should be at the opera at this critical juncture, especially after his recent pep-talk on the royal house of Prussia at
Schloss Klessheim.

Then he spoke, briefly and to the point. I was to contact Signor Himmler at once and inform him that he, the Duce, had decided to form a Leibstandarte of his own. Signor Himmler was to waste no time in sending officer and NCO instructors, guns, ranks and whatever else was needed for the setting-up of such a division. Then he asked how long it would take. I had no idea, and once again I sensed that he was amused. I stammered something about 'a few weeks', but this was not good enough. I was enjoined to see that he got his division at once—today rather than tomorrow. He had already instructed the head of the Fascist Militia, General Enzo Galbiati, to earmark the flower of the young Fascists under his command for the new division. I was further enjoined to run an eye over this youthful élite and work in close collaboration with Galbiati.

I promised to do as I was told, feeling highly dismayed. I had never helped to set up a German division, let alone an Italian one. At the same time, I was furious that the dictator had not thought of all this at Klessheim, where he could have received far more expert and detailed information from Heinrich Himmler. However, that was his affair. With a *'Mi fido di Lei, caro Dollman'*, I was graciously dismissed. I wondered whether to return to Orpheus and Eurydice, but my Bavarian, if not Prussian, sense of duty prevailed. In this Austro-Bavarian frame of mind, I decided to find someone who could shoulder the responsibilities of my new office, and quickly settled on Ambassador von Mackensen, who was an honorary SS-Brigadeführer.

Von Mackensen was touched by my frankness and my tactful desire to spare him the repercussions of the renewed struggle for power which would inevitably have flared up between Himmler and Ribbentrop, his chief, if I had transmitted Mussolini's instructions to Berlin direct. We drafted a report together. He was adept in drafting such communications, and he also knew the devious channels through which they could reach Himmler without giving offence to Ribbentrop.

Such was the birth of 'M' Division, Mussolini's personal bodyguard, which distinguished itself by its inactivity on the night of 25–26 July 1943, when Benito Mussolini was incarcerated in a Carabinieri barracks on the King's orders. I did not dream then that anyone would ever suggest that I take command of it and lead it on Rome in an attempt to liberate him—but more of that later.

The next few weeks were devoted to 'divisional tasks'. I inspected the young Fascist recruits and was gratified by the confidence which they seemed to repose in my military ability. I went to meet the anti-aircraft guns, mortars, Tiger tanks and other weapons as they arrived. I also welcomed the instructors that came with them, all of whom were veterans of the Russian campaign and most of whom were disabled. Unlike the Italians, they guessed at once that I had no idea what I was doing, and enjoyed the joke hugely. Then came the proud day when the Italian Leibstandarte was reviewed, first by the ambassador and me and then by Mussolini and his entire staff. The Duce beamed, the Chief of the General Staff scowled, and the men of the division, Italians and Germans, glowed with pride—but too late. By that time— it was 10 July 1943—the Allies had landed in Sicily.

Only nine days later, under the impact of this landing and other unpleasant developments, the two dictators held another surprise meeting, this time on Italian soil. I reproduce my contemporary account below. It was the last occasion on which Mussolini met his German friend as Duce del Fascismo and head of the Italian government. When they next met, in September of the same year, the man who thanked Adolf Hitler for his release from the Gran Sasso by German paratroops under the command of Otto Skorzeny was destined to be an eagle freed from captivity but bereft of talons.

'Treviso-Feltre, 19 July 1943.

'The Italian Foreign Ministry had picked a strange location for the conference. First to reach the airfield at Treviso, a provincial town in Northern Italy, was Benito Mussolini, who had piloted his own plane there to welcome Field Marshal Kesselring, Ambassador von Mackensen, and the members of their staff. Hitler and his entourage, who looked worried and out of sorts, were greeted with chill and unwonted formality by a guard of honour drawn from the Italian air force.

'The Italian Chief of the General Staff, Ambrosio, scarcely

bothered to observe the conventions when greeting his German allies. The members of Hitler's personal bodyguard advanced on me in all their splendour and bombarded me with questions about the existence or non-existence of security precautions. Their mood did not improve during the long drive from Treviso to the enchanting Renaissance villa owned by Gaggia, the Italian financier, at Feltre. Indeed, their suspicions were only heightened by the sight of the gentle deer grazing on the green lawns, the golden pheasants and peacocks stalking round the classical statues, the groaning tables laid beside cool streams for the delectation of the guests. General Ambrosio's soldiers lurked behind tree and bush, and the precipitous slopes of the Alps loomed around us on every side. It was a perfect setting for a trap. With pistols cocked, Hitler's handful of trusty henchmen ringed the villa. They were convinced that a new Bartholomew's Day massacre was in the offing, and my assurances to the contrary were rejected with condescending smiles.

'What they did not know was that Ambrosio and Bastianini, backed by the usually bland Italian Ambassador to Berlin, Alfieri, had spent the luncheon interval trying to persuade their dictator to present Hitler with an ultimatum. Under this, Italy would abrogate the Pact of Steel unless granted immediate and effective military assistance in Sicily and large-scale support by the German air force.

'Their efforts were unavailing. Back in the conference room, Hitler presented a tediously detailed account of all the military blunders and sins of omission so far committed by his Italian ally. Instead of receiving aid, planes, anti-aircraft guns, heavy artillery, tanks and mortars, the Duce had to listen, for hours on end, to allegations that he had been consistently deceived by his own generals as to Italy's military strength and state of preparedness ever since the outbreak of war. The distressing word "Greece' was mentioned, and for the first time the German corporal told the Italian corporal in plain terms that this ill-starred campaign was responsible for the difficulties that had arisen in Russia. The Italians gathered round their pale, tired, nervous Napoleon with ominous expressions, and I had a momentary feeling that all of us, the dictators and their entourages, would leave this *buen retiro*

as captives of the icy-mannered General Ambrosio—to the joy
and delight of His Majesty in Rome.
'Though lost itself, it may have been Rome that saved us.
Adolf Hitler had just reached a climactic stage in his recrimina-
tions when an elegant Job's messenger in the person of an air force
officer violated protocol by bursting in excitedly with a slip of
paper in his hand. He reported, in a tone which spoke of fire,
smoke and destruction, that the Eternal City had just suffered its
first heavy air-raid of the war. Mussolini sprang to his feet. His
friend, long accustomed to such unpleasant announcements,
calmly remained seated. After the Italians had conferred together,
the Duce turned to Hitler. Realising that he had to do something
for Mussolini's shattered nerves, the Führer muttered something
about unshakable confidence in victory and the dispatching of
air squadrons and divisions to Sicily, without, however, going
into greater detail. This brought the conference to an end.
'Ambrosio's soldiers disappeared, Hitler's trusty bodyguards
released their safety-catches, and we all drove back to Treviso.
No one took any more notice of us. Rome burned blood-red
against the gloomy back-cloth of the Italians' thoughts, and
Mussolini and his men heaved an audible sigh of relief when the
German plane bore its load northwards again. The dictators' handshake was as brief as their farewell gaze.
'Then a miracle occurred. Benito Mussolini was tired of Job's
messengers and Adolf Hitler, tired of the whole inauspicious
day. Donning a snow-white flying suit, he strode towards the
aeroplane which he was to pilot back to Rome. On the gangway
he turned and faced us, staring down at the astonished Field
Marshal Kesselring, the speechless Mackensen, the contemptu-
ously smiling Ambrosio, the despondent gentlemen of the Italian
Foreign Office. With eyes aglow and hand raised in the Fascist
salute, he took leave of us like a man bound for a victory celebration. I thought of Nero, and how gladly he would have undertaken the same journey, not to set light to Rome but to see it in
flames.
'But Benito Mussolini was no Nero. He was a beaten man
seeking encouragement in a gesture, just as he had sought it before
the March on Rome in 1922. He did not know that this was to

be his last imperial salute, and that five days later he would be a prisoner at his place of destination.

'I was sorry for him, but I was even sorrier for Rome, which I loved with every fibre of my being.' (*Written on 28 July 1943*)

VIII

TWENTY-FOUR FATEFUL HOURS

I COULD not have prevented the abortive conference of 19 July, still less the bombing of Rome by the Allies, but I had at least done something. I had travelled to Treviso on a secret mission, and the person who had entrusted me with that mission was Donna Rachele Mussolini, the wife of the Italian dictator.

I had never met her before, but few people in Rome apart from her family and immediate circle ever came into contact with her. Donna Rachele had remained steadfastly in character throughout her life—no mean feat for the wife of a dictator. She had grown up in the humblest circumstances, and her father's pocket had not run to more than two classes at primary school. As a child she had been employed by a gardener at a wage of three lire per month. Writing of her youth, she recalls:

> Very early in my childhood I learned to get up at five a.m. and stay on my feet all day long, and ever since then I have found it impossible to sit still for more than ten minutes at any one time. Even when we lived in the Villa Torlonia (*Mussolini's private residence in Rome*), I found it simply impossible not to help my maidservant with the housework in spite of my husband's exhortations. ('Do you really have to tire yourself out?' he used to say.)

Donna Rachele never entertained, never went anywhere. The court saw her very seldom, the diplomatic corps and her husband's ministers and their families never. A true peasant-woman from the hot-blooded, passionate Romagna, she lived exclusively for her husband and children, whom she watched over with Argus-eyed vigilance. The most amusing stories about her private intelligence and surveillance network used to circulate in Rome. Her agents were the police constables assigned to guard her, her housemaids, gardeners and washerwomen, the traders in the public markets where she still did her own shopping in person, and all who had been convinced Fascists in the Party's heyday but were now disillusioned by the growth of corruption among their former leaders and the increasing incompetence that went with it. She loved as ardently as she hated, and I have always cherished the highest admiration for her. I am certain that much, if not everything, would have gone differently if Mussolini had heeded her warnings before it was too late.

I was first caught up in the cogs of the Mussolini machine at the end of June 1943, when my old friend Buffarini-Guidi, ex-Secretary of State for the Interior, informed me that Donna Rachele wished to speak to me at his home in the strictest confidence. I was forbidden to tell anyone, even Herr von Mackensen, and had to slink into the house through the rear entrance before being conducted to Buffarini's library, where Italy's second lady received me.

I had often seen Queen Empress Elena and admired her Slav beauty and the regal bearing which even her bad taste in clothes could not disguise, but I had never found her *simpatica*, nor had she ever attempted to hide how much she disliked the Germans. Donna Rachele made absolutely no pretence of being smart. Her get-up was that of a middle-aged provincial woman in her Sunday best. She had plenty of poise, however, and demonstrated it when she graciously gave me her hand and thanked me for calling on her. Then she sat down, but only for the prescribed ten minutes. It was stiflingly hot in the beautiful room, which was lined from floor to ceiling with expensive leather-bound editions of the Roman classics. Like us, Donna Rachele was perspiring. The scant traces of make up on her cheeks melted, and her handkerchief soon proved inadequate to stem the tide. Buffarini-Guidi disappeared and came back with one of his wife's dainty wisps of lace, so much more elegant than anything Donna Rachele possessed. Mussolini's wife rummaged in her scuffed old handbag, looking for something—presumably her powder. She failed to find it and sighed. Her strongly-boned peasant's face looked worn and tired, but her keen eyes never lost their sparkle. Suddenly, she jumped up and began to pace rapidly to and fro. We got up too, of course. The plump ex-minister leant against a collected edition of the letters of Cicero, to whom he bore such a strong inner resemblance, while I found myself standing beneath Virgil's *Aeneid*, which had bored me since childhood. I was not bored now.

What followed was the shrewdest and most passionate philippic I had ever heard. The weary middle-aged woman before me became transformed, minute by minute, into a second Livia, a second Cassandra. In denunciatory tones, she presented a full and accurate picture of the disasters confronting Italy, Fascism, her husband and her family. I listened—uncharacteristically—with bated breath.

The tirade lasted nearly an hour. Donna Rachele began by inveighing against her husband's former henchmen, who were, she said, only waiting for an opportunity to desert the sinking ship. She described the luxury surrounding her and other wives of the old guard, and asked where it came from. She castigated the new ministers, and Buffarini-Guidi, who had not previously been one of her confidants, gave a gratified nod. She spoke of her profound lack of faith in the royal court of Victor Emmanuel III in particular, and complained of the incomprehensible apathy of her husband, who regarded treachery on the King's part as out of the question.

We continued to sweat. The lukewarm lemonade which our host brought in—the most that Donna Rachele drank was an occasional glass of Romagna wine—did nothing to alleviate our condition, but we hung spellbound on her words. The word 'treason' recurred time and time again in her monologue. She described most of the senior military leaders as traitors, referred to their English and American family connections, and predicted that, thanks to their treachery, Sicily would fall very quickly if the Allies landed. I recalled her prediction only too vividly a few weeks later.

She then came to the 'bane' of her family. I froze for a moment, scarcely able to believe my ears. Her words amounted to a death-sentence passed on her own son-in-law, the handsome, charming, effetely elegant Crown Prince of Fascism—Galeazzo Ciano, Edda's husband.

'He was the one who brought unhappiness into our family. With him, luxury, social fads and high living take priority over the Party and over us all. I am fully aware that his lady-friends at the golf-club know all there is to know, and I am equally aware that his vanity and ambition mean more to him than his links with our family—but Edda will always be a Mussolini. She is one of us, even though she often seems to have turned into a Ciano under Galeazzo's influence. I have finished now, my dear Dollman. I know what you are going to ask me, so I will answer your question in advance.

'Why am I telling you all this rather than the Duce? I have tried to, again and again, but when he comes home at night, tired and drained of energy, I can't bring myself to worry him with all the treachery around him—not now his health is so poor. I just serve him his favourite meals, as far as he is allowed to eat them, and try to hold my tongue. I think back on our happy years in the Romagna, when we were still nobodies, and long for my old home. Will we ever see it again?'

Buffarini-Guidi raised his plump beringed hands supplicatingly to the evening sky beyond the library windows, which had at last been opened. I continued to lean against Virgil, waiting for the inevitable. It came.

'So I now ask you, my dear Dollman, to inform Signor Hitler of all this in my name, in my name alone. I can't do it myself— I hardly know him—but I'm sure you can. You must do it, because I know that you love Italy like a second home.

'*A rivederci e tante grazie.*'

She nodded to Buffarini-Guidi and gave me a clean but unmanicured hand. Then she mopped the sweat from her brow, dropping her handkerchief as she did so. I picked it up, but before I could hand it to her she had gone, so I put it in my pocket. I keep it to this day—laundered, of course—in remembrance of a great lady before whom queens and princesses could have curt-seyed without demeaning themselves.

Buffarini-Guidi returned after a while, and we had something stronger to drink. I explained to him that I was not in a position to fly to Signor Hitler at an hour's notice and pass on Donna Rachele's home-truths. In the first place I had no aeroplane, and in the second place I would have to go 'through the proper channels', which meant informing Hans Georg von Mackensen, German Ambassador to Rome. Buffarini-Guidi repudiated the latter suggestion with horror and implored me to find some way of conveying the information to Signor Hitler direct. I promised to try. Having made some notes at home, I bided my time until the Treviso conference. I then handed my memorandum to one of Hitler's aides, whom I knew fairly well, and begged him to pass them on to his lord and master. I never heard anything more, so I do not know if he did as I asked. If he did, Adolf Hitler must have been astonished to note how accurate Donna Rachele's prophecies were. After landing in Sicily on 10 July the Allies made steady progress, aided by a series of betrayals, and on 25 July King Victor Emmanuel III fulfilled yet another of her Cassandra-like predictions.

*   *   *

On the day Hitler and Mussolini engaged in their vain and pointless discussion at the Villa Gaggia in Feltre, Rome was bombed. The Pope and the King did their best to bring aid and comfort to the devastated quarter of the city, but the icy reception accorded to His Majesty probably dispelled his last lingering doubts as to how he should act. Surrounded by an agitated crowd, His Holiness prayed for the faithful with hands raised to heaven, but the Cumaean Sibyl would probably have enjoyed a greater success if she had suddenly appeared and predicted a speedy end to the war.

Instead of damaging government buildings or the palaces of the wealthy, Allied bombers had hit the Church of San Lorenzo and the populous districts of Tiburtino and Porta Maggiore. It must have been scant consolation to the Western airmen to learn that they had also destroyed the grave of John Keats in the cemetery beside the Pyramid of Cestius, a fact which hardly influenced the course of the war but at least injected a note of ironical amusement into the atmosphere of universal distress. I visited the 'Alfrediani' in their shattered homes and was met by morose and angry faces. When I asked if everyone in the neighbourhood felt as they did they replied in chorus that the days of Benito Mussolini and Fascism were numbered, and that I ought to think seriously about going into hiding with them.

I remembered Donna Rachele's plea and hoped that my aide at Treviso had done his job. Returning home in a very depressed state of mind, I found Signorina Bibi bent over an English grammar. This not only failed to raise my spirits but filled me with dark new forebodings. I tried to contact the former Ambassador to London and current President of the Fascist Chamber, Dino Grandi, with whom I was on fairly amicable terms. I knew that he had long been head of the anti-Mussolini front and was by far the most intelligent of the Fascist leaders. In the past he had spoken to me, if not with candour, at least as frankly as any Italian could have who wished to convey his meaning without compromising himself. Now, however, he declined to see me—yet another indication of sentiment in the week immediately preceding 25 July 1943.

I asked myself whether I ought to try something else and came to the conclusion that the best policy was to do nothing. Hitler had conferred with Mussolini, Rome boasted an over-staffed German embassy, there was a special attaché responsible for all police and security matters, and the military were represented by their own generals. What was I supposed to do? I had already taken the only step open to me by passing on Donna Rachele's appeal. Nevertheless, when I heard of the surprise session of the Fascist Grand Council called by the Duce for the evening of 24 July, I did something more. I assured Herr von Mackensen that I would tap all my contacts and connections for a definite picture of what had happened as soon as possible after the meeting had adjourned. I was thinking mainly of Buffarini-Guidi, who, though no longer a minister, was still a member of the Council. I kept my word, unaware that my report would prove the indirect cause of the ambassador's downfall. I have always regretted that my one attempt to do something of genuine political importance should have injured a man who had always taken such a friendly and paternal interest in me.

On the evening of 24 July I went for my usual stroll on the Monte Pincio. The Eternal City looked much as it always did at this hour and time of year. Leaden sirocco clouds hung over St Peter's as the sun sank slowly behind the dome in a lilac-grey haze. It was oppressively close, and not many people were emulating my attempt to snatch a breath of air from the warm breeze that blew feebly from the direction of the sea. Two figures caught my eye, however. One belonged to Princess Ann-Mari Bismarck, whose fresh Swedish beauty was quite unaffected by Rome's notorious south wind, and her companion was Filippo Anfuso, formerly Ciano's principal private secretary but now Italian Ambassador in Budapest. He had lost something of the outward glamour which had made him the darling of Rome's feminine socialites, and looked far more worried and serious than I had ever seen him. We strolled up and down the terrace for a few minutes while Anfuso painted a highly gloomy picture of what was happening down in the Palazzo Venezia. He was outraged that Mussolini should have dismissed the Moschettieri, or praetorian guards, who usually guaranteed his personal safety. Anfuso was not a member of the Grand Council, but he hinted that he would know what to do if he were. Before I could question him further, the Princess changed the subject. Perhaps she was bored, perhaps it was too sultry, perhaps she was reluctant to see her gallant escort embroiled in a matter of such delicacy. Whatever the reason, I never heard what Filippo Anfuso would have done in Mussolini's place.

I walked home in a thoughtful mood, to find a message awaiting me. Its gist was that Buffarini-Guidi would expect me '*in ogni caso*'—come what may—at a well-known restaurant in the old quarter of the city at noon next day. I also found Signorina Bibi there, not poring over an English grammar this time but busy with some very dry Martinis and a Roman prince of exalted name and station. They were so deep in conversation that they did not hear me come in. I never discovered what they were talking about, but I guessed later on, when Don Francesco enthused to me about his lonely, far-flung castles, some of which I knew, and extolled their inaccessibility.

Don Francesco was a good friend of mine. He was also one

of the few Roman aristocrats who acknowledged that even the German race produces a few ladies and gentlemen. I still marvel at little Bibi's fabulous rise in the world, which took her from Alfredo and his friends, via me, into the rarified world of the Roman palazzi, one of the loveliest of which she now occupies in her capacity as a princess and Don Francesco's wife. It irks me that I am not a Balzac. I am sure he would have turned Bibi's life into an enchanting novel under some such title as 'The Lily of Rome'.

Next morning—Sunday morning—the city lay under a mantle of divinely blue sky. Nothing seemed to have changed. Those who could drive down to the sea to bathe did so, and those who could not stayed in Rome, cursing the war and petrol rationing for keeping them at home.

Before meeting Buffarini for lunch, I decided to drive to the Palazzo Venezia, Mussolini's official place of work and scene of the previous night's meeting of the Fascist Grand Council. Plain-clothes policemen were lounging around as usual, easily distin-guishable by their pomaded hair and garish ties; and Vincenzo Agnesina, head of the Duce's personal security guard, was in his office, also as usual. We had been on many trips together, the last one being to Klessheim in April. He had me shown in at once, and we chatted away for some time as if nothing had hap-pened. We discussed the weather and deplored the oppressive July heat. I inquired after his family and he responded with some trivialities of his own devising. Casually, I mentioned the Council meeting and asked how the Duce was. Agnesina's shrewd, inscrut-able eyes studied me for a moment. Then he replied: *'La situ-azione è quasi invariata'*—'The situation is virtually unchanged'. His *'quasi'* was quite enough to startle me, as he quickly noted. He went on to tell me that *'Sua Eccellenza'* was closeted with the Japanese Ambassador, having previously had a scene with Albini, Buffarini-Guidi's successor as Secretary of State for the Interior. The terms 'His Excellency', and 'scene' were equally significant. Agnesina had never before referred to Mussolini as His Excellency in my presence, and I concluded that the magic word Duce must already have lost its appeal, even for the police.

Slightly reassured by the news that Buffarini-Guidi had spent

several hours with His Excellency that morning, I thanked Agnesina and wished him an uneventful Sunday. It was almost noon,
and time to set off for my appointment at the Ristorante San Carlo
in the Corso.

Once again it seemed that nothing had happened. I was greeted
by deferential waiters and conducted to a small private room,
sealed off from the other patrons of the establishment, where
Buffarini-Guidi and his friends were awaiting me. I have often
been embraced by men in Italy. It is a friendly masculine custom
there and has no erotic significance, even if inhibited German
imaginations refuse to acknowledge the fact and Sigmund Freud
has associated the practice with pre- and post-natal complexes.
I have seldom been embraced so often, however. First came the
portly little ex-minister, then his colleague at the Ministry of
Education and Public Worship, then the President of the Supreme
Court, and, finally, two or three other members of the Fascist
inner circle. I rejoiced in their embraces, reflecting that a hug
from a high court judge was a comparative rarity. We drank a
large number of Campari-and-sodas while I listened to the tragic
story of the previous night as retailed by the Duce's three leading
loyalists. Although Buffarini-Guidi kept interrupting his colleague
Biggini and Biggini kept interrupting the high court judge, I
eventually gathered that everything—but everything—had gone
awry.

There is no need for me to expand upon this night of conspiracy and betrayal, which Mussolini himself described with
laconic brevity in his *History of a Year, Disclosures about the
Tragic Events of 25 July—8 September 1943*. To cut a long
story short, I knew by the time the hors d'œuvres arrived that
nineteen members of the Grand Fascist Council had voted against
the Duce and his existing policies and seventeen in favour, with
two abstentions. The spaghetti was accompanied by a description
of Dino Grandi's agenda and the roast chicken by loyal outbursts of fury at Galeazzo Ciano and his treachery. The appearance of cheese and dessert was the signal for a loyal toast by all
present, and I had no choice but to drain my glass in Benito
Mussolini's honour.

It was nearly 3 p.m. by this time. Gripping Buffarini-Guidi

by the arm, I begged him to accompany me to Herr von Mackensen, who was most anxious to see him. I stressed the importance
of this mission and promised him some strong coffee, as much
Napoleon brandy as he could drink, and one of his favourite
cigars. We left at once.

Rome still wore its usual Sunday appearance. Mussolini remarks in the book mentioned above that 'the face of Rome could
be seen to blanch on the afternoon of 25 July. Cities have faces,
too. They reflect the stirrings of their soul.' I cannot say I noticed
anything special, except that it was even hotter when we left the
Ristorante San Carlo and the few passers-by looked even more
disgruntled. At about the time Buffarini-Guidi and I were driving
to the embassy, the Duce was visiting Tiburtino, the quarter that
had been particularly badly hit by the air-raid of 19 July. I do
not known if he blanched during this visit, but he had reason
enough.

The Villa Volkonsky, once a parting gift from the fickle Tsar
Alexander I to his ex-mistress, Princess Volkonsky, looked dead
and deserted. Our only greeting was the cacophonous screech of
the ambassador's pet peacocks, whose baneful significance I had
often warned him of. Herr von Mackensen received us in his
study, looking grave and dignified. A superb tapestry on the red
damask walls told the story of Alexander the Great, Darius and
the beautiful Roxana. Buffarini-Guidi was not impressed. There
were no embraces this time, merely a long handshake followed
by brandy, coffee and cigars. Von Mackensen asked his visitor
for an account of the previous night's events and me for a translation thereof, even though he knew Italian extremely well and
I would much have preferred to go for a bathe in the embassy
swimming-pool.

It was cool in the large room. No ray of sunlight penetrated
the darkened windows, but the gloom only accentuated the tragic
and dramatic nature of the scene which Buffarini now enacted
for us. He played it magnificently, pacing up and down the room
on his short legs as if he were bestriding the rostra of ancient
Rome. He had shed his jacket. All he needed was a toga, and
the great conspiracy of the Ides of March 44 BC would have come
alive once more.

Buffarini gave a personal imitation of all the principal actors. He played the dictator, pale and ill, watching the growing defection around him with weary immobility. He portrayed the fanatical eloquence of Dino Grandi, the bearded ringleader, and quoted as his climax the resolution which Grandi had the effrontery to hurl into the face of his erstwhile lord and master:

'That the head of government shall request H.M. the King, to whom the hearts of the entire nation turn in loyalty and devotion, to take the supreme initiative for the honour and salvation of the Fatherland, that is, to assume supreme command of land, sea and air forces; an initiative granted him by our institutions, which have, throughout our national history, been the glorious heritage of the exalted house of Savoy.'

And so on. No further reference to Benito Mussolini.

Buffarini mimed the dictator again, a motionless figure listening mutely to the frenzied attacks of a man who only a few weeks before had been begging Mussolini to persuade the King to invest him with the highest royal order, the Collar of the Annunziata.

Next in line was the Duce's son-in-law. Buffarini, who had never liked Ciano, threw himself wholeheartedly into a classic traitor's role. He imitated the way the renegade's eyes flinched and reproduced his self-conscious turns of phrase as he laid all the blame on Italy's German ally, not sparing his father-in-law's feelings in the process. I thought of the glamorous peacock Ciano had been in May 1939, when the Pact of Steel was signed in Berlin, and of all the enthusiasm he had shown then. Mussolini apparently listened to him with mounting horror and contempt.

Others followed Ciano's lead, though none of them, to judge by Buffarini's dramatic performances, was a Brutus. Von Mackensen tapped away at his typewriter without respite, only pausing to refill our brandy-glasses. Buffarini now came to the midnight adjournment of the Fascist Grand Council, when the Duce had retired to his study for a quarter of an hour. He now played himself, re-enacting the moment when he implored the dictator to arrest his opponents while they were still in the conference chamber. The Duce merely shook his head disgustedly, and the session was resumed. Nearly two years later, during my last audience with Benito Mussolini beside Lake Garda in April 1945, I asked him why he had watched and listened to the conspirators without taking any action. He crossed his arms and fixed me with his large eyes.

'Confronted by so much human vileness, my dear Dollman, I was too tired.'

It was a magnificent reply, in my view, except that his apathy cost him his freedom and Italy the war.

Buffarini continued his series of impressions. It would be tedious to list all the individuals he portrayed. With few exceptions, they were petty traitors who were apprehensive about their future and sought to cloak their fear and ambition in a mantle of patriotism. They did not include any character of the exalted greatness of Shakespeare's Brutus, and history was right to reward them with their lives but not with renewed power and glory.

Then came the final act. In a melancholy voice, Buffarini enumerated the votes cast against Mussolini. He drew himself up commandingly as he became the Duce's mouthpiece, only to subside once more:

'You have conjured this government crisis into being yourselves. The meeting is adjourned. I give you a "salute to the Duce".'

The meeting in Mackensen's study was also drawing to a close. The ambassador requested Buffarini's views on the situation as it now stood. Buffarini pronounced it extremely grave but not hopeless, provided that Mussolini, who was not bound by the result of the vote, took vigorous action. What this ought to have consisted of we never learned, because at that moment he was called to the telephone. He came back wearing an agitated expression, and informed us that the Duce would shortly be received in audience by the King at the latter's request. He concluded his report by flinging his arms to heaven and whispering:

'*Mamma mia!*'

Mackensen tried to reassure him. As a former aide to August Wilhelm, the Kaiser's son, and a trusted servant of Empress Auguste Victoria, he found the idea of treachery on the King's part as inconceivable as Mussolini did. He forgot that the Italian court was not the court of Prussia and that Victor Emmanuel III was not Wilhelm II. Buffarini and I remained sceptical. Then

Buffarini announced that he had to pay an urgent visit to Donna Rachele at the Villa Torlonia. He gave me a meaningful look which I carefully avoided. After all, what could I have said to him about Donna Rachele's mission in the presence of the ambassador?

It was now about 5 p.m. The ambassador picked up his type-written sheets and went off to contact Ribbentrop by teleprinter. Von Mackensen's report reached its destination just as Benito Mussolini became a prisoner of his King and Emperor. The German Foreign Minister was wild with fury when he heard the news, but only a clairvoyant could have foreseen that Victor Emmanuel III would take a mere twenty minutes to get rid of the man whom he had entrusted with the destinies of Italy since 1922 and pack him off to a Carabinieri barracks by ambulance, a royal prisoner.

At almost the same time, I was visiting the head of the Fascist Militia, General Enzo Galbiati, at his Rome headquarters. I had expected to find it a fortress bristling with armed men, but I was mistaken. I was saluted in the courtyard by a few listless individuals, one of whom wearily condescended to escort me to the general's office. Having had enough dramatics for one day, I heartily welcomed the prevailing air of lassitude. I was kept waiting, a thing which had never happened before, but eventually the general bustled in, looking fresh and alert. He had just returned from escorting the Duce through the bombed-out quarter of the city, and was full of excitement. Public enthusiasm had been intense, he told me. I said nothing, remembering my visit to the Alfrediani.

Then I asked him what he proposed to do with his militia and, more especially, with 'M' Division, its Waffen-SS instructors, Tiger tanks, anti-aircraft guns and other weapons. He rolled his eyes like the Duce—their sole point of resemblance—and declared:

'*Marceremo!*'—'We shall march!' When I inquired when, wherefore and whither, his disarming response was: '*Sempre pronti*'—'Always ready'.

I held my peace and allowed myself to be deluged with slogans which I knew by heart, e.g. 'Our life belongs to our Duce. He can rely on his Militia to the last drop of blood. Duce, command! We will follow!' It was a wearisome and unnerving monologue. To cut it short, I ventured to ask what would happen if the Duce were not in a position to issue any orders. General Enzo Galbiati, a nice young man and certainly no coward, was nonplussed.

'The Duce will always be there to command!'

It was hopeless. Galbiati was so youthfully naive and so confident that he was only there to follow, obey and march in response to orders that I refrained from jolting him into an awareness of present reality. Instead, I suggested a trip to the division, which was stationed at Sutri, just outside Rome, but this was no good either, because he was expecting orders from the Duce.

He was wasting his time, not that either of us realised it yet. I drove home, intending to wrestle with the problem alone on my beautiful terrace overlooking the Piazza di Spagna.

I had still not reached any conclusion when Bibi rushed breathlessly upstairs to tell me that Don Francesco, her prince, had telephoned to say that His Majesty had ordered Mussolini's arrest and entrusted Marshal Pietro Badoglio with the formation of a new government. Remembering my translation of Badoglio's *Abyssinian Campaign* and the photograph on my desk, I decided to drive back to the Villa Volkonsky at once to await the inevitable Fascist counter-measures.

They never came. The ambassador and his wife, Field Marshal Kesselring's headquarters at Frascati, outside Rome, the footmen, chefs, gardeners and lady's-maids of the embassy—all waited in vain. A small crowd did assemble outside the gates, not to reinstate Benito Mussolini with our assistance, but to hurl cries of derision at the Fascists who sought refuge in the embassy.

I tried to reach Buffarini-Guidi and the other participants in my midday symposium at the San Carlo, but their telephones were as dead as Donna Rachele's at the Villa Torlonia.

On the other hand, Berlin and the Führer's headquarters telephoned incessantly. I have never listened in on so many contradictory, conflicting, furious, complacent, despairing, optimistic telephone calls in my life: 'The Duce must be freed immediately! —How is the Duce and where is he?—The King Emperor and his Marshal are traitors and must be overthrown forthwith! —His Majesty must be questioned about the fate of Mussolini at once.—Marshal Badoglio will not be recognised as head of government.—His Majesty appears to have authorised the formation of a new government legally and in accordance with the Italian Constitution—or has he?—The expected Fascist mass-rising is to be vigorously supported.—I demand the immediate release of Mussolini. Germany would welcome him as a guest.— Can Mussolini regain control with aid of rebellious Fascists?— What is to be done with the King?'

Hans Georg von Mackensen had a great deal of patience, but in the end this proved too much even for him. He suggested that I either convey my impressions to the Führer's Headquarters by telephone or fly there in person, but that was the last thing I wanted to do, so I extricated myself with an allusion to my present indispensability in Rome.

We continued to wait for the Fascists to act, but all they did was to turn up at the embassy, disguise themselves as German air force personnel and drive to Frascati escorted by grinning officers from the Field Marshal's headquarters. They were in a great hurry. In their view, their presence was urgently required in Germany, where they could form a Fascist government-in-exile. The idea of forming a new government in Rome did not appeal to them.

While prominent Fascists were still arriving, disguising themselves and fleeing to Kesselring's headquarters at Frascati, the ambassador made another proposal, to wit, that I should drive to 'M' Division at Sutri, deliver a rousing harangue, and march on Rome at its head. At first I thought I had misheard. No one had ever cast me in a general's role before. For a few moments it seemed as if my hour of greatness had struck—but only for a few moments. Then, to Herr von Mackensen's annoyance, I laughed. My counter-proposal was that we should both drive to Sutri—provided we could find one Fascist of repute to come with us—and jointly lead the division on Rome in a bid to free the Duce. I thought of Buffarini-Guidi, who would undoubtedly have volunteered for the task even though he was as incapable of generalship as I, but I was unaware that he was already a prisoner of the new regime. I thought, too, of Vittorio Mussolini, the Duce's son, though I later gathered from his indescribably naive memoirs that he contemplated every course of action save a *coup de main* in his father's favour.

Finally, I thought of Roberto Farinacci, *Federale* of Cremona and the boldest and most determined Fascist of all. Farinacci had lost an arm in the Abyssinian War, which would be bound to impress the men of 'M' Division. Added to that, at the previous night's meeting of the Grand Council he had proposed a motion affirming that it was 'the supreme duty of all Italians to defend the sacred soil of the Fatherland to the last, and to stand by alliances entered into'.

At that moment, the porter from the lodge materialised like a genie and reported breathlessly that a certain Herr Farinacci was being badly jostled by the mob outside and had asked for asylum in the embassy. I ran downstairs and ordered the gate to be opened. There was nothing the matter with him apart from a torn jacket and a few bruises, but the jacket was part of a civilian suit, which struck me as an unpromising sign. My fears were confirmed. Farinacci gave the ambassador a dignified lecture on his, Farinacci's, obligation to serve the case of Fascism in Germany. Since he was anxious to commend himself to Hitler as future head of the Italian government, he asked to be conducted to Field Marshal Kesselring with all possible haste. He did not mention the Duce, and I was reminded that there had never been much love lost between the two men.

Farinacci, too, declared his intention of leaving the embassy attired as a German airman, which evoked more grins from Kesselring's officers. Just at that moment, to cap everything, the ambassadress appeared on the stairs leading to her private apartments and asked me if our friends needed any women's clothes. If so, she would be glad to oblige. My involuntary guffaw incurred universal displeasure, but the momentary vision of Farinacci leading the doughty lads of 'M' Division back to Rome dressed as a woman was too much for me.

The Fascists and Herr von Mackensen did not share my amusement, and I was glad when Marshal Badoglio finally telephoned on the King's instructions and formally introduced himself as the new head of government. What was more, he gave an assurance that *'la guerra continua'*—'the war goes on'.

Von Mackensen breathed a sigh of relief. He was a strict legitimist, and if the King had nominated a new prime minister in conformity with the Italian Constitution—a prime minister who intended to fight on, what was more—the requirements of law and political common sense had been satisfied.

Berlin and the Führer's Headquarters also calmed down. The ambassador was authorised to take any steps necessary to ensure Benito Mussolini's personal safety, but the methods to be employed were not specified. When questioned on the subject, Badoglio merely replied that he vouched for Mussolini's safety. This was not over-generous, in view of their long association, but it was better than handing him over to the clamorous, jubilant crowds who were now bawling anti-Fascist songs and marching through the streets where they had once acclaimed their Duce with equal fervour.

With the Fascists safe at Frascati and a continued absence of news from the Villa Torlonia, we decided to have supper.

At about the same time, a man was pacing restlessly up and down in the Carabinieri barracks in the Via Legnano. Every now and then he would come to a halt, shake his bald head and roll his eyes furiously, crying: *'Ah, il quarantenne, il quarantenne!'*

The man was Benito Mussolini, and the 'forty-year-old' target of his wrath was his son-in-law, Galeazzo Ciano, who owed him everything, yet had deserted him so ignominiously at the Grand Council meeting twenty-four hours earlier. Could it be that Mussolini was already a prey to the dark thoughts which prompted him to condemn Ciano to death by shooting on 11 January 1944?

Also at the same hour, the peace which had finally descended upon the royal dining-table in the Villa Savoya, where Benito Mussolini had suffered his reversal of fortune that afternoon, was rudely disturbed. Queen Elena, normally so uninvolved in politics, raised her fine dark eyes and fixed them on her husband's face. For once, it was not family or household matters that concerned her. Instead, she proclaimed to the astonished company that she strongly disapproved of what had just occurred at the royal villa.

'Even though my father was only the King of Montenegro, he would never have abused the laws of hospitality, which are sacred to everyone in my country, in the way in which they have been abused in our home today.'

No one spoke. His Majesty rose without a word and brought the meal to an end.

IX

THE SNAKE-PIT

WHEN I graduated in history in the winter of 1926 I regarded Gaius Julius Caesar as Rome's most brilliant mind, Augustus as the wisest of all emperors, Frederick II of Hohenstaufen as a consummation of all Late Medieval culture, and Charles V as a tragic world ruler on whose empire the sun never set. I was prepared to look upon Wallenstein's defection from the Habsburgs as an act of supreme statesmanship inspired by lofty concern for the welfare of the German nation within the tottering Holy Roman Empire—and so on.

My conception of history received its first jolt on the occasion of the Munich Conference of 1938, when I was privileged to take a glance behind the scenes and observe the actors at close quarters. The shattering of my historical ideals progressed at an alarming rate during the career of the Rome-Berlin Axis and reached its climax in the summer of 1943, or, to be more precise, in the period between 25 July, the day of Benito Mussolini's overthrow and imprisonment, and 8 September, when Italy defected from her alliance with Hitler's Germany. By 9 September I would have been quite capable of writing a second thesis entitled 'Perfidy' or 'The Snake-pit'.

These few weeks were characterised by universal betrayal and deception, both by individuals and so-called Great Powers.

Having staged their performance of 25 July with undeniable skill and success, the King and his court busied themselves with the dual task of allaying Hitler's suspicions with assurances that 'the war goes on' while simultaneously preparing the ground for a secret armistice with Italy's erstwhile enemies.

Outwardly, the Führer's Headquarters behaved as though it had implicit faith in the King's pledges and in the various guarantees so lavishly dispensed by the new head of government, Marshal Badoglio. Simultaneously, and on various pretexts, it began to send military reinforcements across the Alps, among them Adolf Hitler's bodyguard.

The ever-faithful Carmine Senise, now back in office as chief of police, re-established his former links with me in memory of our mutual and unforgettable friend Bocchini. He also offered to get me an audience with Badoglio, who had apparently been seized with an intense desire to see his one-time translator again. At the same time, I received overtures from the Palazzo Vidoni, headquarters of the Grand General Staff, where my only contact man in the past had been General Castellano. I was assured of the army's goodwill and loyalty to the alliance—and this at a time when the above-named general was feverishly negotiating with the Allies and planned to travel to Lisbon on 12 August to engage in direct armistice talks.

On 6 August the two Foreign Ministers, Ribbentrop and his newly appointed opposite number Guariglia, formerly Italian Ambassador to Constantinople, accompanied by Field Marshals Keitel and Ambrosio, travelled to Tarvis on the former Austro-Italian border. Despite my dutiful endeavours as an interpreter, the conference turned out to be an impressive display of lies, mistrust and insincerity.

Earlier, towards the end of July, the fate of the Eternal City and certain sections of its population had hung by a thread. Hitler, Himmler and Kaltenbrunner, Heydrich's successor at the Central State Security Bureau, had instructed SS-Hauptsturmführer Otto Skorzeny, head of Group VI S of Department VI of that institution, to land in the vicinity of Rome with forty or fifty picked men. Their mission was to ascertain the captive Mussolini's whereabouts, free him if possible, and try to prevent Italy's defection from the Axis by any available means, not excluding a bloodbath. I was indifferent to the first part of their task. Indeed, after witnessing the funeral of Fascism on the night of 25 July, I regarded the prospect of a come-back by the toothless lion with great misgivings. I was not indifferent to their second task, however, and decided to do all I could to save Rome from a senseless massacre. To this end I acquired an unlikely ally in someone who had hitherto been an opponent of mine, SS-Sturmbannführer Herbert Kappler, the German police attaché in Rome. He was quite as convinced of the folly of this part of Skorzeny's mission as I, and so our incongruous pact was sealed. Here, too, each party worked against the other. The King and Badoglio, the Grand General Staff and those soldiers and diplomats who were agreeable to an armistice with the Allies, Carmine Senise and his policemen, Hitler and his associates in the Third Reich, Ribbentrop and the Foreign Office, Field Marshal Kesselring, Ambassador von Mackensen, Police Attaché Kappler and I—all were involved, more or less deeply and more or less openly, in the tortuous happenings of summer 1943.

To add to the chaos, it occurred to me that I, too, might be able to devise a political plan. Although I had only translated such plans before, I now decided to contact Himmler's Chief of Staff, General of the Waffen-SS Karl Wolff. My aim was to convince him that Fascism in its pre-25 July form should be written off, and that a new and effective Italian cabinet should be held in readiness for the moment when Italy defected from the Axis under Victor Emmanuel III and Marshal Badoglio. My personal 'tip' was Mussolini's long-time Secretary of State for, and later Minister of, Agriculture, Professor of Political Economy Giuseppe Tassinari. The Duce had demonstrated his lack of judgement by severing relations with Tassinari after he had been involved in an exchange of blows with Party Secretary Serena at the Palazzo Venezia in December 1941, even though Tassinari was his ablest associate and a man of unimpeachable character —qualities which are rare enough in any government and almost unique under a dictatorship.

I had been friendly with him and his family—he led a private life which would have commended itself even to Cato the Elder —for years, thanks to my work as an interpreter for his German colleague Darré, Hitler's Minister of Agriculture. This chapter in my interpreter's career forms one of my pleasantest recollections of this period. It took me from the orchards and market gardens of Italy and the problems of pisciculture in East Prussia and the Mediterranean area to the brood-mares of Trakehnen and Rominten and the buffalo herds of Salerno and Maccarese on the Tyrrhenian coast. My connections with Tassinari also gained me some memorable culinary experiences. If I had not been an interpreter, what should I have known of peach-growing in the province of Verona, of the arcana connected with golden Parmigiano and Reggiano, noblest of Italian vintage cheeses, of the vast wine kingdom, of the treasures of the Adriatic and Tyrrhenian Seas? My friend Tassinari ensured that I was kept supplied with choice produce from his ministerial domain all the year round, but that was not the sole reason why I resolved to repay him by trying to stake his claim as successor to the Duce in the event of 'Case X', i.e. if the King's government renounced the German alliance. While the royal envoys were negotiating to this end in Lisbon, I drove to a secret rendezvous in Venice, my old love. This meeting, which almost achieved its object and might well have spared Italy the horrors of civil strife after 8 September 1943, was yet another thread in the tangled web of intrigue in which Italy became enmeshed that summer.

Lack of space forbids a detailed account of all the secret moves, betrayals, deceptions and lies which formed part of this elaborate game, but I should like to record one or two of the more important episodes, if only as a warning to the younger generation not to dabble in politics.

I decided to link my future activities as an interpreter to the person who seemed to offer the best substitute for my lost allies of the past, Arturo Bocchini, Guido Buffarini-Guidi, and Ambassador von Mackensen, whose fate had been sealed at Tarvis. That person was Field Marshal Kesselring, Wehrmacht Commander-in-Chief, Southern Command. My acquaintance with him had so far been limited to a few official functions and embassy receptions, but our rare talks together had convinced me that he was the sort of political general who represents an exception in any army in the world. Although I had been able to chat to him at some length during the Treviso-Feltre conference, I did not guess at the time that he was destined to become my loyal friend and protector and remain so until his death in 1959. It was at his headquarters that I first came into contact with a prominent inmate of the midsummer snake-pit.

Kesselring had established himself at Frascati, once the summer retreat of Roman princes and cardinals. On 27 July, as far as I can remember, I was invited to dine there. I had barely arrived before the Field Marshal introduced me, with a look of unwonted gravity, to a mountainous man in a fur-lined flying jacket which seemed strangely out of place on such a warm summer evening. The giant with the sabre-scarred visage extended a giant hand, and I immediately realised that there was not the slightest possibility of our reaching a mutual understanding. Giants with duelling scars, fur-lined flying jackets and an air which suggested the State Security Bureau were not in my line, just as Germans with Italianised manners and gestures were certainly not in his.

Dinners at Frascati were usually enlivened by verbal jousts between Kesselring and myself, but this one was positively funereal. Also present were General Student of the Luftwaffe, Police Attaché Kappler, and the members of Kesselring's staff. Noticing Kesselring's eye resting on me thoughtfully, I resolved to behave in as German, humourless and arrogant a fashion as I could.

The Field Marshal and his officers adjourned immediately after the meal, leaving me alone with Police Attaché Kappler and the Wagnerian figure in the flying jacket, who was none other than Otto Skorzeny. After a few preliminaries, Skorzeny solemnly enjoined me and Kappler, whose own duelling scars glowed red with joyful anticipation, not to inform anyone of what he was about to tell us, Mackensen and the embassy staff included. I knew at once that I would only keep this promise in so far as it did not violate my position of trust with the von Mackensens. Skorzeny soon came to the point: he was there to find the Duce and set him free. I thought of my Tassinari scheme and tried to look interested. I did not begrudge Mussolini his freedom, even if I did have my own views on an attempt to resuscitate the living corpse of Fascism.

Otto Skorzeny and his men were under orders from the Führer's Headquarters to frustrate Italy's anticipated defection from the Axis by means of a *coup de main*. Their orders further envisaged the arrest, if necessary, of the King, the royal family, the cabinet, senior officers from every branch of the armed forces, and the Fascists who had deserted Mussolini at the meeting of the Fascist Grand Council, notably Galeazzo Ciano and Dino Grandi. In addition, the oracle declared that 'although care must be taken not to kill or injure anyone while these persons are being taken into custody, resistance must be broken'.

This was enough for me. I inquired how many men Skorzeny had with him and was relieved to hear that they numbered between forty and fifty. Even the Germanic and East Roman mercenary leaders who had made sport of the ailing Roman Empire during the days of the great migrations had had larger forces at their disposal. When I asked whether the Field Marshal and Herr von Mackensen had been informed of the second phase of Skorzeny's programme, the response was a grim negative. There conversation rested for the moment. Neither Skorzeny nor I cherished any illusions about our mutual antipathy. The only difference was that I did not have fifty heavily armed and grimly determined men at my command—merely Lupo, my faithful Alsatian dog. However, I proposed to avert a Roman massacre by other means than armed force.

We met for the second time in the police attaché's office, which Skorzeny and his men had meanwhile adopted as their stronghold. Once again, it would have been heroic of me if I had told the State Security Bureau's agent flatly what I thought of his plans for Rome, but I naturally refrained from doing so. I even showed him the location of various ministries and royal palaces on a street map, and pointed out an ill-guarded entrance to the royal palace at the foot of the Quirinal with a tremendous show of secrecy. In short, I did everything to allay Skorzeny's instinctive distrust of me, and I think he soon realised that, if it came to nocturnal raids and gun-battles, I would be less a help than a hindrance.

I then did something which might be described as petty treason. I called on Frau von Mackensen and asked the imperturbable ambassadress to ensure that the women and children of the royal family abandoned their palaces and left Rome as quickly as possible. I told her the truth, knowing that she would keep it to herself. She proved fully equal to the situation, and it only took us a few minutes to reach agreement. Women are far more reliable and determined on such occasions than men, who tend to be encumbered by oaths of allegiance or civic and professional obligations. Before long, I was told that the court had been reduced to its male members, who could fend for themselves and needed neither me nor an ambassadress to help them fight for life and crown.

Next, I was bold enough to invite Kappler, the Third Reich's cool, blue-eyed police attaché, to a private meeting at the home of a Colonel Helfferich, Admiral Canaris's representative in Rome. I selected this venue, which Helfferich readily placed at my disposal, so as to avoid attracting unnecessary attention in German or Italian circles. I told Kappler that I considered his colleague Skorzeny's plans not only impracticable but extremely hazardous. I also conveyed to him that the Italians, and Police Chief Carmine Senise in particular, were fairly well informed about what was in store for their present rulers and had taken countermeasures.

The SS-Sturmbannführer, like Skorzeny a favourite of his chief, Kaltenbrunner, was not a stupid man but a cool and calculating master of his trade. Although he was true to his oath of allegiance and would never have disobeyed a direct order, the orders in question had been issued to Skorzeny, and he no doubt looked upon the whole mission as a highly questionable and gratuitous invasion of his own sphere of command. He disliked me, of that I am sure, but I think he realised that my activities as an interpreter and social butterfly were far less dangerous to him personally than the role which Skorzeny had assumed in Rome on orders from above. In short, he quickly and explicitly declared himself ready to fly to Himmler and advise him against backing Skorzeny's adventurous schemes. We shook hands, cordially for once, and he departed.

He actually went to Himmler, and I suspect that it was only in consideration of past services that the Reichsführer did not have him arrested on the spot. By the time he returned, my need of him had largely evaporated. Chance had intervened, as it usually does at critical moments in history, to the benefit both of me and Rome. I met Sepp Dietrich, ultra-Bavarian commander of the Leibstandarte and the most senior of all Adolf Hitler's mercenaries. I had, of course, come across him before, during my official trips to the Third Reich. Whenever I saw him—squat, thick-set, hard-drinking and tough—I was reminded of the Thirty Years War and the days when men of his type must have formed the backbone of the armies of Wallenstein, Tilly and Gustav Adolf. He was a born soldier of fortune, and what nation in the world can dispense with such men when it comes to the pinch? Only the Italians, perhaps, but no one who knows and loves them would claim that their natural propensities or successes are primarily of a military nature.

Sepp Dietrich, who had reported to Field Marshal Kesselring in his capacity as commander of the Leibstandarte units now in Northern Italy, saw me as a welcome opportunity to sample what Rome had to offer in the way of wine, women and song. With my sights set on other things, I devoted an evening to him.

Behind the Monte Gianicolo, which is known to every visitor to Rome and affords a superb view of the Eternal City, especially at sunset, stood one of my favourite trattorias, the 'Da Scarpone', where frequent visits with Signorina Bibi and the Alfrediani had earned me the status of a 'regular'. It was hardly the time for a party, but that mattered little in view of the mortal danger looming over Rome. Having laid on some Vino di Frascati, a group of folk-singers, a few nice girls and plenty of spaghetti and chicken—in short, a small-scale Oktoberfest *alla romana*—I drove the rude soldier and his aides to the top of the Monte Gianicolo. Warrior-like, but with the true Bavarian's susceptibility to the beauties of Nature, Dietrich began to mellow. Step by step, I carried out my strategic plan: first, a glimpse of the Eternal City glowing in the evening sunlight, then some golden Frascati dispensed by pretty girls, and, finally, huge dishes of spaghetti and chicken accompanied by sentimental songs. By the time we reached the chicken the Leibstandartenführer was enthusing about the delights surrounding us, and after the chicken he listened politely to my description of how the city had been burned by Emperor Nero. Even he had heard evil reports of Nero. Contemptible as 'King Nutcracker', his family and his government were, Dietrich declared, Rome must not fall prey to another Neronian orgy. Glancing round at the wine, women and singers, he lent a ready ear as I took my courage in both hands and painted a grim picture of the probable results of his liege lord's plan. Dietrich dismissed it with a grin as 'typical Hitler bluff'. I felt far less confident of this than he did, but the wine and what went with it was having a mellowing effect on me too. Having stressed the historic importance of saving Rome from destruction, I raised my umpteenth glass to Sepp Dietrich and the Eternal City. The pretty girls raised their glasses too, and the musicians did their best to render Giacomo Puccini's immortal *Inno di Roma*.

It was an historic moment, and I was only glad that Otto Skorzeny and his Nibelungs were not present. I said farewell to the saviour of Rome as the sun was climbing above the distant hills. He promised me that he would give Hitler his views on Rome and the proposed massacre in the very near future, and he kept his word. The men of his Leibstandarte have long been mouldering on battlefields in every corner of Europe and their leader only escaped an Allied death sentence by the skin of his teeth, but Rome survived—as did Otto Skorzeny and the orders which Hitler apparently devised as a piece of bluff. Was it really bluff? Whatever the truth, the nightmare receded for me, at least, when I heard that the Führer's Headquarters and Rome had agreed to hold a meeting at Tarvis on 6 August. If special trains were still running and senior diplomats and soldiers from both sides could sit down peacefully at the same table, the danger could not be as acute as it had been a short while before.

This was the first journey I had undertaken as an interpreter to members of the new Badoglio government. It was also the last. Everything had changed. The long row of coaches had dwindled to three *saloncini* and a dining-car. We left from an obscure suburban station, and there were neither flowers nor truffles on the table. I travelled in one of the coaches with the ambassador —it was our last trip together—accompanied by the German military attaché in Rome, von Rintelen, and one of his officers, Major von Jena. The Italian delegation consisted of the new Foreign Minister, Guariglia, and several of his associates, the Chief of the Grand General Staff, General Ambrosio, and the Italian military attaché in Berlin, General Marras.

We all knew each other with the exception of Guariglia, who had until recently been ambassador to Turkey. The Italians ventured a modified version of the Fascist salute when we met and looked noticeably embarrassed. I shared their embarrassment. As I saw it, the whole conference was merely a hollow sham, an Italian device for gaining time, but, being equally anxious to gain time, I made the best of things. The better this diplomatic and military intermezzo went, the more the danger of direct intervention receded. Consequently, I did my utmost to keep conversation going at dinner by recounting, or translating, episodes from my career as an interpreter—without reference, of course, to Mussolini. The ambassador, who was serious by nature, summoned up a smile, the other diplomats feigned amusement, and the soldiers looked openly bored.

Our special train was the first to pull into the gloomy frontier station at Tarvis. The Italian diplomats lined up along the opposite platform, which was still empty, and began to wave their arms about in a comical fashion. I asked them jocularly if they were doing their morning exercises.

'More or less,' was the reply. 'We're trying the Fascist salute to see if we've forgotten it.'

Joining in my laughter, they expressed the hope that it would put Herr von Ribbentrop in a more conciliatory mood to be greeted in the long-accustomed manner. I strongly encouraged them to perform their little demonstration because I wanted to see his face when they did so.

I was not disappointed. Ribbentrop and Keitel were greeted by a display of callisthenics when they got out. They knew everyone except Guariglia, of course, but they behaved as if they had never met their Italian allies before. All in all, it was an entertaining scene.

The meeting known to history as the Tarvis Conference then began. The diplomats sat in conclave in the German special train, with Dr Schmidt of the Foreign Office acting as interpreter, The soldiers, headed by Keitel and Ambrosio, for whom I interpreted, conferred in the Italian special train. I seemed to be spending more and more of my time with the military, and I was not sorry. As long as they are not actually locked in mortal combat, generals are more congenial people to interpret for than politicians.

As it turned out, battle was almost joined. Ambrosio demanded to know why an endless stream of German reinforcements was pouring southwards across the Brenner, and his German opposite number countered by asking why the Italians were withdrawing their men from Greece and the Balkans. Mutual distrust grew and voices rose in volume. Before long, Keitel and Ambrosio were bellowing orders at each other on an imaginary parade-ground, and I half expected to hear the fatal words 'Duce', 'treason' and 'loyalty to the Axis' burst in the air like shrapnel shells at any moment. However, with the chivalrous support of General von Rintelen, a dignified man with whom I had always been on terms of mutual esteem and respect, I judiciously slanted my translations so as to steer discussion into calmer waters. By midday the generals were debating technical matters, and may even, as professional soldiers, have temporarily believed in the mutual loyalty which was supposed to be part of their stock in trade.

I heard later that the atmosphere in the other Pullman car was quieter but no less uneasy. Ribbentrop was no longer dealing with the despised Ciano, but with a professional diplomat whose intellect was vastly superior to his own. Here, too, the events of 25 July loomed in the background, but all had their own reasons for wishing to postpone an open conflict: the Italians because their negotiations with the Allies were far from concluded, the Germans because their troop movements were far from complete, and I because I hoped to scotch Skorzeny's operation at all costs.

At one o'clock everyone adjourned to the Italian train to have lunch. The meal was a pale shadow of the banquets that used to be served on Mussolini's, Ciano's and Marshal Cavallero's special trains. My copy of the menu, which I have preserved, lists *Bordura di spinaci* and *Pollo di gelatina*, followed by *Macedonia di frutta*.

I doubt if spinach, chicken in aspic and fruit salad would have saved the situation on their own, but the wines were better than the food. Moreover, all those present at table were so visibly fatigued by their morning orgy of lying and so bereft of ideas that they decided to make the best of a bad job.

Ribbentrop demonstrated his faith in the Italians' fighting spirit and loyalty to the alliance by looking as if he were suffering from toothache. Guariglia, who had unblushingly given his word of honour that the new regime was not engaged in clandestine negotiations with the Allies, seemed almost convinced of his own good faith—and this despite the fact that he had, on the orders of the King and Marshal Badoglio, been doing everything possible since 30 July to get such negotiations under way. Chief of the General Staff Ambrosio, a mere novice in the art of dissimulation, did his best to convey that he regarded the German divisions now crossing the Brenner as a welcome addition to Axis fighting strength. Field Marshal Keitel, whose experience of the Führer's Headquarters had taught him a thing or two, pretended to regard the sinister recalling of Italian units stationed abroad in the same light.

In short, the company became positively intoxicated by its own lies and treachery, so much so that Herr von Ribbentrop was finally emboldened to make a sensational proposal. Shortly after 25 July, Rome had tried to appease the Fuehrer's Headquarters by suggesting a conference between the King, the Crown Prince, Badoglio, and Adolf Hitler. Ribbentrop had indignantly repudiated the idea. Now, to everyone's astonishment, he revived it. The rulers of the two countries were to meet on German soil, like lambs grazing peacefully in green pastures, to eliminate all suspicions and misunderstandings once and for all.

I do not know to this day what lay behind the German Foreign Minister's suggestion. Was it a final bluff on the lines of Skorzeny's Operation Alarich, or a convenient way of laying hands on Italy's rulers? Whatever it was, Guariglia retained his composure with Machiavellian skill and referred the matter to Rome, well knowing that current negotiations with the West ruled out any possibility of agreement.

Everyone breathed more easily when the two special trains prepared to depart at about 7 p.m. There was a last-minute sensation when one of Ribbentrop's delegates rushed over excitedly and asked Herr von Mackensen with honeyed charm if he would mind accompanying the Foreign Minister back to Germany. The ambassador's baggage had to be transferred hurriedly, and all I could do was clasp his hand and wish him luck on his unexpected trip to the Reich. Neither of us guessed the dangers that lay ahead of him, nor did we know that he would never again return to Rome as ambassador.

In fact, even though von Mackensen bore absolutely no responsibility for Mussolini's arrest by the King, the Foreign Office and the Führer's Headquarters had not forgiven him for his belated teleprinter message of 25 July, with which I had been so actively associated. It was our last meeting, not that I realised it at the time. I did not see him again before his death in 1946, and should like to take this opportunity of giving renewed thanks for the trust and friendship he bestowed upon me during his term as ambassador in Rome. He may not have been a Talleyrand or a Metternich, but he was a diplomat whose decent, upright character matched his personal convictions.

The wheels of the German train were the first to turn. The Italian diplomats lined up on the platform as before, but this time they only inclined their heads. They did not deem it necessary to give a 'salute to the Duce', a salute to the man before whom they had so often raised their arms in my presence. Their thoughts were with their intermediaries in Lisbon, just as mine were centred on Rome, Skorzeny's plans for it, and my own plans for the future government of Italy, which were claiming more and more of my attention.

As soon as I got back to Rome I contacted my friend Giuseppe Tassinari at Lake Garda and, after warning him to take every possible precaution, proposed a secret meeting in Venice. He agreed.

It was only while preparing my modest coup d'état that I realised how essential it was that there should be no slip-ups. I was not only bypassing Ribbentrop, who was supposed to be kept *au courant* by General Wolff, but circumventing the government now in power at Rome. The man I was going to meet was a prominent Fascist ex-minister, even if he had always belonged to the moderately conservative wing of the Party and was well disposed towards the monarchy, if not to Victor Emmanuel III.

Above all, I was meeting him in order to prepare the ground for a new government, even though the ex-Duce of Fascism was still alive on some island in the Western Mediterranean, alive but a prisoner.

It was too late for second thoughts now. My old flame Marianna had been married for some years to a nice young man who ran a small locanda near the Fondamenti delle Zattere, just behind the Jesuit Church. I had always made a point of visiting the happy couple on my excursions to Venice. Their eldest son was christened Eugenio in my honour, and they regarded me as one of the family. Marianna, who had blossomed into a mature beauty in the style of a Tiepolo model, presided over her trattoria alone. Signor Paolo had been drafted into the navy, and my efforts to secure his release had failed because the Italian navy was not fond enough of the Germans. I got in touch with Marianna and invited myself and a 'business friend' to a *colazione* on the coming Sunday, when her establishment was closed to the general public.

The flight from Rome to Venice was punctuated by exclamations of joy from my Italian travelling-companions every time the radio reported a new Axis setback in Southern Italy. Remembering Tarvis, I found my apprehensions more than confirmed. In the next seat to me was Frau von Weizsäcker, the new ambassadress to the Vatican. My friends the von Bergens had left Rome in June, after performing their ambassadorial duties there for almost twenty-five years. My aerial conversation with the new mistress of the embassy brought home to me how much I would miss her predecessor. She was a decent, puritanically simple woman, and correspondingly boring. She was also an excellent pianist, but her favourite composer was Bach, who has always been beyond me. She expressed the hope that she would see me at the soirées which were to be devoted to the great master's work that autumn and winter. I hoped she would not, and sadly recalled Frau von Bergen's dinner parties—not musical parties, it was true, but sparkling and harmonious affairs none the less.

We landed at our destination. No one followed me as I made my way to Donna Marianna's through a maze of narrow streets, past mouldering palazzi and across disused canals. I received a warm welcome. Little Eugenio was eager for his usual present, and his mother rested her pretty head on my chest for a moment and declared herself *'felicissima'*. I shared her happiness at our reunion until I saw Giuseppe Tassinari's majestic figure appear on the bridge opposite. To simulate an air of informality, he had brought his small son Sergio with him. Marianna welcomed her—or, rather, my—guest with the grace of a Dogaressa and conducted us into the bright little dining-room. Here, on a table covered with a snow-white cloth, old Murano glasses competed for our favour with an array of cold sea-food—lobster, scampi and mussels reposing appetisingly in sauces peculiar to the traditional cuisine of Venice. The festive picture was completed by a large carafe of red Veronese. It was like peace-time. We both laughed, I at the recollection of my spinach lunch at Tarvis, and the minister at this renewed demonstration that one could get the Italians to do almost anything except observe regulations and use their ration cards.

Marianna curtseyed like a character in a Goldoni comedy—the only missing feature was a small orchestra—and withdrew. After the meal we got down to business. I laid all my cards on the table. Only the Germans believe in the hallowed generalisation that all Italians are untrustworthy. During the years I spent shuttling back and forth between Italy and Germany I came across quite as many untrustworthy Germans as Italians, the only difference being that the latter invested their perfidy with more charm.

Tassinari listened to me with polite attention. We at once agreed that the country was on the verge of a separate peace, and that chaos was impending in the German-occupied provinces from Naples northwards. He agreed with me that a come-back by Mussolini, given that he could be found and freed, would be no more than the resurrection of a living corpse, and both of us secretly hoped that the situation would not arise. This being so, I suggested that he form, in consultation with Italy's German allies, a politically neutral government composed of specialist ministers. This government, in which both moderate Fascists and moderate monarchists would be represented, was to remain largely independent of the German army of occupation and the Reich, and was to continue in office until the outcome of the war was finally decided. Tassinari mentioned a number of eminent academics and industrialists whom he proposed to enlist when the time came. They included a personal friend of his on the board of the Fiat works at Turin, Professor Valletta, who is still the real controller of Italy's largest automobile manufacturers. The minister also asked me if I would act as intermediary between his shadow cabinet and the German authorities. I cannot thank the gods enough for having spared me this form of martyrdom!

Having achieved a broad measure of agreement, we discussed the question of liaison in the event of an Italian armistice. I was able to inform him that he and his family were already under the protection of the German High Command. Finally, we drained a glass to the success of our plan, dispensing with the handclasps and ocular pledges of mutual loyalty favoured by dictators on such occasions. They would have been not only superfluous but out of keeping with the picture presented by Marianna when we summoned her and the two boys to join us. She entertained us in her delightful lilting Venetian dialect with all the aplomb of a princess. Then His Excellency departed, complete with son.

Chatting to my old flame afterwards, I learned without undue surprise that the population of Venice could hardly wait for the arrival of a victorious Allied fleet, and that her husband Paolo, now serving on board a cruiser, had no intention of extending our ties of friendship to the sphere of military co-operation. But, whatever happened:

'Nostra casa è Sua casa.' She laid her little head against my melancholy breast once more as she said this. It was a gesture of farewell.

Venice was steaming and glowing with heat, the canals reeked of past centuries, and I grew more and more sad as my hour of departure approached. Recalling all the good times I had enjoyed in the old days at Harry's, the world-famous bar on the Grand Canal, I decided to revive bygone memories. It was a mistake. The bar where all the play-boys and good-time-girls of Europe and America had once congregated was still there, and the Martinis were still as stingingly dry as they had been in the halcyon

days of the Windsors, the Amazonian Rita, and Lord Dorian.
But the leopard was dead, the hedonists dispersed, and the boys
who had mimed Adonis night after night were either slumbering
on the bed of the Mediterranean or interred in the frozen earth
of the Russian steppes. Harry's Bar was not empty, however.
One or two gigolos who had managed by devious means to evade
military service sat around drowsily, waiting for the sound of
Allied gunfire and hoping, no doubt, that the Allied ships would
come equipped with some American millionairesses eager for
male company. Also hanging around were some boys from Lord
Dorian's field of research, equally eager for male company but
with other ends in view.

As for me, I waited for my Martini. It fulfilled my expectations
—unlike Tassinari. I could not know as I sipped it that I would
wait in vain for him to form a government. He missed becoming
head of a new Italian regime, though only by a hair's breadth.

To complete the story of my contribution to the political intri-
cacies of summer 1943, I must move on to the events of September. I had given General Wolff a detailed account of my meeting
in Venice, and after Italy defected on 8 September I left the
responsibility for any further decision to him. A breathless race
against time began. On 11 September, the Duce was released
from his place of detention in Italy's highest mountain, Gran
Sasso in the Abruzzi, with the assistance of German paratroops
under the command of my acquaintance Skorzeny. He was then
flown to Munich via Vienna. The now wingless Italian eagle was
due to render thanks to his friend and saviour Adolf Hitler at
the latter's headquarters on 14 September. On the night of 13–14
September, Tassinari set off by plane for the same destination,
and was received by Hitler an hour before Mussolini's arrival.

Everything went hopelessly awry. Tassinari was very courte-
ously received and allowed to speak for an hour without interruption, but it was the speech of a scholar and academic, not a
fiery political harangue such as the occasion demanded. The only
time he showed any fire was when he came to describe the events
of 25 July.

'This disaster would never have occurred,' he declared, 'if the
Duce had been his old self.'

To everyone's surprise, Hitler merely gave a start and continued to listen in silence to Tassinari's proposals for the formation of a non-party government of experts—the sole means, he asserted, of eliminating the risk of civil war in Italy. Then Tassinari got down to personalities, but only in a negative way. He bitterly condemned his personal enemies among the former Fascists but was very vague on the subject of nominations to his prospective cabinet—in complete contrast to the line he had adopted at our meeting in Venice.

Adolf Hitler's manner became increasingly cool. When the audience was over he turned to Ribbentrop, who was also present, and said:

'Tassinari is a thoroughly decent, good and sincere patriot, I've no doubt, but I'm afraid he's a typical academic and theoretician.'

Did Hitler really pay any attention to Tassinari, or were his thoughts already with his 'best friend'; or, again, was he playing another of his favourite double games? Whatever the truth, the two dictators' melodramatic reunion half an hour later deserved musical backing from the score of Wagner's *Götterdämmerung*.

The Tassinari project was still-born. I do not know if Mussolini was ever fully aware of my abortive attempt to assist at its birth, but if he was he never showed it. I still submit that a great deal of trouble and misfortune would have been avoided if my favourite had taken over the government and the Duce and his family had chosen honourable exile in some German castle or other.

I did not, of course, know all this when I returned from Tarvis. On 21 August I celebrated my birthday at the Villa Volkonsky as a guest of the ambassadress, as I did every year. Frau von Mackensen was extremely worried about her husband, whom Hitler was treating with the same repulsive duplicity which he had once used on her father, Foreign Minister von Neurath, on the occasion of his dismissal in 1938. On a series of pretexts which varied from day to day, the ambassador was being held as a 'guest' at Führer's Headquarters, where the prospect of a return to Rome was constantly dangled before him even though another diplomat had been earmarked for his post ever since the Tarvis conference. A similar fate had overtaken Prince Philipp of Hessen, once Hitler's favourite errand-boy for special missions to Rome. What had once been an asset in the eyes of the dictator, namely, the Prince's privileged position in the royal household as the King's son-in-law, became transformed after 25 July—and even more so after 8 September—into a liability which doomed him to be moved from prison-camp to prison-camp until the end of the war, only one step away from death the whole time.

Every guest at my small birthday party suspected that this would be our last celebration together at the Villa Volkonsky. Nothing could disguise that fact, neither the intoxicating scent of summer roses, nor the summer symphony of bird-song, nor the indefatigable chirping of the crickets. The only entertaining note of the evening—my description of a birthday audience with Carmine Senise at the Ministry of the Interior that morning— had a macabre undertone. The police chief had presented me with a huge toy in the shape of an expensive mahogany box containing the wherewithal for many hours of harmless amusement: an authentic copy of a Monte Carlo roulette wheel, an exquisite pack of patience cards which had once belonged to Princess Paolina Borghese, Napoleon's favourite sister, and— the crowning glory—a delightful baroque chess-set which would have done credit to a museum. I thanked Senise profusely and asked him, with a smile, whether he would like to play a little roulette with me. He responded—with a cryptic jocularity which sent a chill down my spine—by suggesting that we stake our respective heads on a spin of the wheel.

On 2 September Frau von Mackensen left Rome for good, having been ambassadress at the Quirinal since May 1938. She had proved her worth in every situation where it was incumbent upon a woman of poise and a diplomat's daughter to do so. His Majesty had amazed everyone at court banquets by becoming affable and talkative in her presence, and Benito Mussolini, who had held her father in high esteem during his time as ambassador in Rome, confided in her more freely than was his normal practice with the ladies of the diplomatic corps. Even in the case of the Crown Princess, a haughty and avowedly anti-German woman whose tart intelligence was unalloyed with any form of charm, she succeeded in establishing a relationship which a more adroit Foreign Office than Ribbentrop's would have welcomed and exploited as a gift from the gods. Her only 'failure' was a creditable and ladylike one. She did not care for Galeazzo Ciano and his collection of belles, and her aversion to Mussolini's son-in-law became intensified during the State banquet in honour of Hitler at the Palazzo Venezia in May 1938, when he tried to bestow on her a token of esteem which would have been more appropriate to a peasant wedding.

All Germany's official representatives in Rome and Italy turned out to see her off. I attended to the unofficial side of things by bringing along Signorina Bibi, my Alsatian, and the few Roman princes who still dared to consort with Italy's German allies. We stood a little apart from the Weizsäckers, Field Marshal Kesselring and his staff officers, and Rudolf Rahn, von Mackensen's successor. I had never felt lonelier. Baron von Weizsäcker's sparkling blue sailor's eyes appealed to me as little as the thought of his wife's forthcoming Bach season. As to the new ambassador, I knew that he was a cultured and highly intelligent man, but his bushy eyebrows, coupled with the idea that he was to succeed my friend and patron Mackensen, put me—quite unreasonably, I am sure—into a melancholy frame of mind. I watched the Field Marshal closely. He had been a true and chivalrous friend to the departing ambassadress during the difficult weeks that lay behind her, and the deep disfavour into which her husband had fallen had only reinforced his friendly attitude. Now that I had lost my protectors in the two embassies, I once more resolved to place my official services and knowledge of Italy at Kesselring's disposal. I never regretted my decision.

The huge dark bird rose into the air, dwindled, and finally disappeared. The animated conversation between Bibi and the princes momentarily dispelled the gloomy forebodings which filled my mind and were so soon to prove justified.

Another five days of 'snake-pit' lay ahead of me. On 30 August Rahn had officially assumed control of embassy business and granted me an interview. He was cautiously optimistic, and seemed anxious not to do anything which might aggravate the growing crisis. Our conversation was correct in tone, but we found little to say to each other.

Shortly afterwards, General Castellano invited me to call on him at General Staff Headquarters in the Palazzo Vidoni. It was a fortress bristling with men and guns, and for a moment I wondered whether I was destined to leave it under armed guard. My fears were groundless. Castellano, who had secretly returned from Lisbon with the text of the Allied armistice terms on 27 August, embraced me with all the warmth of a comrade-in-arms and begged me to look upon General Staff Headquarters as my future Italo-German liaison centre. I shook his proffered hand with fervour while a morose-looking orderly served the customary vermouth *d'onore*. Since I did not believe a word of the smooth Sicilian's protestations of friendship and my main concern was to get out of the building in one piece, I promised to give Field Marshal Kesselring a full account of the warm and auspicious reception I had been accorded. I would have given a great deal to know what the Italian generals said to each other when I was safely outside again.

I did not learn until much later, of course, that during his armistice mission to Portugal General Castellano had briefed the Allies on the strength and location of every German unit in Italy. He was mistaken if he thought I would be of help to him in this respect, since military dispositions were quite beyond my ken. It should be said at this juncture that, whatever their former rank, unit and colour of uniform, any Germans who claim to have had advance knowledge of 8 September are simply lying. I do not say this because I myself knew nothing, but because my ignorance was genuinely shared by everyone, from Ambassador Rahn and Field Marshal Kesselring down to Police Attaché Kappler, Otto Skorzeny and Colonel Helfferich of Intelligence. Admiral Canaris may—I repeat, may—have known something, but this is just another of the unsolved mysteries in which the Abwehr chief's career abounds. Of course everyone guessed that something was in the wind; of course everyone knew that things could not go on as they were; of course the serpents of treachery, deceit and defection were creeping out of every palace, government office and military headquarters, but no one knew when and where they would strike first.

Signorina Bibi, her prince and the Alfrediani were as much in the dark as everyone else. I came very close to the truth on the morning of the fateful day—how close I did not realise at the time. It was a Wednesday, and the weather was as oppressively hot and sultry as it had been on 25 July. That morning I was informed, in the mysterious manner then in vogue throughout Rome, that someone wished to speak to me urgently in the Forum. Although no names were mentioned, I knew at once that the person in question was an ex-colleague of Bocchini's, a man who had lost his post as a result of 25 July but not his contacts or his nose for information. We had a long-standing arrangement to use the great Caesar's memorial as our rendezvous in case of necessity. We might just as easily have picked the triumphal arch of Titus, but the time for triumphs was past.

I made my way to the Forum alone except for my Alsatian, universally known in Rome as *il lupo*, 'the wolf', although sheep and Pekinese were his only prey. There was no one about. It was far too hot for most people, and Rome's last air-raid had discouraged the general public from walking the streets until nightfall. My confidant was sweating with excitement, and it was not long before I did likewise, first because it was appallingly hot in the Forum and, secondly, because the news he brought me seemed to rob the air of its last breath of coolness.

Two senior American officers had been in Rome since 10 p.m. the previous night, apparently with the intention of putting a pistol to the head of the Italian military leaders. It was like something out of a classical drama. They had been sneaked into Rome in a lorry after an adventurous flight, and had then conducted lengthy discussions with various generals in the Palazzo Caprara, one of the General Staff annexes. After that they had been granted a midnight interview with Marshal Badoglio, not returning to the Palazzo Caprara until 3 a.m. (8 September). My bearer of evil tidings even knew the names of General Eisenhower's envoys: one was General Maxwell Taylor, second-in-command of the American 82nd Airborne Division, and the other an army colonel named Gardiner.

I refrained from inquiring the source of my informant's news. He knew nothing more, but what he knew was quite enough. It was clear, even to a mind as unmilitary as mine, that the not-so-secret appearance in Rome of two senior American officers portended something of unusual, nay, crucial importance. Above all, I knew Badoglio. Like the true Piedmontese he was, he retired to bed with the punctuality of a clock, and nothing irritated him more than nocturnal interruptions. He was seventy-two years old, and the past few weeks had cost him quite enough sleep already. Taylor's mission must be sensational indeed if the generals in the Palazzo Caprara and the elderly Marshal in his official villa were prepared to risk an encounter between officers in American uniform and German army personnel or Skorzeny's men.

I mentally invoked Caesar's ghost, but the Italian opposite me was quite as knowledgable on the subject of *coup d'état* and conspiracy as the dictator of ancient Rome. He assured me that these nocturnal discussions could mean only one thing, namely, that Victor Emmanuel and Badoglio would very shortly be deserting their allies—probably within the next twenty-four hours. He implored me to 'do something', and I decided to do what I could. Having thanked him, I drove to the Vatican Embassy to have a talk with Teddy von Kessel, the shrewdest diplomat there. I found him with the beautiful daughter of Count Welczek, former-ly German Ambassador in Madrid and Paris, Princess Aldobran-dini, whose first reaction to the news was to commend her hus-band's palatial villa in Frascati and his huge flocks of sheep to my protection.

Her concern was timely, because we heard shortly afterwards that Frascati had been almost razed to the ground by an Allied air-raid. Miraculously, Kesselring's villa was only slightly dam-aged, even though my 'friend' General Castellano had obligingly ringed the Field Marshal's headquarters in red on an aerial map which the Allies had given him in Lisbon.

While Princess Aldobrandini hurried back to burning Frascati, her villa and her sheep, I pondered on my interview in the Forum and my forthcoming visit to Kesselring's headquarters, where I was due to dine that evening. I felt more than ever certain that the game of intrigue had reached its climax. After discussing the situation with Signorina Bibi, I appointed her guardian of my books and other treasured possessions, including an extensive collection of photographs, menus, invitations and souvenir booklets acquired during my travels as an interpreter. I also gave her my signed photograph of Benito Mussolini and told her to hide it behind a photograph of herself as a young girl, where no one would guess at its existence. She smiled mysteriously and imprinted a tender kiss on my forehead. Then, just as I was about to leave for the Field Marshal's dinner-table, I switched on the radio and heard:

The Italian government recognises the impossibility of continuing the unequal struggle against a superior foe, and has, with a view to sparing the people further grave misfortune, requested General Eisenhower, supreme commander of the Anglo-American forces, for an armistice. This request has been granted.

In consequence of this, all hostile action against Anglo-American forces by Italian forces is to cease everywhere. The latter will, however, react against any attacks from another source.

The voice belonged to Marshal Badoglio—I remembered his unmistakably Piedmontese accent from the days when I used to translate for him. I regretted that the interview which I had planned to have with him in the next few days would not now take place. It would no doubt have provided him with an opportunity to assure me, as he had assured others that, 'la guerra continua'.

Whistling to my bodyguard, Lupo the Alsatian, I drove first to the Villa Volkonsky. The oasis of peacocks, roses and chirping crickets was in a state of turmoil. Pale-faced diplomats of every rank scurried to and fro carrying bundles of papers, apparently bent on organising an auto-da-fé. They scarcely deigned to recognise me, perhaps because they were afraid I would demand a seat in the special train which the ambassador had, in accordance with international law, requested during his farewell interview with Foreign Minister Guariglia.

The ambassador, who was busy burning documents, received me and gave me a brief account of his last audience at the Palazzo Chigi. Guariglia later described the encounter as follows:

Rahn entered my office calmly, a sign that, despite his suspicions, he was still not fully convinced that the armistice had actually been signed. My statement to this effect came as a grave blow to him, and his anger was clearly apparent. He made no reply, and slammed the door behind him.

That was the end of the Axis, at least where the Italian Foreign Ministry was concerned. The ambassador was obviously relieved when I told him of my decision to join Kesselring at Frascati, and wished me luck. I wished him and his special train the same. The other embassy staff, soldiers included, were so pressed for time and so busy with their plans for departure that we had no opportunity to exchange valedictory remarks. I walked through the magnificent gardens once more, remembering all the happy hours I had spent there and privately cursing the white peacocks as they raised a plaintive and discordant cry in honour—or execration—of the armistice. Finally, I shook hands with the humbler members of the embassy staff, and this time our mutual salutations were sincerely meant.

Then I drove off to Frascati in the gathering twilight. The trip took barely an hour in normal times, but on this occasion it took rather longer. After 25 July my friend Senise had given me some papers guaranteeing me free passage anywhere inside Italy. With these in my pocket and Lupo at my side, I felt doubly armed. I soon discovered to my regret that Lupo only bristled and bared his huge fangs when he scented the proximity of sheep. As for the numerous patrols which flagged us down, he gave them a friendly reception, too inured to the sight of uniforms to be affected by Badoglio and his treachery.

Senise's signature worked wonders. Detectives, policemen and other personnel entrusted with carrying out the terms of the armistice saluted in a friendly fashion and allowed me to pass. I began to breathe more easily, but my relief was premature. Not far from my destination an awesome-looking road-block had been erected, and even Senise's permits failed to get me through. A company of the Royal Carabinieri was drawn up on either side of the road. The men's manner was correct but cool, and nothing could shake their royalist sympathies. It occurred to me that Benito Mussolini had been a prisoner of just such men on the night of 25–26 July, and the recollection was not a cheering one. The only thing which had any effect on Carabinieri was a Prussian, soldierly tone of voice—and I was no stranger to the sound. Divesting myself of what has been called my Italianate charm, I assumed an equally glacial manner and demanded to be taken to the officer in charge. I inquired his name and rank, and almost spoilt my act by smiling when I heard that Major Pensabene was in command—not only because Pensabene means 'think well' but because the major had been a frequent guest at Signorina Bibi's parties. My acquaintanceship with him had taught me that he was a conscientious Carabinieri officer but not averse to enjoying himself. I walked into his temporary office, and was gratified to see my escorts give a start of surprise when they heard his cheerful words of welcome. He offered me a cigarette and aroused further surprise by telling his orderly to open a bottle of wine from the town I was trying to get to.

Pensabene inquired after Bibi and her prince, and I flattered him by commending them to his protection. I also requested permission to continue my journey, simultaneously hinting that the Field Marshal would undoubtedly send out a search-party if I did not turn up for dinner, and that the search-party's first objective would no less undoubtedly be the road-block under his command. Finally, I made a casual reference to the meaning of his name, which made him laugh. Being an Italian, he was susceptible to omens. He had obviously 'thought well' when he raised his glass and said:

'Caro Dollmann, alla Sua fortuna—ma anche all mia! You may have occasion to "think well" on my behalf sometime—who knows? One more thing: tell the Field Marshal that we are only doing our duty, and that not all of us have forgotten the years of alliance.'

I toasted him in return. The barrier was raised as soon as I emerged with Pensabene beside me. His Carabinieri saluted smartly, and I continued on my way to Frascati. The Field Marshal and his staff were obviously pleased to see me safe, sound, and in possession of the latest news from Rome. I am sure Kesselring's staff officers had already placed bets on whether or not I would take refuge with them. Soldiers are not great judges of human nature as a rule, and they had no idea how glad I was to be with them rather than in the overcrowded diplomatic train.

I was pressed to describe my morning oracle in the Forum. Maxwell Taylor's name had an electrifying effect. Everyone was convinced that Eisenhower would never have sent such a senior paratroop commander to Rome if a large-scale airborne landing were not on the cards. Feverish preparations were made to counter such a landing, which would very probably have decided Rome's fate in favour of the Allies. Unfortunately, Kesselring's staff officers knew nothing of the chaos prevailing in the city, nothing of the royal family's removal to the more easily defended War Ministry, nothing of the failure by Badoglio and his generals to provide for the city's defence. They did not know, either, that the 135 transport planes which were standing by at French North African airfields, ready to lift advance elements of the American 82nd Airborne Division to the Roman airfields of Furbara and Cerbeteri, would never take off.

The secret envoy who had been dispatched by Eisenhower to Rome on the night of 7–8 September 1943 was second-in-command of the 82nd Airborne. Who, in the course of that dramatic evening at Frascati, could have forecast that God, in his inscrutable wisdom, would destine the same officer to head the Pentagon in July 1962? General Taylor was the first senior American officer I ever came into contact with, if only through the medium of Julius Caesar's ghost. The second was Colonel, later General, Lemnitzer, who ultimately succeeded General Norstad at NATO Headquarters, also in July 1962. It was Lemnitzer who, in a villa at Ascona in March 1945, conducted the first secret military talks on the subject of an armistice for the German forces in Italy, talks which had been initiated at the beginning of the same month.

X

MY FIGHT FOR ROME

For a night and a day uncertainty reigned, both at Frascati and in the world at large. Once again, the fate of the Eternal City hung in the balance. No less than six Italian divisions had taken up positions round Rome to oppose any German counter-moves and enforce the armistice terms solemnly proclaimed by Badoglio on 8 September. If the large-scale airborne invasion which Taylor had mooted to the shocked and sleepy Marshal during the night of 7–8 September had actually taken place, Kesselring and the slender forces under his command would undoubtedly have been lost. Their fate would also have been sealed, one presumes, if the six Italian divisions had been in a full state of combat readiness, but they were not. Some of them were as unreliable as the old 'M' Division, which Galbiati had failed to lead into Rome on 25 July. This now bore the name 'Centauro' and was under the command of the King's son-in-law, Count Calvi di Bergolo. The remaining units were more reliable from Badoglio's point of view, but they all lacked ammunition, equipment and, above all, unified command and a concerted plan of action.

I attended my first conference at Frascati on the evening of 9–10 September, feeling very military and appropriately self-important. In the course of discussion, the Field Marshal asked me if I thought he ought to allow for the possibility of an armed rebellion by the population of Rome. On the strength of almost fifteen years' experience of the Italian mentality I felt able to reassure him. The Romans have often demonstrated in the course of their turbulent history that they dislike rising, whether in the morning or against an enemy.

They only rose against their Caesars when the latter's willingness to ply them with bread and ciruses waned, and Cola di Rienzo's popular insurrection in the Middle Ages was an isolated exception. The Roman populace did not drive out Charles V's mercenaries in response to the notorious *sacco di Roma*, nor did they ever rise in revolt in the course of centuries marked by gross and unparalleled mismanagement of the *patrimonium Petri*. They had not vented their wrath on Benito Mussolini on 25 July, and I assured Kesselring that their reaction this time would be similar: they would merely wait with folded arms to see whose hands their city fell into, the British and Americans, with the Badoglio government trailing pitifully along in their wake, or the Germans. My assertion was greeted with smiles, but the Field Marshal himself believed me. He backed my judgement a second time in March 1944, when the situation again hung by a thread after the Allied landing at Anzio, near Rome. Once again, universal expectations of a Roman uprising proved to be unfounded.

The far from cheerful mood which reigned at the Field Marshal's headquarters during the night of 8–9 September and for most of the following day underwent a considerable change when news arrived of the royal family's flight and Badoglio's assumption of power. Just as Wilhelm II had preferred to make for the shelter of the Dutch frontier in his special train instead of setting an honourable seal on his career, so King Victor Emmanuel III of Savoy abandoned the attempt to defend Rome and his crown. Like the Kaiser's decision, that of Victor Emmanuel spelt the inevitable doom of his dynasty. The escape itself was just as contemptible and just as inefficiently and precipitately carried out as its historical prototype, the flight of the unfortunate Louis XVI and his even more unfortunate queen to Varennes. At 5.10 a.m. on 9 September, while we at Frascati were waiting for the King to take command of his six divisions and march on the Field Marshal's headquarters, several cars drove into the courtyard of the War Ministry, where the royal family had sought refuge the night before. Their Majesties climbed in accompanied by Crown Prince Umberto, whose father had persuaded him—much against his better judgement—to flee with them. Also in the party was the new head of government, Marshal Badoglio, once more wrested from his slumbers at an untimely hour.

And so the Savoys fled from the city where they had been established since 1870. The King and Queen never saw it again, and their rather more charming and intelligent son only returned for the space of the May Monarchy, as his brief reign was nick-named. At that very moment, bereft though they were of sover-eign, commander-in-chief, ammunition and equipment, isolated units of the King's forces were engaging the Germans in brisk but hopeless combat.

For the Savoys it was the end of the road; for the people of Rome a further demonstration of their already legendary histor-ical good fortune.

'His Majesty left Rome with a heavy heart. He hoped to guar-antee the continued existence of the Badoglio government in co-operation with Italy's new allies; above all, he hoped to spare the Eternal City the horrors of war.' Thus wrote the King's devoted aide, General Puntoni, of the decision of a man who, throughout his long reign since 1900, had displayed the prover-bial cunning of his house, the parsimony of the Piedmontese, and—for a brief hour—the exalted courage of another member of his line, Prince Eugene of Savoy. In November 1917, after the disastrous battle of Caporetto and the break-through at Isonzo, Victor Emmanuel had averted the threatened collapse of the Italian lines of defence at a conference between the erstwhile Allies at Peschiera, attended by Lloyd George, Painlevé and Franklin-Bouillon. There was no question of this in 1943. His Majesty's decades of subservience to Fascism had robbed him of any such heroic impulses and accustomed him, like his personal friend, the last Tsar of all the Russias, to the circumscribed family life of a country nobleman.

I acted as Victor Emmanuel's interpreter several times, even though he had a good knowledge of German. It was no pleasure. Probably because of his bad teeth, His Majesty scarcely deigned to open his mouth and spoke with extreme indistinctness. He never went beyond routine courtesies—not that this was surpris-ing. He knew only too well how much his imperial cousin Wilhelm

II had scorned him on account of his small stature, and how much more Hitler despised him as a medieval curb on the activities of his great and good friend Benito Mussolini. All in all, he had no reason to love the Germans.

His flight quickly put paid to Italian resistance in the vicinity of Rome, but he did the Eternal City at least one inestimable service by leaving it a parting gift in the person of his son-in-law, Count Calvi di Bergolo. This once renowned horseman and cavalry officer, who had greatly displeased Victor Emmanuel by marrying Yolanda, his prettiest daughter, in 1923, entered into negotiations with Field Marshal Kesselring on 9 September, and these negotiations led to a cessation of hostilities on the following day. As I predicted, the inhabitants of the capital emulated their ancestors' approach to the tumults and disturbances of ancient Rome by playing the part of interested but passive spectators. They watched paratroops advancing into the Colosseum with the alert attention once bestowed by their forbears on Christians being burnt to death on the same site. They wanted a German defeat, of course, but what they wanted most of all was the counter-manding of Badoglio's hated proclamation that the war would go on. Now that an armistice was, by their reckoning, in force, they wanted to see their uniformed sons home again as quickly as possible. Their wish was devoutly shared by the soldiers, and the valiant resistance put up by individual units round Rome did not alter that fact.

It is still uncertain what prompted Count Calvi to negotiate with Kesselring. Whether he acted on secret instructions from the fleeing monarch, as the Italians later alleged, or from a real-isation of the hopelessness of the struggle, or out of a wish to 'spare Rome the horrors of war', his true motives will probably never be known. He certainly behaved in an intelligent and far from cowardly manner. Later on, when his position in Rome became untenable, I did my utmost to ensure that his honour was safeguarded and his future made as tolerable as possible. Despite the greatest initial difficulties, he was able to spend the closing stages of the war, first in a castle in Piedmont and later with his family in Switzerland.

By the morning of 11 September, matters were far enough

advanced for me to leave my place of temporary exile and return to Rome, whose shimmering outlines I had glimpsed with such nostalgia from the vine-clad hills of Frascati during the past two days. There had been ample time for me to ponder on my personal future, and I had finally decided to throw in my lot with Field Marshal Kesselring. Before leaving, I suggested that he might find some use for my knowledge of Italy. I had lost two ambassadors, Mackensen and Bergen, my friend Buffarini-Guidi was a prisoner of the Badoglio regime in Rome, the Tassinari project was still in the air, and Benito Mussolini was shrouded in the mists of the Gran Sasso. Kesselring at once fell in with my proposal and said he would contact General Wolff, who had since 8 September been invested with the majestic and megalomaniac title of 'Supreme SS and Police Commander in Italy'. Kesselring and his title suited my purposes better. My ambition was to stay in Rome as long as possible, and I was less likely to achieve it with General Wolff than with the Commander-in-Chief, Southern Command.

Persuasively, as I believe, I outlined to Kesselring the necessity of abandoning Rome to the Allies, primarily on political and moral grounds, and urged him to follow out the intentions of another field marshal, Rommel, who regarded Rome as so much strategic ballast. I received a sympathetic hearing. Indeed, from then on Albert Kesselring readily lent an ear to problems which would have been beyond the comprehension of most soldiers. I cannot say that this interview made me feel like the future saviour of Rome, a role later assumed by far greater and more important men from every walk of life. Everyone saved Rome, from His Holiness Pope Pius XII to the humblest priest, from neo-Fascists to Resistance fighters. Far be it from me to begrudge them my admiration. My own modest contribution was not inspired by their lofty ethical and moral ideals, but stemmed mainly from a desire to remain in Rome for as long as humanly possible, to linger with Signorina Bibi on my terrace overlooking the Spanish Steps, to stay with my friends of both sexes in every stratum of society. I wanted to go on visiting my favourite little trattorias with the Alfrediani, who needed me more than ever now, to go on drinking the golden wine which hailed from the little town whose hospitality I had enjoyed between 8 and 11 September, during my brief spell in exile. Above all, I wanted to avoid being closeted in an office with a bunch of stupid secretaries or posted to a German headquarters where I would be surrounded by orderlies and equally stupid superiors. So far, I had managed to remain as free and independent as it was possible for a German in Italy to be, and Kesselring, who probably shrank from incorporating me in his staff except in a supernumerary capacity, was prepared to guarantee my freedom.

I felt sure that Wolff would sanction the proposal. Apart from the fact that the Field Marshal carried great weight, I had often tried to convince Wolff of how much Rome meant, both to me and in general.

I returned to Rome in triumph and without any recourse to the services of Major Pensabene. The ubiquitous detachments of paratroops not only placed no obstacle in my path but sped me on my way. In the Piazza di Spagna mothers and daughters welcomed me with tears of joy, just as they would have welcomed General Eisenhower if he had billeted himself on them. My handsome gander Mario, originally a gift to the table from Bibi's prince but now a universal pet, waddled eagerly to meet me with wings flapping, and observed time-honoured tradition by nipping my Alsatian's tail. Cuno von Gandersheim, to give the dog his pedigree name, was the only creature not to welcome our return home, principally because exile at Frascati had afforded him unparalleled opportunities for pursuing stray sheep.

We sat down to a table laden with delicious *spaghetti alla romana*. I had brought along one or two nice young paratroop officers whom I had met in Frascati—so genuinely young and nice that Signorina Bibi forgot her disappointment at not being able to try out her newly acquired English on some nice young Britons and Americans. As Kesselring had already informed me, these youthful heroes were under orders to co-operate with Police Attaché Kappler next morning in liberating the senior Fascist dignitaries whom Marshal Badoglio had incarcerated in Forte Bocca, a military prison.

The paratroop officers were most insistent at first that I should join them in this Homeric operation. I thought of Buffarini-

Guidi, who was one of the prisoners, then of Marshal Cavallero and General Galbiati. The others I knew less well. I ought at least to have helped to release Buffarini-Guidi, but the young officers gradually forgot about the necessity for my presence and it was ultimately decided that I should take charge of arrangements for a 'liberation lunch' at the German Embassy. I do not know what contributed most to this decision—the good food, the even better wine, or Signorina Bibi's slightly disdainful smile at the idea of my being involved in a military operation. At all events, I did not take part—although, in view of the peaceful way in which the captives were handed over, I might just as well have done.

At 2 p.m. next day I was waiting for them in the grounds of the Villa Volkonsky. There were no peacocks left to greet me. They had all fallen prey to the appetite of the occupying troops, who had apparently found them tough eating. An army lieutenant of classical education complained bitterly to me that the banquets of the ancient world must have been a fraud. He had forgotten that the ancient Romans only ate peacocks' tongues in special sauces, and was disappointed that the wherewithal for a culinary experiment in that direction no longer existed.

A convoy of German jeeps squealed to a halt outside the embassy. The heavily armed paratroops who were manning them grinned as their passengers got out. I almost grinned too, but remembered in the nick of time that I was on the brink of an historic moment.

With due composure I went to meet the shambling scarecrows whom I had so often seen in glittering, bemedalled uniforms. Their faces were unshaven now, their shirts soiled, their trousers torn. The platinum ring which had once excited Hermann Göring's admiration adorned Buffarini-Guidi's hand no longer, and Cavallero, who had resembled an industrial tycoon in uniform, now had the shabby appearance of an unsuccessful commercial traveller. Only Galbiati, who still looked as if he were waiting for orders, held his empty head high.

They all rushed forward to kiss and embrace me, much to the amusement of the paratroopers, who obviously thought we were all mad and almost dropped their sub-machine-guns in surprise.

It was a singularly Italian and rather unappetising form of martyr-dom, but not one which I could decently evade. I did not count the hugs and kisses I received because, apart from the three principal figures, the party included numerous other generals and Fascists of my acquaintance.

Buffarini told me in a whisper that he was the only responsible member of the party, and pointed to the Marshal. Cavallero really did give an impression of bewilderment—almost of mental dis-order. Only a nervous breakdown could have accounted for the fact that he brought the ensuing meal to an end in the time-honoured way, by proposing the health of the fugitive King coupled with that of the Duce. I managed to quell the tumult that broke out by announcing to the assembled company that Benito Mussolini had just landed at an airfield near Rome, bound for Vienna. To men who had heard no news since the day of their imprisonment, this came as a fanfare of trumpets. There was a yell of exultation. The former Colonial Minister, who boasted a lion's head on his wall at home, could scarcely contain him-self, and Galbiati pictured himself at the head of a new division. Only Cavallero blanched, and his face turned even paler when I told him that he and his companions were to be driven as guests of the Field Marshal to a hotel on the edge of Frascati, whence they would be flown to Germany next day. He was the only one who did not want to go. Knowing, as I did, that Kesselring not only held him in high esteem but had selected him as supreme commander of the reorganised Italian armed forces, I could not understand his reluctance. What neither the Field Marshal nor I knew at this stage was that Cavallero had sent Badoglio a mem-orandum from Forte Bocca, informing him that he, Cavallero, had devised a plan for ousting the Duce as early as autumn 1942. Since, in the nature of things, the author of the memorandum knew of its existence, his attack of nerves was understandable. It would have been even more pronounced if he had known that the worthy Badoglio, who detested him, had deliberately left this memorandum lying on his desk before embarking on his precipit-ate flight on the morning of 9 September. Or did he guess? Treach-ery is a risky business, and the last thing a traitor should do is commit his perfidy to paper. I was amazed when I learned the truth, not because I had never regarded Cavallero as a rock of constancy, but because I had credited him with more intelligence. We calmed the agitated man, and he eventually accompanied the rest of the party to Frascati, where Kesselring was waiting to confer with him.

I never saw him alive again. He did not join the others on the flight to Germany on 13 September, but spent the afternoon visiting his sick wife. That evening he was Kesselring's guest at dinner. The Field Marshal, who describes the scene in his memoirs (*Soldat bis zum letzten Tag*, Athenäum-Verlag, Bonn, 1953), hinted to Cavallero that Hitler had always regarded him with particular favour and that he would undoubtedly recommend him to Mussolini as War Minister. 'Count Cavallero looked exceedingly grave during dinner, but I put it down to the excitement of the past few weeks and the fact that he had just taken leave of his wife.'

Only Cavallero knew why he looked so grave. He must have been thinking of his memorandum and of the effect it would have on Mussolini if he learned of its contents. He spent the night of 13–14 September pacing restlessly up and down his room, and dawn found him wandering in the grounds of the superbly situated hotel. It was at the hotel that I saw him for the last time, just as the morning sun was beginning to gild the Roman Campagna and the vineyards of Frascati. Cavallero was seated in an armchair with his dead eyes fixed on the distant dome of St Peter's. He was leaning forward slightly, and the revolver with which he had ended his life had slid to the ground, where it lay gleaming dully like some noxious reptile. It was a scene of tragic grandeur. But for his open eyes, Cavallero might have been sleeping peacefully, far removed from all earthly passions and earthly cares.

I cannot provide him with a better epitaph than the following lines from Kesselring's memoirs:

I respected Count Cavallero and lent him my unqualified support because I had found him to be a staunch friend of the Axis who believed that the furtherance of our common interests would greatly benefit Italy, to whose service he devoted his life, unreservedly and in the face of all opposition. A man of well above average gifts and excellent military qualifications, he combined shrewd diplomatic skill with a high degree of vigour, and was, in my opinion, the only one of his contemporaries capable of bringing the Italian armed forces into line with the Italian war economy. I say this advisedly, in full cognisance of his inherent weaknesses and of the great hostility which he aroused in a certain section of the officer corps of the Italian armed forces.

The historic 'liberation lunch' and the surprise announcement of Mussolini's release had not filled me with anything approaching the rapture felt by the assembled ex-Fascists. Skorzeny's daredevil exploit exactly coincided with my attempt to realise the Tassinari project, which I had evolved without any inkling that the Lazarus of the Gran Sasso would stage a sensational return from the dead. I accordingly used the time which remained before the guests' departure to acquaint Buffarini-Guidi with my plan. With a quickness of reaction which far exceeded that of most German and Italian politicians, he told me that the liberated Duce would never agree to my bright idea. He had nothing against the ex-Minister of Agriculture personally, however unappealing he found the man's dry professorial objectivity, total lack of interest in intrigues and cabals, and Catonian integrity and incorruptibility. I explained that it was only Buffarini's restricted freedom of movement which had prevented me from communicating with him on the subject of my proposals for a Tassinari government. He was too much of an Italian to believe this, but assured me with an equal show of sincerity that he would have acted just as I had. In view of our genuine friendship, I was able to tell him—truthfully this time—that his conduct on 25 July and subsequent detention by Badoglio had provided the Führer's Headquarters with a proof of his loyalty which would, at the very least, be bound to secure him the Ministry of the Interior. I asked him to convey my greetings to General Wolff and anyone else I knew, and we raised a glass of champagne, not to the Duce, but to Buffarini-Guidi's future tenure of the Ministry of the Interior.

I then addressed myself to a handsome, elderly man who had not arrived until after lunch was over. With grey hair dishevelled by the wind and imposing head held high, he looked like a great general from the days of the Roman Republic. He was, in fact, Marshal Rodolfo Graziani, a man whose military career had alternated between triumph and disaster. Now in his early sixties, he had been Viceroy of Abyssinia from 1936 to 1937, and one of his victories had earned him the title of Marchese di Neghelli. Because of the bitter emnity that existed between him and his fellow-marshal, Badoglio, he had been leading a peaceful life of retirement on his beloved country estate at the foot of the Abruzzi from 1941 until the present time. As a result, few of us knew him well.

Graziani wore an expression which implied that 8 September had been a divine judgement in his favour and against his rival. We exchanged a few polite words, and I assured him—boldly taking Kesselring's name in vain—that the Field Marshal would be enchanted to see him in the near future. I had no idea that Rodolfo Graziani was destined to become Republican Fascist War Minister in Mussolini's re-formed government, nor that he would be commander-in-chief of the new armed forces and, later, commander of the Ligurian Army Group. He did not forget my courteous reception, and his goodwill was a great help to me later on, when I had to interpret for him and Kesselring under extremely difficult conditions.

In the end, the ex-prisoners drove off to Frascati with Cavallero, and Graziani returned to his country village, leaving the embassy temporarily deserted. It remained in the undisputed possession of the paratroops and the new German Military Commandant of Rome, General Stahel, until Ambassador Rahn and his closest associate, Consul Möllhausen, landed in Rome at 5 p.m. Rahn I already knew, of course, but his colleague was a stranger to me. We shook hands appraisingly, establishing—in that one moment—a friendly, loyal and co-operative relationship which endured to the bitter end. Möllhausen's mother came from the South of France and his father from Prussia. He had dark, melancholy eyes and a pale skin, and was, all in all, the precise opposite of the Ribbentrop ideal. Rahn, who helped Möllhausen in his career, later described him as 'loyal, shrewd, vehement, sensitive and happy-go-lucky, quick to understand and misunderstand'. This apt description exactly corresponds to my own impression of him during his time as Consul-General and Deputy Ambassador in Rome. It was small wonder that I took to him immediately. At dawn on 14 September 1943 Marshal Cavallero put a classic end to the life he had gambled away; at midday Tassinari gave his abortive performance at the Führer's Headquarters; shortly afterwards the two corporals celebrated their reunion by shedding tears—not crocodile tears, for once—of emotion and joy. Now began the complex task of forming a government for the new 'Italian Social Republic' under the leadership of a newly resurrected Duce.

I did not witness the unedifying scramble which ensued, but Buffarini-Guidi was a champion player of political musical chairs, and it was enough for me to know that he was on the spot. Most of those who were invited to join the cabinet declined, thereby displaying an admirable measure of political instinct. There were almost no gib names. Buffarini may have been Cicerorian but he was not a demagogue whom the masses would follow with glad cries. That only left Rodolfo Graziani, legendary ex-Viceroy of the lost Abyssinian Empire, whose body still harboured the bullets of the would-be assassin who had once shot at him in Addis Ababa. Half hero, half martyr has always been the perfect recipe for popularity, especially in Italy, but even the grey-haired marshal was reluctant at first. Indeed, he revealed a capacity for indecision which made his earlier military reverses understandable and his victories incomprehensible.

By 23 September the time for a final decision had come. Mussolini had already telephoned from Munich and designated Graziani as Commander-in-Chief and War Minister in his new cabinet. There was no one for him to command as yet except the soldiers who had hot-footed it home after 8 September and the units which had been captured by German troops and interned in German prison-camps, but War Ministers have to toe the line whether they like it or not. Later on, Graziani allowed me to take a look at his diary. The page for that fateful 23 September bore the following entry:

23 September—Thursday.
In Rome. In the morning I saw C., who told me of the difficulties

of forming a government and the lack of suitable personalities. I refused point-blank.

Then to the German Embassy. My name was already on the new government list. My sacrifice was complete. Lunched at the embassy.

That is my drama, and that is the unvarnished truth.

Unfortunately, soldiers' diaries are as inaccurate as those of diplomats. The elderly hero did not behave quite like Iphigenia approaching the sacrificial altar. On the contrary, he conducted a heated argument with Ambassador Rahn and General Wolff, who had also hurried to Rome from Mussolini's new base of operations at Lake Garda. Graziani, who wanted to irritate his colleague Badoglio by accepting the appointment but was unwilling to make the supreme sacrifice, entrenched himself behind his oath of loyalty to the fugitive Victor Emmanuel. This prompted Rahn, in best snake-pit manner, to accuse the King of breaking his own word and betraying the officers and men who had been left in the lurch as a result of his flight. Ably seconded by Wolff, the ambassador went on to paint an alluring picture of how the Anglo-Saxons would be driven from Italian soil, but still the new Napoleon hesitated. At that moment an embassy secretary came in to report that it was two minutes to twelve—i.e. two minutes before the official announcement of Mussolini's new cabinet was due to be broadcast. Rahn appealed to Graziani as 'saviour of the Fatherland', and finally, on the dot of midday, the agitated marshal nodded his acquiescence.

Whether attributable to the ambassador's powers of persuasion or his own weak-mindedness, Graziani's decision earned him years of imprisonment under the post-1945 government, involved him in an interminable trial and ruined his health, although he ultimately escaped with his life.

Buffarini-Guidi, who was also present in the embassy, breathed a sigh of relief. I did too, even though I had lost my candidate for the Ministry of Agriculture, who had been approved by both Rahn and Wolff. An agricultural expert who had been at the Ministry in Tassinari's time, he decided at the last moment in favour of a quiet life in the country. I sympathised with him, and we have remained good friends ever since.

The midday broadcast did not, it is true, proclaim my protégé Tassinari as head of the new government, but I had the satisfaction of hearing that Buffarini-Guidi was to be Minister of the Interior, Tringali-Casanova Minister of Justice, and Biggini Minister of Education. Their loyalty had borne dividends. They were the three men who had lunched with me on 25 July, the three who, unlike so many others, had put Mussolini under an obligation by keeping faith with him the night before.

The ensuing lunch at the Villa Volkonsky passed off in an idyllic atmosphere thanks to Buffarini's social expertise, the martial dignity of the newly sacrificed commander-in-chief, Rahn's experience in handling abnormal situations, and my dutiful efforts as an interpreter. Thinking of Tassinari, I glanced at Wolff, but he gave me a reassuring nod. He had apparently managed to survive the failure of the project without losing prestige in the eyes of Mussolini, whose personal safety was now his prime responsibility.

The Villa Volkonsky had lost some of its charm. Paratroops were encamped on its English-style lawns, transforming the embassy into a sort of fairground which had little in common with the formal atmosphere that had prevailed there in the time of Herr von Mackensen. All the ladies had gone. Their day was past, at least where the German Embassy was concerned, although the princesses, countesses and society women who had belonged to the vanished Count Ciano's circle cultivated me with unwonted enthusiasm.

There were some amusing interludes, for all that. A few days after his inaugural lunch the new War Minister roused me from my slumbers in a state of high excitement. It seemed that the subterranean passages near his house were swarming with foreign invaders, whom he could clearly hear from his cellars. He lived close to the catacombs of Sant'Agnese, and I knew from my earlier studies that they were full of chambers once used as assembly-places by the early Christians. Graziani requested my assistance, and I could hardly refuse to give it.

Not having any armed men at my disposal, I rang the Military Commandant of Rome, General Stahel. He thought I was playing a practical joke on him at first. However, when I told him that

I would have to contact Kesselring direct if he did not help me, he became more amenable and summoned me to the embassy. There he read me a soldierly lecture on the difference between German and Italian field marshals and dispatched me to the catacombs with a force of twenty-five heavily armed and highly unenthusiastic paratroopers. Graziani was waiting for us, attired not as a marshal but in a multicoloured silk dressing-gown which was probably a relic of his viceregal days in Addis Ababa. He gave the paratroopers a report on the situation and a plan of his cellars, and withdrew.

Glancing at the plan, I saw the words '*cantini di vini*'. If the wine-cellar was where the sinister noises were coming from, that was where the hypothetical British agents must have established their hypothetical headquarters. I roused the flagging spirits of my men with allusions to the rich alcoholic rewards awaiting them in the cellar below, and they became considerably more eager for the fray. The operation to which we later gave the symbolic name 'Operation R' then began.

With all the skill and cunning of seasoned veterans, the paratroopers made their way into the former catacombs on which the Villa Graziani stood. The closer we got the more distinctly we could hear scratching, scrabbling, squeaking noises, and I began to suspect that the old man upstairs might be right after all. Then the advance-guard opened an iron door, and a roar of laughter went up as their torches shone on a half-gruesome, half-comical scene: hundreds and hundreds of huge, ancient rats with hairless tails and evil red eyes had adopted Graziani's wine-cellar as their headquarters, and were now baring their sharp and poisonous teeth furiously at the intruders.

The paratroopers wrought frightful havoc among them. The rats clung to their positions grimly, but they eventually gave up, and the survivors scampered off into the next subterranean passage uttering shrill squeals of rage. The floor was red with blood and frightful corpses lay everywhere. The fat-bellied bottles which had been caught by the hail of bullets also dripped red. The victors clumped around in their heavy boots, kicking their dead foes into corners. In the name of the Marshal, whose permission I should have asked first, I followed ancient custom by giving them the run of the remaining stocks of bottles under the supervision of their sergeant-major, while I went upstairs to report to Graziani. The Marshal did not believe me at first, but he could not help laughing when the truth sank in. Still laughing, he accompanied me to the cellar and presented his deliverers with a pair of superb hams from another catacomb which the rats had so far failed to discover. Then we all went home.

This concluded 'Operation R', originally conceived as a round-up of British spies in the catacombs of Sant'Agnese, but from then on a staple item in my interpreter's repertoire of amusing anecdotes.

Far less amusing was my last encounter with a member of the Italian royal family, namely Count Calvi di Bergolo. As I have already mentioned, the Count was a son-in-law of the fugitive king and had done Rome an invaluable but insufficiently appreciated service by entering into negotiations with Field Marshal Kesselring during the critical days immediately after 8 September. He had since been appointed Italian Commandant of Rome, that is to say General Stahel's opposite number. In view of the continuing state of tension, the German military authorities deemed it necessary to ask the Count whether he recognised Mussolini's new government, based at Salò on Lake Garda, and whether he would repudiate his father-in-law's former status as supreme military commander. General Stahel asked me to accompany him on this embarrassing and pointless mission. I agreed to do so as a favour, but only on condition that when Count Calvi refused the German request, as he inevitably would, he was treated with the courtesy due to an officer and allowed to retain his arms.

The brief but dramatic proceedings were conducted in the manner prescribed. The two generals duly met, escorted by their respective staffs, and the Italian promptly and emphatically ruled out any possibility of further loyal co-operation on the new basis. Beckoning me over, he asked me to inform his visitors that they were addressing His Majesty's son-in-law and that, as such, he had no choice but to say no. When apprised of this, General Stahel informed the Count that he would have to be interned in Germany under honourable conditions. He was allowed to keep his sword, but his pistol was taken away. This being against the terms of my agreement with Stahel, I assured the Count that his side-arm would be returned to him—which, after some hesitation, it was. I then accompanied him and his ADC to the train which was to convey him to Germany. It was my last personal encounter with a member of the house of Savoy until the war's end, and we wished each other luck.

Count Calvi's fortunes did not improve until General Wolff managed, with difficulty, to impress on Kaltenbrunner, the head of the Central State Security Bureau, that his internment should be of an honourable nature. He was subsequently permitted to spend the rest of the war in a château in Piedmont, waiting for the moment when he could cross the frontier into Switzerland. He had better luck than his ill-fated sister-in-law, Princess Mafalda of Hessen, who fell prey to a vile trick on the part of SD agents and died in tragic circumstances at Camp Flossenbürg in 1944. She owed her death to Hitler's maniacal detestation of the house of Savoy, which had been instilled in him mainly by Goebbels. Her tragic end will always be an ineffaceable blot on the name of the Third Reich and its rulers. When Kesselring and I inquired the whereabouts of this kind and charming princess we were officially told that she was in good health and living in a villa belonging to her husband. I did not learn of her true fate until 1945.

A sort of peace descended on Rome. The inhabitants awaited the advent of better times in a spirit of passive resistance which prompted them to scrawl on their walls:

'*Non vogliamo ne Tedeschi ne Inglesi. Lasciateci piangere da soli.*' ('We don't want the Germans or the British. Leave us to weep in peace.')

They continued to weep until 4 June 1944, and the intervening winter was the saddest Rome had known for many a century.

My own connection with the formation and first moves of the new government culminated in a summons to escort the newly fledged ministers, headed by '*il terribile vecchio*'—'the Old Terror', as Marshal Graziani was irreverently known—on a visit to their puppet-master's erstwhile Sans Souci, the medieval fortress of Rocca delle Caminate. The castle had been presented to the

Duce in his heyday by the fiery and excitable provincials of Romagna. He was a son of their soil like Pietro Nenni, the man who was later to hold the Italian political scales in balance. Now, after a brief spell of exile at Schloss Hirschberg, near Munich, he had returned to the green hills of Romagna on 25 September and called his first cabinet meeting for two days later.

On 26 September a long column of cars left Rome and headed north. I have forgotten most of the ministers, none of whom carried much weight except for Graziani, Buffarini, Tringali-Casanova and Biggini, but I still cherish pleasant memories of Fernando Mezzasomma, Minister of Popular Culture and the Parsifal of the party. Mezzasomma was one of the few genuine idealists I ever met in the course of my varied career, and he emulated a number of other idealists in 1945 by dying a dignified and honourable death for the sake of his ideals. I regret to say that I also remember Finance Minister Pellegrini, whose appalling servility and Byzantine deviousness fitted perfectly into the *opéra bouffe* atmosphere of Lake Garda.

It was dark when we got to the castle. I recalled that this was where Mussolini used to retire, at crucial moments in his political career, to ponder on whether to be or not to be. If only he had done so before plunging into war on 10 June 1940! How much tragedy and misfortune he might have spared himself and his people if he had first strolled, lost in meditation, along the battlements of his castle or across the vine- and olive-clad slopes surrounding the Rocca!

There was a dismal air about the castle. Someone had evidently ransacked the place after 25 July, because a female member of the Mussolini family had to serve up the spaghetti on cracked dishes and broken plates. On the other hand, someone did manage to conjure up some dust-laden bottles of bitter-sweet, fiery red Romagna wine from the cellars. Everyone was tired, and all Buffarini's sugar-coated tranquillisers could not dispel my misgivings about the trip. I had no idea whether the dictator knew of my Tassinari initiative or not, and my spirits sank still further when I was informed that the great man, who did not appear that night, wished to see me before the cabinet met next morning. However, what with the magnificent wine, the sight of the pale moon above the battlements and the tangy scent of the surrounding hills, I abandoned myself to the medieval, Macbethian atmosphere and forgot my personal worries.

Next morning saw me in Mussolini's study, a large room commanding a view of the beautiful but all too often blood-soaked approaches to the castle. The resurrected dictator looked old, tired and wan, and only his eyes retained their old Palazzo Venezia fire. His desk, a heavy baroque piece, was littered with the papers which heads of government always leave lying around as proof of their own importance. He extended his hand with an affable smile and thanked me for accompanying the party. As always in his presence, I found myself falling under his spell, and gathered with some relief that we were not, as far as could be seen, going to talk about Tassinari. I congratulated him on his release from the Gran Sasso and reassumption of power, but he dismissed my remarks with a gesture of resignation and the light in his eyes grew dim. Then he came to the subject of the interview, which turned out to be Rome and the Romans. With a momentary access of animation and vehemence, he demanded to know precisely how the Eternal City and its inhabitants had behaved on 25 July and 8 September. He asked for the truth and got it. He listened in silence as I spoke, and his thoughts were not hard to fathom. Having spoken quietly until then, he now addressed me as if he were haranguing a crowd from the balcony of the Palazzo Venezia.

'All the same,' he exclaimed, 'all the same! Rome must remain in our hands in spite of the Romans. Without Rome, the new Italian Social Republic is a mere trunk, a fragment without a base.'

He was wide awake now, and speaking from the heart. If I wanted to remain in Rome, as I did at all costs, I would have to make the most of this moment. He asked me what the field marshals thought of the problem. I was able to report, truthfully, that Rommel, who was in command in Northern Italy, wanted to abandon Rome and defend Italy from the Apennines. I was also able to assure him that Kesselring, C.-in-C., Southern Command, intended to hold Rome and the South for as long as possible.

I had said my piece. Mussolini stared past me at the hills of his native countryside. Then he pulled a memorandum pad towards him and began, without hesitating or pausing for thought, to make notes in his characteristically forceful handwriting. I sensed that the future of Rome was at stake, and the moment has lived with me to this day.

After a minute or two he stopped writing and removed his glasses. It was the first time I had seen him wearing them, and they made him look even older and more weary. Then he read me what he had written, the gist of which was as follows:

'While I am unacquainted with the plans of the German High Command, I should like to stress the vital necessity of holding Rome. Coming after the abandonment of Naples, the loss of Rome would have immense repercussions on Italy and the world at large. In this respect, I would give prime consideration to the political and psychological aspect of such a step. As to the military aspect, the fall of Rome would leave the enemy in possession of the thirty airfields in Central Italy. This would facilitate not only the bombing of Central Germany and its South-Eastern areas but attacks on the Danube Basin and the Balkans. It would be a great piece of good fortune if Rome could remain in our hands, at least for the duration of the winter.'

He looked up at me with the triumphant air of a child anticipating a good report. There was something boyishly naive about him at such moments, and I warmed to him even more when I compared him with his friend Adolf Hitler, who was completely lacking in this quality. He told me that he would shortly be sending Marshal Graziani to Hitler with a personal letter and a memorandum in the form of a *nota militare* on the subject of Rome. The Marshal would also be instructed to negotiate with the Führer's Headquarters on the reorganisation or reconstruction of the Italian armed forces within his sphere of command.

'And you, *caro Dollman*, will go with him. Rome has become your home too, despite the Romans' behaviour on 25 July and 8 September.'

I had never accepted a mission more gladly or with a fuller heart. For the next five minutes Mussolini was quite his old self again. He led me to the window and showed me the view, reminiscing about his hard and austere childhood in the Romagna. I think he would rather have gone on reminiscing to me than devote himself to his cabinet meeting, but the ministers were already making their presence felt in the ante-room, where Graziani's imperious voice dominated those of his colleagues.

I thanked the Duce for seeing me, feeling shamefully aware that his faith in me was unmerited. Perhaps he never knew how much I had hoped that the eagles of Zeus would bear him off to Olympus on 25 July 1943 and never bring him back.

On 13 October we took to the air ourselves—Marshal Graziani and Mussolini's letters, his aide, Lieutenant-Colonel Zingone, and I. Piloting us was Captain Gerlach, the man who had been mainly responsible for Mussolini's release from the Gran Sasso. Gerlach's return flight in a Fieseler Storch was one of the most daring exploits of the Second World War, even though his fame has been dimmed by the blaze of publicity which was kindled round Skorzeny on the instructions of Goebbels. We were all crammed into a plane of an entirely new type, and for the un-known meteorological reasons the flight took much longer than had been foreseen. As a result, we drank correspondingly more of the cognac which the Marshal had brought with him in large quantities. I shall never again drink on board an aeroplane with-out making a prior inspection of its facilities. This one had none, and Columbus cannot have yearned for the coast of America more ardently than we longed to see the airfield at Rastenburg, near the Wolf's Lair. By the time it hove in sight we were at the limits of our resistance to the calls of Nature. As we came in to land, I saw that a guard of honour and military band had turned out to greet the War Minister and Commander-in-Chief of Mussolini's new republic, but the old warrior was magnificent. We climbed out, stalked past the erect figure of Field Marshal Keitel, past the guard of honour, past the band and its anthems of welcome, and made for the shelter of a wall.

The band was still playing when we reappeared, the guard of honour trying not to grin, and Keitel and his staff still standing to attention with hands raised in salute. Soldiers are soldiers, however. They win battles without turning a hair and lose them with equal fortitude. As though nothing had happened, Graziani strode along the ranks, which had turned to stone again, shook his German colleague by the hand, and greeted the other members of the reception committee.

The ensuing lunch at the Führer's Headquarters is said to have been a cheerful affair. We were not invited, so I cannot say whether the grim-faced lord and master of the Wolf's Lair enjoyed himself too. It was not until late afternoon that Hitler received us in his private bunker. I can do no better than reproduce Graziani's impressions of him, as seen through Italian eyes:

Hitler met me at the door. I had last seen him in 1938 on the occasion of his trip to Rome. He looked fifteen years older, and his appearance was far from imposing. His ash-grey jacket of Austrian cut and First World War style, long black trousers and flat, brilliant polished shoes gave him the appearance of a monk in lay clothing. He stooped as he walked, and his eyes had lost their hard brilliance and looked almost dead. The transparency of his hands and face completed the priestly picture, which bore no relation to that of a war leader of such importance. Then he said: 'You did right to accept your post. It is impossible for a soldier to stand aloof from the field of action and honour.'

A fire was burning in the hearth in Hitler's study, illuminating the faces of those present: Hitler, Marshal Graziani, Field Marshal Keitel, General Jodl, Lieutenant-Colonel Zingone, and me. The ice which had separated the Führer's Headquarters from Italy, particularly in the military sphere, was soon broken. Graziani was neither a managing director in uniform like Cavallero nor a foxy intrigant like Badoglio. To Hitler and his associates, he was a straightforward, honourable soldier and a man of courage—and it took courage to be the first senior Italian officer to visit the Wolf's Lair since Italy's defection on 8 September and the overnight disintegration of the Italian army. Graziani produced Mussolini's memorandum on Rome from a sealed envelope and Hitler opened it. He behaved as if he understood it, but then handed it to me with instructions to translate it for him after the meeting was over. This would be no great effort since I already knew its contents, so I devoted myself to the technical points which were now being raised in connection with the new army of the Italian Social Republic. German doubts about the renewed fighting spirit of the former royal army were not only great but justified. The Italian forces, which had always obeyed under compulsion but never from inner conviction, even before 25 July and 8 September, were now to be asked to swallow a second dose of unpleasant medicine under the leadership of their Phoenix-like Duce. The Italian plan envisaged a gradual process whereby Mussolini's military dreams were to be fulfilled first by four, then eight, and, finally, twelve divisions. Graziani suggested that volunteers should be released from the camps which had been set up to accommodate Badoglio's disarmed soldiers in Germany. Keitel and Jodl favoured the mobilisation of call-up groups in Italy, and I almost laughed aloud when I thought of the probable results of such a policy. Hitler, who had been staring into the fire, began to speak of his own glorious soldiers, their feats of arms, their contempt for death, their implicit and unbroken faith in victory. Graziani may have been a simple soldier, but he was enough of an Italian to avoid making a clear-cut decision. Instead, he fell back on the need to consult Mussolini. At the Duce's name Hitler came to life again. He signified his agreement, sent greetings to 'my friend', and promised to produce a written reply to the Rome letter by next morning.

Our leave-taking was markedly cordial, but we all felt relieved when the audience was over. The Italians went off to have dinner in Keitel's special train, our accommodation for the night, and I sat down to my translation. The text roughly corresponded to what I had heard at Rocca delle Caminate, except that it was more forcibly expressed and laid even greater emphasis on Rome. I made a painstaking translation of it and handed it to Keitel. He was delighted, but then he always was. Remembering that he had daily access to the Führer, only in a menial capacity, I went on to tell him how closely Mussolini associated his personal and political future with the defence of Rome. He promised to inform Hitler of this, as did General Jodl, Chief of the Wehrmacht Command Staff, with whom I chatted after dinner. Jodl was not only a Bavarian, like me, but a former friend of my old patron, General Otto von Lossow, and a lover of Rome. He was a typical product of the General Staff, intelligent but inscrutable, and it was impossible to form a clear picture of his personality.

He kept his word, at least where Rome was concerned. Next morning, before our return flight, he and Keitel both assured me that the Führer had already familiarised himself with the contents of the Duce's letter and had instructed Field Marshal Kesselring accordingly. In addition, the *terribile vecchio* was given a sealed reply to deliver to his lord and master at Lake Garda.

We landed safely at Verona on 16 October, this time without any pangs of physical discomfort. Graziani hurried off to see Mussolini and I flew on to Rome. The evening sun was just sinking behind the dome of St Peter's when I entered the city. I had never done so in a happier frame of mind. For a moment I too felt like the saviour of the Eternal City. Above all, my personal wishes had been granted. Unencumbered as I was by any strategic or military considerations, why should I not have felt satisfied?

Then came the ill-fated Roman winter of 1943–4. The people of Rome bemoaned their fate more loudly and with less justification than the Jews besieged in Jerusalem or the starving burghers of Calais. The dramatic slogans on walls and buildings multiplied. Of course the Romans had reason to weep. The Eternal City was bereft of all its glitter, all its glamour, all forms of profane—and, to a large extent, sacred—entertainment. Shops and bars closed early, food became scarce and uninteresting, and there was no one left to treat the pampered citizens to the bread and circuses they had enjoyed under Mussolini and, to a lesser degree, the Savoys. The German commandant, General Mältzer, liked to style himself King of Rome, but the poor Duke of Reichstadt would have turned in his grave if he had ever met his titular successor. Mältzer ruled Rome like a carousing, gormandising Germanic governor from the age of the great migrations. He was not brutal—just laughable. The real master of Rome, SD-Führer Herbert Kappler, whose power and prestige had grown enormously, tolerated him because he wore Kesselring's uniform, but Mältzer took good care not to engage the head of the Security Police in serious conflict.

Kappler was as narrow-minded as his supreme chief, Himmler. He was incorruptible as Robespierre and professional as it was possible to be. Nothing escaped his steely blue eyes, and the ladies of Rome, having made an initial attempt to beguile him with their Ciano-schooled charms, had long since abandoned the hopeless struggle and returned, disappointedly, to me. The only trouble with me was that I did not wield Kappler's power. He respected my working relationship with the Field Marshal's headquarters outside Rome, but a man who had no executive staff or armed men at his disposal could never mean more to him, for all Kesselring's patronage, than a drawing-room soldier. In that capacity he was prepared to tolerate me. He smiled at my patient reception of the princesses and other ladies who came to me with requests that their property should be protected by Kesselring's decree from the depredations of the hungry, thirsty soldiers who tramped past their castles and country estates; he turned a blind eye to the tyres, petrol and other items which the great ladies of Italy still considered so vital to their continued existence, and which I 'organised' for them; he never did anything to impair my contacts with the Vatican; and, finally, he respected my status as liaison officer to General Wolff, another man whom he undoubtedly regarded with secret amusement.

Although Kappler would scarcely have approved of my contacts with the Alfrediani, it was from them that I heard what was really going on in Rome. They escorted me to market early in the morning and showed me mothers lamenting over their hungry babies because there was virtually no milk. They took me on a tour of the once luxuriant fruit and vegetable stalls and pointed accusingly at the bare counters. They took me to the Giardini del lago, formerly the private garden of the Borghese princes and now Rome's favourite park, and complained that the military authorities were proposing to instal a vehicle park in the middle of the ancient groves, fountains and temples. I not only commiserated with them on the threatened loss of this horticultural gem but succeeded in saving it—plane-trees, cypresses, fountains, temples and all.

What was far more important, it was through them that I learned something of the dark forces which were beginning, as in the days of Spartacus, to equate justice with violence and brutality. The new Fascism of the Salò Republic had spewed up several champions of this philosophy and installed them in the offices of the Rome Party Secretariat. A triumvirate consisting of two boorish Party bosses and a refined little count with degenerate instincts established a sort of subterranean revolutionary tribunal in the Palazzo Braschi, an old papal palace famed for its magnificent marble staircase. No one ever heard the screams of those who were whipped and tortured in its cellars, but everyone in Rome quaked at its very name. Signorina Bibi, now closer to the Alfrediani than ever before, introduced me to a friend of hers who had escaped from the place. With the mute gesture of a tortured slave, he pulled his shirt up for me to see—and the Marquis de Sade would have trembled with delight. I was due at a routine conference at Kesselring's headquarters on the Monte Soracte that evening. The Field Marshal trembled when he heard my report, but with rage rather than delight, and the unpleasant goings-on ceased shortly afterwards. This episode did not enhance my popularity in neo-Fascist circles, but the Alfrediani rallied round me in a solid phalanx.

One evening in November, Signorina Bibi came back from her English lesson at a neighbouring convent and told me that a young man 'of great family' urgently wanted to speak to me. She was so enthusiastic, partly about him and partly about his great family, that I agreed to see him at once. An extremely handsome young man entered the room. He spoke so softly that I did not catch his name at first, but Bibi interpreted with such zeal that I soon grasped the full picture.

It was the son of Count Cini, whom I had met several times officially and once informally. Vittorio Cini had been Mussolini's last Minister of Transport, but not, like the majority of his colleagues, because he wanted something out of Fascism or needed the Duce's patronage. He was as immeasurably rich as only an Italian or Spanish nobleman can be. He owned large hotels, factories, shipping lines—everything, in fact, which can contribute to the wealth of a commercial or industrial magnate. There were castles, villas and art collections of his everywhere. In Ferrara he owned a palazzo of the Este period furnished in contemporary style, at Monselice one of the loveliest castles in Italy, and in Venice itself an Aladdin's Cave of a palazzo beside the Grand Canal to which Anna Morosini did not, I regret, supply me with an entrée. Apart from that, he not only resembled a virile condottiere of the fifteenth century but had the courage of his breed. I have already described how much this aspect of Cini's character impressed Reich Marshal Göring in autumn 1942—Göring, who was once a man of courage himself but whom no one had had the courage to stand up to for years. My most recent encounter with Count Cini was at a lunch given by the Marchese Medici del Vascello, an ex-Secretary of State, in June 1943. On that occasion he had complained bitterly of Mussolini's lack of technical and military competence:

'I have only one wish, and that is to hand back my post as quickly as possible to the man who literally forced it on me. The Duce needs no experts. Whatever the subject, he always knows best.'

He resigned shortly afterwards, a step which the events of 25 July and 8 September encouraged both the Italian and German authorities—though it was absolutely no concern of the latter—to construe as high treason.

Cini's son Giorgio now stood before me, pouring out his story with a mixture of agitation and despair. His father's health and very existence were in dire peril. He had been taken to Dachau, and only the promptest action could save him. Giorgio was close to tears, and, since he was younger than his father and just as handsome, Bibi wept with him. I too might have wept at the desperate complexity of the situation, but considerations of prestige forbade it. The whole affair was beyond my competence. It rested with Kappler and his superiors, and even Kesselring would be powerless to intervene in a case of this sort.

Giorgio Cini implored me to have a word with his mother. Accompanied by Bibi, who insisted on coming too, we drove at once to his home and held a council of war there. The Countess had been Italy's loveliest and most popular film star in her youth and is still remembered under her professional name, Lydia Borelli. She received us in a veritable museum of jade, and I immediately endeared myself to her by enthusing about her treasures, which were among the finest of their kind in Europe. She was dressed entirely in black and looked like Mary Stuart during the early years of her imprisonment. It struck me then that it would take a *mise-en-scène* worthy of Schiller to secure her husband's release. Herr Kappler had no feeling for such things, of course, but General Wolff was his official superior in Italy, and Wolff loved meetings with a melodramatic flavour. As luck would have it, he was due in Rome in a few days' time, so I worked out a programme for the interview which I proposed to arrange on the Countess's behalf.

She appeared at the appointed place, a hotel owned by her husband and favoured as a home from home by the Germans, wearing her celebrated black pearls and a small veil which made her look even more like Mary Stuart. Giorgio had seen to the champagne, and Bibi acted as a sort of lady-in-waiting.

The General, briefed on what lay ahead but not unduly attracted by the prospect, gradually succumbed to the magic of the scene. The *grande dame* before him was probably the richest woman in Italy apart from Donna Virginia Agnelli and the Duchess of Torlonia. Her black-clad figure, the charm of her gentle voice and her heartfelt grief all conspired to allay his suspicions. He promised to make inquiries in Berlin, and eventually sanctioned my proposal that Giorgio and Bibi should be sent off to Munich at once to see that all was well with the detainee. Then I thought of Kappler. Remembering that he collected Etruscan antiquities, I ventured to ask if there would be any objection to young Giorgio's offering him a gift of this nature when he paid the requisite routine call at his office. Wolff could not help smiling, and I realised that even Gestapo chiefs had their Achilles' heel.

Herr Kappler was presented with an Etruscan sarcophagus. He not only approved the young couple's passports and travel permits but gave them a letter of recommendation to the camp commandant at Dachau. Wolff interceded for them in Berlin, and no objections were lodged against the visit in that quarter either, at least in the first instance.

Giorgio and Bibi set off, armed with pre-Christmas presents, passports and genuine gold coins, and it was not long before Count Cini's living conditions improved. Forgetting that she had already switched her attentions to English, Bibi charmed sentries, guards and camp personnel of every rank with her delightful smile and enchanting German. Her companion made good use of his gold coins, and his father was soon transferred from prison cell to hospital bed, and from there to Switzerland.

The Countess, now restored to the youthful radiance of her halcyon film-star days, celebrated the young people's return by throwing a party whose extravagance would have horrified Victor Emmanuel. There was even a necklace for Bibi, not particularly valuable but undeniably of eighteenth-century origin. It came from the Bulgari brothers, who were the largest jewellers in Rome and personal friends of the Cini family. They were the Cartiers and Fabergés of the Eternal City, and their underground vaults contained, *inter alia,* as many treasures as the Russian kinsfolk of the reigning Queen had managed to salvage from the wreck of Tsarist Russia. They knew the history of every tiara, necklace and bracelet and the fate of every grand duchess who had ever worn it. Their treasures were buried so deep in the heart of Rome that the subterranean tributaries of the Tiber could be heard rushing past. The two brothers, of whom one, Costantino, was a treasure-hunter and story-teller straight out of the Arabian Nights, used to accompany their reminiscences by serving age-old cognac, thereby dispelling the grey cares and sorrows of every-day life in Rome for hours on end.

I have not told this story because I feel in any way entitled to congratulate myself on Count Cini's release. It was my duty to help as a fellow human being, and I tried to do my duty by the mothers, sisters and girl-friends of the Alfrediani out of a precisely similar sense of obligation. I detest *soi-distant* saviours and martyrs, and only include the Cini story here because it contributes to my picture of war-time Rome in the winter of 1943–4.

What also contributes to this picture is the fate of another leading Fascist, which I was only able to follow from afar. I refer to the tragic end of that erstwhile darling of the gods and Alcibiades of Fascism, Count Ciano, who was executed at Verona on 11 January 1944. We never liked each other, in so far as our differences in rank and station permits me to talk in such terms. Perhaps we were too alike, too self-absorbed. We also knew that we were somewhat more prepossessing than most of the fat, bloated and unattractive figures that dominated that world of Fascism and National Socialism.

When news first reached Rome of Ciano's imprisonment at Mussolini's behest, my thoughts returned to the part which I had been called on to play in helping him and his wife to escape from Rome in August 1943. Despite the unworthy way in which Ciano had betrayed his father-in-law and protector at the Grand Council session of 24–25 July, the new Badoglio regime had placed the couple under house arrest in their elegant two-floor apartment in the Via Angelo Secchi. The clouds above their heads grew darker week by week, and anyone with experience of contemporary Italy knew that house arrest might easily be a prelude to something worse. Galeazzo Ciano was too pure-bred an Italian to cherish any illusions about his future fate as the fallen Duce's son-in-law and former Foreign Minister.

But to return to mid-August 1943. I received a visit from a smartly dressed man whose civilian clothes did not disguise the officer beneath. He handed me a note:

Dear Dollmann,

The bearer of this, a family friend, is instructed to convey my regards and a request which I should be grateful if you would fulfil.

Yours sincerely,

Edda Ciano-Mussolini

What followed was an exciting midsummer adventure in which Edda was cast as Marie Antoinette and I as her would-be rescuer, Mirabeau. I went for a stroll near the Ciano home with my faithful and unsuspecting dog. Unlike Ciano, Edda and her children enjoyed walking-out privileges. She emerged for a breath of cool evening air. My car was waiting round the corner. I drove past, she climbed in, and we made for the home of some friends, a rendezvous which I had selected as being suitably unsuspicious. Mussolini's daughter behaved precisely as her intimates had expected her to behave when it came to a pinch. Questionable as some aspects of her married life had been in the past, she now became all wife and mother. Her every thought and emotion was centred on a wish to save her husband and children, and the present fate of her father received only fleeting mention.

We did not take long to reach a decision. This was that I should use my influence with Field Marshal Kesselring to secure the immediate availability of a special aeroplane for the Cianos' flight from Rome—a flight which would undoubtedly take them to Germany. I stressed this more than once. Edda was far too shrewd not to grasp what I meant, but she declared that her husband would be quite agreeable to this plan if his first choice of asylum, Spain, were ruled out. I further stressed that this exhausted my own powers of intervention. Herr Kappler and his experienced staff would be responsible for the technical aspect of the flight, its preparation and implementation. I asked her if she would be willing for me to arrange a second meeting, this time with Kappler. I felt sorry for her when she said yes. The Mussolinis had sunk low indeed if the Duce's favourite daughter was ready to meet a man like Kappler in secret, with a view to fleeing from a city in which she had occupied the centre of the political and social stage for so many years.

Kappler and his aide-de-camp were present at our second meeting, which took place shortly afterwards. He was extremely grateful to me for entrusting him with a mission so dear to his own devious heart. Two days later, one of his men turned up at the Cianos' residence dressed in civilian clothes and armed with a huge bouquet of flowers for the lady of the house. His actual job was to fill the capacious pockets of his overcoat with sundry articles of value which the Cianos were particularly anxious to save.

Early on the morning of 23 August, in the midst of a city as hostile to the Count as to his German helpers, the operation got under way.

As always in such cases, the guards presented the main obstacle, even if they were drawn from the well-behaved ranks of the Royal Carabinieri. Fortunately, this was Italy, and even the Cianos' sentry found it impossible to resist the wiles of Edda's lady's-maid indefinitely, especially when lured into a neighbouring park by promises of a seductive nature.

The Carabiniere and the lady's-maid duly disappeared and

Edda and her children set off on their morning walk, rather more heavily laden than usual, leaving the house deserted save for Ciano. Then, with a punctuality which did Kappler credit, a fast sports car drew up at the corner of the street. Wearing a pair of large green-tinted glasses, Ciano made a last hurried exit from the house which had for so many years opened its doors to ambitious diplomats and aristocratic play-boys, elegant women and attractive young girls. The Countess, who had meanwhile been picked up by another car, met him in the courtyard of the Deutsches Heim, and the whole family was loaded into a truck and conveyed to the airfield. The Mozartian mood of the escape changed to one of Wagnerian gloom.

Galaezzo Ciano caught a last glimpse of his beloved golf-course from the air. I do not know what passed through his mind as he gazed at it, but he can hardly have been thinking along the right lines. If he had been, he would never have embarked on a journey which would take him into the domain of Ribbentrop, who was his mortal enemy, or of Adolf Hitler, who despised him.

The Cianos' escape from Rome, their subsequent stay in Bavaria, their meetings with Donna Rachele and Mussolini himself, and Ciano's wild hopes and schemes—all this came back to me when I heard of his landing and arrest at Verona on 2 November 1943.

I had no part in the grim drama which now unfolded under Benito Mussolini's supreme direction. No one consulted me this time, no one delivered any secret notes. Rome was far away, and the gunfire from the Southern Front drowned the ill-aimed rifle-shots which hit Rome's erstwhile darling in the back as he sat roped to a chair. He died more nobly than he had lived. Mussolini could have averted his death by a stroke of the pen, but he was only human. Perhaps his mind returned, in that fatal moment of decision, to his solitary night in the police barracks in Rome, when he paced restlessly up and down like an enraged and wounded lion, crying: '*Ah, il quatantenne, il quarantenne!*' Quite why he failed to save Ciano despite impassioned pleas from Edda, his favourite child, will never be established with any certainty.

I should like to conclude the story of the Ciano tragedy by emphasising that, for once, the Germans were not responsible—neither for his return to Italy, nor for his death sentence, nor for his execution. They too could have saved him, of course, but they were haunted by the betrayal of September 1939.

All these tragedies, whether they concerned Ciano or Cini, distressed princesses, starving washerwomen or tortured Alfrediani, receded into the background when, in the early hours of 22 January 1944, the Allies landed in force at Anzio and Nettuno, only an hour or two from Rome. I was roused shortly afterwards by a call from Kesselring's headquarters and instructed to report to him immediately. My interview lasted rather longer than headquarters expected. It did not end until I had convinced the Field Marshal that my place was in Rome and not with him. He was surprised at first—almost affronted—but he quickly understood. He was one of the few senior officers who possessed political flair, a respect in which he differed widely from the two other field marshals then on Italian soil, Rommel and Richthofen. He expected the landing to coincide with a mass insurrection in Rome which would take his meagre forces in the rear. I cherished no such fear, thanks to the friendly relations I had maintained with my old crowd of friends from the Campagna. They had repeatedly assured me that the Romans would never rise in revolt until the last German soldier had left the city and the Allied liberators were at the gates, garlanded with flowers and ready to march in. Knowing the Romans, I took my friends at their word. If the people of Rome had not risen on 9 September, when fighting broke out in the neighbourhood of the city, they would not do so now. They had learnt how to get their own way without resorting to revolt or insurrection, first under the Caesars and later under the Popes, and they had got their own way ever since the days of the great Augustus. I vouched for them at that early morning interview, and the Field Marshal accepted my assurance with a relief which was not shared by his staff.

I proved to be right. Morning, noon and night, the streets preserved their Sunday calm. I guessed, as I walked them, that His Holiness was praying, like me, that the people of Rome would leave the decision to God rather than try to force it themselves. The streets remained quiet and the Romans ate what spaghetti they had—made of white flour for choice, brown at a pinch. I drove a short way down the Anzio road, and what I saw, or, rather, did not see, almost made me regret my guarantee to Kesselring. Even I, with my unmilitary instincts, was astonished not to meet any armoured columns racing towards Rome. All I saw were a few weary-looking German units composed—in default of anything better—of men discharged from a hospital where they had been recuperating from the results of nocturnal self-indulgence in Rome. Undoubtedly, one of the Allies' greatest tactical blunders was their failure to push on to Rome with all the forces at their disposal. On any reckoning, they could have entered St Peter's Square by noon that day and shortened the war—at least in this theatre of operations—by a year or more.

Instead, they stopped to unload their supplies, which were lavish enough to distract anyone from the idea of a lightning advance on Rome. Unfortunately for them, the German units rushed to the scene by Kesselring during the late afternoon, night and following day banished the possibility of an armoured parade through St Peter's Square, and the inhabitants of Rome had to wait until next June before supplies of Lucky Strikes and Camels finally arrived.

On the whole, they waited with good grace. True, there were tragic incidents in the Via Rasella and Fosse Ardeatine, but the treacherous shooting of thirty-four German policemen was not the work of the Romans. As every fair-minded and unprejudiced Italian will admit, it was the work of the Communist wing of the Resistance movement. Similarly, the shooting of hostages in a proportion of ten to one—a form of retaliation which was not only excessive but politically inept—was not the work of Kesselring and his staff but the result of a direct order from Hitler himself. Neither Hitler nor Jodl nor Keitel appeared to grasp that the Führer's Headquarters had thereby fulfilled the Roman Communists' secret but ardent wish to sow mortal emnity between the Eternal City and the Germans. However, dictators and their advisers are probably immune to such considerations.

From the moment when the heavy naval guns at Anzio became clearly audible in Rome, I knew what my final task there must be: first to ensure that it was abandoned without a fight, and, secondly, to establish contact with Pope Pius XII, who was making unremitting attempts to save Rome from destruction with all the divine and earthly resources at his command. Once Rome had been abandoned this would enable me or, rather, the German High Command to get in touch with the authorities who really mattered in Northern Italy, now that the neo-Fascist government at Lake Garda was daily losing ground: that is to say, with the Cardinals of Milan, Florence and Bologna. Only through them would it still be possible to maintain contact with the Vatican via the Papal Nunciature in Bern.

Almost every German who was ever in Rome now claims to have saved the city from becoming a battle-ground. Everyone saved Rome, from field marshals to private soldiers, from the Ambassador to the Holy See to the lowliest German official. In fact, the credit belongs to two people alone, namely, Pope Pius XII and Field Marshal Kesselring. In its indefatigable endeavours to save Rome from destruction by all the direct and indirect means open to it, the Vatican received every possible assistance from the ambassador accredited to it by Hitler, Herr von Weizsäcker. The same can be said of Consul-General Eitel Friedrich Möllhausen and his superior, the Ambassador Plenipotentiary at Lake Garda.

His Holiness was naturally the main recipient of divine aid in this noble contest. As C-in-C., Southern Command, Kesselring had the guns and soldiers, but his task was even harder. Not only had the Führer decreed that Rome should be defended, but Benito Mussolini, too, had felt called upon to throw his belligerent weight into the scales. Furthermore, there were important strategic and military arguments against quitting Rome without a fight. Its abandonment would greatly impede the Fourteenth Army's withdrawal, thereby sacrificing human lives which might be spared if all the Tiber bridges were blown up.

'It was my irrevocable decision to avoid fighting in and around Rome.' Thus wrote the Field Marshal in his memoirs, *Soldat bis zum letzten Tag*, and the many conversations I had with him about the fate of the Italian capital and seat of the Vatican enable me to confirm his words. Kesselring never wavered for a moment, and this stand alone would have been enough to earn him a place of honour in any country but Germany. He did not waver even when Mussolini suddenly remembered that he still had a say in what went on, and sent one of his prefects to call on me in Rome. The Duce's emissary was Signor Zerbino, a man of great personal integrity. He begged me to secure him an immediate interview with Kesselring at Monte Soracte and act as his interpreter. He was very secretive, but I eventually discovered what his liege lord wanted out of the Field Marshal: it was nothing less than an assurance that Rome would be defended, house by house, street by street, palace by palace. I was so horrified that I boldly asked whether people at Lake Garda had lost their heads. Didn't they realise what the destruction of Rome, even if only partial, would mean to the world at large? What was the Pope to do—emulate his Medici forerunner, Clement VII, by taking refuge in the Castel Sant'Angelo at dead of night and calling on the Swiss Guard to defend him and the Vatican?

Signor Zerbino eyed me pityingly. 'The Duce's view is that the war cannot be run like a museum tour if it is to be won at all. Besides, if need be, he has agreed to concentrate his defence on the Tiber bridges—which he trusts have all been mined long ago.'

Thinking of the unique Via Giulia and its glorious palaces, of the Bridge of Sant'Angelo and the churches, all of which would doubtless make splendid gunnery targets, I said no more and drove out to Monte Soracte alone. Kesselring was shocked at first, but on second thoughts he decided that Mussolini's intervention might, after all, prove extremely helpful to his plans for saving Rome. Had I any advice to offer?

I suggested that he see Signor Zerbino and thank him for this unexpected offer of assistance from Lake Garda. The Duce must state how many divisions would be available for his plans and also—needless to say—assume personal command of the battle for Rome. I assured the Field Marshal that he would hear no more, and promised to provide a colourful translation of his proposals.

All went according to plan. Signor Zerbino departed in high good humour and we never heard another word about Mussolini's

Tiber-based Holy War. The bridges were never blown, even though their demolition would have presented no problem, and Rome was abandoned on the night of 4 June. Not a single inhabitant, palace, museum or church suffered.

The Zerbino interlude was one more token of how essential it was to obtain an interview with the head of Catholic Christendom before direct contact with the Vatican was lost. I have only twice taken part in a political manœuvre of such importance. The other time was in Switzerland and Northern Italy in the spring of 1945. Also involved on that occasion were the American secret service under Allan W. Dulles, the Swiss General Staff, the top SS and police chiefs of Italy, a field marshal and numerous generals, a Papal Chamberlain and Knight of Malta, and a German ambassador plenipotentiary. This dangerous game, whose code-name was 'Sunrise Crossword', led on 28 April 1945 to the surrender of the German armies in Italy and the Italian units attached to them.

The game I entered upon in April and May 1944 was equally exciting but not so dangerous. The players included His Holiness Pope Pius XII, the Superior of the Salvatorian Order, Dr Pfeiffer, a cardinal of the Curia, a prominent Roman society woman, Field Marshal Kesselring's personal medical officer and, once again, the top SS and police chiefs in Italy. The main credit must go to the lady in question, for without her and her untiring efforts to keep the ball rolling General Wolff would never have obtained his audience with Pope Pius XII at the Vatican on 10 May 1944.

I christened the operation 'Farnese' in honour of my old sixteenth-century friend Cardinal Alessandro Farnese, who had gained me my first access to the Vatican Library so long ago.

Donna Virginia Agnelli, widow of the Turin Fiat heir, was the daughter of Prince Borbone del Monte and an American woman who had attained legendary status in Roman society. Harnessing the vast wealth of the Agnelli to her highly individual tastes, she had transformed her Roman home into a jewel casket of unique beauty.

Donna Virginia could not have found a more appropriate retreat than the Villa del Bosco Parrasio at the foot of the Gianicolo. An oasis in the middle of Trastevere, the oldest and most populous quarter of the Eternal City, it had once, at the close of the seventeenth and beginning of the eighteenth centuries, been the headquarters of a bizarre society of literary and scientific amateurs who used to dress up as shepherds and try to re-create the atmosphere of bygone Arcadia. This democratic republic of literati included cardinals, members of the Papal court and great noblemen and their ladies, and it was this villa with its ancient grounds that Donna Virginia had chosen as her Roman residence. The little theatre which gave off the ornately decorated reception rooms still survived, and on the floor above were Donna Virginia's private quarters, with their superb view of the dome of St Peter's—a view which may well have played a decisive part in our Farnese undertaking.

During the inter-war years Donna Virginia had been the hub of a select and slightly snobbish set. Crown Prince Umberto could be seen at her home, together with members of the court and prominent Roman literary figures headed by Curzio Malaparte. They all preferred to speak English together, and the lady of the house was destined to suffer for her Anglophile tendencies. Times had changed since 8 September, even for someone who bore the Fiat name, and there was no Bocchini in Rome to smile indulgently at the whims of a queen of industry.

I had several times tried, with an attempt at the Bocchini smile, to convince Donna Virginia that the altered situation in Rome rendered it advisable for her to conduct her interminable telephone calls and cocktail party chatter in Italian, but she merely smiled her own celebrated smile and asked me if I had suddenly joined the neo-Fascists. She then steered conversation to her favourite subject, which was Rome and how to save it. We eventually agreed that the only authority fitted to act as supreme spokesman for the suffering people of Rome was the Vatican, that last bulwark against the ever-mounting, all-consuming tide of war. The Pope, we decided, must consult some wielder of earthly authority with a view to securing Rome's future. Kesselring had to be ruled out for various reasons, much as we should have liked to play such a trump card, but General Wolff, the senior SS and police chief in Italy, had shown growing concern over the fate of Rome. We shuffled our 'Farnese' cards, and

Donna Virginia duly drew the ace like the accomplished player she was. She ordered champagne—French champagne, of course —and we drank to our joint success. It was her last glass for some time.

Shortly afterwards, Benito Mussolini's police got tired of tapping her hour-long Anglo-American telephone conversations, which made it only too clear that she and her clique welcomed the thunder of gunfire from Anzio and Nettuno and were diligently practising the V-sign so as to be in vogue when their boyfriends marched into Rome in triumph.

Donna Virginia was moved to another villa. It was hardly like being in prison, but her movements were severely restricted. She was clever enough—what Roman lady would not have been, under the circumstances?—to advise me of her misfortune. I, in turn, urgently advised her to contract a throat infection, and promised to see that she was transferred to a hospital. She fell ill at once and was duly hospitalised. Two policemen were posted outside her door day and night, but they were young men and Romans to boot. How, in the hour of crisis, could they have been expected to resist the wiles of a Roman lady who bore the name Agnelli?

Anxious to proceed with care, I interested Kesselring's young and charming medical officer in the case. We were on very good terms, and he promised to help. He came to Rome wearing an air force uniform covered in medals, and we drove to the hospital to see our patient. Whether at death's door or not, she looked quite enchanting in her Venetian lace bed-jacket. The policemen were overwhelmed with pity for their captive and awe at the sight of my uniformed companion, whom they mistook for Kesselring in person. He examined Donna Virginia and wrung his hands. Then he offered her his arm and conducted her, still attired in lace but with a silk scarf round her neck, past the stiffly saluting guardians of the law to my car, which was waiting outside. We celebrated Donna Virginia's release in the suite which had been booked for her at the Hotel Excelsior. She was given a medical certificate plastered with rubber stamps, and no one ever examined her throat again. The policemen disappeared too, possibly to join the resistance movement—who knows?

In any case, Donna Virginia saw her miraculous deliverance from the direst peril as yet another sign from Heaven that she must devote herself with renewed vigour to the task of saving Rome—in other words, of obtaining General Wolff an audience with the Pope. I gathered from the confused titbits of information which reached me that it was not a simple matter, but by the beginning of May 1944 arrangements were complete. Cardinal Caccia-Dominioni, Dr Pfeiffer of the Salvatorian Order, divine providence, and Pius XII in his infinite wisdom—all had finally yielded to the tireless pleas of Donna Virginia and her influential friends among the nobility and in the world of finance. All that now remained was to get hold of Wolff, who as yet had no inkling of his good fortune. I decided that it would be best to present him with a fait accompli on his next visit, and this was precisely what I did.

As Weizsäcker, the German Ambassador to the Vatican, later corroborated at Nuremberg, General Wolff 'had long entertained a wish to spare the Catholic Church as far as possible and be of service to it'. Knowing this, and realising, too, that Wolff's attitude would be favourably influenced by an intimate little supper party on the eve of the great event, I invited a few attractive women who were as ready as Donna Virginia to place themselves at the service of the Eternal City. Just before they arrived, I startled the General by informing him that His Holiness would be awaiting him in his private apartments on the morning of 10 May. He was to wear civilian clothes, because—as Donna Virginia had told me—'His Holiness has expressed the fullest appreciation of the official difficulties that may arise.'

Most human decisions are unfathomable, and those of generals are no exception. I still do not know how many different motives prompted Wolff to accept this strange and memorable invitation. He himself attributed his decision to the dictates of conscience alone. I was quite indifferent to his motives provided he went, which he did. Since he naturally had no civilian clothes with him, he borrowed a smart suit of mine. It was rather small for him, I fear, and he did not feel particularly happy in it. His mood did not improve when Monsignor Pfeiffer and I conducted him across St Peter's Square, which was guarded—or watched, which ever one preferred—by our own troops. He brightened as we passed the colourful Swiss Guards, who saluted us, and we mounted the baroque staircase leading to the ante-rooms of Pius XII's private library.

I stayed behind in one of these rooms while Pfeiffer escorted Wolff to the Pope. It was not a boring three-quarters of an hour. Ante-rooms are instructive places, and my mind returned pleasurably to the times I had spent waiting for interviews with Bocchini, Senise and Buffarini.

Before long, Monsignor Pfeiffer came hurrying back, full of the gracious way in which His Holiness had risen from his desk to greet them. Pfeiffer then inquired after Donna Virginia, and I was able to assure him that she was in the cathedral, praying for the success of the audience.

The better part of an hour passed before our civilian-clad general appeared. He was wreathed in smiles, and spent the short trip back to the Salvatorian Convent telling us what a deep and unforgettable impression the Pope's personality had made on him. He seemed delighted at His Holiness's happy reminiscences about his time as Papal Nuncio in Munich and Berlin and at the deep sympathy which he had evinced for the trials and tribulations of the German people. He told us that Pius XII had been outspoken in his opposition to Roosevelt's call for un-conditional surrender, which he regarded—at best—as likely to prolong the war. Finally, he informed us with evident satisfaction that the Pope had expressed a wish to talk to him again as soon as possible, and accompanied this information with a meaningful gesture which we were at liberty to construe as we thought fit.

Wolff's account concluded with an amusing description of his ceremonial leave-taking. Long years of habit made him raise his hand in the Nazi salute, but the Pope had merely greeted the gesture with a gently indulgent smile. Pfeiffer smiled too, and consoled Wolff by telling him that the Pope must have realised that it had 'just slipped out'.

As a little epilogue to this exchange of courtesies, the Superior of the Salvatorian Order told Wolff that His Holiness had a personal request whose fulfilment would be regarded as token of goodwill. It concerned the son of Professor Vasalli, an old friend and former fellow-student of the Pope. Vasalli junior had deeply distressed his parents and the Vatican by joining the left-wing of the Roman resistance movement, and had fallen into Kappler's hands. He was safely restored to the Vatican authorities, who returned the favour by keeping him out of mischief for the duration of our presence in Rome.

This eventful morning was crowned by a lunch with Herr von Weizsäcker, Ambassador to the Holy See, who was dismayed by the fact that he had not been informed of the audience in advance. He even speculated sadly that it might cost him his job, until General Wolff leapt into the breach and declared himself ready to inform Ribbentrop personally. There was a brief slanging-match at Schloss Fuschl shortly afterwards, and all was well again, not only with Ribbentrop but also—curiously enough —with Himmler, who interpreted Wolff's audience as a sort of compliment to himself and his SS empire.

The audience did not, in the nature of things, yield any concrete results, though it might well have done had not Rome fallen almost immediately afterwards, on 4 June. Its psychological effect on Wolff was considerable, however, and it undoubtedly influenced his attitude in spring 1945, when the German forces in Italy were negotiating an armistice. From my point of view, it enabled me to obtain letters of recommendation to the Milan Curia and, more particularly, to the man who acted as political go-between for Cardinal Ildefonso Schuster. These letters of recommendation made it possible for me to establish contact not only with the Curia of Milan but with other high ecclesiastical authorities in Northern Italy. My relations with them have been exhaustively described by Schuster in his brief but informative book *Gli ultimi tempi di un regime*.

All this lay in the future, however. What concerned me at the moment was the sinister music of the naval guns at Anzio, which grew louder and more menacing every day. I persuaded Donna Virginia to take Signorina Bibi north with her, but Bibi's prince was staying put like a true Roman, so Bibi decided to stay too. I said goodbye to her on 4 June itself, just before all the Romans, true and otherwise, cast themselves eagerly at the feet of their liberators.

A woman's instinct is traditionally better than a man's. Perhaps I should have stayed to welcome the conquering heroes as they made their triumphal entry. All the Alfrediani advised me to, and they were not alone in this. On the other hand, I do not think that by staying behind I should have won the hand of a Roman princess and a palace to go with it. That sort of success is reserved for women like Bibi, who combine the gentleness of one of the doves in St Peter's Square with the sagacity of a snake from the Roman Campagna.

Before setting off alone, I drove out to Frascati to see the Field Marshal, who was also in the throes of departure. He looked pale and exhausted. I congratulated him, in the name of all the decent people in the world, on having spared Rome. We shook hands, and he instructed me to report to his new headquarters in the neighbourhood of Florence.

Escorted by my Roman chauffeur and my German wolf-hound, the only faithful companions remaining to me, I took a last walk up the legendary hill which had once been sacred, first to the gods of the underworld and then to Apollo, the hill celebrated in verse by Horace and Virgil. The youthful emperor Otto III, son of the Greek Empress Theophano, had died at its foot at the age of twenty-two. He too had been driven out of Rome, and he too had been making for the north. This was food for thought in itself, but my mood became even more thoughtful when I reached the little monastery of San Silvestro at the top of the hill, where King Carloman, son of Charles Martel, had spent the latter part of his life in retreat.

With a final look at the broad expanse of the Roman Campagna and the dull glint of St Peter's dome in the distance, I retraced my steps.

XI

CUR NON? – WHY NOT

[Motto of Gilbert du Motier de La Fayette,
Marshal of France in the reign of King Charles VII]

MY SPIRITS sank lower with every kilometre I put between me and Rome, accompanied by the badly mauled remnants of the Fourteenth Army and subjected to incessant fighter-bomber attacks. The game I had played since 1927 was up, at least where humour, irony and deeper meaning were concerned. I had certainly done my best, together with Kesselring, Rahn, Möllhausen and Weizsäcker, to save the focus of my life and ideals from destruction, but was that enough? And what now? Looking into the weary, sweat-stained faces of the soldiers who shared my ditch by the roadside, I heard them tell of the latest battles, of the terrible fighting in and around Anzio and Nettuno, of their longing—their grim and desperate longing—to bid the war a last farewell and go home. To them, if not to me, every kilometre they retreated was a kilometre nearer their goal. Suddenly, in the course of that harrowing journey, I realised what I had to do, or at least what I had to try to do.

Although it had long been clear, even to a behind-the-scenes participant like me, that the final phase of the Second World War had arrived, I had always shut my eyes to this not over-brilliant piece of deduction and dismissed it from my mind as far as possible. The time for self-deception was now past. Thinking back on the papal audience of 10 May, I remembered that my contact at the Curia, Dr Pfeiffer, had urged me to accept some letters of recommendation to the cardinals of Milan, Florence and Bologna. They bore the handsome old seals of various papal offices, but Pfeiffer's parting words had given me a fair idea of their contents:

'You have a mission, my dear Dollmann, and people trust you. You have a certain amount of influence with Field Marshal Kesselring, and he trusts you too. Use this opportunity to do everything in your power to mitigate the horrors of the Italian civil war which, unbeknown to you, is raging in the North. One more thing: bear in mind that Germany has lost the war and that you must therefore do all you can to shorten it. Only the will of God can bring it to an end.'

Since this was the tenor of my final interview with Dr Pfeiffer, the letters which he had pressed into my hand must be couched in similar terms. Only the immediate future would show what use I could make of them and who would help me in my task, but such were the thoughts that dominated my mind during the sad journey to Tuscany.

I again succeeded, just as I had done after the Italian armistice of 8 September 1943, in thwarting all well- or ill-meant attempts to transplant me into the tragic environment of Mussolini's shadow-regime at Lake Garda. If I ever fought for anything in my life, that thing was personal freedom. Even during my time as interpreter to the two dictators and their minions, I achieved my object with remarkable success. My assignment to Kesselring was another milestone on the same road, though it still strikes me as truly miraculous that a field marshal should have had so much sympathy and understanding for a point of view like mine.

I reached Florence towards evening. The Field Marshal had established his new headquarters at Monsummano, a peaceful little spa in the neighbourhood. Once again, I was in luck. Mussolini's durable Minister of the Interior, Buffarini-Guidi, was waiting for me in one of the big hotels beside the Arno. Ever young in heart, Buffarini was a native of this former domain of the Grand Dukes of Tuscany, where his passion for political manœuvre, cabals, intrigues, and good food and drink would undoubtedly have earned him a prominent position at the court of the Medici. We sat talking for a long time, and his Machiavel-

lian mind seized on my letters of recommendation with enthusiasm. He expounded a future programme in which everyone and
everything was to play a part except the government of the Salò
Republic, whose Minister of the Interior he was. Little though it
accorded with his unheroic exterior, Buffarini-Guidi bravely insisted that no harm must come to Mussolini, displaying a sense
of personal loyalty which not only did him credit at the time
but endured until both men met their tragic end. At this stage,
however, murder and mob violence were far from our thoughts.
Kesselring still had his armies, even if they were in urgent need
of recuperation, and Benito Mussolini still controlled Italy's main
agricultural and industrial provinces—at least to the extent that
his German allies permitted him to wield authority over them.

The night was far advanced and a bright Tuscan moon was
gilding the melancholy cypresses when Buffarini-Guidi let slip
the word 'Switzerland'—quite casually, much as Machiavelli
might have done. Zürich and Berne, he said with a smile, possessed
all the right ingredients for future peace, including a papal nunciature and America's main intelligence bureau in Europe. Then
he sighed, gazing dreamily at the yellow moon as it glided behind
the cypresses.

Next morning I drove to Monsummano, the gout and rheu-
matism spa, and reported to Kesselring. He did not discuss military matters with me—he never did. Instead, he concentrated on
the problems posed by the civil war that was raging throughout
Northern Italy, the allied problems of guerilla warfare, and the
relations between the army, the civil population, and the
official government authorities at Salò. He asked for a picture of
the situation in Florence and, as usual, gave me a free hand to do
whatever I thought best. Just as I was leaving he called me back
and suggested that I call on the German Consul-General in Florence, Dr Gerhard Wolf, and the general commanding the anti-
aircraft defences, Max von Pohl, whose headquarters were also
near Florence.

As it happened, Kesselring's suggestion was superfluous. I had
known Wolf for years. Having been a guest at gatherings of historians and art historians in his Florentine villa, I knew that he
was almost as passionately in love with Florence as I was with

Rome. Although not on good terms with Kappler or the security services, he was an old and intimate friend of Rudolf Rahn, German Ambassador Plenipotentiary to the Lake Garda regime. As for General von Pohl, a Knight of Maximilian Joseph of Bavaria, I owed my acquaintanceship with him to my mother's social connections in Munich. I knew that he possessed both courage and intelligence—a rare combination, as anyone would agree. My weeks in Florence brought me into contact with both men, and I should like to record a brief account of my experiences with them.

Wolf's consulate had become a mobile aid post. His help and advice was sought by anyone who had anything to fear from the police headquarters run by a certain Herr Alberti or the torture-chambers of Signor Carità. Foremost among his protégés was Crown Prince Rupprecht of Bavaria, whom Hans Georg von Mackensen had assisted in the most generous manner until his recall from the German Embassy in Rome—without, it must be said, reaping any gratitude.

Wolf's main clients in Florence were the friends and associates of Bernhard Berenson, the world-famous authority on art who was their acknowledged leader. 'B.B.' or 'Bibi', as the distinguished old gentleman was known to his intimates, wielded power of life and death over authentic and less authentic Italian masterpieces of the Early and High Renaissance. In view of his Jewish origins, he had been spirited away in the nick of time to one of the countless old villas round Florence. His place of asylum belonged to the Marchese Filippo Serlupi, the ambassador accredited to the Vatican by the miniature republic of San Marino, and it was thus armed with diplomatic privileges and immunities which even Messrs Alberti and Carità deemed it unwise to violate.

As soon as the Marchese heard of my special status at Kesselring's headquarters he bombarded me with invitations to sample the joys of Tuscan cooking and Tuscan chianti from the vineyards of the Medici. San Marino, itself gravely threatened by the tide of war, thus played a part in deflecting the Damoclean sword which now hung over Florence as it had once hung over Rome. What would happen when German troops withdrew, as they would in the forseeable future? Would it be possible to save the bridges over the Arno as well as those over the Tiber, and if so at what price? Such were the questions uppermost in the minds of all Florentines, notably their ageless cardinal, Dalla Costa.

Serlupi was undoubtedly responsible for my being summoned, late one evening, to the Archbishop's Palace beside the Baptistry. It was like a scene from the time of Savonarola. Apart from the absence of flickering torches and piles of faggots, the interview might just as well have taken place in the days of the great hell-fire preacher, and Elia Dalla Costa seemed to be a man of the same calibre, both outwardly and inwardly.

Having received me with measured courtesy in a library filled with massive pigskin tomes, he began by thanking me, on behalf of the inhabitants of the city, for having protested to Kesselring about the sadistic techniques of arrest and torture employed by Major Carità, whose behaviour grossly belied his name. This, however, was not the principal reason for my nocturnal audience.

A slow flush spread over the Cardinal's pale and ascetic face as he spoke of the grave concern which he and everyone in Florence felt for the city's future. He volunteered to discuss the matter with the Field Marshal in person as soon as I could arrange a meeting. In fact, personal intervention on his part would have been the surest way of bringing about just what he hoped to avoid: the military defence of Florence. Hitler and his closest associates were constantly reproaching the Field Marshal for his 'soft' attitude towards the Italians. If Führer's Headquarters heard that he had interviewed a cardinal, the result would be the exact opposite of what Dalla Costa hoped. I tried to convey this to him with the requisite tact, and my years of practice in dealing with ecclesiastical dignitaries at Rome stood me in good stead.

Dalla Costa favoured me with a faint but sympathetic smile and at once agreed to my counter-proposal, namely, that I should brief Kesselring on the problems raised by the city's defence with Consul Wolf's backing. Thanks to the Field Marshal, Florence had been made an open city since February 1944, so there was a chance that its inviolability might be preserved by a similar renunciation on the part of the Allies. This concluded the audience. The spiritual head of the city of the Medici introduced me to his secretary, a young *monsignore*, and asked me to keep in touch with him.

I drove out to see Kesselring next day, accompanied by Wolf. The Field Marshal agreed that a personal meeting with the Cardinal would be both dangerous and inexpedient, but he was glad to know that Dalla Costa and his contacts would back negotiations with the Allies on the joint preservation of Florence. At the same time, he left us in no doubt that if the plan fell through he would be forced to cover his retreat by laying demolition charges. He was, of course, referring to the Arno bridges, notably the Ponte Vecchio and Ammanati's dreamlike masterpiece, the Ponte S. Trinità. It was not the first time a soldier like Kesselring had been overburdened with responsibility. He was neither an artist nor an art historian, and the lives of his soldiers naturally meant more to him than the beauty of the bridges whose demolition would cover their withdrawal and so help them to survive. Although I left Florence before it was abandoned by German troops, it did at least emerge during my talks with the Field Marshal that he was prepared to save one of the bridges. It was not my fault that he decided in favour of the more popular but artistically far less meritorious Ponte Vecchio. The necessity for such a decision would have been avoided altogether if Allied Headquarters and Field Marshal Alexander had given a clear and concise reply to the Cardinal's negotiation proposals instead of indulging in vague and military unacceptable phraseology.

'I really didn't know I should ever be called upon to wage war in a museum,' Kesselring remarked during one of my visits to Monsummano, but this was just what he was being asked to do. I never appreciated his discernment—the discernment of an artistic and literary layman—more than I did during those weeks in Florence, when I was taxing his patience with my highly unmilitary requests. There was so much that could and must be protected or brought to safety. Wolf and Serlupi were tireless in their endeavours. Once, it was a clump of cypresses which had been selected as an artillery position. How could Kesselring and his staff be expected to know that Petrarch had kissed his Laura beneath those same historic trees? Again, how could they know what store art historians set by Pietro Tacca's four bronze Turkish slaves, which had adorned the statue of Grand Duke Ferdinand I at Leghorn before being evacuated to the Villa di Poggio. Any young tank corps lieutenant might have ordered his troop to run them down without knowing what they were, since they lay half embedded in the ground beneath a thin layer of sand, where a tank would have made short work of them. Remembering that the villa had once witnessed the tragic love and marriage of the legendary Grand Duke Francis I and his wife Bianca Capello, the expert poisoner, I recounted their colourful story while dining one evening at the Field Marshal's headquarters. The unfortunate Moors benefited as a result. They were removed from the danger-zone and now adorn the statue in Leghorn once more.

On another occasion I was invited to dine at the headquarters of General of the Air Force von Pohl. This gathering, which was highly illustrative of the mood prevailing among senior army and air force officers in June 1944, was described by the general himself in a report written in the officers' prisoner-of-war camp at Cinecittà, Rome, on 15 August 1945. The report is now in London, together with his other papers. What follows is the unabridged text of a carbon copy in my possession:

Max Ritter von Pohl,
General of the Air Force.
Rome, 15 August 1945.
Political discussion with Dr Eugen Dollmann in 1944
I was filled with mounting anxiety about Germany's future in the first half of 1944. There were growing signs of internal dis-integration in the National Socialist regime on the one hand, and, on the other, of a decrease in our military strength. Any sober-minded observer had to recognise the danger of total collapse in the foreseeable future.

It became clear to me that only a radical change in the system could save us and, more especially, pave the way for peace on reason-able terms. I realised at the same time that the obstacles to such a goal were very considerable. The liquidation of all democratic institutions in Germany ruled out the most natural solution, which was to consult the people. The forcible elimination of the regime by a strong mass movement was equally out of the question, since any attempt to influence the people in that direction would in-evitably have been nipped in the bud by the superlative National

Socialist police system. Finally, any operation undertaken by military commanders was doomed to fail as long as the regime still exercised full control over an unimpaired Party organisation and propaganda machine.

To me, the only practicable alternative seemed to be a seizure of power by a combination of military and political leaders who either controlled the key government posts or could easily gain possession of them. It is undeniable that the Party originally comprised many idealistically-inclined National Socialists endowed with the requisite qualities of leadership and moral courage. Although never a National Socialist nor in close contact with the Party myself, I felt confident that some of these men must still exist. Suitable candidates were more readily available on the military side, especially as many of the older members of the officer corps were at last beginning to waver in their once blind faith in the supreme command.

I was naturally aware that, as General Officer Commanding the Air Force in Central Italy, subordinated to the Second Air Force, I could neither organise such an operation nor exert a decisive influence on it. On the other hand, I wanted at least to salve my conscience by trying to explore the ground at an appropriate stage and putting forward suggestions, so as to make myself available if need arose.

Bearing this in mind, I sought an exchange of views with Dr Eugen Dollmann. Social and informal contact with him in Munich and Rome had satisfied me that he was a thoroughly decent type, and his status as political adviser to General Karl Wolff and Field Marshal Kesselring was bound to have given him a certain insight into the workings of politics.

This conversation, which took place at my headquarters near Florence at the end of June 1944, lasted several hours. Our initial discretion and reserve yielded to complete candour, and I was delighted to find that our views broadly coincided. I even learnt to my surprise that similar ideas were already being mooted with caution by senior but unspecified members of the SS.

One particular point of agreement between us was that the main responsibility for Germany's grave predicament lay with Adolf Hitler, whose disastrous foreign policy had plunged Germany into war with almost the whole of the civilised world. He had insisted on assuming military command, totally overestimating his own capabilities, and he had failed. He had bred bossism and corruption, and finally, as a complete autocrat, he had increasingly cut himself off from all rational advice.

He and the Party leaders responsible (to the best of my recollection, we mentioned names such as Ribbentrop. Göring, Streicher, Esser and Christian Weber), would have to be eliminated and replaced by a decent government which the Allies could accept as a partner in peace talks and which would later have to reorganise the German State—though we only touched on this briefly.

We both considered that this task could only be carried out jointly by the armed forces, under the leadership of Rommel or some other big name, and the SS, which was the only Party organisation that could be regarded as essentially intact. Unfortunately, Dollmann had to concede that Himmler lacked both the moral fibre and high sense of responsibility which would enable him to embark on such a venture and break away from the Führer. He did hint, however, that General Wolff, then commanding the SS and police forces in Italy, might be the man for such an undertaking, and that he would almost certainly make himself available as soon as he was convinced of Himmler's unsuitability and reluctance to act. He suggested that he should arrange a strictly confidential meeting between Wolff and me, and I gratefully accepted his offer.

This meeting was postponed, unfortunately, because Wolff was then on sick leave, and the first few days after his return were naturally claimed by his official duties.

Then came 20 July, which put us all in a difficult position because the Party's internal espionage and surveillance system was immediately tightened up to an enormous extent. Quite innocuous remarks or the laying of insufficient emphasis on National Socialist sentiments were enough to set the Gestapo in motion, and the successful campaign launched against the officer corps by Goebbels was an additional factor.

I met Dollmann again in the second half of August, and we agreed that no further development of our plans was possible under existing circumstances. Wolff and I reached a similar conclusion when we met in Fasano at the end of September and briefly discussed the situation. Wolff confirmed that his verdict on our leaders and their policies broadly corresponded with my own views as conveyed to him by Dollmann, and had done so for a long time past. He emphatically agreed with me, however, that popular sentiment and the Party's security measures temporarily precluded a solution of the kind discussed. As soon as an opportunity presented itself, we would reopen the lines of thought that had already been broached.

Our discussions did not, therefore, yield any concrete results. The only positive advantage may have been that Wolff knew he could count on my co-operation when he embarked on preparations for the armistice in spring 1945.

Sighed, von Pohl

So much for General von Pohl's deposition, recorded at the Intelligence Service Centre in Rome in August 1944. Von Pohl made only one major omission. His view was that the senior members of the German officer corps should be bypassed during the preparation and implementation of a putsch against the existing regime. Although, as a professional soldier, he belonged to this class, he told me flatly that it would be quite incapable of carrying out a coup d'état against higher authority. Any undertaking of this kind would have to originate within the Party itself, in this instance, Himmler and his SS. It was then conceivable that, once the inner circle of the Party oligarchy—Hitler included —had been purged by the Reichsführer-SS, the officers would in their turn decide to overthrow Himmler, to whom they were not bound by oath. It was a somewhat intricate and very German putsch theory whose roots went back to Martin Luther and his no less German concept of authority. Whether or not it was destined to become a historical reality was decided by the drama of 20 July, whose latter stages I witnessed in the company of Benito Mussolini and his senior ministers.

The Salò Republic's Head of State had spent several days touring Germany, and the meeting which took place on this momentous day in German history was intended to be the final item of his schedule. After inspecting his new army, i.e. the four divisions—San Marco, Monterosa, Littorio and Italia—which were currently being trained on German soil, Benito Mussolini was due at the Führer's Rastenburg headquarters on 20 July 1944 for talks on the future employment of these units. It was well known that the formation of these new divisions had been beset by a series of difficulties, the events of 8 September 1943 having convinced Hitler and his associates that all Italians with the exception of the Duce were, to a greater or lesser extent, traitors.

The tired and ailing dictator was far more interested in his new 'army' than in other, far more important problems confronting his puppet regime. As I have already said, Mussolini had a disastrous hobby: he loved to play soldiers. He resembled his German fellow-corporal in this respect, except that the latter, for all his undeniable blunders and miscalculations, possessed a far greater aptitude for this dangerous pastime. In addition, Hitler's military commanders were abler than the contemporary Italian generals, few of whom would have risen above field rank in Moltke's day.

Nothing about Hitler aroused his Italian co-dictator's envy more than his soldiers, and this was the fatal origin of their curious friendship, which was based on a truly Freudian mixture of love and hatred. Everything the Führer had—Stukas, tanks, submarines, countless divisions, paratroops, élite corps—the Duce wanted too, heedless of his limited resources and the total lack of interest and enthusiasm evinced by the overwhelming majority of his people, who had entered the war on 10 June 1940 with perceptible reluctance and ill-concealed distaste.

In pursuit of his Napoleonic dreams, Mussolini had celebrated the conquest of Abyssinia by getting a docile parliament to appoint him and King Victor Emmanuel the two first marshals of the new empire, thereby provoking one of the gravest constitutional crises that had occurred since he came to power. Victor Emmanuel became his avowed enemy from that day forth, and ultimately settled accounts with him by arresting him on 25 July 1943. In September of the same year, already weakened by its ill-starred participation in the Second World War, the Italian army was rent asunder. Thousands upon thousands of Italians were transported to Germany and confined in camps or forced to work for the Nazi war economy. Volunteers drawn from the sad survivors of Mussolini's toy army were then grouped in four divisions and licked into shape by German instructors. Such were the units which the Duce was now called upon to inspect and present with regimental colours.

The Italian and German organisers of this military function viewed its approach with mixed feelings. What would it be like, this first encounter between the fallen dictator and the ill-officered, ill-equipped soldiers whom he had led from one defeat to the next in his capacity as first marshal of the empire? Contrary to the arrogant and apparently unshakable belief of many Germans, the Italian private soldier and his superiors of low and medium rank were not cowards—indeed, they had given of their best in North Africa and Russia under the most inauspicious physical and psychological conditions. Would they now, brimming with hatred and thirsting for revenge, hurl themselves at the man responsible for their past and present misfortunes, and tear him to shreds?

They certainly hurled themselves at him, but not as I had imagined they would, and they almost tore him to shreds, but not in the way I had anticipated.

From Florence, where I had again been indulging in neo-Medicean day-dreams, I was hurriedly summoned to join the Duce's party at Mattarello near Trento. Here I met a new Mussolini. I had last seen him during the trip from Rome to Schloss Klessheim in April 1944. On that occasion, his first meeting with Hitler since the founding of the ill-fated Salò Republic, discussion had centred mainly on the question of Italian internees in Germany and on Mussolini's innumerable complaints about the collateral government which had been established at Lake Garda by the Germans. When Hitler, who had been wolfing multi-coloured pills throughout the interview, finally allowed his last remaining friend and ally to get a word in, the result was a rare display of temperament and political fireworks.

This time the Duce had donned the austere mental garb of a Roman stoic, and seemed to have taken the philosopher-emperor Marcus Aurelius as his model. Marcus Aurelius was, in fact, an admirable choice at this juncture, as long as one equated his concern at the inroads of barbarian hordes with the two dictators' fears of an imminent and decisive irruption by Russia and the Western Allies into the Third Reich and that part of Italy which was still under Mussolini's jurisdiction.

The great man was quiet and taciturn, and displayed a human dignity which banished the memory of his former posturings and pomposity. The first thing he did after welcoming me aboard the special train was to ask if I knew my Plato. I was compelled to say no. I had read Plato's *Symposium*—merely out of literary curiosity—but this was the one work in which Mussolini evinced no particular interest. He gave me a pitying smile, showed me the other works by Plato in his travelling library, and then treated me to an interesting but untopical lecture on his new pet author. Since most of what he said was new to me and he had had few chances of airing his German since September 1943, I listened to his philosophy lesson in silence. I enjoyed it, but wondered if he intended to favour his troops with a dissertation on the same theme.

Although my doubts and misgivings about the whole trip were hardly dispelled by all this talk of Plato, they proved to be unfounded. Wherever the dictator-turned-philosopher showed himself to his new praetorians he was greeted with a storm of applause. But were these eruptions of Latin temperament really aimed at him, the Duce of bygone days, or were they meant for a man who, to these despairing, uprooted playthings of an unpredictable fate, personified their poor, despised, betrayed homeland?

It was not jubilation of the sort that accompanied Napoleon from Elba to Paris, when the watchword was Napoleon and only Napoleon. I suspect that the general enthusiasm was directed less at Mussolini than at Italy—the place where the wives, children and mothers of these German-trained soldiers lived, the place where there was chianti and spaghetti and sun and blue sky.

I am certain that Benito Mussolini laboured under no illusions about his soldiers' true sentiments, which only enhanced my admiration for the Platonic calm and shrewd scepticism with which he managed to overcome this dilemma in his speeches to them. He himself entitled his platform address to the commanders of one division '*dialogo quasi Socratico*', and I privately christened another of his rhetorical feats '*De Gratitudine*'—'On Gratitude.' I remember it to this day.

It was at Sennelager, where the horizon is bounded by that forest rich in memories for every Roman, the Teutoburger Wald. Marshal Graziani, Mussolini's military travelling-companion, opened with a dramatic allusion to the lost legions of Emperor Augustus, which Varus had led to ignominious defeat there—a loss which the latter-day Germani were now making good by training and equipping four new Italian divisions. The legendary old man with the tangled shock of white hair—a genuine Blücher *alla italiana*—was greeted with applause which was as enthusiastic as it was unmilitary.

Benito Augustus had listened, grave-faced and motionless, to

his marshal's fiery effusions. Now came his historic moment. It
bore no relation to what the officers and NCOs, young and old,
sympathetic and indifferent, calm and excited, had been expecting.

Without once raising his voice to the old pitch, without em-
ploying any of his old dictatorial gestures, the great man of yore
delivered a brief but masterly speech on the subject of contemporary gratitude.

Sennelager and the German training area seemed to dissolve
around us as the battle-flags of Fascist Italy fluttered once more
over the soil of Spain and Abyssinia, as the warships of her once
mighty fleet cleft the waters of the Mare Nostrum, as the white-
uniformed Albanian Guard marched through the streets of Rome
to the sound of martial music, bound for guard duty at the royal
palace. The solitary man on the rostrum went on to recall the
gold wedding-rings which the mothers and wives of Italy, led by
Queen Elena, had sacrificed on behalf of the army, the vast
empire which Fascism and its army had carved out for the sake
of the over-populated motherland, the marshals and admirals
who owed their gold braid and medals to him, Mussolini. The
word 'betrayal' recurred again and again. Who had not betrayed
him and Fascism? Only from the men gathered around the platform—and here the unemotional voice rose almost imperceptibly
—only from them did he not expect betrayal.

'What do I ask of you, veteran officers and men of a new army?
Only gratitude—enough gratitude to do your duty by a native
land which, after all that has happened since 8 September 1943,
can only be called the Italian Social Republic. I am well aware
that many if not most of you would obey without question if
the watchword were: With you, Benito Mussolini—yes! With
your Fascism of former times—no! *Ufficiali, soldati Italiani*, after
what I have just said, can you dissociate Benito Mussolini from
his past career, from the creation of the Empire, from the conquest of Abyssinia and Albania?'

They could not. They cheered, hugged one another with tears
in their eyes, and hurled their caps into the air: their native
land, their motherland, had spoken. The fallen dictator who had
been summoned back to life by Hitler and Skorzeny's paratroopers

greeted his last triumph with an impassive face, while the German instructors stared dumbfounded at the unmilitary chaos in the hall muttering: 'These Italians, these Italians!'

Then the tumult died, and the man who had aroused it and his Italo-German entourage boarded the special train, where he was again at liberty to devote himself to Plato. He left us in no doubt that the foregoing scene would exercise a profound effect on the interview which he was due to have with his companion in misfortune, Adolf Hitler, at the Wolfsschanze next day, 20 July. As it turned out, fate decreed otherwise.

The day dawned humid and sultry. There was nothing pleasurable about the train journey, which was constantly interrupted by air-raid warnings. The only moment of relief came during one of our enforced halts, when Mussolini climbed out to stretch his legs. Like fugitives from the pages of Grimms' Fairy-tales, a party of children emerged from a clearing in the woods and presented him with some fresh raspberries, gazing timidly up at him as if he were the wolf in the story of Little Red Ridinghood. Then we journeyed on towards the East.

Mussolini sent for me, perhaps because he had had enough of Plato for the time being. He wanted me to help him revive old memories—memories of his last visit to the Wolf's Lair at the end of August 1941, when he was still the triumphant Duce del Fascismo and the Axis had been within an ace of victory over Soviet Russia and, in all probability, the Western World. He spoke of his aeroplane flight to newly captured Uman, of the rapturous welcome accorded him on the sunflower-bordered high roads of the Ukraine by the first Italian troops to have been dispatched there at his behest. He made no mention of what had happened to his Italian 'Grand Army'. Did he realise that most of these men had frozen or starved to death in the snow-fields or been transported to Siberia as living skeletons?

I do not know, but his new-found interest in Plato and philosophy had not immunised him against attacks of martial ambition. He outlined his agenda for the forthcoming conference. The main item was to be the active employment of his new army in the North Italian theatre of operations on equal terms with Kesselring's forces. He was in the middle of his war-game when Baron

Dörnberg, who was accompanying the party as Ribbentrop's *chef de protocole*, appeared at the door. He looked worried, and apologised for the fact that there would have to be yet another delay. No further explanation was offered, and we remained stationary on an open stretch of line not far from Görlitz, the small station serving the Führer's Headquarters, for nearly an hour before getting under way again. Mussolini vainly solicited information from his ambassador to Berlin and I did the same with Baron Dörnberg, but he merely wagged his red beard apologetically.

At last the train drew slowly into Görlitz. Gone were the gorgeous red carpets, the flags, garlands and military bands of former times. The only concomitants of this dismal reception were a grey-blue sky, a few scattered rain-drops and the mournful rustle of fir and pine.

The Führer of the Greater German Reich was standing on the platform with his paladins behind him, as of yore. He wore a long black cape, and his cap was pulled low over his face. That was all I saw as I leapt out and stationed myself beside him before the visitor from Lake Garda could descend from his carriage. It was part of my interpreter's duties to do this, and I always comforted myself with the thought that if the war went badly I might be able to find a job with the railways.

A moment later we were face to face with Benito Mussolini.

'Duce, a few hours ago I experienced the greatest piece of good fortune I have ever known!'

Hitler extended his left hand, and I saw that he was wearing his right arm in a sling.

It was about 3.30 p.m.

We soon learned the nature of Hitler's good fortune when he gave a brief account of how he had escaped assassination by a hair's breadth at 12.50 p.m. that day. Mussolini shook hands with Göring, Ribbentrop, Bormann and—needless to say—Heinrich Himmler, who was convulsed with agitation. Himmler soon set off with Hitler and Bormann on the short trip from the station to the Wolf's Lair, while Mussolini had to content himself with Göring, Foreign Minister Mazzolini and Ambassador Anfuso with Ribbentrop, and old Marshal Graziani with his colleague Keitel. Before long we were standing in front of the ruins of the so-called Tea-house where the midday conference had taken place. It was a room measuring sixteen feet by forty-one, and in its centre stood a map-table long enough to accommodate five people standing side by side. The whole place was a picture of havoc and devastation.

The two dictators sat down, one on an upturned box and the other on a rickety chair, looking vaguely like the characters from some Shakespearian tragedy. The man who had just cheated death delivered a monologue while Mussolini rolled his staring eyes to and fro as only he knew how. Divine providence was invoked. It was claimed that the Führer's invulnerability would have inspired Wagner to compose a new version of *Siegfried*, and, since he was so manifestly a darling of the gods, joint victory was assured. The frightful chaos surrounding us, the scent of death and destruction and the sight of the man who had escaped it virtually unscathed—was this not confirmation of the miracle to come? Being a guest and a true son of the South with a truly Latin fondness for signs and omens, Benito Mussolini needed no convincing of this.

I well remember that I was equally impressed, and anyone who claims not to have been is either a liar or a fool. One of the two lords of light and darkness must genuinely have intervened in the course of world history a few hours before. Whether it was the Devil or God Almighty I did not presume to decide, nor, fortunately, was I called upon to do so.

There was plenty of interpreting for me to do after Hitler had finished his account of the explosion. The rest of the afternoon was devoted to talks and discussions. Ribbentrop conferred with Mussolini's diplomatic advisers, Count Mazzolini and Filippo Anfuso, while Marshal Graziani held a council of war with Keitel and Jodl.

Hardly anything new emerged. Hitler, who delivered another monologue on the political and military situation, advocated a brutal and ruthless intensification of the war in the interests of final victory. He also dropped a few hints about secret weapons, one of whose tasks would be to effect the total destruction of London. Benito Mussolini painted a grim picture of partisan attacks and civil war in the South, only coming to life when he remembered his new army, two divisions of which he wanted thrown into action immediately. He handed his friend a three-page memorandum, drafted on board the train, which dealt with the vexed problem of the Italian soldiers interned in Germany who had not volunteered for service with the four new divisions. Hitler accepted Mussolini's proposals in favour of these hundreds of thousands of Italians, and the Duce's eyes shone with their old fire.

All these points had often been raised and discussed before, however. The only new feature was that there had at last been a putsch against Hitler in his own Reich, and that the Italians need no longer suffer taunts about 25 July and 8 September in silence. I was well enough acquainted with Messrs Mazzolini, Anfuso and 'Old Terror' Graziani to know that their ill-concealed smiles, smug expressions of sympathy and glib references to miracles of every description were symptomatic of deep private satisfaction at the events of the day. It was understandable that they should welcome the sudden application of the word 'traitor' to senior German officers, when it had hitherto been applied exclusively to their compatriots, but their reaction left a bitter after-taste.

It became even more bitter when we at last adjourned for the traditional tea-party, which was a positively ghoulish affair. Mussolini's son, the fat and foolish Vittorio, who disliked conferences as much as he liked his stomach, appeared from somewhere, and we assembled round a large tea-table in one of the huts which had not been damaged by the explosion. I sat in my usual position between the dictators, and the exalted Italian and German guests distributed themselves round us. The table was laid with painstaking neatness and tended by the usual blue-eyed SS boys in white jackets. But for the conversation of the Germans present, no outside observer would have guessed that only the intervention of the gods had made the tea-party possible at all. As it was, they all talked, led by Göring, Dönitz, Ribbentrop and Keitel. It suddenly occurred to them why ultimate victory had so far eluded their grasp: the whole thing was a conspiracy on the part of the generals. Conversation reverted to the generals again and again, and Goering, with an air of probity which matched his spotless white uniform, announced in deadly earnest that the same treacherous generals had secretly been withdrawing their best combat troops from the front line.

There were going to be big changes. Dönitz affirmed this on behalf of his blue-jackets, Ribbentrop on behalf of his diplomats —who came in for some scathing remarks from Göring, even on this solemn occasion—and Martin Bormann, the éminence grise, on behalf of the Party.

Absolved of all responsibility now that the generals had conveniently shouldered it for them, they noisily proclaimed their faith in ultimate victory. I looked round the table during this demonstration of loyalty. Mazzolini and Anfuso were exchanging amused glances, Graziani was vainly trying to impress Keitel with the story of his escape from assassination at Addis Ababa, Vittorio Mussolini was busy with his third slice of cake, and his father was nervously crumbling a piece of the same cake and moulding it into little figures. I turned to Hitler, thinking to engage him in conversation with his friend, but abandoned the idea at once. Watching him as he sat huddled in his chair like some inanimate idol, dull eyes gazing into infinity, I felt sure that, whatever the next few moments brought forth, it would not be polite tea-table conversation.

Minutes of uneasiness and apprehension elapsed before the storm finally burst. Outside, a light rain pattered unceasingly on the window-panes. All eyes were fixed on the motionless figure who alone could break the spell.

Then it came.

'Never have I felt more strongly that providence is at my side— indeed, the miracle of a few hours ago has convinced me more than ever that I am destined for even greater things and shall lead the German people to the greatest victory in its history. But I shall crush and destroy all the treacherous creatures who tried to stand in my path today. Traitors in the bosom of their own people deserve the most ignominious of deaths—and they shall have it! I shall wreak vengeance—inexorable vengeance—on all who were involved in this, and on their families, if they aided them. I shall exterminate this whole brood of vipers once and for all! Exterminate them, yes, exterminate them . . .'

The Furies of the Third Reich fled the close and stuffy room with a rustle of wings. The vision of revenge faded, leaving Hitler staring into the distance with an even paler face and eyes drained of fire.

With the unerring instinct of his race, the Duce realised that it was up to him to seize the initiative and save the situation. He laid his hand on Hitler's and looked into his eyes with a gentle, endearing smile, and Hitler abruptly awoke from his reverie. Someone opened the outside door. The rain had stopped, and Hitler told me to send for the Duce's coat. I must have looked surprised, because he told me that a fresh east wind generally sprang up in the late afternoon. The Duce was used to a soft climate, and Hitler did not want him to risk catching cold. I sent someone for the coat, secretly reflecting that a cold was the least of Mussolini's worries—and ours.

I handed the Duce his plain grey-green army greatcoat and was rewarded with raised eyebrows. When I translated his host's solicitous remarks, his proud response was in the spirit of the Caesars: 'Caro Dollmann, un Duce in un momento come questo non prende un raffreddore!' (At a time like this, a Duce does not catch colds!)—but he put his coat on all the same.

It got later and later. We learned that Goebbels had telephoned in high excitement and that events in Berlin seemed to be coming to a head. We paced nervously up and down in front of the tea bunker. I could not understand why we did not leave, but supposed there must be a good reason. Perhaps we were not at liberty to leave at all . . .

Eventually, towards evening, the tension was dispelled by another telephone call from Goebbels. Hitler beckoned the Duce to his side. After exchanging a few words with Goebbels, he addressed himself to the commanding officer of the Grossdeutschland Guard Battalion, who was in the Propaganda Minister's office and had actually been entrusted by the conspirators with the task of arresting him.

'Major Remer, do you recognise my voice?'

'Yes, my Führer.'

'Major Remer, I am uninjured. You are under my direct command until the Reichsführer-SS arrives in Berlin to take up his new appointment as Commander-in-Chief, Replacement Army. Until then, your job is to quell all resistance at all costs and by every means!'

'Yes, my Führer.'

The die was cast. This historic telephone conversation had set a final seal on the events of 20 July 1944, and we could depart.

Adolf Hitler accompanied us back to Görlitz station. One pale and ageing man, with his cap pulled even lower over his face, extended his left hand to another pale and ageing man. The two incongruous friends gazed deep into each other's eyes once more, as in the days of their glory, but the light in those eyes was extinguished, almost as though they guessed that this was their last meeting.

Safely back on board the special train, Mussolini thanked me for my services with his customary courtesy, adding: 'It doesn't matter what happens to a putsch, as long as it doesn't fail.'

I should have liked to reply: 'Excellency, what a pity that the putsch of 25 July 1943, which cost you your freedom and spelt the end of Fascism, succeeded so well.'

Instead, I preserved an equally polite silence while the rattling wheels sped us back through a half-destroyed Germany to the idyllic shores of Lake Garda.

*   *   *

After the Wolf's Lair, with its dramatic first rehearsal for Germany's *Götterdämmerung*, Lake Garda seemed like the Elysian fields. Cypress groves and citrus orchards bordered its delightful shores, and fairy-tale bowers of blossom surrounded the gleaming white villas in which the members of the new Salò Republic and the German protectors had installed themselves. As Head of State, Benito Mussolini occupied a château-like villa belonging to the Milan industrialist Feltrinelli at Gargnano. My old friend Buffarini-Guidi, now Minister of the Interior, lived at Maderno, and General Wolff was based at Fasano. Wolff's immediate task after the Duce's arrival—hardly a military assignment—was twofold: first, to ensure his personal safety, and, secondly, to restore him as quickly as possible to the arms of Clara Petacci, his Roman mistress. Mussolini had made it quite clear to his security chief that he could neither live nor rule without her. Accordingly, the Signorina also moved into a villa beside Lake Garda. This far from modest establishment was poetically named 'Fordalisa', but the locals had christened it the Villa dei Morti because its inmates were hardly ever to be seen. The Signorina and her villa were also assigned an SS guard, and competition for this Homeric vigil was understandably keen.

All went well until war broke out between the two queens of Mussolini's heart. Schiller would have turned green with envy at this conflict, beside which the confrontation between Elizabeth and Mary Stuart paled into insignificance.

After the dramatic events in Germany, the whole affair resembled a piece in the *opéra bouffe* style of, say, Cimarosa's *Secret Marriage*. Discounting Mussolini, I believe I was the first person to receive an authentic and colourful account of it immediately after the curtain had fallen on the last act.

Buffarini often invited me to the government guest-house beside the lake at Maderno. On this particular occasion I waited vainly for my host until, three hours late, the fat little Minister of the Interior finally put in an appearance. Breathless, dishevelled and bathed in perspiration, he tottered in and flung himself down on the sofa with a groan, having first—to my surprise—tossed aside something which looked suspiciously like a revolver. Then he moaned:

'*Queste donne, ah, queste donne!*' ('These women, these women!')

To my even greater surprise, I learned that the ladies in question were Donna Rachele Mussolini and Signorina Clara Petacci.

It was some time before he recovered himself sufficiently to tell me his story. Although he found it far less amusing than I did, he did not take offence at my laughter. Slowly, I grasped what had happened. I had known, even in Rome, that my Machiavellian friend had for years been compelled to perform feats of acrobatic agility in order to keep the two exalted ladies at bay without losing the confidence of one or the favour of the other.

Every tightrope has to break sometime, however, and he had come to grief at last.

Although Claretta's affair with Benito—'my Ben', as she used to call him—had been common knowledge throughout Rome and Italy for years, Donna Rachele, the faithful guardian of Mussolini's hearth and home, had not, on her own submission, learned of it until her husband's arrest on the fateful night of 25–26 July 1943. Hard as I find it to believe this, I would not venture to doubt the word of a woman whom I always regarded as head and shoulders above the thoroughbred fillies in her son-in-law's stable. Be that as it may, her husband's daily visits to the Villa dei Morti while in exile at Lake Garda finally exhausted her patience. What was more, she feared the worst for her family and the Republic at the hands of the Petacci clan, who were reputed to be hatching all kinds of dark financial and political schemes. To cut a long story short, one hot and thundery August afternoon not long after our return from the Wolf's Lair she surprised her husband by announcing her intention of paying a call on his mistress. Benito, whose stay at Lake Garda had taught him the Christian virtue of forbearance, merely shrugged and said: 'If you must.' Thus armed, the proud Romagnola, who was a native of the same hot-blooded North Italian province as her husband, decided to enlist Buffarini as chief witness for the prosecution.

The plump little minister, who would far rather have lunched with me and listened to my report on the Wolf's Lair, was virtually abducted from his office and forced into the passenger seat of Donna Rachele's small car. Two Romagnolese bodyguards followed in another car.

Pulling up outside the Petacci villa, they knocked and rang until an SS officer came to tell them that he could not admit them. There was a moment of stupefaction. Then Donna Rachele, no longer in the first flower of youth, launched an attack on the tall wrought-iron grilles covering the windows. She continued to rattle them vainly until the unfortunate Minister of the Interior at last managed to gain admittance.

The officer who had been so unwelcoming conducted the unwanted visitors to a small room guarded by two of Clara's German bodyguards.

At length the door opened and the Pompadour of Fascism,as she was popularly known, made her entrance. She sank into an armchair with a flimsy handkerchief fluttering from her hand. Donna Rachele opened her attack with the interesting but not over-tactful question: 'Are you Signora or Signorina?' Disconcerted, Clara admitted to the former designation. Then the storm broke with a vengeance. Donna Rachele brooked no form of interruption or contradiction once she got under way—this I knew from my own experience. Having stressed the critical position in which Benito and his Republic now found themselves, she requested her frail adversary to leave him alone, refrain from taxing his physical and mental resources, and bring her scandalous sojourn at Lake Garda to an end.

Here Clara threw her first faint. Buffarini hurriedly fetched a bottle of brandy, but she recovered herself and did her best to save the little that remained to be saved. She impressed on Donna Rachele how charmingly Benito had always spoken of 'his Rachele', but this was the last thing Donna Rachele or any other married woman would have wanted to hear from a rival. Donna Rachele waxed vociferous, and Clara closed her eyes again. It may not have been another swoon. Perhaps she was merely wondering how to hit her visitor where it hurt most. If so, her deliberations bore fruit.

'Ben can't live without me.'

That shaft went home. Despite Buffarini-Guidi's efforts to restrain her, Donna Rachele hurried to the telephone. A moment later, Clara heard her beloved confirm that he had known of his wife's proposed visit and had done nothing to prevent it. She preserved her tenuous hold on life with another glass of brandy.

The conversation, which had already lasted for hours, neared its climax and, consequently, its end. Donna Rachele, who had not been reared in a princely palazzo but was well provided with basic human instincts, pulled all the stops out. Fury-like, the corpulent, over-blown matron turned on her young and beautiful rival and rent her as she would have rent the flimsy chiffon handkerchief she was holding.

'You'll come to a bad end! Everyone hates and despises you —I warn you!'

The wife of the Duce and mother of his children leapt to her feet, flushed and trembling. She conjured up a picture of the frightful end awaiting Clara in the Piazzale Loreto in Milan, as described in a threatening letter from a partisan. She achieved her object. Donna Rachele's adversary buried her face in her crumpled handkerchief and burst into tears, then swooned again. Victory was complete and the honour of Romagna saved.

Followed by the distraught Buffarini, Donna Rachele stalked proudly out of the house. Ordering him into the seat beside her, she drove off without another word and dropped him at the house where I had been waiting for him for so long. She had had enough of him, and she was enough of a woman to realise what a double-dealing game he had been playing all these years. Buffarini's ministerial days were numbered, hence his pitiful condition when he returned and described the torment of the past three hours with all the eloquence of a modern Cicero.

Donna Rachele drove home to the Villa Feltrinelli. Benito spent the whole evening with his lioness, stroking her hand and begging her forgiveness. The upshot was that Clara stayed on, not at the Villa Fiordalisa but in a wing of the château which Gabriele d'Annunzio had built beside Lake Garda. She suited the place, and the great portrayer of the soul of woman would undoubtedly have devoted a novel to her if he had known her. Her romance with 'Ben' endured to the bitter end—an end in which she played her part with a loyalty and devotion which ought to exempt her from the rebukes and reproaches of posterity. I shall never forget her proud response when I urged her to catch one of the last flights to Spain at the beginning of April 1945.

'Never,' she said. 'I loved Benito when times were good. I shall love him even more now that they are bad.'

I had had my fill of *opéra bouffe* performances beside Lake Garda, even if they were presented by an all-star cast. Apart from that, it was time for me to resume my duties with Kesselring, who had since moved to San Andrea, another small spa near Parma. I had enough to do there, since Mussolini had announced his intention of paying a military call on the Field

Marshal in his capacity as Head of State, and arrangements for the forthcoming visit had to be made.

Having consoled the crestfallen Minister of the Interior with an assurance that I would do everything in my power to buttress his precarious position, I drove to Reggio Emilia. Friends had secured me new quarters there in the Villa Roncina, which belonged to an elderly countess named Brazza. I shall have more to say about her and why I accepted her hospitality elsewhere in this chapter. The villa was equidistant from Lake Garda, Kesselring's new headquarters, and Milan, the seat of the Milanese Curia, but it possessed still other advantages.

Kesselring devoted a long evening to me. Much as my account of the battle royal between Donna Rachele and Clara Petacci amused him and his staff, he listened to my description of the Wolf's Lair on 20 July in deadly earnest. Unlike the military commanders in France and Belgium, Kesselring was not privy to the conspiracy, even though one of the ringleaders, Goerdeler, had once tried to establish contact with him. Everything had remained quiet in his area on 20 July. Kesselring's soldierly interpretation of his oath of allegiance to Hitler was unshakable, but he utterly condemned the system of revenge and retribution which was now being instituted. When he heard that two of his staff officers, one of very senior rank, had been involved in the conspiracy, he did all he could to remove them from the line of fire. He succeeded with the utmost difficulty, a fact which deserves to be recorded in view of the extremely unfair criticism levelled at him in later years by his own countrymen.

Mussolini and Marshal Graziani turned up to see him a few weeks later, accompanied by only a handful of officers. There was the usual guard of honour, the usual discussion of the current situation, and the usual consensus of opinion that the situation was extremely grave and would become even graver, especially if Field Marshal Alexander followed up the capture of Florence by pushing on vigorously, with the whole of his far superior forces, before autumn and winter arrived. Mussolini pored over the map-littered table as in days gone by, and one could see how relieved he was to get away from his marital and extra-marital worries. He comported himself in a modest, natural, unbombastic way, and generally behaved as befitted an ally of dwindling importance. To the despair of Kesselring and his staff, however, he refused to be dragged away from his military hobby. Graziani proposed one of his pet tactical exercises. It came to nothing, as usual, because there were not sufficient forces available, and with this brilliant display of generalship the war-game on the green baize table came to an end.

There followed an intimate little *rinfresco*, complete with some choice wines from the Reggio Emilia district procured by me. They prompted Mussolini to explain why Parma, Reggio and Modena, the richest of all Italian provinces, bred such bloodthirsty and violent inhabitants. He attributed it to the potent wine, strong Parmesan and pungent spices which the natives of these fortunate regions consume from childhood onwards.

'They're too full-blooded and they've always been extremists. They were the boldest of my Fascists in 1922, when I marched on Rome and Italy was Socialist. Now, because they live in the Salò Republic, they're Communists. Wherever there's a whiff of blood, there they are. They're too well off, that's what it is.'

I was in the distressing position of being able to contribute some really ghastly details of torture, mass murders along the Via Emilia, nocturnal raids—in short, of the Italian civil war. Mussolini, who had never been a torturer, executioner, or deviser of horrors, looked grim. Seizing this unique opportunity, I begged him to back my attempts to mitigate these orgies of revenge and hatred as far as it was in my power to do so. Kesselring at once fell in with my suggestion, and I received permission to report direct to Lake Garda and establish contact with the Salò authorities.

Then Mussolini drove off, doubtless reluctant to return to the Amazonian warfare raging at Lake Garda. Although I saw him again at various formal conferences, I only had one more private interview with him. This meeting, which took place on 6 April 1945, shortly before his tragic death, remains one of my most impressive memories of a man whose greatest error was his lovehatred for Adolf Hitler and the unnatural alliance with the Third Reich that sprang from it.

There had been a German-Italian military conference in his

study at the Villa Feltrinelli that morning. My private name for it was the Thermopylae Conference. General Baron von Vietinghoff, Kesselring's successor as C.-in-C. Southern Command, headed the German side, and the Italians were represented by Graziani, the handsome Filippo Anfuso, formerly Mussolini's ambassador in Berlin and now his last Foreign Minister, and Alessandro Pavolini, a one-time poet who now commanded the dreaded Brigate Nere, or Black Brigade. Also present were Ambassador Rudolf Rahn and General Wolff. Benito Mussolini presided.

Pavolini wanted to take the remnants of the neo-Fascist forces, notably his black gods of vengeance from the Brigade, and make a last desperate stand in the Valtelline Valley. No preparations had been made, of course. Justifiably outraged by the idea itself and the lack of organisation behind it, the Germans shook their heads. Their opposition was reinforced by the knowledge that the negotiations being conducted with the Americans in Switzerland by General Wolff and myself—negotiations whose primary aim was to avert any such lunatic last-minute massacre—were almost complete. It should be added that, because of the machinations of the Petacci clan, we had not ventured to inform Mussolini of this move.

The 'Epic of the Fifty Thousand', as Pavolini rapturously christened his scheme, petered out in recommendations to set up a number of committees to study the question of arms, supplies, and defensive positions—and this on 6 April 1945! The Duce started to play soldiers again, but lack of military knowledge compelled him to fall in with the proposals of Vietinghoff and the others.

Of the hypothetical 50,000, a mere hundred or two joined their Duce on his last northward march on 27 April, only to fall into the hands of the Dongo partisans. This, however, was still three weeks away.

When the Thermopylae Conference was safely over and the German delegates had left the room looking understandably relieved, Mussolini called me aside and said he wanted to see me again at four that afternoon—alone, he added meaningfully. I felt uneasy. Even though we had done and were still doing all we could to associate him and his Fascists in the Swiss surrender talks with Allen Dulles, neither Vietinghoff nor Wolff nor I had ever discussed the matter openly with him. The two generals adjured me to absolute secrecy. They did not care how I extricated myself from this awkward predicament as long as I kept my mouth shut. Trusting my luck, which had always proved more effective than my intelligence, I presented myself at the door of Mussolini's small study in the Villa Feltrinelli at 4 p.m. precisely.

'*Che ospite raro al nostro Garda!*'—'What a rare visitor to our Lake Garda! ' was his opening remark.

The lord and master of Salò was affability itself, but this only intensified my misgivings. He asked the usual routine questions about the situation in Northern Italy, praised my role as a mediator, and seemed determined to keep conversation on a general plane.

Why had he sent for me?

I expected the bomb to burst at any moment. Any moment might bring an inquiry about my visits to Switzerland from March onwards, about my contacts with US intelligence agents in Lugano and Zürich—in short, about the surrender talks.

Time passed and still no question came. Gradually, it dawned on me that he just wanted a chat. It was a charming and typically Latin gesture which would never have occurred to a German in his predicament. He reminisced about our joint trips, conferences, meetings, about his summer visit to the Ukraine, the Brenner talks, Hitler's tour of Italy in May 1938.

Finally, he came to September 1938 and the Munich Conference. The quiet, even tenor of his voice yielded to sudden animation. It was as if the walls of his place of exile rang with the joyous fanfare of the guard of honour that had greeted his arrival, as though Adolf Hitler's invincible war-planes once more circled in the sky above the open car that took the two dictators to the station at midnight, after the conference had reached a peaceful conclusion; as though he could once more hear the deluded masses hailing their supposed deliverance with a storm of cheers.

'That was my great day. I was the only one who spoke and understood all the languages. All eyes were on me, not on Mr

Chamberlain or Monsieur Daladier. It was an occasion worthy of the Caesars—do you remember?'

I remembered it with pleasure, and agreed that he had indeed played a part worthy of Julius Caesar. He interrupted me excitedly:

'What a play—the greatest thing Shakespeare ever wrote!'

He went on to speak of 25 July 1943 and the fact that the gods had omitted to warn him in advance. Rising, he stationed himself behind his massive desk, which almost filled the room, and declaimed:

'Caesar shall go forth: the things that threaten'd me
Ne'er look'd but on my back ; when they shall see
The face of Caesar, they are vanished.'

In a quieter tone, he quoted Calpurnia's warning:

'Caesar, I never stood on ceremonies,
Yet now they fright me . . .
O Caesar, these thing are beyond all use,
And I do fear them!'

With a sorrowful smile, he concluded:

'Donna Rachele was the only one who warned me. She begged me not to venture into the King's lair, but:

'Cowards die many time before their deaths ;
The valiant never taste of death but once.'

It was a memorable moment. I had never heard *Julius Caesar* performed in Italian, let alone by an actor of this calibre. I was fascinated. I, too, forgot that the war was lost, that I was negotiating with the enemy in Switzerland, and that the Caesar opposite me was probably destined to die no more pleasantly than his classical forbear.

Then the curtain fell. I had seen Mussolini's eyes glow for the last time. The fire in them died, and he wearily resumed his seat, looking old and ill. Silence reigned for a moment. Although my fear of awkward questions had receded, Mussolini did have one last surprise in store for me.

It seemed that he had been deeply impressed by Hitler's fleeting reference to German secret weapons at the Wolf's Lair on 20 July 1944—so impressed that, even on 6 April 1945, he was still convinced of the necessity to stand fast and fight to the last. A chill ran down my spine, and my brief access of enthusiasm for the Duce waned abruptly.

Opening a drawer, he pulled out the draft of a letter which he had written on his return from the Reich. In it, he requested Hitler to leave his troops in Italy for a year or two after the successful termination of hostilities so that the Salò Republic could secure a firm hold on the country from the Brenner to Sicily.

It only needed one of his old dictatorial maxims, e.g. 'Better a day as a lion than a hundred years as a sheep', and I should have been spirited back to Rome as it was on the day when he proclaimed the founding of the Empire. I rose with the customary '*auguri*' and begged him not to leave Lake Garda. We still believed that our negotiations in Switzerland might save his life provided he remained close at hand.

On 18 April, despite solemn assurances that he would not do so, he set off for Milan and the death which it was beyond our power to avert.

*   *   *

Between Donna Rachele's duel and Clara Petacci and the farewell performance described above, that is to say, between August 1944 and April 1945, I was based at the Villa Roncina. This was my so-called heroic period, or so I thought at the time. Heroic or not, it was certainly eventful, and it brought me into direct contact with human passions, vices and emotions of which I had been only fleetingly aware during my young days in Munich, my many visits to the cultural institutes and drawing-rooms of Rome, and my journeys as an interpreter in luxurious special trains. So far, death had only revealed itself to me through the medium of map-tables or casualty reports; now I came face to face with it in all its naked horror. The internecine strife raging in the Central and North Italian provinces defended by Kessel-

ring's troops and nominally administered by the Salò Republic
ran the gamut of all the virtues and vices inherent in human
nature. All types were represented, from the Marquis de Sade to
St Francis of Assisi, from the torturers of the Inquisition to the
rifle-toting Amazons of the Spanish Civil War. However sublime
and patriotic the motives which may sometimes have inspired the
deeds and misdeeds of these people, there was nothing sublime
about their actuality.

The Villa Roncina was situated in the middle of an extensive
area which had earned the unlovely name of Triangolo della
Morte. The Triangle of Death ran through the provinces of
Romagna, Modena, Reggio Emilia and Parma, and was traversed
by the Via Emilia. The cross-roads of this ancient Roman high-
way were piled high with victims of the hydra-headed monster
of civil war, left there as a mutual deterrent by the two warring
camps. The blood-streaked bodies lay there stinking in the summer heat because no one, whether neo-Fascist or partisan, dared
to cart them away. The appalling methods of torture employed
in the prisons of the Salò Republic were rivalled only by the
painful inquisitorial techniques of partisan interrogators. Sensitive parts of the body were singed with red-hot irons and soles
branded with horse-shoes, orgies of beating were a regular part
of interrogation, and shootings had become so commonplace that
they no longer caused a stir.

While driving through the area one night I pulled up outside
a brightly lit farmhouse off the sinister Via Emilia, hoping for a
meal and a rest. The farm proved to be an outpost of the Brigate
Nere. The young black-shirts eagerly invited me to join their
crowded table. Glasses of sparkling Lambrusco heightened the
feverish mood of my hosts. There they were, Mussolini's last
remaining fanatics, loyal to a man, convinced of their own and
their Duce's historic mission, confident of final victory, and only
too well acquainted with the inexorable savagery of fratricidal
war. In many cases, bands of Communist guerillas had shot their
fathers and mothers, carried their sisters or fiancées off to the
mountains as spoils of war, taken the last cow from their stables.
Descriptions of these atrocities flew thick and fast, hoarse young
voices intoned oaths of vengeance, old Fascist marching-songs

were sung. From somewhere outside, or so it seemed to me, came faint moans and the distant sound of weeping.

The mystery was soon solved. Someone whispered something to the commander of the group, a young dark-haired lad of about twenty. Tension mounted, and cries of 'At last!' rang out on every side.

My hosts poured out of the room, leaving me behind. A moment later the German NCO who was acting as my armed escort rushed in and beckoned me to follow. We hurried through a small door into another room, half stable, half hay-barn. The dim light of a paraffin lamp fell on the naked white bodies of two girls who were each lashed to a bench in the middle of the room, face upwards. A boy with the smile of an angel of death —the same boy who had just told me at table how his whole family had been massacred in the course of a single night—was busily emptying the contents of two jars on to the bodies of his defenceless victims.

Muffled cries of '*Pietà, pietà!*' rent the air. 'Mercy?' came the retort. 'Why mercy? Because you whores denounced my family to your comrades as Fascists and sent them to their deaths—why mercy?'

He was still at work when another young Fascist entered the stable leading a bearded billy-goat and a huge white Campagna sheep-dog. The Walpurgisnacht orgy proceeded with lightning rapidity. Inflamed with hatred and revenge, passion and wine, the young men crowded round the two benches and the motionless bodies strapped to them. The animals leapt on the girls, who had been smeared with butter and scattered with salt. A savage war-chant rang out, drowning the half-voluptuous, half-maddened shrieks of the victims.

It lasted only a few moments. Then the German NCO drew his pistol, shot the frantic animals, and untied the ropes. The black-shirts gave the girls back their clothes and we drove them to the nearest German military post, where we were relieved of further responsibility for them. I sent a direct report to Mussolini's secretariat and to Buffarini-Guidi, and a few days later I heard that this particular picket of the Brigate Nere had been disbanded.

My next mission was to drive far into the mountains, there

to exchange a couple of hundred German soldiers who had fallen into a partisan trap for the same number of Red guerillas in German hands. I welcomed the assignment, but decided to go accompanied by a monsignor on the staff of the Bishop of Reggio Emilia, clad in full clerical regalia. Somewhere in the Apennines I was greeted, solemnly and punctiliously, by a guard of honour with red neckerchiefs and fists raised in the Communist salute, and was invited by the 'C.O.' to join him at a table laden with richer fare than I had ever enjoyed at the royal palace in Rome.

The meeting was a complete success. It was agreed that the German soldiers should be delivered at a pre-arranged spot in the mountains where the captured partisans would also be waiting. I learned one or two interesting things, notably that the partisan leader and his daredevil guerillas would far rather be fighting with the Germans against the capitalist Allies if only the Germans had not allied themselves with the *cadavere vivente*, or the Living Corpse, as Mussolini was disrespectfully known. We parted on the best of terms, and the guard of honour turned out again for my benefit. My ecclesiastical companion attributed it all to his prayers.

Kesselring was probably thinking of this episode when he made the following reference to me in his memoirs:

Had it not been for Standartenführer Dr Eugen Dollmann, who maintained the closest contact with senior Italian circles, enjoyed my fullest confidence, and recklessly ventured into partisan-controlled areas without an escort, many of my precautionary measures would have come into effect too late—if, indeed, they could have been taken at all.

I did not, of course, go unescorted. I was accompanied not only by a monsignor and his prayers but by an ex-Communist from Modena, who was driving.

Although I only heard the cry *'Evviva la guerra!'*—'Long live war!'—once during my Roncina period, it remains one of my saddest and most enduring memories of those months. One day, while I was driving through the province of Modena, there was a severe air-raid. Being in the the vicinity of one of the Salò

Republic's prisons, I decided to take cover there. Just at that moment, the agitated warders opened the outer gates and a stream of pale and emaciated convicts in tattered prison uniform poured forth. A few soldiers who were also seeking shelter on the premises volunteered to restore discipline and good order in the prescribed manner. I ought to have encouraged them in their efforts, but then one poor devil flung his bony arms to heaven and screamed:

'Long live war—we're free! '

It was like a scene from Dostoevsky's *House of the Dead*. Aided and abetted by me, the pitiful scarecrows vanished in all directions. Whatever they were, whether murderers, pimps or thieves, the war had at last achieved something of value. Breathlessly, they told me their stories, swore to repent and reform their lives, promised to pray for me. I hope they did so, because my peculiar rescue operation earned me universal opprobrium. If the Field Marshal had not taken me under his wing yet again—even though he did not know his Dostoevsky—I should probably have been put in one of the empty cells in Modena penitentiary. For all that, I still look upon my irresponsible action as one of the few good deeds I have ever performed.

And so my life at the Villa Roncina went on. Bishops and *monsignori*, generals and military commanders, duchesses and peasant women, neo-Fascists and partisans came and went. Calls for help flooded in from all quarters, including one from the villa which Giuseppe Verdi had built with the proceeds from his operas at Busseto, where he led the comfortable life of a gentleman farmer. I was able to prevent it from being turned into an artillery park, thereby saving the original scores of his works which were stored there, his piano, and the villa's unpretentious late nineteenth-century furnishings. No objections were raised at Kesselring's headquarters this time.

Before concluding this account of my rescue operations, successful and otherwise, I should like to mention one which I still regard today—quite immodestly—as the most important and worth-while mission I undertook at this stage in my life.

During September and October 1944 I was visited with increasing frequency by the only Italian of my acquaintance who had no charm and never laughed. He resembled a citizen of Sparta rather than Athens or Rome. Whether it was warm or cold, whether the sun was shining or the autumn wind whistling across the broad plains, he always wore ceremonial black and looked like a Grand Almoner of the Spanish royal court. His name was Capitano Ghisetti, and I had known him in Rome.

Ghisetti had fought bravely in the East and been awarded the Iron Cross while serving with the Julia Division, which, like the entire Italian corps in Russia, received far less credit than it deserved. He stayed on in Rome after 8 September 1943, and had lent me every possible assistance in my attempts to safeguard the city's future.

What I did not know was that he extended similar assistance to agents of the CIC, or Counter-Intelligence Corps, who were also in the city—yet another indication of my superficiality and irresponsibility. It was at their request, so I learned later, that he followed me to Northern Italy. He presented himself at the Villa Roncina as a close friend of Monsignore Professore Don Bicchierai, who was an influential member of the Milan Curia and a confidant of Cardinal Ildefonso Schuster. His Eminence had been very favourably inclined towards Fascism in general and Benito Mussolini in particular. Like Pope Pius XI, another native of the Milan area, he too had looked upon the Duce as a man sent by providence.

There was a certain connection between 'providence' and the plans which Ghisetti now began to discuss with such wearisome solemnity. Our talks culminated in a memorandum which he gravely handed me on behalf of the Cardinal on 14 October. It was highly confidential, of course, and I only quote the main passages, as reproduced in Schuster's *Gli ultimi tempi di un regime* (Milan, 1946, p.35):

The Catholic Church regards the systematic destruction of public utility installations (gas and electricity works, etc.), together with that of industrial plant, as a prerequisite of Bolshevik infiltration into Italy. This threat to living conditions on the one hand and industrial potential on the other is intended to create disorder and unemployment. This is the basis upon which the masses are to be won, first for Communism and then for Bolshevism.

It is in both the Italian and German interest to examine whether, in view of the general situation, there is any possibility of averting these systematic acts of destruction.

There has never been any fundamental or explicit refusal on the German side to participate in an agreement which would not only further material interests but benefit the German forces' reputation for humanity and civilisation.

His Eminence Cardinal Schuster requests you to mediate to this end with Field Marshal Kesselring, supreme commander of the German armies operating in Italy.

For his part, His Eminence likewise offers to play the part of a mediator and act as guarantor of an agreement between the German armies in Italy and the Comitato Nazionale di Liberazione (Northern Italy), with the following aim:

The German troops in Italy will refrain from the systematic destruction of all industrial or other installations of public utility, in so far as these do not represent objectives of military importance. His Eminence includes under this heading: electricity and gas works, water mains, reservoirs, factories, etc. Installations of tactical importance do not fall within this definition.

For their part, the partisan groups of the National Liberation Committee will refrain from any hostile act or sabotage against German troops. Isolated incidents and cases of indiscipline shall not be allowed to prejudice this agreement.

My Grand Almoner rounded off the Cardinal's proposal with the following appeal, doubtless inspired by the Cardinal himself via Don Bicchierai:

As an Italian, I consider it my duty to transmit this communication to you and lend it my fullest support. I know that I have never turned to you in vain on behalf of my native land and my fellow-countrymen. If you declare your willingness to convey this communication to the Field Marshal, and if these proposals strike you as generally worthy of discussion, please be good enough to inform me when and where you wish to meet Monsignor Bicchierai with a view to further discussion of any difficult points.

Thank you for being kind enough to bestow your attention on this memorandum.

Yours,

Ghisetti

A complicated exchange of letters ensued. I briefed Kesselring as fully as possible and was instructed to maintain contact and keep my lines of communication open. However, not even a cardinal of Schuster's calibre could go very far without paying heed to one factor which weighed heavily with the partisan groups, namely, the Allies.

'Providence' ravelled and unravelled the threads of destiny still further. One evening in December I was invited to dinner by Tuninetti, the Prefect of Pavia. He introduced me to an elegant gentleman with a smile of great charm, and I knew at once why I had been asked. Baron Parrilli, as this cavalier and *homme du monde* was called, was also known to me from my Rome days, if only by reputation. Rumour had it that he was a great *bon viveur* and woman-chaser, and he looked like a character in a late nineteenth-century French novel. Just to complete this scintillating picture, I must add that Parrilli was a Knight of Malta, a Papal Chamberlain, and the son-in-law of Milan's leading industrialist. His contribution to our meeting was a case of French champagne, which he was passionately fond of. It soon loosened his tongue. Quite simply, he wanted me to help him arrange a trip to Switzerland—no easy matter for an Italian citizen of the Salò Republic, especially in view of the close watch kept on the frontiers by the Germans. When I inquired the object of his journey, his response was couched in Delphic ambiguity.

Parrilli spoke of the old friends he hoped to see there, of North Italian industrial interests and the like. The first glimmer of light came when he began to talk about the speech which Mussolini had delivered to a fanatical crowd in Milan's Teatro Lirico on 16 December, a few days earlier. He asked me what I thought of the Duce's avowed intention to defend the Po valley tooth and nail, street by street and house by house, thereby turning Northern Italy into a blood-stained battlefield.

I replied that I thought it was a crazy speech—just as crazy as the Duce's similar outbursts in the spring of 1944, when he had advocated fighting to the death in and around Rome. After gazing earnestly into my eyes for a full minute, Parrilli asked whether this was merely my personal opinion, or whether it was shared by Field Marshal Kesselring and General Wolff.

Feeling that I had gone far enough, I challenged him to go and ask the two gentlemen the same question to their face, and volunteered to accompany him.

'You'll be hearing from me soon, my dear Dollman,' he replied, raising his glass. 'Let us drink to the preservation of the Po valley.'

I did so gladly. A veil was drawn across the subject, and conversation turned to the baron's romantic escapades.

In the latter part of February I heard that he had actually travelled to Switzerland. This news reached me almost at the same time as a report from my friend Ghisetti that Don Bicchierai had also gone there to contact the Nunciature at Berne on the subject of our discussions and of the memorandum which had been passed to me. I heard nothing more from anyone for some time.

It was not until after the war that I discovered what Parrilli was planning to do in Switzerland and how far he had made use of me for his own purposes. A book has been written about the few months immediately preceding the surrender of the German armies in Italy at Caserta on 29 April 1945—not an impartial or faultless book, but a book written by an Italian journalist: Ferruccio Lanfranchi's *La Resa degli Ottocentomila con le memorie autografe del Barone Luigi Parrilli* (Milan, 1948).

The 'eight hundred thousand' were Kesselring's armies, which were still fighting in Northern Italy in February and March, and the few Italian units attached to them. Baron Parrilli's visit to Switzerland at the end of February 1945 was primarily concerned with them, and with Hitler's scorched earth directive, which was due to come into effect if these troops retreated northwards from the Po valley. While in Switzerland he met his old friend Professor Max Husmann, whose acquaintance I also made at a later date. Husmann, who ran two large boys' academies modelled on the English public school, was a twentieth-century Erasmus imbued with a spirit of humanity. He engineered a meeting between Parrilli and a senior member of the Swiss military intelligence service, Max Waibel, then a major on the General Staff. After a great deal of feverish activity, feelers went out, via him, to President Roosevelt's special delegate in Switzerland, Allan W. Dulles, head of the OSS or Office of Strategic Services in Berne and Zürich.

Roosevelt's European representative greeted these overtures from a—to him—unknown Italian nobleman with caution. Instead of meeting him personally, he sent his close associate Gero von Schulze-Gaevernitz. Parrilli recalls in his memoirs that my name was mentioned during this interview. Gaevernitz immediately pricked up his ears, and the upshot was a suggestion that I should drive to Switzerland with Parrilli at once to meet representatives of the OSS there.

I knew nothing of this until Parrilli arrived back in Italy and asked me to meet him in Milan on 1 March. I remembered Gaevernitz well, of course. As I have already related, I had met him in Rome in autumn 1940 at the home of Herr von Clemm, the German Embassy's adviser on economic questions. Our conversation had been extremely informative, if rather depressing, and its comparison of American production statistics with those of Nazi-controlled Europe had led us to hope, vaguely, that it would be possible to keep the United States out of the war. Since Gaevernitz's reasons for quitting the Third Reich were mainly racial, our meeting had not been without its dangers, especially as Herr Kappler kept a close watch on the activities of all foreigners in Rome. Such was the extent of my memories of Herr von Gaevernitz. I was not aware of the nature of his political duties in Dulles's organisation.

The Baron was understandably delighted that our acquaintanceship dated back so far, and opened a new bottle of Veuve Cliquot to celebrate this unlooked-for piece of good fortune. I think he expected me to drive to Switzerland with him at once, because he seemed very disappointed when I told him that I was quite ready to undertake the trip, but only with the permission of Dr Rudolf Rahn, German Ambassador Plenipotentiary to the Salò Republic, and of General Wolff. He was not discouraged, however, and thanked me effusively for my goodwill—which was, in any case, all I had to offer.

In the above-mentioned book Lanfranchi describes my part in the affair as follows:

The surrender at Caserta was instigated and arranged by General Wolff, but it was Dollmann who paved the way for it, and Dollmann was a diplomat, not a soldier. He spoke good Italian and knew Rome, where he had lived for a number of years before the war. Cultured, elegant and enterprising, he possessed all the attributes needful for a successful career in the world of diplomacy.

So much for the polite remarks of Signor Lanfranchi, whom I did not meet until after the war in Switzerland, where he interviewed me in 1950. He described the German-Swiss-American adventure which lay ahead of me in the following terms:

Undoubtedly the finest thing Dollmann did, not only on behalf of Italy but for Germany and humanity, was that he acted as one of the instigators of and foremost participants in the secret negotiations with the Americans, which were aimed at securing the surrender of the German troops in Italy—the surrender of the eight hundred thousand.

To be the hero of a surrender is not something for which laurels are awarded—far from it—but I had never set much store by laurels in the course of my career. No such vain ambitions preoccupied me as I drove to Lake Garda on 2 March, the day after my champagne rendezvous with Don Luigi Parrilli, in response to an urgent request from Messrs Wolff and Rahn to call on them dressed in my 'smartest civilian suit'.

I realised what this meant. My interview with the two men lasted for some hours, in the course of which time I received the marching orders and general instructions I had been expecting. They related to a meeting whose outcome would, I suspected, depend less on my alleged intelligence than on chance and good luck.

Early on the morning of 3 March I met Baron Parrilli at Chiasso station. His Swiss confederates appeared on the other side of the frontier and waved to us. It was like something out of a spy film, and I apparently contributed to the drama of the occasion by wearing what Lanfranchi describes as '*un cappellino alla Eden del miglior periodo, alquanto pretenzioso*'—'a little hat in the style of Eden's best period, a trifle pretentious'.

I cannot remember, but it is quite possible. Perhaps it was my emulation of Eden that inspired Lanfranchi to praise my diplomatic ability. Confronted by the sort of journey and undertaking that lay ahead of me, one man carries a revolver in his pocket, another wears a pretentious hat.

Cur non?–why not?

INDEX

Abyssinian Empire, 166
Acquasanta golf-club, 105, 186, 198
Agnelli, Virginia (daughter of Prince Borbone del Monte), 298–303
Agnesina (Commander of Mussolini's bodyguard), 208, 224
Albini (Minister of the Interior), 207, 224
Aldobrandini, Princess, 257
Aldrovandi-Marescotti, Count Luigi, 62
Alexander (Field Marshal), 310, 330
Alexander VI (Pope), 95
Alfieri, Dino (Propaganda Minister), 161–3, 203
Alfredo (Dollmann's friend from Trastevere), 140–3
Ambrosio (Chief of General Staff), 202, 207–8, 213–15, 236, 243–6
Anfuso, Filippo (Ciano's secretary), 172–4; (Ambassador) 223, 320–1, 323, 332
Attolico, Bernardo (Ambassador), 133–5
Attolico, Eleonora (Ambassadress), 104, 115–16, 131–3, 135, 156

Badoglio, Pietro (Marshal), 50, 163, 230, 232–3, 256–7, 258, 263, 269, 271
Balbo, Italo (Air Marshal), 119–27
Bastianini (Foreign Minister), 207, 211
Berenson, Bernhard (Art historian), 308

Bergen, Diego von (Ambassador), 63–5, 140, 248
Bergen, Eva von (Ambassadress), 65–8, 248
Bianchi (Fascist), 120
Bibi, see Maria Celeste
Bicchierai, Monsignore, 340–1, 343
Biggini (Court judge), 225, 275
Bismarck, Count Albrecht von, 172
Bismarck, Princess Ann-Mari von, 171–3, 198, 223
Bismarck, Prince Herbert von, 172
Bismarck, Princess Johanna von, 172
Bismarck, Countess Marguerite von, 172
Bismarck, Otto von (Chancellor), 172
Bismarck, Prince Otto von, 171–3
Blackshirts, 120, 336
Bocchini, Anna, 194–5
Bocchini, Arturo (Chief of Police), 42, 52–5, 97
  and Himmler, 73–4, 82–92, 125, 194–5
  and Clara Petacci, 80
  and Eva Braun, 116–17, 139, 155
  Pact of Steel, 168, 170
  and Kersten, 179–80, 185
Borelli, Lydia (film star), 288
Borgia, Lucrezia, 95
Bormann, Martin, 138, 320, 323
Bouhler, Frau, 157, 162
Braun, Eva (Hitler's mistress and wife), 116–17, 130
Brazza, Countess, 330
Brigate Nere, 336–7

Buffarini-Guidi (Secretary of State), 97, 178, 185, 199, 202
  and Donna Rachele, 218–21, 223, 225–9, 266, 268–9, 271, 273–5, 306–7, 325, 326–9
Bulgari Brothers (jewellers), 290
Bülow-Schwante (Chief of Protocol), 113
Burckhardt, Carl J. (Swiss historian), 96
Byron, Lord, 145

Caccia-Dominioni (Cardinal), 301
Calvi di Bergolo, Count, 262, 265, 277–8
Canaris (Admiral), 255
Carità (Major), 308–9
Casanova-Tringali (Minister of Justice), 275
Casati, Marchesa Luisa, 149–50
Castellano (General), 236, 255, 257
Cavallero, Count (Chief of General staff), 201–2, 268–71, 272–3
Chamberlain, Arthur Neville (Premier), 128, 131
Chierici, Renzo (Police Chief), 210
Ciano, Countess Edda, 66–8, 137, 172–4, 181–2, 291–3
Ciano, Count Galeazzo, 100–1, 104
  and Balbo, 120–1
  Munich Conference, 127, 132, 137, 139
  and Ribbentrop, Pact of Steel, 153–60
  and Ribbentrop, Fuschl Castle, 164–8
  and Sir Percy Loraine, 169–70, 171
  with the Bismarcks, 172–4
  and Kersten, 178–81, 182–3, 186
  and Himmler, 196–7
  at Rastenburg, 201
  Ambassador to the Vatican, 206, 210
  Donna Rachele's opinion, 220
  Fascist Council, 225, 227, 233
  and Frau von Mackensen, 254

flight to Bavaria, return, execution, 290–4
Cigna, Gina (singer), 113
Cini, Count Vittorio (Minister of Transport), 200, 287–8
Cini, Countess, 288–90
Cini, Giorgio, 287–90
Colonna, Princess Isabella, 138, 168
Croce, Benedetto (philosopher), 31
Curtius, Ludwig (archaeologist), 20

Daladier, Edouard (Minister-President), 127, 130, 169
Dalla Costa, Elia (Cardinal), 309–10
Daluege (Police General), 195
Darré (Minister of Agriculture), 237
De Bono (Fascist), 120
De Cesare (Mussolini's secretary), 207
De Vecchi (Fascist), 120
Dietrich, Sepp (Commander of Hitler's bodyguard), 241–3
Dollmann, Dr. Eugen, remarks on him in books, 77–9, 303, 338, 344–5
  Hitler's view on his interpreting, 144
  negotiations with the Americans, 332–4
Dönitz (Grand Admiral), 208, 322–3
Dörnberg, Baron (Chief of Protocol), 320
Dulles, Allen W. (OSS–Europe), 175, 298, 333, 343–4

Eagle's Nest, 167
Eduard, Duke of Saxony-Coburg-Gotha, 96
Eisenhower (General), 258, 261
Elena, Queen, 138, 145, 233–4, 264

Farinacci (Fascist), 232
Farnese, Alessandro (Cardinal), 19
Farnese (Isle), 163
Feltre Meeting, 213–16
Feltrinelli (Industrialist), 325

Filangieri, Count (archivist), 33
Fischer, Edwin (pianist), 105
Fouché (Napoleon's Police Chief), 79–80
François-Poncet, André (Ambassador), 128, 171
Franz Joseph I, Emperor, 14
Fuschl Castle, 164

Gaggia (financier), 214
Galbiati, Enzo (General of Militia), 212, 229–30, 268–9
Gamelin, Maurice Gustave (General), 170
Gardiner (Colonel), 256
Gaevernitz, see Schulze-Gaevernitz
Gerlach (pilot), 282
Gestapo, 313
Ghisetti (Capitano), 340–1, 343
Gigli, Benjamino (singer), 113, 118
Goebbels, Magda, 104, 156
Goebbels, Joseph (Propaganda Minister), 108, 161
20 July 44, 161
Goerdeler, Karl, 20 July 44, 330
Göring, Emmy, 156
Göring, Hermann (Reich Marshal), and Hassell, 48–9
and Balbo, 123
Munich Conference, 128, 132
Pact of Steel, 158
in Sicily, 199–200
at Klessheim Castle, 208–9
20 July 1944, 320, 322–3
Grand Fascist Council, 225
Grandi, Dino (President of Fascist Chamber), 222, 225, 227
Graziani, Rodolfo (Marshal), 271–9, 282–5, 317, 320, 323, 330–1, 332
Guariglia (Foreign Minister), 236, 243, 245–6, 258–9

Hassell, Frau von (Ambassadress), 45–6
Hassell, Ulrich von (Ambassador), 45–9, 100–1

Helfferich (Colonel), 241
Hess, Rudolf (Hitler's Deputy), 100
Heydrich, Reinhard (State Security Bureau Chief), 80, 91–7
and Himmler, 97, 159
and Kersten, 175
Himmler, Heinrich (Reichsführer-SS), and Bocchini, 74–91, 194–5
and Heydrich, 97, 108
with Balbo in Tripoli, 121–3, 131–2, 138
and Kersten, 175–80
and Ciano, 196–9
at Klessheim Castle, 209–10, 241
Wolff's papal audience, 303
Himmler, Marga, 121–2, 125
Hitler, Adolf, and Mussolini at Stra, 49, 161, 104
in Italy, 1938, 107–15
and Balbo, 123–4
Munich Conference, 127–30
on Dollmann's interpreting, 144
Pact of Steel, 156–8, 162
and Ciano at Fuschl Castle, 165–8
blinded, 178
Brenner Meeting, 182–3, 187
with Mussolini in Russia, 188–93
at Rastenburg, 203–5
with Mussolini at Klessheim Castle, 208–9, 316
Feltre Meeting, 213–15
and the liberated Duce, 251–2, 278
and Graziani, 283–4, 295
defence of Rome, 296, 309, 312
20 July with Mussolini, 320–5
Hohenberg, Carl F. Clemm von (Attaché), 173–5
Husmann, Max (Swiss Professor), 343
Interpreter, art of, 144
Italian Social Republic, 273
Jena, von (Major), 243
Jodl (General), 283–4, 321
20 July 1944, 320–25

Kaltenbrunnér, Ernst (Head of State Security Bureau), 278

Kappler, Herbert (Police Attaché), 91, 175, 181, 237, 239, 241, 267, 285–6, 289, 292, 303, 344
Karinhall, 123
Keats, John, 140, 221
Kehr, Paul (Prussian Hist. Inst., Rome), 20
Keitel, Wilhelm (Field Marshal), 208–9, 236, 244, 246, 282–4, 321–3
Kempka (Hitler's chauffeur), 192
Kersten, Felix (physician), 175–81
Kessel, Teddy von (Diplomat), 257
Kesselring, Albert (Field Marshal), 199, 213, 215, 238–9, 254, 257, 260–1, 262–3, 265–7, 269–70, 280, 294, 296–7, 304, 306–7, 310, 330–1, 342
Klessheim Castle, 206
Ko, Dr (Chinese physician), 176
Kraus, Clemens (conductor), 106
Kühlmann, Richard von (Secretary of State), 65
Laval, Pierre Etienne (Minister President), 201
Lemnitzer (General), 261
Loraine, Sir Percy (Ambassador), 169, 183

'M' Division, 212
Mackensen, Hans Georg von (Ambassador), 101–3, 140, 151–2, 158, 170, 207, 212, 213, 215, 226–9, 231–3, 246–7, 252, 308
Mackensen, Wini von (Ambassadress), 103–7, 116, 139, 232, 240, 252–4
Mafalda, Princess of Hesse, 278
Malaparte, Curzio (writer), 299
Mältzer (General), 285
March on Rome, 119–20
Maria Celeste, Princess (née Rossi, named Bibi), 72, 117–18, 140–1, 143, 179, 186, 198, 222, 223–4, 256, 267–8, 287–90
Maria José, Crown Princess, 105, 112–13, 138

and Frau Scholtz-Klinck, 152–3
and Frau von Mackensen, 253
Marras (Military Attaché), 243
May Monarchy, 264
Mazzolini, Count (Foreign Minister), 320–1, 323
Medici del Vascello, Marchesa Olga, 151–3, 288
Meissner, Dr (State Secretary), 210
Messe (Italian Commander in Russia), 191
Mezzasomma, Fernando (Minister of Culture), 279
Mitford, Unity (Hitler worshipper), 130
Möllhausen, Eitel Friedrich (Consul-General), 272–3, 296
Mommsen, Theodor (historian), 44
Morosini, Countess Anna, 145–7
Munich Conference, 127–32
Munthe, Axel (writer), 140
Mussolini, Benito (Duce), with Hitler at Stra, 49
entry into the war, 106, 187
Hitler's visit in 1938, 107–15
March on Rome, 119–20
Munich Conference, 128–32, 136–7, 333
Pact of Steel, 155, 165, 169
in Russia, 188–193
at Klessheim Castle, 206–210, 316
bodyguard, 211–13
Feltre Meeting, 213–16
Grand Fascist Council, 227–9
the King's prisoner, 230, 233, 315
liberated, 251
and Frau von Mackensen, 253, 269
in Munich, 273
in Italy again, 279
defence of Rome, 296–7
in Salo, 307, 325
inspecting new divisions in Germany, 314–19
with Hitler on 20 July 1944, 320–5
and Kesselring, 330–1, 332, 342
Mussolini, Bruno, 189
Mussolini, Edda, see Ciano, Edda

Mussolini, Rachele, 217–21, 229
and Clara Petacci, 326–9
Mussolini, Vittorio, 232, 322–3

Napoleon, 79
Neurath, Konstantin von (Foreign Minister), 102, 107

Pact of Steel, 155, 158, 165–9, 214
Palazzo, Braschi, 287
Palazzo, Caprara, 257
Palazzo, Chigi, 104, 169, 196
Palazzo, Venezia, 106, 110, 211, 224
Parrilli, Baron Luigi, 342–5
Pavolini, Alassandro (writer), 332
Pellegrini (Finance Minister), 279
Pensabene (Major), 260
Petacci, Clara (Mussolini's mistress), 80
and Donna Rachele, 326–9
Pfeiffer, Dr (Cardinal), 298, 301–2, 305–6
Philipp, Prince Eulenburg, 149
Philipp, Prince of Hesse, 109, 118, 253
Pittalis (Consul-General), 133
Pius XI, 117, 138
Pius XII, 169, 296, 298, 301–3
Pohl, Max von (General), 307–8, 311–14
Puntoni (General), 264

Rahn, Rudolf (Ambassador), 254, 258–9, 272, 274–5, 308, 332, 344–5
Rastenburg (Hitler's Headquarters), 201–2, 282, 314
Raubal, Geli (Hitler's niece), 129
Ribbentrop, Joachim von (Foreign Minister), 105, 108–9, 134
and Ciano, Pact of Steel, 153–60
and Ciano, Fuschl Castle, 164–8, 171, 203
on the USA, 204
at Klessheim Castle, 208–10, 236

Tarvis Conference, 244–6
Wolff's papal audience, 303
20 July 1944, 320–3
Ribbentrop, Frau von, 104, 116, 156
Ricci, Renato (President of Balilla), 68–71, 207
Rintelen, von (General), 207, 243, 245
Rita (crank American in Venice), 147–9
Rocca delle Caminate (Castle), 278–9
Röhm putsch, 49
Rome-Berlin Axis, 55, 154
Rommel, Erwin (Field Marshal), 199, 266, 280
Rosalba, Duchess, 38
Rossi, Maria Celeste, see Maria Celeste
Rossi, Stefania (Dollmann's landlady), 140
Rundstedt (Field Marshal), 191
Rupprecht, Crown Prince of Bavaria, 308

Salò Republic, 325
Salon Kitty (Berlin), 159
Schirach, Baldur von (Youth Leader), 68–71
Schmidt, Dr (interpreter), 165, 244
Scholtz-Klinck, Gertrud (Women's Leader), 150–3
Schulze-Gaevernitz, Gero von (US Secret Service), 174–5, 344
Schuster, Ildefonso (Cardinal), 303, 340–1
Senise, Carmine (Police Chief), 81, 98–9, 196, 209, 210, 236, 241, 253
Sennelager (training area), 317–18
Serena (Party Secretary), 237
Serlupi, Marchese Filippo, 308–10
Sermoneta, Leone Caetani, Duke of, 56
Sermoneta, Vittoria Caetani, Duchess of, 55–62, 138
Skorzeny, Otto (Mussolini's liberator), 236, 239–41, 251, 282

South Tyrol, 110
Spanish Civil War, 166
Spanish Steps, 140
Stahel (General), 272, 275, 277–8
Stalin, 133
Stalingrad, 203, 205
Starace, Achille (Party Secretary), 150–3, 155, 168
Starhemberg, Prince, 44
Steinmann, Ernst (Hertziana), 20
Strauss, Richard (composer), 106
Student (General), 239
Sunrise Crossword, 298

Tacchi-Venturi (Jesuit), 25, 47, 186
Tarabini (General of Militia), 203
Tarvis Conference, 244–7
Tassinari, Giuseppe (Minister of Agriculture), 237–8, 247–52, 271, 273–4
Taylor, Maxwell D. (General), 256–7, 261
Tirpitz, Alfred von (Grand Admiral), 65
Tuninetti (Prefect), 342

Umberto, Crown Prince, 138, 197, 263–4

Vasalli (professor), 302–3
Victor Emmanuel III, King of Italy and Wilhelm II, 60–2
and Frau von Mackensen, 105
Hitler's visit in 1938, 107–14
the March on Rome, 120, 138, 182, 219
Mussolini prisoner, 229–35, 315
flight, 263–5
Vier Jahreszeiten (Hotel), 124, 130, 162
Vietinghoff, Baron von (General), 332–3
Villa Madama, 197
Villa Savoya, 233
Villa Torlonia, 217
Villa Volkonsky, 226, 258, 268, 275
Waibel, Max (Swiss Major), 343
Waldau, Gusti (actor), 162
Walterspiel, Adolf (hotelier), 124
Weizsäcker, Ernst Baron von (Ambassador), 254, 296, 301, 303
Weizsäcker, Frau von (Ambassadress), 248
Wilhelm II, 60–2, 145–6
Wilhelm, Crown Prince, 62
Wilhelmina, Queen of Holland, 176
Windsor, Duchess of, 104
Wolf's Lair, 282
Wolf, Gerhard (Consul-General), 307, 310
Wolff, Karl (General of Waffen-SS), 91, 124, 251, 267, 274–5, 278, 289
papal audience, 298, 301–3
negotiations with the Americans, 298, 332–3, 345, 312–13, 325

Yolanda (daughter of Victor Emmanuel), 265

Zerbino (Officer), 297
Zingone (Lt.-Colonel), 282–3